THE CHAOS MACHINE

THE CHAOS MACHINE

THE INSIDE STORY OF HOW
SOCIAL MEDIA REWIRED
OUR MINDS AND OUR WORLD

MAX FISHER

Little, Brown and Company
New York • Boston • London

Little, Brown and Company
Hachette Book Group
1290 Avenue of the Americas, New York, NY 10104
littlebrown.com

First Edition: September 2022

Little, Brown and Company is a division of Hachette Book Group, Inc. The Little, Brown name and logo are trademarks of Hachette Book Group, Inc.

The publisher is not responsible for websites (or their content) that are not owned by the publisher.

The Hachette Speakers Bureau provides a wide range of authors for speaking events. To find out more, go to hachettespeakersbureau.com or call (866) 376-6591.

ISBN 9780316703321

LCCN 2022941585

10 9 8 7 6 5 4 3 2 1

MRQ-T

Printed in Canada

To Mom and Dad, for getting me here
To Jordan, for seeing me through

Contents

Author's Note

This book is based on interviews with hundreds of people who have studied, combated, exploited, or been affected by social media, as well as with workers and executives in Silicon Valley. In some cases, for readability, a source's name and title may appear in the Notes section rather than in the narrative. All interviews were conducted on the record save one, with a third-party moderator who asked to remain pseudonymous. I reviewed pay stubs and corporate files that confirm his account.

The book also draws heavily on academic research, court records, and many other primary sources, which are listed in the Notes as supporting evidence for every figure or assertion presented in the narrative, as well as for any quote that I did not report myself. A handful of statements draw on scholarly research that has not yet been published outside this book. In these cases, a brief overview of the findings, methodology, and authorship appear in the Notes section.

THE CHAOS MACHINE

prologue

consequences

WALKING INTO FACEBOOK'S headquarters can feel like entering the Vatican: a center of power shrouded in secrecy and opulence that would shame a Russian oligarch. The company had spent $300 million alone on building number 21, an airy steel and glass playground of gardens, patios, and everything-is-free restaurants that I visited in late 2018. Between meetings, a two-story mural on a back wall caught my eye, reminding me of a famous Chinese artist who'd recently been featured at the Guggenheim Museum. I asked the PR rep who was minding me if it had been deliberately painted in his style. She laughed politely. It was no mimicry; the artist had been flown in to do an original on Facebook's walls. So had dozens of other artists. All around me fabulously paid programmers hustled down hallways adorned by priceless murals.

In my bag, stuffed between notepads, was my ticket in: 1,400-plus pages of internal documents, from regions across the globe, that revealed Facebook's unseen hand in setting the bounds of acceptable politics and speech for two billion users worldwide. To the insider who'd leaked them to me, the files were evidence of the company's sloppiness and shortcuts in trying to stem the growing global turmoil that he believed its products exacerbated, or even caused. To me, they were even more than that. They were a window into how Facebook's leadership thought about the consequences of social media's rise.

Like many, I had initially assumed social media's dangers came mostly from misuse by bad actors — propagandists, foreign agents, fake-news peddlers — and that at worst the various platforms were a passive conduit for society's preexisting problems. But virtually everywhere I traveled in my reporting, covering far-off despots, wars, and upheavals, strange and extreme events kept getting linked back to social media. A sudden riot, a radical new group, widespread belief in some oddball conspiracy — all had a common link. And though America had yet to explode into violence, the similarities to what was happening back home were undeniable. Every week there was another story of a Twitter conspiracy overtaking national politics, a Reddit subculture drifting into neo-Nazism, a YouTube addict turning to mass murder.

And Donald Trump's unexpected victory in 2016 had been attributed, in part, to social media. Though the role of the platforms remained poorly understood, it was already clear that Trump's rise had been abetted by strange new grassroots movements and hyperpartisan outlets that thrived online, as well as Russian agents who'd exploited social media's reality-distorting, identity-indulging tendencies. This global pattern seemed to indicate something fundamental to the technology, but exactly what that was, why it was happening, or what it meant, nobody was able to tell me.

At the other end of the world, a young man I'll call Jacob, a contractor with one of the vast outsourcing firms to which Silicon Valley sends its dirty work, had formed much the same suspicions as my own. He had raised every alarm he could. His bosses had listened with concern, he said, even sympathy. They'd seen the same things he had. Something in the product they oversaw was going dangerously wrong.

Jacob, slight and bookish, had grown up in love with the internet and had been tinkering with computers for years. The technologies seemed to represent the best of the United States. He'd looked up especially to web moguls like Mark Zuckerberg, Facebook's CEO and founder, who argued that connecting the world would make it better. When Jacob landed a job with an outsourcing agency that reviewed user content for Facebook and Instagram, one of several that the company employs worldwide, it felt like becoming part of history.

Every day his team clicked through thousands of posts from around the world, flagging any that broke a rule or crossed a line. It was draining but necessary work, he felt. But over some months in 2017 and 2018 they had noticed the posts growing more hateful, more conspiratorial, and more extreme. And the more incendiary the post, they sensed, the more widely the platforms spread it. It seemed to them like a pattern, one playing out at once in the dozens of societies and languages they were tasked with overseeing.

Moreover, they believed that their ability to constrain this rising hate and incitement was hamstrung by the very thing that was supposed to help them: the dozens of secret rulebooks dictating what they were to allow on the platforms and what to remove. To Facebook's more than two billion users, those rules are largely invisible. They are intended to keep the platforms safe and civil, articulating everything from the line between free expression and hate speech to the boundaries of permissible political movements. But as the rulebooks proved inadequate to stemming harms that were often ginned up by the platform itself, and as corporate oversight of this most unglamorous part of the business drifted, the worldwide guides had sprawled to hundreds of confusing and often contradictory pages. Some of the most important, on identifying terrorist recruitment or overseeing contentious elections, were filled with typos, factual errors, and obvious loopholes. The sloppiness and the lacunae suggested a dangerous disregard for a job that Jacob saw as a matter of life and death, and at a time when the platforms were overflowing with extremism that increasingly bled into the real world. Just months earlier, in Myanmar, the United Nations had formally accused Facebook of allowing its technology to help provoke one of the worst genocides since World War II.

Jacob recorded his team's findings and concerns to send up the chain. Months passed. The rise in online extremism only worsened. He clocked in and out, waiting at his terminal for a response from headquarters, far away in America, that never came. He had an idea. It would mean cracking the security system at work, secreting confidential files abroad, and convincing the media to broadcast his warnings for him — all in the hope of delivering them to the screen of one person: Mark Zuckerberg, founder and CEO of Facebook. Distance and bureaucracy, he was sure, kept him from reaching the people in charge. If only he could get word to them, they would want to fix things.

Jacob first reached me in early 2018. A series of stories I'd worked on, investigating social media's role in spinning up mass violence in places like the small Asian nation of Sri Lanka, struck him as confirmation that the problems he'd observed on his screen were real — and had growing, sometimes deadly consequences. But he knew that his word alone would not be enough. He would need to siphon Facebook's internal rulebooks and training documents from the computers at his office. It wouldn't be easy — the machines were heavily locked down and the office closely monitored — but it was possible: a year earlier someone had managed to pass some of the files to *The Guardian,* and more were later leaked to *Vice News.* Jacob built a program to secrete the files out, encrypting and washing them to remove digital fingerprints that might trace back to him or even the country where his office was located. He transferred some to me through a secure server. A few weeks later I flew out to gather the rest and to meet him.

Facebook, on learning what I'd acquired, invited me to their sleek headquarters, offering to make a dozen or so corporate policymakers available to talk. All were tough-minded professionals. Some had accrued sterling reputations in Washington DC, in fields such as counterterrorism or cybersecurity, before joining the Silicon Valley gold rush. Others had impressive backgrounds in human rights or politics. They were hardly the basement hackers and starry-eyed dropouts who had once governed the platforms — although it would later become clear that the dorm-room ideologies and biases from Silicon Valley's early days were still held with near-religious conviction on their campuses, and remained baked into the very technology that pushed those same ideals into the wider world.

A strange pattern emerged in my conversations at Facebook's headquarters. An executive would walk me through the challenge that consumed their days: blocking terrorists from recruiting on the platform, outmaneuvering hostile government hackers, determining which combinations of words constituted an unacceptable incitement to violence. Nearly any question I posed, however sensitive, yielded a direct, nuanced answer. When problems remained unsolved, they acknowledged as much. No one ever had to check their notes to tell me, say, Facebook's policy on Kurdish independence groups or its methods for distributing hate-speech rules in Tagalog.

I found myself wondering: with such conscientious, ultra-qualified people in charge, why do the problems for which they articulate such thoughtful answers only ever seem to get worse? When rights groups warn Facebook of impending danger from their platform, why does the company so often fail to act? Why do journalists like me, who have little visibility into the platforms' operations and an infinitesimal fraction of their staffing or budget, keep turning up Facebook-born atrocities and cults that seem to take them by surprise? But at some point in each interview, when I would ask about dangers that arose not from bad actors misusing the platform but from the platform itself, it would be like a mental wall went up.

"There's nothing new about the types of abuse that you see," the company's global-policy chief said when I asked about the platform's consequences. "What's different here is the amplification power of something like a social media platform," she said. "As a society, we're still quite early in understanding all the consequences of social media," the company's head of cybersecurity said, suggesting the primary change wrought by the technology had simply been to reduce "friction" in communication, which allowed messages to travel faster and wider.

It was a strangely incomplete picture of how Facebook works. Many at the company seemed almost unaware that the platform's algorithms and design deliberately shape users' experiences and incentives, and therefore the users themselves. These elements are the core of the product, the reason that hundreds of programmers buzzed around us as we talked. It was like walking into a cigarette factory and having executives tell you they couldn't understand why people kept complaining about the health impacts of the little cardboard boxes that they sold.

At one point, talking with two employees who oversaw crisis response, I dropped out of reporter mode to alert them to something worrying I'd seen. In countries around the world, a gruesome rumor was surfacing, apparently spontaneously, on Facebook: that mysterious outsiders were kidnapping local children to make them sex slaves and to harvest their organs. Communities exposed to this rumor were responding in increasingly dangerous ways. When it spread via Facebook and WhatsApp to a rural part of Indonesia, for instance, nine different villages had separately gathered into mobs and attacked innocent passersby. It was as if this rumor were some mysterious virus that turned normal communities into bloodthirsty swarms, and that seemed to be emerging as if from the platform itself. The two Facebookers listened and nodded. Neither asked any questions. One commented vaguely that she hoped an independent researcher might look into such things one day, and we moved on.

But versions of the rumor continued to emerge on Facebook. An American iteration, which had first appeared on the message board 4chan under the label "QAnon," had recently hit Facebook like a match to a pool of gasoline. Later, as QAnon became a movement with tens of thousands of followers, an internal FBI report identified it as a domestic terror threat. Throughout, Facebook's recommendation engines promoted QAnon groups to huge numbers of readers, as if this were merely another club, helping to grow the conspiracy into the size of a minor political party, for seemingly no more elaborate reason than the continued clicks the QAnon content generated.

Within Facebook's muraled walls, though, belief in the product as a force for good seemed unshakable. The core Silicon Valley ideal that getting people to spend more and more time online will enrich their minds and better the world held especially firm among the engineers who ultimately make and shape the products. "As we have greater reach, as we have more people engaging, that raises the stakes," a senior engineer on Facebook's all-important news feed said. "But I also think that there's greater opportunity for people to be exposed to new ideas." Any risks created by the platform's mission to maximize user engagement would be engineered out, she assured me.

I later learned that, a short time before my visit, some Facebook researchers, appointed internally to study their technology's effects, in response to growing suspicion that the site might be worsening America's political divisions, had warned internally that the platform was doing exactly what the company's executives had, in our conversations, shrugged off. "Our algorithms exploit the human brain's attraction to divisiveness," the researchers warned in a 2018 presentation later leaked to the *Wall Street Journal*. In fact, the presentation continued, Facebook's systems were designed in a way that delivered users "more and more divisive content in an effort to gain user attention & increase time on the platform." Executives shelved the research and largely rejected its recommendations, which called for tweaking the promotional systems that choose what users see in ways that might have reduced their time online. The question I had brought to Facebook's corridors — what are the consequences of routing an ever-growing share of all politics, information, and human social relations through online platforms expressly designed to manipulate attention? — was plainly taboo here.

The months after my visit coincided with what was then the greatest public backlash in Silicon Valley's history. The social media giants faced congressional hearings, foreign regulation, multibillion-dollar fines, and threats of forcible breakup. Public figures routinely referred to the companies as one of the gravest threats of our time. In response, the companies' leaders pledged to confront the harms flowing from their services.

They unveiled election-integrity war rooms and updated content-review policies. But their business model — keeping people glued to their platforms as many hours a day as possible — and the underlying technology deployed to achieve this goal remained largely unchanged. And while the problems they'd promised to solve only worsened, they made more money than ever.

The new decade brought a wave of crises. The Covid-19 pandemic, racial reckoning and backlash in the United States, the accelerating rise of a violent new far right, and the attempted destruction of American democracy itself. Each tested the platforms' influence on our world — or revealed it, exposing ramifications that had been building for years.

In summer 2020, an independent audit of Facebook, commissioned by the company under pressure from civil rights groups, concluded that the platform was everything its executives had insisted to me it was not. Its policies permitted rampant misinformation that could undermine elections. Its algorithms and recommendation systems were "driving people toward self-reinforcing echo chambers of extremism," training them to hate. Perhaps most damning, the report concluded that the company did not understand how its own products affected its billions of users.

But there were a handful of people who did understand and, long before many of us were prepared to listen, tried to warn us. Most began as tech-obsessed true believers, some as denizens themselves of Silicon Valley, which was precisely why they were in a better position to notice early that something was going wrong, to investigate it, and to measure the consequences. But the companies that claimed to want exactly such insights stymied their efforts, questioned their reputations, and disputed their findings — until, in many cases, the companies were forced to acknowledge, if only implicitly, that the alarm raisers had been right all along. They conducted their work, at least initially, independently of one another, pursuing very different methods toward the same question: what are the consequences of this technology? This book is about the mission to answer that question, told in part through the people who led it.

The early conventional wisdom, that social media promotes sensationalism and outrage, while accurate, turned out to drastically understate things. An ever-growing pool of evidence, gathered by dozens of academics, reporters, whistleblowers, and concerned citizens, suggests that its impact is far more profound. This technology exerts such a powerful pull on our psychology and our identity, and is so pervasive in our lives, that it changes how we think, behave, and relate to one another. The effect, multiplied across billions of users, has been to change society itself.

Silicon Valley can hardly be blamed for the psychological frailties that lead us to do harm or to act against our own interests. Nor for the deep cultural polarization, in America and elsewhere, that primed users to turn these new spaces into venues of partisan conflict, destroying any shared sense of welfare or reality. Even its biggest companies cannot be blamed for the high-tech funding model that gave rise to them, by handing multimillion-dollar investments to misfit twentysomethings and then demanding instant, exponential returns, with little concern for the warped incentives this creates. Still, these companies accrued some of the largest corporate fortunes in history by exploiting those tendencies and weaknesses, in the process ushering in a wholly new era in the human experience. The consequences — though in hindsight almost certainly foreseeable, if someone had cared to look — were obscured by an ideology that said more time online would create happier and freer souls, and by a strain of Silicon Valley capitalism that empowers a contrarian, brash, almost millenarian engineering subculture to run the companies that run our minds.

By the time those companies were pressured into behaving at least somewhat like the de facto governing institutions they had become, they found themselves at the center of political and cultural crises for which they were a partial culprit. You might charitably call the refereeing of a democracy bent on its own destruction a thankless task — if the companies had not put themselves in positions of such power, refused responsibility until it was forced on them at the point of a regulatory gun, and, nearly every step of the way, compromised the well-being of their users to keep billions of dollars in monthly revenue flowing. With little incentive for the social media giants to confront the human cost to their empires — a cost borne by everyone else, like a town downstream from a factory pumping toxic sludge into its communal well — it would be up to dozens of alarmed outsiders and Silicon Valley defectors to do it for them.

One

Trapped in the Casino

1. *The Sky Is Falling*

RENÉE DIRESTA HAD her infant on her knee when she realized that social networks were bringing out something dangerous in people, something already reaching invisibly into her and her son's lives. No one in her immediate circle had children, so she had joined online groups for new parents, looking for counsel on sleep training or teething. But the other users, though mostly friendly, she said, occasionally slipped into "flame wars" that were thousands of posts long, and all over a topic she'd rarely encountered off-line: vaccinations.

It was 2014, and DiResta had only recently arrived in Silicon Valley, there to scout startups for an investment firm. She was still an analyst at heart, from her years both on Wall Street and, before that, at an intelligence agency she hints was the CIA. To keep her mind agile, she filled her downtime with elaborate research projects, the way others might do a crossword in bed.

Her curiosity provoked, she began to investigate whether the anti-vaccine anger she'd seen online reflected something broader. Buried in the files of California's public-health department, she realized, were student vaccination rates for nearly every school in the state — including the preschools she was considering for her son. What she found shocked her. Some of the schools were vaccinated at only 30 percent. "What on earth is going on?" she asked herself. She downloaded ten years' worth of records. The trend during that period — a steady increase in opt-outs — was clear, she told me. "Holy shit," she thought, "this is really bad."

With rates so low, outbreaks of diseases like measles or whooping cough became a grave danger, putting everyone's children at risk. She called her state senator's office to ask if anything could be done to improve vaccination rates. It wasn't going to happen, she was told. Were vaccines really so hated? she asked. No, the staffer said. Their polling showed 85 percent support for a bill that would tighten vaccine mandates in schools. But lawmakers feared the extraordinarily vocal anti-vaccine movement — comprising young California parents gripped by paranoia and rage — that seemed to be emerging from Twitter, YouTube, and Facebook.

"That was what really sent me down this rabbit hole," DiResta said. "For six months, no joke, from 8:00 p.m. to 2:00 a.m., this was what I did." In time, that rabbit hole led her not to any secret hand behind the anti-vaccine movement but, rather, to the very social networks on which it had arisen. Hoping to organize some of those 85 percent of Californians who supported the vaccination bill, she started a group — where else? — on Facebook. When she bought Facebook ads to solicit recruits, she noticed something curious. Whenever she typed "vaccine," or anything tangentially connected to the topic, into the platform's ad-targeting tool, it returned groups and topics that were overwhelmingly opposed to vaccines. And something else: when she targeted her ads to display for California moms, the users who received them responded with a flood of anti-vaccine invective. It was as if her real-life community's pro-vaccine views had been inverted online.

Curious, she joined a handful of anti-vaccine Facebook groups. Their users seemed to live and breathe social media, circulating YouTube clips and coordinating Twitter hashtag campaigns. Most expressed genuine anguish over what they believed to be a vast conspiracy to pump their children's arms with dangerous shots. But if they represented only 15 percent of Californians, why were they so dominant here? Soon, DiResta noticed Facebook doing something strange: pushing a stream of notifications urging her to follow other anti-vaccine pages. "If you joined the one anti-vaccine group," she said, "it was transformative." Nearly every vaccine-related recommendation promoted to her was for anti-vaccine content.

"The recommendation engine would push them and push them and push them."

Before long, the system prompted her to consider joining groups for unrelated conspiracies. Chemtrails. Flat Earth. And as she poked around, she found another way that the system boosted vaccine misinformation. Just as with the ad-targeting tool, typing "vaccines" in Facebook's search bar returned a stream of anti-vaccine posts and groups. Even though mainstream health and parenting pages often had groups with many more members, those results showed up farther down.

DiResta had an inkling for what was going on. She'd held a fascination with computers since childhood, when her father, a biomedical engineer who worked in cancer research, had taught her to code at age nine. She'd owned an early-1980s Timex machine that played simple games. In high school in New York, engineering engaged her love of creative problem-solving as well as the clean absolutes of math. She interned at MRI labs, helping to program computers for processing brain-scan imagery.

"I really liked the idea that you could build your way to a solution," she said. "I like the rigor. I like the logic." And computers were fun. Freewheeling chat rooms on America Online, the dial-up internet service, provided thrillingly randomized connections. Forums for esoteric shared interests, like DiResta's favorite band, Nine Inch Nails, felt like real communities. In college she majored in computer science but decided against a graduate degree, opting instead for work in intelligence and finance. Still, when the dust from the financial crisis settled, she got in touch with friends at Google. Come out West, they said.

Though her investment work in Silicon Valley focused on hardware, she'd picked up enough about social media to understand what she'd found in her Facebook searches. The reason the system pushed the conspiratorial outliers so hard, she came to realize, was engagement. Social media platforms surfaced whatever content their automated systems had concluded would maximize users' activity online, thereby allowing the company to sell more ads. A mother who accepts that vaccines are safe has little reason to spend much time discussing the subject online. Like-minded parenting groups she joins, while large, might be relatively quiet. But a mother who suspects a vast medical conspiracy imperiling her children, DiResta saw, might spend hours researching the subject. She is also likely to seek out allies, sharing information and coordinating action to fight back. To the A.I. governing a social media platform, the conclusion is obvious: moms interested in health issues will come to spend vastly more time online if they join anti-vaccine groups. Therefore, promoting them, through whatever method wins those users' notice, will boost engagement. If she was right, DiResta knew, then Facebook wasn't just indulging anti-vaccine extremists. It was creating them.

"I felt like Chicken Little, telling people the sky was falling," she said. "And they were looking at me like, 'It's just some social media post.'" But what DiResta had discerned was that there was something structurally wrong with the platform. Friends in the Valley got in touch with her to say they were noticing strangely similar disturbances across all sorts of online communities. She sensed a common set of dynamics at play, perhaps even a common origin point somewhere in the bowels of the social web. And if this was the effect on something narrow like school vaccination policy or video game discussions, what would happen when it reached politics or society more broadly?

"I was looking at it and saying, 'This is going to be such a disaster,'" she recalled.

It was a journey that would eventually take her to the trails of the Islamic State and Russian military intelligence. To State Department meeting rooms and a congressional witness table. And to a set of shocking realizations about social media's influence on us all. But it started in California, fighting an online fringe she did not yet realize represented something much deeper and more intractable.

Almost certainly, no one at Facebook or YouTube wanted to promote vaccine denial. The groups represented such a tiny slice of their empires that any ad money they brought in was likely trivial. Zuckerberg, in a tacit response to the problem, wrote in 2015 that "the science is completely clear: vaccinations work and are important for the health of everyone in our community." But the technology building this fringe movement was driven by something even the company's CEO could not overcome: the cultural and financial mores at the core of his entire industry.

2. *American Galápagos*

LESS THAN A century ago, the Santa Clara Valley, in central California, was a sleepy expanse of fruit orchards and canneries, specked by the occasional oil derrick. That began to change in 1941, when the Japanese navy struck Pearl Harbor, setting in motion a series of events that remade this backwater into one of the greatest concentrations of wealth the world has ever known.

The story of that transformation, which bears little resemblance to the hacker legends or dorm-room tales that pass for Silicon Valley's mostly self-invented lore, instilled the Valley with cultural and economic traits that were built into the products that increasingly rule our world. And it began with a wave of pioneers who played a role as crucial as any of the engineers or CEOs who came after them: the military-industrial complex.

After Pearl Harbor, the Pentagon, preparing to push into the Pacific but fearing another surprise attack, dispersed military production and research across parts of the West Coast that still had a touch of the frontier to them. One such location was Moffett Field, a largely disused air-base on a protected bay, shielded by the Santa Cruz Mountains. When the war ended, the war machine stayed, repurposed for the ever-escalating stand-off with the Soviet Union. Planning for nuclear war, the Pentagon encouraged contractors to shift vital projects away from major population centers. The aerospace giant Lockheed complied, moving its missiles and space division to the quiet Santa Clara Valley, just behind hangar three on Moffett Field. Much of the Cold War arms race was conducted from its campus. Apple co-founder Steve Wozniak, like many of his era, grew up watching a parent head to Lockheed every morning.

Equally important was an unusual new academic research center, just a few miles away. Frederick Terman, the son of a psychology professor at then-unremarkable Stanford University, spent World War II at Harvard's labs, overseeing joint military–academic research projects. He returned home with an idea: that this model continue into peacetime, with university scientists cooperating instead with private companies. He established the Stanford Research Park, where companies could work alongside academic researchers.

With Cold War contractors already next door, there were plenty of takers. The arrangement drew talented scientists and graduate students from back East, offering them the chance to get in on a lucrative patent or startup. University research departments usually toil, at least in theory, on behalf of the greater good. Stanford blurred the line between academic and for-profit work, a development that became core to the Silicon Valley worldview, absorbed and propagated by countless companies cycling through the Research Park. Hitting it big in the tech business and advancing human welfare, the thinking went, were not only compatible, they were one and the same.

These conditions made 1950s Santa Clara what Margaret O'Mara, a prominent historian of Silicon Valley, has called a silicon Galápagos. Much as those islands' peculiar geology and extreme isolation produced one-of-a-kind bird and lizard species, the Valley's peculiar conditions produced ways of doing business and of seeing the world that could not have flourished anywhere else — and led ultimately to Facebook, YouTube, and Twitter.

The chance migration that seeded much of the Valley's technological DNA, like an adrift iguana landing on a Galápagos shore, was a cantankerous engineer named William Shockley. At Bell Labs, perhaps the most prestigious of the East Coast research firms, he'd shared a 1956 Nobel Prize for pioneering new semi-conductive transistors. The tiny devices, which direct or modify electrical signals, are the building blocks of modern electronics. Shockley became convinced he could beat Bell's methods. When his mother's health declined, he returned home, the same year as his Nobel, to care for her and start his own transistor company. His hometown just happened to be Palo Alto, five miles from Moffett Field. His transistor design called for replacing the conventionally used germanium with silicon.

Shockley, who had a reputation for being difficult and arrogant, struggled to convince Bell engineers to follow him. Besides, even with money flowing from the Pentagon, few scientists with any pedigree wanted to relocate to the backwater of San Jose. So he hired talented engineers with backgrounds that limited their opportunities in Boston: nongraduate, immigrants, Jews. Some, like Shockley, were brilliant but difficult to work with. It established Valley startups, forever after, as the domain of self-starter misfits rising on raw merit — a legacy that would lead its future generations to elevate misanthropic dropouts and to excuse toxic, Shockley-style corporate cultures as somehow essential to the model. Within a year of Shockley's launch, though, his talent all quit. His "fondness for humiliating his employees," his knee-jerk rejection of any idea not his own, and his inclination toward extremes — he later embraced eugenics and called Black people genetically inferior — was too much to endure.

For the defectors, the easy and expected thing would've been to bring their innovations back East, where the rest of the industry still lay. Instead, perhaps for no better reason than California weather, they got East Coast financing and stayed put. Because they happened to be based in the Santa Clara Valley, that was where future semiconductor investment and talent came as well. The little industry thrived thanks to the mass of engineers already in town for Lockheed, ensuring top-flight recruits for any promising startup. And the Stanford Research Park put cutting-edge research within easy reach.

That pool of talent, money, and technology — the three essential ingredients — would be kept in the Valley, and the rest of the world kept out, by an unusual funding practice: venture capitalism. Wall Street money mostly stayed away. The products were too esoteric and the market too opaque for outside financiers. Seemingly the only people able to identify promising ideas, the engineers themselves, provided startup funding. Someone who'd made some money on their own project would hear about a new widget getting designed across town and grant seed money — venture capital — for a percentage stake.

The arrangement went beyond money. An effective venture capitalist, to safeguard an investment, would often take a seat on the company's board, help select the executive team, even personally mentor the founder. And venture capitalists tended to fund people whom they trusted — which meant people they knew personally or who looked and talked like them. This meant that each class of successful engineers reified their strengths, as well as their biases and blind spots, in the next, like an isolated species whose traits become more pronounced with each subsequent generation.

As semiconductors developed into the circuit board, then the computer, then the internet, and then social media, each technology produced a handful of breakout stars, who in turn funded and guided the next handful. Throughout, their community remained a commercial-cultural Galápagos, free to develop its own hyper-specific practices for how a business should work, what constitutes success, and what responsibilities a company has to its customers and the wider world.

The consequences of their model, in all its peculiarities, would not become apparent until Shockley's successors assumed, in the form of social media giants, indirect control over us all. But the first indications were already emerging by the mid-2000s, as Silicon Valley began tinkering with a bit of hardware more complex than any semiconductor or computer: the human mind.

3. Against News Feed

IF YOU HAD to pinpoint the dawn of the social media era, you might pick September 2006, when the operators of a dorm-grown website, Facebook.com, made an accidental discovery while trying to solve a business problem. Since launching the site two and a half years earlier, they'd run a modestly successful entry in the modestly successful social media industry, in which users maintained personalized profile pages and did little else. At the time, Facebook had 8 million users, impressive for a bunch of kids barely old enough to drink, but not enough to guarantee survival. Even Friendster, already seen by then as a catastrophic failure, had about 10 million. So did LiveJournal. Orkut had 15 million. Myspace was nearing 100 million.

Facebook's two competitive advantages were coming to look like liabilities. Its clean design made it visually appealing but less lucrative than ad-stuffed LiveJournal or Myspace. And its exclusivity to college campuses had won it a large share of a market that was both limited and cash-poor. The company had tried expanding to workplaces, but few workers signed up. What self-respecting adult would put their professional life on a website for college kids?

User growth had stalled when, that summer, a life raft appeared: Yahoo offered to buy Facebook for $1 billion. The internet giant was bringing in at least that much in revenue every quarter. But its web-portal business was growing obsolete and the company was casting around for new growth markets. Social media seemed promising. But to much of the industry's surprise, after months of negotiation, Zuckerberg turned it down. He did not want to get off the startup roller coaster and, at age twenty-two, become a cog at ossifying, unhip Yahoo. However, denying employees pulling all-nighters a chance to retire rich in their twenties left Zuckerberg under tremendous pressure not only to turn Facebook around but to succeed so wildly that Yahoo's billion would seem small.

Part two of his two-part plan was to eventually open up Facebook to anyone. But the failed expansion to workplaces made it uncertain that would succeed, and might even be counterproductive if it drove out college kids, which was why so much rested on part one. He would overhaul Facebook's homepage to show each user a personalized feed of what their friends were up to on the site. Until then, you had to check each profile or group manually for any activity. Now, if one friend changed her relationship status, another posted about bad pizza in the cafeteria, and another signed up for an event, all of that would be reported on your homepage.

That stream of updates had a name: the news feed. It was presented as a never-ending party attended by everyone you knew. But to some users it felt like being forced into a panopticon, where everyone had total, unblinking visibility into the digital lives of everyone else. Facebook groups with names like "Students Against Facebook News Feed" cropped up. Nothing tangible happened in the groups. Joining signaled your agreement; that was it. But because of the site redesign, each time someone joined, all of that person's friends got a notification on their feed alerting them. With a tap of the mouse, they could join, too, which would be broadcast in turn to their friends. Within a few hours, the groups were everywhere. One attracted 100,000 members on its first day and, by the end of the week, nearly a million.

In reality, only a minority of users ever joined. But proliferating updates made them look like an overwhelming majority. And the news feed rendered each lazy click of the "join" button as an impassioned shout: "Against News Feed" or "I HATE FACEBOOK." The appearance of widespread anger, therefore, was an illusion. But human instincts to conform run deep. When people think something has become a matter of consensus, psychologists have found, they tend not only to go along, but to internalize that sentiment as their own.

Soon, outrage became action. Tens of thousands emailed Facebook customer service. By the next morning, satellite TV trucks besieged Facebook's Palo Alto office, as did enough protesters that police asked the company to consider switching off whatever had caused such controversy. Some within Facebook agreed. The crisis was calmed externally with a testy public apology from Zuckerberg — "Calm down. Breathe. We hear you" — and, internally, with an ironic realization: the outrage was being ginned up by the very Facebook product that users were railing against.

That digital amplification had tricked Facebook's users, and even its leadership, into misperceiving the platform's loudest voices as representing everyone, growing a flicker of anger into a wildfire. But, crucially, it had also done something else: driven engagement up. Way up. In an industry where user engagement is the primary metric of success, and in a company eager to prove that turning down Yahoo's billion-dollar overture had been more than hubris, the news feed's distortions were not just tolerated, they were embraced. Facebook soon allowed anyone to register for the site. User growth rates, which had barely budged during the prior expansion round, exploded by 600 or 700 percent. The average amount of time each person spent online grew rapidly, too. Just thirteen months later, in the fall of 2007, the company was valued at $15 billion.

I have come to think of this as Silicon Valley's monolith moment, akin to the scene at the beginning of Kubrick's *2001: A Space Odyssey*, when a black pillar appears before a clan of chimpanzees, who suddenly learn to wield tools. The breakthrough sent Facebook leaping ahead of competitors it had previously lagged far behind. Others went extinct as a new generation arose in their place.

When the news feed launched in 2006, 11 percent of Americans were on social media. Between 2 and 4 percent used Facebook. Less than a decade later, in 2014, nearly two thirds of Americans used social networking, among whom Facebook, YouTube, and Twitter were near-universal. That year, halfway through the second Obama term, a significant threshold was crossed in the human experience. For the first time, the 200 million Americans with an active Facebook account spent, on average, more time on the platform (forty minutes per day) than they did socializing in person (thirty-eight minutes). Just two years later, by the summer of 2016, nearly 70 percent of Americans used Facebook-owned platforms, averaging fifty minutes per day.

These systems hooked so many users so effectively that, by then, the market value of Facebook, a free-to-use web service with almost no physical products or consumer services, exceeded that of Wells Fargo, one of the world's largest banks. That same year it also surpassed General Electric and

JPMorgan Chase, then, by the end of 2017, ExxonMobil. Ever since, two of the world's largest companies have been Facebook and Google, another mostly free web service that makes much of its money from ads, particularly on YouTube, its subsidiary.

Long after their technology's potential for harm had been made clear, the companies would claim to merely serve, and never shape or manipulate, their users' desires. But manipulation had been built into the products from the beginning.

4. The Casino Effect

"WHEN FACEBOOK WAS getting going, I had these people who would come up to me and they would say, 'I'm not on social media,'" Sean Parker, who had become Facebook's first president at age twenty-four, recalled years later. "And I would say, 'Okay, you know, you will be.' And then they would say, 'No, no, no. I value my real-life interactions. I value the moment. I value presence. I value intimacy.' And I would say, 'We'll get you eventually.'"

Parker prided himself as a hacker, as did much of the Silicon Valley generation that arose in the 1990s, when the term still bespoke a kind of counterculture cool. Most actually built corporate software. But Parker had cofounded Napster, a file-sharing program whose users distributed so much pirated music that, by the time lawsuits shut it down two years after launching, it had irrevocably damaged the music business. Parker argued he'd forced the industry to evolve by exploiting its lethargy in moving online. Many of its artists and executives, however, saw him as a parasite.

Facebook's strategy, as he described it, was not so different from Napster's. But rather than exploiting weaknesses in the music industry, it would do so for the human mind. "The thought process that went into building these applications," Parker told the media conference, "was all about, 'How do we consume as much of your time and conscious attention as possible?'" To do that, he said, "We need to sort of give you a little dopamine hit every once in a while, because someone liked or commented on a photo or a post or whatever. And that's going to get you to contribute more content, and that's going to get you more likes and comments." He termed this the "social-validation feedback loop," calling it "exactly the kind of thing that a hacker like myself would come up with, because you're exploiting a vulnerability in human psychology." He and Zuckerberg "understood this" from the beginning, he said, and "we did it anyway."

Throughout the Valley, this exploitation, far from some dark secret, was openly discussed as an exciting tool for business growth. The term of art is "persuasion": training consumers to alter their behavior in ways that serve the bottom line. Stanford University had operated a Persuasive Tech Lab since 1997. In 2007, a single semester's worth of student projects generated $1 million in advertising revenue.

"How do companies, producing little more than bits of code displayed on a screen, seemingly control users' minds?" Nir Eyal, a prominent Valley product consultant, asked in his 2014 book, *Hooked: How to Build Habit-Forming Products*. "Our actions have been engineered," he explained. Services like Twitter and YouTube "habitually alter our everyday behavior, just as their designers intended."

One of Eyal's favorite models is the slot machine. It is designed to answer your every action with visual, auditory, and tactile feedback. A ping when you insert a coin. A ka-chunk when you pull the lever. A flash of colored light when you release it. This is known as Pavlovian conditioning, named after the Russian physiologist Ivan Pavlov, who rang a bell each time he fed his dog, until, eventually, the bell alone sent his dog's stomach churning and saliva glands pulsing, as if it could no longer differentiate the chiming of a bell from the physical sensation of eating. Slot machines work the same way, training your mind to conflate the thrill of winning with its mechanical clangs and buzzes. The act of pulling the lever, once meaningless, becomes pleasurable in itself.

The reason is a neurological chemical called dopamine, the same one Parker had referenced at the media conference. Your brain releases small amounts of it when you fulfill some basic need, whether biological (hunger, sex) or social (affection, validation). Dopamine creates a positive association with whatever behaviors prompted its release, training you to repeat them. But when that dopamine reward system gets hijacked, it can compel you to repeat self-destructive behaviors. To place one more bet, binge on alcohol — or spend hours on apps even when they make you unhappy.

Dopamine is social media's accomplice inside your brain. It's why your smartphone looks and feels like a slot machine, pulsing with colorful notification badges, whoosh sounds, and gentle vibrations. Those stimuli are neurologically meaningless on their own. But your phone pairs them with activities, like texting a friend or looking at photos, that are naturally rewarding.

Social apps hijack a compulsion — a need to connect — that can be even more powerful than hunger or greed. Eyal describes a hypothetical woman, Barbra, who logs on to Facebook to see a photo uploaded by a family member. As she clicks through more photos or comments in response, her brain conflates feeling connected to people she loves with the bleeps and flashes of Facebook's interface. "Over time," Eyal writes, "Barbra begins to associate Facebook with her need for social connection." She learns to serve that need with a behavior — using Facebook — that in fact will rarely fulfill it.

Soon after Facebook's news-feed breakthrough, the major social media platforms converged on what Eyal called one of the casino's most powerful secrets: intermittent variable reinforcement. The concept, while sounding esoteric, is devilishly simple. The psychologist B. F. Skinner found that if he assigned a human subject a repeatable task — solving a simple puzzle, say — and rewarded her every time she completed it, she would usually comply, but would stop right after he stopped rewarding her. But if he doled out the reward only sometimes, and randomized its size, then she would complete the task far more consistently, even doggedly. And she would keep completing the task long after the rewards had stopped altogether — as if chasing even the possibility of a reward compulsively.

Slot machines leverage this psychological weakness to incredible effect. The unpredictability of the payout makes it harder to stop. Social media does the same. Posting on Twitter might yield a big social payoff, in the form of likes, retweets, and replies. Or it might yield no reward at all. Never knowing the outcome makes it harder to stop pulling the lever. Intermittent variable reinforcement is a defining feature of not only gambling and addiction but also, tellingly, abusive relationships. Abusers veer unpredictably between kindness and cruelty, punishing partners for behaviors that they had previously rewarded with affection. This can lead to something called traumatic bonding. The victimized partner finds herself compulsively seeking a positive response, like a gambler feeding a slot machine, or a Facebook addict unable to log off from the platform — even if, for many, it only makes them lonelier.

Further, while posting to social media can feel like a genuine interaction between you and an audience, there is one crucial, invisible difference. Online, the platform acts as unseen intermediary. It decides which of your comments to distribute to whom, and in what context. Your next post might get shown to people who will love it and applaud, or to people who will hate it and heckle, or to neither. You'll never know because its decisions are invisible. All you know is that you hear cheers, boos, or crickets.

Unlike slot machines, which are rarely at hand in our day-to-day lives, social media apps are some of the most easily accessible products on earth. It's a casino that fits in your pocket, which is how we slowly train ourselves to answer any dip in our happiness with a pull at the most ubiquitous slot machine in history. The average American checks their smartphone 150 times per day, often to open social media. We don't do this because compulsively checking social media apps makes us happy. In 2018, a team of economists offered users different amounts of money to deactivate their account for four weeks, looking for the threshold at which at least half of them would say yes. The number turned out to be high: $180. But the people who deactivated experienced more happiness, less anxiety, and greater life satisfaction. After the experiment was over, they used the app less than they had before.

Why had these subjects been so resistant to give up a product that made them unhappy? Their behavior, the economists wrote, was "consistent with standard habit formation models" — i.e., with addiction — leading to "sub-optimal consumption choices." A clinical way of saying the subjects had been trained to act against their own interests.

5. The Sociometer

A YEAR AFTER launching the news feed, a group of Facebook developers mocked up something they called the "awesome button" — a one-click expression of approval for another user's post. Zuckerberg nixed the idea several times, believing it would divert users from more engaging behaviors like posting comments. It became "considered a cursed project because it had failed so many Zuck reviews," wrote Andrew Bosworth, one of the developers of the news feed, who later became a Facebook vice president. After a year and a half in limbo, a new team took over what was now the "Like" button. In user tests, Bosworth wrote in a post recalling the episode, they found that the button increased the number of comments. When Zuckerberg saw that, he relented.

In early 2009, a product manager named Leah Pearlman, who'd worked on the feature since shortly after joining Facebook at age twenty-three, published a post announcing it as "an easy way to tell friends that you like what they're sharing on Facebook with one easy click." Traffic surged immediately, well beyond internal expectations. But user behavior changed, too. For all the Nir Eyals and Sean Parkers deliberating about addict users, this was, as with the news feed and so many developments to come, another episode of social companies stumbling into even more powerful psychological hacks they did not understand.

That little button's appeal, and much of social media's power, comes from exploiting something called the sociometer. The concept emerged out of a question posed by the psychologist Mark Leary: what is the purpose of self-esteem? The anguish we feel from low self-esteem is wholly self-generated. We would not have developed such an unusual and painful vulnerability, Leary reasoned, unless it provided some benefit outweighing its tremendous psychic costs. His theory, now widely held, is that self-esteem is in fact "a psychological gauge of the degree to which people perceive that they are relationally valued and socially accepted by other people."

Human beings are some of the most complex social animals on earth. We evolved to live in leaderless collectives far larger than those of our fellow primates: up to about 150 members. As individuals, our ability to thrive depended on how well we navigated those 149 relationships — not to mention all of our peers' relationships with one another. If the group valued us, we could count on support, resources, and probably a mate. If it didn't, we might get none of those. It was a matter of survival, physically and genetically.

Over millions of years, those pressures selected for people who are sensitive to and skilled at maximizing their standing. It's what the anthropologist Brian Hare called "survival of the friendliest." The result was the development of a sociometer: a tendency to unconsciously monitor how other people in our community seem to perceive us. We process that information in the form of self-esteem and such related emotions as pride, shame, or insecurity. These emotions compel us to do more of what makes our community value us and less of what doesn't. And, crucially, they are meant to make that motivation feel like it is coming from within. If we realized, on a conscious level, that we were responding to social pressure, our performance might come off as grudging or cynical, making it less persuasive.

Facebook's "Like" feature, some version of which now exists on every platform, is the equivalent of a car battery hooked up to that sociometer. It gives whoever controls the electric jolts tremendous power over our behavior. It's not just that "likes" provide the social validation we spend so much of our energy pursuing; it's that they offer it at an immediacy and scale heretofore unknown in the human experience. Off-line, explicit validation is relatively infrequent. Even rarer is hearing it announced publicly, which is the most powerful form of approval because it conveys our value to the broader community. When's the last time fifty, sixty, seventy people publicly applauded you off-line? Maybe once every few years — if ever? On social media, it's a normal morning.

Further, the platforms added a powerful twist: a counter at the bottom of each post indicating the number of likes, retweets, or upvotes it had received — a running quantification of social approval for each and every statement. This was how even LinkedIn, a résumé-hosting bulletin board, became a networking site and sold to Microsoft for a deal worth $26.2 billion. It had added badges to users' profiles indicating the size of their network. "Even though at the time there was nothing useful you could do with LinkedIn, that simple icon had a powerful effect in tapping into people's desire not to look like losers," B. J. Fogg, the head of Stanford's Persuasive Tech Lab, has said. But by 2020, even Twitter's co-founder and then-CEO, Jack Dorsey, conceded he had come to doubt the thinking that had led to the Like button, and especially "that button having a number associated with it." Though he would not commit to rolling back the feature, he acknowledged that it had created "an incentive that can be dangerous."

In fact, the incentive is so powerful that it even shows up on brain scans. When we receive a Like, neural activity flares in a part of the brain called the nucleus accumbens: the region that activates dopamine. Subjects with smaller nucleus accumbens — a trait associated with addictive tendencies — use Facebook for longer stretches. And when heavy Facebook users get a Like, that gray matter displays more activity than in lighter users, as in gambling addicts who've been conditioned to exalt in every pull of the lever.

Pearlman, the Facebooker who'd helped launch the Like button, discovered this after quitting Silicon Valley, in 2011, to draw comics. She promoted her work, of course, on Facebook. At first, her comics did well. They portrayed uplifting themes related to gratitude and compassion, which Facebook's systems boosted in the early 2010s. Until, around 2015, Facebook retooled its systems to disfavor curiosity-grabbing "clickbait," which had the secondary effect of removing the artificial boost the platform had once given her warmly emotive content.

"When Facebook changed their algorithm, my likes dropped off and it felt like I wasn't getting enough oxygen," Pearlman later told *Vice News*. "So even if I could blame it on the algorithm, something inside me was like, 'They don't like me, I'm not good enough.'" Her own former employer had turned her brain's nucleus accumbens against her, creating an internal drive for likes so powerful that it overrode her better judgment. Then, like Skinner toying with a research subject, it simply turned the rewards off. "Suddenly I was buying ads, just to get that attention back," she admitted.

For most of us, the process is subtler. Instead of buying Facebook ads, we modify our day-to-day posts and comments to keep the dopamine coming, usually without realizing we have done it. This is the real "social-validation feedback loop," as Sean Parker called it: unconsciously chasing the approval of an automated system designed to turn our needs against us.

"It is very common for humans to develop things with the best of intentions and for them to have unintended, negative consequences," Justin Rosenstein, a former Facebook engineer who'd also worked on the Like button, told *The Guardian*. "If we only care about profit maximization, we will go rapidly into dystopia," he warned. "One reason I think it is particularly important for us to talk about this now is that we may be the last generation that can remember life before."

6. The Slingshot

FOR ALL THE weight that attention and approval exert over users like Pearlman, and all the addictive pull of casino-like badges, the single most powerful force on social media is identity. It's the stimulus that performs best on the technology's systems and that its systems are therefore engineered to activate and engender above all else. Expressing identity, sharpening identity, seeing and defining the world through its lens. This effect remade how social media works, as its overseers and automated systems drifted toward the all-consuming focus on identity that best served their agendas.

To understand identity's power, start by asking yourself: What words best describe my own? Your nationality, race, or religion may come to mind. Maybe your city, profession, or gender. Our sense of self derives largely from our membership in groups. But this compulsion — its origins, its effects on our minds and actions — "remains a deep mystery to the social psychologist," Henri Tajfel wrote in 1979, when he set out to resolve it.

Tajfel had learned the power of group identity firsthand. In 1939, Germany occupied his home country, Poland, while he was studying in Paris. Jewish and fearful for his family, he posed as French so as to join the French army. He kept up the ruse when he was captured by German soldiers. After the war, realizing his family had been wiped out, he became legally French, then British. These identities were mere social constructs — how else could he change them out like suits pulled from a closet? Yet they had the power to compel murderousness or mercy in others around him, driving an entire continent to self-destruction.

The questions this raised haunted and fascinated Tajfel. He and several peers launched the study of this phenomenon, which they termed social identity theory. They traced its origins back to a formative challenge of early human existence. Many primates live in cliques. Humans, in contrast, arose in large collectives, where family kinship was not enough to bind mostly unrelated group members. The dilemma was that the group could not survive without each member contributing to the whole, and no one individual, in turn, could survive without support from the group.

Social identity, Tajfel demonstrated, is how we bond ourselves to the group and they to us. It's why we feel compelled to hang a flag in front of our house, don an alma mater T-shirt, slap a bumper sticker on our car. It tells the group that we value our affiliation as an extension of ourselves and can therefore be trusted to serve its common good.

Our drive to cultivate a shared identity is so powerful that we'll construct one even out of nothing. In one experiment, researchers assigned volunteers one of two labels by a simple coin toss, then had them play a game. Each showed greater generosity to others with the same label, even though they knew the division was meaningless. The same behavior has emerged in dozens of experiments and real-world situations, with people consistently embracing any excuse to divide between "us" and "them" — and showing distrust, even hostility, toward those in the out-group. During lunch breaks on the set of the 1968 movie *Planet of the Apes*, for instance, extras spontaneously separated into tables according to whether they played chimpanzees or gorillas. For years afterward, Charlton Heston, the film's star, recounted the "instinctive segregation" as "quite spooky." When the sequel filmed, a different set of extras repeated the behavior exactly.

Prejudice and hostility have always animated this instinct. Hunter-gatherer tribes sometimes competed for resources or territory. One group's survival might require the defeat of another. Because of that, social-identity instincts drive us to distrust and, if necessary, rally against out-group members. Our minds compel those behaviors by sparking two emotions in particular: fear and hate. Both are more social than you might think. Fear of a physical threat from without causes us to feel a greater sense of camaraderie with our in-group, as if rushing to our tribe for safety. It also makes us more distrustful of, and more willing to harm, people whom we perceive as different. Think of the response to the September 11 attacks: a tide of patriotic flag-waving fervor and an alignment of fellow feeling, but one that was also followed by a spike in anti-Muslim hate crimes.

These are deeply social instincts, so social media platforms, by turning every tap or swipe into a social act, reliably surface them. And because the platforms elevate whatever sentiments best win engagement, they often produce those instincts in their most extreme form. The result can be an artificial reality in which the in-group is always virtuous but besieged, the out-group is always a terrifying threat, and virtually everything that happens is a matter of us-versus-them.

Social media's indulgence of identity wasn't obviously harmful at first.

But it was always well known. In 2012, a left-wing activist raised money from co-founders of Facebook and Reddit to start Upworthy, which produced content tailored to spread on social media. By continuously testing what traveled most widely, Upworthy reverse-engineered a formula for virality. Numbered lists did well. So did "curiosity gap" headlines that begged to be clicked: "You'll Never Guess What This Coach Said to Cheer Up His Players." But one formula proved especially effective: headlines promising to portray the user's implied in-group (liberals, usually) as humiliating a reviled out-group (creationists, corporations, racists). "A Man Slams a Bigoted Question So Hard He Brings Down the House."

Meanwhile, scores of newspapers were downsizing or shuttering, their business models gutted by the internet. Upworthy, on almost no budget, had gained an audience several times as large as any newspaper's. A desperate industry took note. Entire organizations rose or reorganized around chasing virality. *BuzzFeed* became an internet giant on list-based articles indulging users' desire for social-identity affirmation: "28 Signs You Were Raised by Irish Parents" or "31 Things Only People from a Small Town Will Understand."

In 2014, I was one of several *Washington Post* reporters to start Vox, a news site intended to leverage the web. We never shaped our journalism to please social media algorithms — at least, not consciously — but headlines were devised with them in mind. The most effective approach, though one that in retrospect we should have perhaps been warier of using, was identity conflict. Liberals versus conservatives. The righteousness of anti-racism. The outrageousness of lax gun laws. "Identity was the slingshot," Ezra Klein, Vox's founder, wrote about digital media in a book on polarization. "Few realized, early on, that the way to win the war for attention was to harness the power of community to create identity. But the winners emerged quickly, often using techniques whose mechanisms they didn't fully understand."

Often, that meant hyperpartisan provocateurs, for-profit click farms, outright scammers. Unconstrained by any fealty to fairness, accuracy, or the greater good, they ran up huge audiences by indulging, or provoking, identity conflicts. The consequences might not have seemed, at first, to extend much beyond the internet. But warnings of a most terrible form, and in retrospect of the greatest possible clarity, had been coming in for years, from a part of the world where the stakes could not have been higher and the attention paid to it lower.

7. *The Ride of Your Life*

WHAT HAPPENS WHEN an entire society goes online at once, transitioning overnight from life without social media to one dominated by it? Such an experiment might sound impossible, but it happened. Its name is Myanmar.

"I'm convinced that you all are in for the ride of your life right now," Eric Schmidt, Google's longtime CEO, told a roomful of students in an early 2013 visit to the southeast Asian country. "The internet will make it impossible to go back."

For decades, this Texas-sized country of tropical forests, paddy-filled river deltas, and Indian Ocean coastline had been shrouded in some of the most complete isolation of any nation on earth. A paranoid military junta imposed near-total bans on the internet, cell phones, foreign media, and international travel. Torture and repressive violence were executed with the worst combination of incompetence and cruelty. In 2011, the aging leader was replaced with yet another dour-faced general, Thein Sein, but Sein turned out to have reformist leanings. He urged exiles to return home, eased media restrictions, and released political prisoners. He distanced himself from China, Myanmar's increasingly imperious northern neighbor, and opened talks with the United States. Sanctions were lifted and elections scheduled; in 2012, Barack Obama became the first sitting U.S. president to visit.

A supporting but highly visible player in the country's opening, welcomed by both Myanmar and American leaders, was Silicon Valley. Rapidly bringing the country online would, they promised, modernize its economy and empower its 50 million citizens, effectively locking in the transition to democracy. A few months after Obama's visit, Schmidt, acting as the Valley's ambassador-at-large, landed in Yangon, Myanmar's historic capital, to announce big tech's arrival. Flanked by the American ambassador, he told the student audience, "The internet, once in place, guarantees that communication and empowerment become the law and the practice of your country."

Myanmar's leaders believed in Silicon Valley's vision as well. A state-run newspaper admonished its citizens that "a person without a Facebook identity is like a person without a home address." The country moved online almost instantaneously. From 2012 to 2015, internet-adoption rates exploded from 0.5 percent to 40 percent, mostly through cheap smartphones. SIM card prices dropped from $1,500 to $1.50.

Facebook played a prominent role. Through deals with local companies, it arranged for smartphones to come preloaded with a stripped-down Facebook app. In poorer countries like Myanmar, where average incomes are around $3 a day, cell-phone data can be prohibitively expensive. To overcome this obstacle and thereby win the race to capture the world's poorest two or three billion customers, Facebook and other American tech companies began "zero-rating" — essentially, subsidizing the entire population by striking deals with local carriers to waive charges for any data used via those companies' apps. Myanmar was an early test case and, for Facebook, a staggering success. A huge proportion of the country learned to message and browse the web exclusively through Facebook, so much so that many there remain unaware that any other way to communicate or read news online exists.

I first arrived in Myanmar in early 2014, landing in Yangon to report on the country's tenuous transition to democracy. It felt like a place frozen in the early 1960s, when military rulers had cut it off from the outside world. Power outages were common and modern technology rare; the first international ATMs were only just being installed. Crumbling British colonial offices, overtaken by ivy, still dominated the city center. Many downtown streets were unpaved and, in the early mornings, filled with hundreds of barefoot monks. The orange- and crimson-robed clergy, revered by the deeply pious Buddhist majority, are everywhere in Myanmar.

Shuttling between interviews with politicians and activists, I came to see Myanmar's future as shakier than it had been portrayed. The military still held vestiges of power that it seemed reluctant to surrender. Among the clergy, an extremist fringe was rising. And its newly available social media was filling with racism and conspiracies. Online, angry talk of traitorous minorities felt ubiquitous.

A worrying name kept coming up in my conversations: Wirathu. The Buddhist monk had been imprisoned for his hate-filled sermons for the past decade and had just been released as part of a general amnesty. He'd immediately joined Facebook and YouTube. Now, rather than traveling the country temple by temple to spread hate, he used the platforms to reach much of the country, perhaps multiple times per day. He accused the country's Muslim minority of terrifying crimes, blending rumor with shameless fabrication. On Facebook especially, his posts circulated and recirculated among users who took them as fact, creating an alternate reality defined by conspiracy and rage, which propelled Wirathu to a new level of stardom.

A Stanford researcher who had worked in Myanmar, Aela Callan, met with senior Facebook managers in late 2013 to warn them that hate speech was overrunning the platform, she later told the reporter Timothy McLaughlin. For a country with hundreds of thousands of users, and soon millions, Facebook employed only one moderator who could review content in Burmese, Myanmar's predominant language, leaving the platform effectively unsupervised. The managers told Callan that Facebook would press forward with its Myanmar expansion anyway.

In early 2014, Callan relayed another warning to Facebook: the problem was worsening, and with it the threat of violence. Again, little changed. A few months later, Wirathu shared a post falsely claiming that two Muslim tea shop owners in the city of Mandalay had raped a Buddhist woman. He posted the names of the tea sellers and their shop, calling their fictitious assault the opening shot in a mass Muslim uprising against Buddhists. He urged the government to raid Muslims' homes and mosques in a preemptive strike — a common demand of genocidaires, whose implied message is that regular citizens must do what the authorities will not. The post went viral, dominating feeds across the country. Outraged users joined in the froth, urging one another to wipe out their Muslim neighbors. Hundreds rioted in Mandalay, attacking Muslim businesses and owners, killing two people and wounding many more.

As the riots spread, a senior government official called someone he knew at the Myanmar office of Deloitte, a consulting firm, to ask for help in contacting Facebook. But neither could reach anyone at the company. In desperation, the government blocked access to Facebook in Mandalay. The riots cooled. The next day, officials at Facebook finally responded to the Deloitte representative, not to inquire after the violence but to ask if he knew why the platform had been blocked. In a meeting two weeks later with the government official and others, a Facebook representative said that they were working to improve their responsiveness to dangerous content in Myanmar. But if the company made any changes, the effect was undetectable on its platform. As soon as the government lifted its virtual blockade, hate speech, and Wirathu's audience, only grew. "From at least that Mandalay incident, Facebook knew," David Madden, an Australian who ran Myanmar's largest tech-startup accelerator, told McLaughlin, the reporter. "That's not 20/20 hindsight. The scale of this problem was significant and it was already apparent."

Either unable or unwilling to consider that its product might be dangerous, Facebook continued expanding its reach in Myanmar and other developing and under-monitored countries. It moored itself entirely to a self-enriching Silicon Valley credo that Schmidt had recited on that early visit to Yangon: "The answer to bad speech is more speech. More communication, more voices."

Two

Everything Is Gamergate

1. A New Era

IT WAS AUGUST 2014, a month after the Mandalay riots. Zoë Quinn was raising a glass with friends at a San Francisco bar, marking her twenty-seventh birthday, when the social web came crashing down on her with such terrible force that it altered the trajectory of the internet and nearly everything that emerged from it thereafter. Her phone buzzed with a text from a friend: *You just got helldumped something fierce.* A programmer named Eron Gjoni had posted to his blog a rambling, 10,000-word narrative of their brief relationship and breakup, which included screenshots of private emails, text messages, and Facebook messages.

Quinn, a Technicolor-haired video game developer, was a familiar presence on geek forums and social platforms. She had won glancing critical attention for indie art pieces like *Depression Quest*, a text-based simulation of navigating clinical depression, and for her outspoken feminism. She posted frequently, and sometimes stridently, in support of a cause then gaining momentum among like-minded game-makers and journalists: broadening gaming's appeal and fan culture beyond its traditional enclave of young male geeks. But some online gaming circles seethed at feminist transgressors who sought, they believed, to corrupt the hobby that had become, amid a world that struck many early social media obsessives as hostile and confusing, a kind of safe space. This was more than a debate over whether prince-rescues-buxom-princess games could make room for offbeat entries like Quinn's, or even for girl gamers; it was about a geek male identity whose adherents saw themselves as under attack. Gjoni's narrative of anger and resentment resonated with their own.

One particular detail from Gjoni's post had swirled through video game forums, onto mainline platforms, to Quinn's friends, and back to her phone. Gjoni claimed that she had slept with a video game reviewer in exchange for positive coverage of *Depression Quest*. His accusation was easily debunked; the supposedly ill-gotten review did not even exist. But the truth hardly mattered. Users on gaming subsections of the message board 4chan, a center of nerd culture, and especially on Reddit, a sprawling discussion site that had become a teeming megalopolis at the heart of the social web, embraced Gjoni's claim as vindication of their mistrust, setting the narrative for the platforms' millions of users.

Gjoni's post was also read as encouraging the rough justice often embraced on the social web: collective harassment. So much so that a judge later forbade him from writing anything further about Quinn. And indeed, if harassment was Gjoni's goal, his post had the desired effect. "i just want to see zoe get her comeuppance," one 4chan user wrote in a chat organizing the effort to, as another put it, "make her life irrepairably horrible," even "harassing her into killing herself."

"I tried to focus on the conversation at the table," Quinn later wrote, "but the agitated rattling of my phone was the only thing I could hear. It was like counting the seconds between thunderclaps to see how far away the storm is and knowing it's getting closer."

She slipped home to track the hate pouring in online. Already, hundreds of messages urged her to kill herself and pledged to torment her family if she did not, their threats made credible with lists of relatives' addresses and phone numbers. Some circulated photos of her edited into pornography. Others posted personal details like her Social Security number, demonstrating their power to reach into her life. "If I ever see you are doing a pannel at an event I am going to, I will literally kill you," one wrote. "You are lower than shit and deserve to be hurt, maimed, killed, and finally, graced with my piss on your rotting corpse a thousand times over."

Fury at Quinn and the supposedly corrupt gaming press overtook much of 4chan and Reddit, then YouTube. Across all three, huge communities grew obsessed with the made-up scandal they termed Gamergate. But what had begun as another internet-trolling episode, if an unusually large one, gradually became something more, something new. Gamergate altered more than the lives of its targets. It sent the extremes of the social web smashing against mainstream American life, forever ending the separation between digital and nondigital spaces, between internet culture and culture.

It also launched a new kind of politics, defined by social media's foundational traits: a digital culture built around nihilistic young men, Silicon Valley dreams of destructive revolution, and platforms designed in ways that supercharge identity into a matter of totalizing and existential conflict. Other communities, whether as niche as organic-hippie Facebook moms or as large as the American political right, were already following a similarly antagonistic trajectory. Gamergate itself was just a first iteration, but one that carried within it the seeds of others to come. Violent "incel" extremists, a rejuvenated and reimagined far right, and its youth-friendly alt-right offshoot all drew on Gamergate, as did a transformative strain of another movement just beginning to form: Trumpism. Among analysts and journalists who tried to understand this new era, when the rules governing the social web came to govern all of us, a shorthand took hold: "everything is Gamergate."

It would take another year before most beyond Gamergate's immediate wake — which ripped quickly across the media, entertainment, and virtually any online community — felt the consequences. But at first it was about vengeance, about web-dwelling men and boys who felt left behind by American life, exacting revenge on whomever the social networks where they found refuge had trained them to blame.

"If you think your enemy is a symbol and not a person, suddenly there's a bunch of inhuman shit you have the emotional bandwidth to do," Quinn later told an interviewer. "And I know because I've been an asshole. If Gamergate had happened to somebody else, years earlier, I probably would've been on the wrong side. As a shitty teenager with mental illness that had a misogynist streak and loved video games? Yeah."

Over the next several months, Gamergaters targeted dozens of people who spoke out in Quinn's defense, who criticized their methods or online-gaming culture, or who were so much as rumored to be involved in the conspiracy of which they had convinced one another. They turned on like-minded female writers and reporters, inflicting a level of destruction not even social media's sharpest critics then considered possible. One favored method was "swatting" — calling 911 with stories of a hostage-taking at the target's home to prompt, often successfully, a SWAT team raid that, in the confusion, might end with police shooting the target or their family. (In 2017, police arrested a man who'd called in a fatal swat-ting over an online-gaming dispute. He was sentenced to twenty years in prison as part of a plea deal over a separate bomb threat he'd made. Two other serial swatters, each responsible for dozens of false reports, mostly over online-gaming arguments, have faced arrest. Otherwise, online harassers rarely face legal consequences. Though law enforcement has begun to take such activity more seriously, it is time-consuming to investigate and, because it is so decentralized, is nearly impossible to stop or deter. By the time that police might track down a harasser's identity, much less act, the harassment is usually over. And prosecuting one or two especially egre-gious harassers, while restorative for the victim, does little to prevent another hundred users from reproducing the same effect.) Women at game companies, presumed complicit, were targeted as well. Some, fear-ful of exposing their children to harm, quit the field entirely.

When an industry-news site accused Gamergaters of rendering game culture "kind of embarrassing," users flooded the site's biggest advertiser, Intel, with phony complaints, briefly convincing the corporate giant to pull its ads. They did the same to *Gawker*. Reporters on what had previ-ously been the long-quiet gaming beat learned to wipe personal informa-tion from the web and, when unwanted attention came to them, alert family members to the possibility of death threats or cyberattacks.

"The thing that really pushed me over the edge was when what became Gamergate targeted Samantha Allen, who was writing for Polygon," Brianna Wu, an independent game developer, later told me. "They literally ran her out of her job. So it wasn't online drama. It was women having their careers destroyed."

Wu's Mississippi drawl was a constant on industry panels and podcasts, where, long before Gamergate, she'd urged reform of the industry's more boyish tendencies. With Gamergate targeting her friends, she felt compelled to speak up. She expected some blowback but not the ferocity of the response. Throughout late 2014 and early 2015, thousands spammed her with graphic images and insults, making the platforms that she relied on to promote her work all but unusable. Death threats were accompanied by floor plans of her house and photos of her family. A friend tipped her off to forums where users were urging one another to carry the threats out for real.

"I'm sure some of it was just an intimidation tactic," she said. But one threat in particular made her worry that some might be sincere. Even years later, she recalled every word: "Hey bitch, guess what? I know where you and Frank live. If you have any kids, they're going to die too. You did nothing worthwhile with your life. I'm going to cut off your husband's tiny, Asian penis and rape you with it until you bleed." When she contacted law enforcement, they counseled her to leave her home. Several months in, a YouTuber posted a video of himself in a skull mask, flashing a knife he pledged to use against Wu. The incident was written into an episode of *Law & Order: Special Victims Unit*. "Ice-T murders Logan Paul on a rooftop to save the character based on me. I swear to God, I didn't believe it when I heard it," she said with a laugh. The threats have continued. Shortly before we spoke, in June 2020, a brick had crashed through her window.

As Gamergate entered the public consciousness, Wu leveraged connections at social networks to lobby them, at the least, to curb the harassment campaigns emerging from their systems. But the Silicon Valleyites she spoke to, mostly young white men, seemed never to have considered that hate and harassment might have real consequences, much less how to curb them. "It's not because they're villains," she said. "They just don't have a certain lived experience a lot of women, and queer people, and people of color have."

The least responsive companies were Facebook, which would not engage with her at all, and Reddit, one of the places where Gamergate had started. The more that Wu interacted with the platform operators or explored the poison emanating from their sites, the more she suspected a wider danger. "Software increasingly defines the world around us," she wrote in early 2015. Platforms and apps "create our social realities — how we make friends, how we get jobs, and how mankind interacts." But they had been designed with little input from people outside of the Valley's narrow worldview or demographic. "These systems are the next frontier of human evolution, and they're increasingly dangerous for us," Wu concluded, adding, in a sentiment that was considered overstated at the time, "The stakes couldn't be higher."

That transformation had been set in motion forty years earlier, with a generation of Silicon Valley computer makers who saw themselves as revolutionaries destined to tear down the American status quo in its entirety, and who built social networking, very explicitly, as the tool by which they would do it. But their new digital society, envisioned as eventual replacement of all that'd come before, was engineered less for liberation than for anger and conflict, thanks to an original sin of Silicon Valley capitalism and, in the 1990s, a fateful twist in toy economics. The result was a digital world already coursing, by the early 2000s, with a strange mix of male geek chauvinism and, though it was initially dismissed, far-right extremism.

Gamergate announced our new era, of American life shaped by social media's incentives and rules, from platforms just beyond the outskirts of mainstream society. Within a few years, those platforms would grow Gamergate and its offshoots into nationwide movements, carry them into the homes of millions of digital newcomers, and mobilize them into a movement that would, very soon, ride into the White House.

2. *The Revolutionaries*

THE FORMATIVE DAYS of the computer revolution coincided with a period of terrible turbulence in American life. Assassinations, riots, defeat in Vietnam, and the disgraced resignation of Richard Nixon stirred up a deep hostility to centralized authority as well as a counterculture whose wild-eyed extravagances seemed appropriate for the times. But although marketers would later rewrite the computer era into one of iconoclastic dreamers, it actually began with people like Douglas Engelbart, a Naval research engineer. Through the 1960s, Engelbart, backed by grants from NASA and the Pentagon, toiled on a machine that used semiconductors to store and display information. But unlike IBM-style punch-card behemoths, it would be easy enough for nonexperts to use.

The device that Engelbart finally showed off in a 1968 public demonstration displayed the first graphical interface. It also included the first-ever mouse. It could even exchange information with other machines by modem. His demo set off a storm of excitement in the Valley, which saw the makings of a brand-new industry. Public intellectuals, steeped in the countercultural excitement of the moment, announced the device as a step toward dismantling power structures and building a new society from the bottom up. *Future Shock*, a 1970 mega-bestseller, predicted a "technological revolution" empowering individuals above institutions. The sociologist Ted Nelson, a friend of Engelbart's, wrote *Computer Lib/Dream Machines*, whose title ("Lib" short for *liberation*) and cover image of a single raised fist conveyed much of the message.

The mythology took quick purchase in an industry ready to redefine itself. In 1971, a business periodical coined the term "Silicon Valley," referencing the silicon-transistor business launched a decade earlier by William Shockley and his disciples. The next year, a glowing profile of a Valley corporate research office ran in, of all places, *Rolling Stone*. It portrayed the engineers as longhaired eccentrics who would bring us "freedom and weirdness" through a product — the computer — that most people had encountered only as dull, forbidding machinery at their office or university.

Engineers around the Valley were happy to internalize the flattery as truth. Forever after, typing code into a terminal was no longer commercial product development, it was "hacking." "We are really the revolutionaries in the world today — not the kids with the long hair and beards who were wrecking the schools a few years ago," Gordon Moore, a co-founder of Intel, told a reporter. As counterculture eccentricities receded in the rest of America after Nixon's resignation, they held in the Valley, thanks in part to the 1974 arrival of the Altair 8800, the first computer small and cheap enough for home use. The machines were "open," meaning that anyone with the know-how could modify or swap out components. Valley engineers formed after-hours tinkering clubs with names like Homebrew Computer Club and People's Computer Company. In newsletters and regular gatherings, they codified their revolutionary self-image into something like doctrine. PCC's newsletter ran technical guidance alongside treatises on the coming libertarian utopia.

Homebrew's meetups produced a generation of startups, among them Apple Computer. As personal computers expanded beyond the niche hobbyist market, Apple vaulted ahead of its competitors, thanks to its technology and, especially, marketing. It sold the "freedom and weirdness" image to baby boomers as simultaneously nostalgic — echoing '60s counterculture — and aspirational. In 1984, with business skyrocketing year over year, it ran a Super Bowl spot of a woman hurling a hammer at a video screen of a totalitarian overlord. Consumerism as revolution; hacker anarchism suffused with the unashamed capitalism of the Reagan '80s. "It's dangerous," historian Margaret O'Mara said, "because the myth becomes Silicon Valley's reality."

Talk of smashing power structures was, at first, mostly rhetorical. But a handful of zealots built those ideals, taken to an almost millenarian extreme, into something they called the WELL, the first social network of real consequence. It had grown out of a magazine run by a former Ken

Kesey associate named Stewart Brand, who'd spent the '60s driving between California's hippie communes selling supplies out of his truck. He'd called it the Whole Earth Truck Store. On settling in the Santa Clara Valley, he converted it, in 1968, into the Whole Earth Catalog. The name was a joke: it advised readers on how to make the products on their own, alongside articles promoting hippie communalism.

Copies were ubiquitous in early Silicon Valley. Steve Jobs later called it "one of the bibles of my generation." Brand, having absorbed the Valley's promises of liberation, used his magazine, and hippie cred, to repeat it back to them as a mandate: only you can finish what the '60s started. "I think that hackers," Brand told a 1984 industry conference, "are the most interesting and effective body of intellectuals since the framers of the U.S. Constitution." When a teleconferencing company pitched Brand on spinning his magazine into a message board, he launched the Whole Earth 'Lectronic Link, or WELL. His friends in the industry's upper reaches all joined and much of the Valley followed, turning it into an unmissable center of activity.

The site's founders imagined it as the realization of their dreams of an anarchist utopia. A near-absence of rules, they believed, would lead to a self-governing community in which ideas rose or fell on merit. In reality, as cantankerous and combative engineers rushed in, the loudest voices and most popular opinions dominated, but because the WELL's architects represented both, they took this as confirmation that their intellectual meritocracy worked. Forever after, the internet-era architects who'd first gathered on the WELL would treat raw majoritarianism as the natural ideal, building it into every subsequent social network through today. Raucous debate became seen as the purest meritocracy: if you couldn't handle your own or win over the crowd, if you felt harassed or unwelcome, it was because your ideas had not prevailed on merit.

The WELL's users, seeded throughout the industry, went on to build the consumer web in its image: unregulated, ungoverned, free to use, implicitly designed for the male geeks who'd filled its seminal forum.

These were not just websites. They were a cyber society lifting us above the outdated ways of the physical world. "We reject: kings, presidents, and voting. We believe in: rough consensus and running code," David Clark, one of the architects of the web, said in 1992.

In 1996, a former WELL board member wrote the web era's defining document, "A Declaration of the Independence of Cyberspace." Addressed to "Governments of the Industrial World," it announced, "You have no sovereignty where we gather." The web would be "a civilization of the Mind," ruled by the collective will of its users. It was an ideology that quickly pervaded the broader culture, enshrined in films such as *The Net* and *The Matrix*, which portrayed programmers as the new counterculture vanguard, kung fu rebels who would break the chains of human bondage.

The manifesto enshrined one ideal in particular: total freedom of speech. As on the WELL, this was to be the web's mechanism for self-governance, first commandment, and greatest gift to the world. Its precepts remain the foundational text of the social media industry. "Our general counsel and CEO like to say that we are the free speech wing of the free speech party," Twitter's chief in the UK had said. Zuckerberg called free speech "the founding ideal of the company."

But it is the long-held ambition to finally realize a root-and-branch revolution that most animates the Valley's underlying ideology, a prophecy that social media companies see themselves as destined to carry out. While Apple was an "innovation company," Facebook was a "revolution company," a then-twenty-two-year-old Zuckerberg told a potential hire. He told a TV interviewer, "We're kind of fundamentally rewiring the world from the ground up," a pledge he formalized in a letter to shareholders. Facebook could and should do this, he believed, because it was run by engineers, whose purity of vision would see them through. "There's this fundamental thing that at an early age you looked at something and felt like: This can be better. I can break down this system and make it better," Zuckerberg once said on a trip to Nigeria, where he pledged that Facebook would help advance all of Africa. "I do think that's the engineering mindset — it may even be more a value set than a mindset." But that ideal-ism — the belief that whichever startups won the most users could and should remake all of society — reflected a hubris that would prove cata-strophic. "The reason we nerds didn't fit in was that in some ways we were a step ahead," Paul Graham, the investor whose incubator had launched Reddit, once wrote. Future Valleyites were "consistently unpopular" as kids, he argued, because "we were already thinking about the kind of things that matter in the real world, instead of spending all our time play-ing an exacting but mostly pointless game like the others."

But even more important than the Valley's belief in a grand mission was the sorts of engineers its investors elevated to lead their revolution, and in whose image the world would be remade. "They all seem to be white male nerds who've dropped out of Harvard or Stanford and they absolutely have no social life," John Doerr, a legendary tech investor, once said of successful founders, calling this the "pattern" he used to select investees. Likewise, Graham has said he looks for "nerds" and "idealists" with "a piratical gleam in their eye," who "delight in breaking rules" and defying social niceties. "These guys want to get rich, but they want to do it by changing the world." Peter Thiel, a founder of PayPal and the first outside investor in Facebook, had urged elevating antisocial contrarians. "Individ-uals with an Asperger's-like social ineptitude seem to be at an advantage in Silicon Valley today," he wrote in an influential book on startups. "If you're less sensitive to social cues, you're less likely to do the same things as every-one else around you." Investors considered this archetype to represent an extreme form of meritocracy — based solely on results, so pure it existed above petty diversity concerns. In reality, those results, Doerr's "pattern" bearing out, simply reflected a tech culture that was hostile to anyone out-side of a long-held male geek misanthrope ideal.

"There's not a lot of value placed on social niceties," Margaret O'Mara told me. "There's a tolerance for weirdness, in part because weird people have a proven track record. That's the other dimension of Silicon Valley culture. It's like everyone was an asshole." This Valley archetype derived from its founding companies: Shockley Semiconductor Laboratory and the electrical-component supplier Hewlett-Packard. Both were defined by their cantankerous founders' disdain for conventional corporate life and management structures, which kept them from moving out East. They cultivated office cultures that were ruthlessly competitive and zealously anti-hierarchical, giving engineers free rein and loose oversight. And they recruited anti-establishment curmudgeons in their own image, with pedigrees too informal and personalities too difficult for genteel IBM or Bell Labs. Eventually, because argumentative, self-driven dropouts seemed to be everywhere, the Valley took that personality as a sign of genius.

In most industries, such quirks would be diluted, over time, by new arrivals and subsequent generations. But as is so often the case in the Valley, the hidden force behind everything, setting both the culture and the economics, was venture capitalism. The practice of engineers becoming VCs who pick the next generation of dominant engineers kept the ideological gene pool incestuously narrow.

Even today, Shockley is only four or so steps removed from virtually every major figure in social media. One of his first hires, an engineer named Eugene Kleiner, later cofounded Kleiner Perkins, the investment firm that hired Doerr. Doerr in turn seeded Amazon and Google, where his advice — lessons he'd learned from Shockley recruits — became the basis of YouTube's business model. Another Doerr protégé, Netscape founder Marc Andreessen, became a major investor in and board member of Facebook, and personal mentor to Mark Zuckerberg. He co-founded a venture firm that seeded, among others, Slack, Pinterest, and Twitter.

There are dozens of these interconnections, all among a tiny pool of like-minded investors and founders. Yishan Wong, Reddit's chief during Gamergate, had come up at PayPal, whose alums guided much of the social media era. One of PayPal's first executives, Reid Hoffman, used his windfall to found LinkedIn and invest early in Facebook. He introduced Zuckerberg to Thiel, who became Facebook's first board member.

Thiel, further parlaying his PayPal success, started a fund that launched major investments in Airbnb, Lyft, and Spotify. Throughout, like many leading investors, he imposed his ideals on the companies he oversaw. In the 1990s, he co-authored a book, *The Diversity Myth*, calling the purposeful inclusion of women or minorities a scam that stifled free intellectual pursuit. "Max Levchin, my co-founder at PayPal, says that startups should make their early staff as personally similar as possible," Thiel wrote. "Everyone at your company should be different in the same way — a tribe of like-minded people fiercely devoted to the company's mission."

This, more than race or gender alone, was the rigid archetype around which the Valley designed its products: ruthless, logical, misanthropic, white, male geeks. For much of the industry's history, this predilection affected few beyond the women and minorities who struggled to endure its workplaces. But with the advent of the social media era, the industry was building its worst habits into companies that then smuggled those excesses — chauvinism, a culture of harassment, majoritarianism disguised as meritocracy — into the homes and minds of billions of consumers.

3. Trolling

THE REVOLUTION CAME quickly, extended by broadband into virtually every town and suburb. It brought, as promised, near-total freedom, at least for those who were welcomed in. But what its architects did not understand was that all communities — especially those largely free of formal rules or authorities — self-govern by social mores of some kind. And the norms and values that they'd encoded into the early web turned out to guide its millions of early adopters toward something very different than the egalitarian utopia they'd imagined.

At the dawn of what we now call internet culture, in 2009, a thirteen-year-old kid in suburban Dallas named Adam set out on a journey through the depths of the social web that would overtake much of his life. He had heard the word *meme* somewhere, googled it, and landed on a blog called *I Can Haz Cheezburger?* It drew two million daily viewers for cat photos overlaid with childlike text meant to be in the cat's voice ("i maked you a dinner but i eated it").

Adam was drawn to one post — a series of memes and screenshots — that recounted a story. A pair of videos, the post said, had surfaced on You-Tube showing two boys abusing a cat named Dusty. The clips drew outrage, especially on a message board called 4chan, whose users could be mischievous. They pledged justice for Dusty; one identified the You-Tube video-maker as a fourteen-year-old from Oklahoma. Another claimed he'd alerted local police, though authorities later said they had identified the video's origins on their own. The video-maker and his brother were charged with animal cruelty; 4chan filled with posts celebrating the victory as their own.

Adam was enthralled. People just like him had turned the act of clicking around on the internet into a thrilling adventure and a bonding social experience. "These guys saved a kitty? You bet your ass that drew me in," he recalled. "The vigilante-justice aspect of it helped define what 4chan is for me." He started spending hours a day on 4chan, whose unusual features had made it wildly popular with early internet adopters. Anytime a user wanted to start a new thread, they had to upload an image, which kept the platform filled with user-made memes and cartoons. Long before Snapchat and others borrowed the feature, discussions automatically deleted after a brief period, which enabled unseemly behavior that might've been shunned elsewhere. So did the site's anonymity; nearly all posts are marked as written by "Anonymous," which instills an anything-goes culture and a sense of collective identity that can be alluring, especially to people who crave a sense of belonging.

"At school, I was always the outcast type," Adam said during one of our late-night conversations about the internet's darker reaches, through which he'd offered to guide me. He had struggled with depression and anxiety since childhood. But on 4chan, he felt welcomed and understood. Night after night, its denizens entertained one another with raucous threads and elaborate pranks that were "some of the most fun I've had online," he said.

And he felt safe there in a way he didn't in the real world, where, by his own admission, he was "a pretty strange person" and "kind of a shut-in." His bedroom in his mother's house, where he still lives in his mid-twenties, was "littered," in his words, with "merch" from a 1990s video game. Whereas mentioning his depression off-line invited worried looks and adult interventions, on 4chan he could open up to others who seemed to share his loneliness.

In a photo of himself he sent me, he wore a vintage gaming T-shirt and hip black glasses half-obscured by shaggy brown hair. He did not look like someone who would need to retreat to byzantine social networks to make friends or meet girls. But he is shy in person, he told me, due to a lisp and a stutter. Both were exacerbated by hearing loss when he was a teenager and, more recently, by anxiety. He still finds verbal communication difficult and doesn't work. "I am a NEET, my man," he said, using a British government term for someone "not in employment, education, or training" that, online, has become a self-identifier for those who feel left behind.

Like many longtime residents of the deep social web, he was wary of talking to reporters, whom he saw as representing the grown-up establishment that wanted, he believed, to control him and shut down his cherished digital home. But a trusted intermediary, a source of mine whom he'd contacted about a decade after joining 4chan, had put us in touch. For all Adam had enjoyed about the forums and their "mostly anonymous silly fun," he conceded that "the darker corners where anti-social behavior leaks into the real world" worried him, adding, "I saw it from the beginning. I'm a Jew and half the site thinks I shouldn't exist." He wrestled over how fully to embrace the worldview that saturated the platform. Its culture of anger and conspiracy helped him make sense of a disorienting world that seemed arrayed against him. That the grievances were collective helped him feel that he belonged. But the unchecked extremes bothered him, particularly when people got hurt.

"Ultimately," Christopher Poole, 4chan's founder, said in 2008, "the power lies in the community to dictate its own standards." Poole, then a reedy twenty-year-old, belonged to a growing community of web hobbyists — programmers, bloggers, grad students — building Silicon Valley's "civilization of the Mind." But after all the heady '80s hacker conferences and '90s-era manifestos, by the 2000s the web's inhabitants were mostly interested in having fun. Suburbanites stuck at home after school, too young to drive, spent hours online. The internet's promise of total freedom appealed especially to kids, for whom off-line life is ruled by parents and teachers. Adolescents also have a stronger drive to socialize than adults, which manifests as heavier use of social networks and a greater sensitivity to what happens there. Poole had started 4chan when he was just fifteen. Kids who felt isolated off-line, like Adam, drove an outsized share of online activity, bringing the concerns of the disempowered and the bullied with them.

That culture was, at first, one of creation and silliness — cat videos and cartoons — though it also tended to be mischievous and transgressive. Drawing on a web culture dating back to the WELL, fun meant being free of society's rules and sensitivities and thumbing your nose at the outsiders who didn't get it. That was how pranks — a pastime already cherished by young men everywhere — became the early web's defining activity.

In one stunt organized on 4chan, users hijacked an online contest in which schools competed to win hosting a Taylor Swift concert, and directed victory to a center for deaf kids. In another, users posted a 4chan inside joke, derived from some late-night meme session, on a message board for Oprah Winfrey's TV show, writing, "Our group has over 9000 penises and they are all raping children." Winfrey somberly quoted the line on air. "A lot of the humor," Adam said, "comes from the act of pushing limits and spreading your reach into more mainstream places that seem untouchable." Getting one over on a world that treated them like outcasts.

Things sometimes escalated into outright sadism. In 2006, users discovered that, in the wake of a thirteen-year-old boy's suicide, the victim's friends had posted remembrances on his Myspace page. Users mocked the misspellings and childlike earnestness. Some hacked the page to change the boy's profile photo to an image of a zombie. Others prank-called his parents, which continued for more than a year. If grown-ups and classmates found such affairs off-putting, all the better.

Transgressing ever-greater taboos — even against cruelty to grieving parents — became a way to signal that you were in on the joke. "When you browse 4chan and 8chan while the rest of your friends are posting normie live-laugh-love shit on Instagram and Facebook," Adam said, "you feel different. Cooler. Part of something niche." The joke might be a photo of scatological pornography. A video of a grisly murder. A racial slur posted to get a rise out of people, daring them to take it seriously. Laughing off the material — or, better yet, one-upping it — affirmed that you shared the club's knowing, cynical detachment. And it recast their relationship with the outside world: it's not society rejecting us, it's us rejecting society.

These two unifying activities, flaunting taboos and pulling pranks, converged to become trolling. A '90s message board had defined trolling as posting comments "for no other purpose than to annoy someone or disrupt a discussion," possibly named after "a style of fishing in which one trails bait through a likely spot hoping for a bite." Since the days of the WELL, web users had entertained themselves by seeking to provoke one another. On networks like 4chan, it often became something darker: acts of collective abuse in which the point was to delight in someone else's anguish.

The thrill of getting a reaction out of someone even had a name: *lulz*, a corruption of the acronym for "laugh out loud." There was almost no limit on who could be targeted or how viciously; the Silicon Valley dream of freedom from laws and hierarchies had become, online, freedom from social and moral codes as well. The community had created its own standards, as Poole hoped, but around the organizing incentive of all social media: attention.

Most platforms are built around a putatively neutral belief that attention indicates value. Reddit and Twitter elevate posts based on how many users endorse them with upvotes or retweets. Facebook and YouTube place this authority with algorithms. Either version flattens all forms of attention — positive or negative, ironic or earnest, whether it made you laugh or made you angry, indulged your intellectual curiosity or your prurient instincts — into one pure metric: up or down.

Boards like 4chan do the same, though more organically. Anonymity and the churn of content encourage users to seek out one another's attention as aggressively as they can. Unchastened by the social constraints of the off-line world, each user operates like a miniature Facebook algorithm, iteratively learning what best wins others' attention. One lesson consistently holds. To rise among tens of thousands of voices, regardless of what you post, it is better to amp up the volume, to be more extreme.

In 2010, one of the community's most cherished attacks targeted an eleven-year-old girl. Users had seen posts circulating on Myspace, where she was active, reporting that she had told friends she was romantically involved with the twenty-five-year-old front man of a local band. Myspace users mocked her for, they assumed, making it up. She posted angry responses, then a YouTube video telling her "haters" she would "pop a glock" in their mouths.

4chan users, delighting in her clumsy and emotional reaction, set out to elicit more. She'd lied, refused responsibility, and now would be put in her place. They bombarded her with harassing Facebook and Myspace messages, fake pizza deliveries, and prank calls, which they recorded and uploaded to 4chan for more lulz. A post on "How to troll" her advised: "Tell her to kill herself," and "Tell her dad that we are going to beat her up," and to circulate revealing photos of her.

She posted a second video, in which she sobbed as her foster father shouted at her invisible tormentors, "Guess what, your emails will be caught and you will be found." It thrilled 4chan users — proof that they were getting through. The harassment worsened. In a final video, she gave in, conceding all accusations and pleading for mercy. The incident became legend on the social web: justice, and lulz, achieved. Her videos circulated over and over, attracting millions of views. The local band she'd named in her initial posts recorded a song celebrating her humiliation: "My name and reputation won't be the target of a slut / I'll be on top of the world and you'll be cutting yourself fucked."

Years later, she told police that, when she was ten years old, the band's front man had repeatedly molested and raped her. As with many victims of child abuse, shame and confusion had led her to tell friends it was consensual. Amid an FBI investigation, nearly two dozen others came forward with similar stories. Yet the episode is still celebrated on 4chan and similar sites, where users have continued to harass her across the web for more than a decade.

The shamelessness was characteristic; 4chan users "regularly framed their activity as a kind of public service," the cultural theorists Whitney Phillips and Ryan Milner once wrote. They saw themselves as drawing on the social web's founding mission: tear down the broken old ways and replace them with a world of self-policing free speech and ruthlessly independent thinking. Tricking Oprah into warning her viewers about a nonexistent sex cult would, they told themselves, teach people to question authority figures and official accounts, "an outcome they prodded along by taunting, gaslighting, and deceiving targets," Phillips and Milner wrote. "Many joked that they deserved a thank-you for their efforts."

"Trolling is basically internet eugenics," Andrew Auernheimer said in 2008. Auernheimer was a 4chan superstar: an anarchist hacker, shameless provocateur, and merciless tormenter of the site's chosen enemies. The interview itself was a troll, daring readers to take offense at Nazi invocations: "Bloggers are filth....We need to put these people in the oven!" Rants like Auernheimer's hinted at something new emerging from the early social web. The culture of provocation, the gleeful rejection of established moral codes, had created what Phillips and Milner called "the perfect conditions for bigotry to spread stealthily, tucked away within things that didn't seem polluted at all."

Auernheimer bragged of his role in a harassment campaign against the tech blogger Kathy Sierra. She'd called for 4chan comment sections to be moderated, enraging users who saw this as an assault on internet free speech. He posted Sierra's Social Security number and home address amid a deluge of death threats, circulated photos of her children edited into pornography, and posted messages in her name soliciting sex, bringing strange men to her door day and night. She was driven completely from public life. Sierra had little incentive to attempt to bring charges. Few in the justice system considered online harassment, however extreme, to cross into criminality, and any public response surely would've just brought more attacks.

Auernheimer also began posting conspiracy-filled, anti-Semitic YouTube "sermons" that he claimed were satirical, but whose calls for "blood in the streets" sounded awfully sincere. At the time, the Auernheimers of the web were treated as boyish mischief-makers. To the extent that anyone paid attention, it was often to laud them. In 2010, *TechCrunch*, Silicon Valley's all-but-official in-house publication, granted Auernheimer a public-service award. It was a show of solidarity with Auernheimer's hacking group, which was under FBI investigation for stealing 114,000 private email addresses through an iPad vulnerability.

At a party for Auernheimer the night before his criminal sentencing, "journalists drank alongside hackers, activists, eyepatch-wearing documentarians, and candy-haired girls with lip rings," according to an account in *Vice*. The next morning, the *Vice* writer brought a Guy Fawkes mask to the courtroom, explaining, "I went because his conviction was wrong, and my friends and I cared for him." The next year, Auernheimer joined *The Daily Stormer*, a prominent neo-Nazi forum founded and populated by 4channers, where he posted a photo revealing a fist-sized swastika tattoo on his chest.

Poole, wary of 4chan's darkening reputation, imposed the lightest of restrictions. Extreme hate speech and harassment were still allowed, but confined to a few subsections. It turned those sections into trolling red-light districts, inviting droves of lookie-loos, some of whom liked what they saw and stayed. Still, some considered even this as a betrayal. One, a software developer named Fredrick Brennan, started a 4chan spinoff, 8chan, which he billed as a "free-speech-friendly" alternative. Users, including Adam, poured in, deepening a collective identity of defiant outsiderdom that became home to some of the greatest horrors of the internet era.

As the 2000s ended, chan communities migrated to the glossier platforms then rising in popularity. Like waves of colonists, they landed on the virgin soil of Facebook, YouTube, and Twitter. Chan culture, expressed in memes and in-jokes now as recognizable as Mickey Mouse, infused the platforms, whose engagement-maximizing features and algorithms absorbed and reified its most extreme tendencies, then amplified them to a world that had no idea what was coming.

4. Gamers

WHEN JOHN DOERR, the kingmaking tech investor, unveiled Kleiner Perkins's $250 million fund for social media startups in late 2010, the person he chose to stand next to him was Bing Gordon. A self-described lacrosse jock, then in his fifties, Gordon sported a frat-boy shag and laced his corporatespeak with "dude" and "awesome." Before joining Kleiner as an investor, his CV had one bullet spanning 1982 to 2008: Electronic Arts, a video game company. "We're making a blue-ocean bet that social is just beginning," Gordon said at the unveiling, flanked, in a show of Kleiner's power, by Mark Zuckerberg and Jeff Bezos.

Gordon's presence reflected a then-widespread belief: the social media industry would operate like the video game business. Gordon told an industry conference a few months later that there were "three themes that you CEOs need to master," listing mobile, social, and, with a fist pump, "gamification." From the beginning, social media platforms borrowed heavily from video games. Notifications are delivered in stylized "badges," which Gordon told the audience could double a user's time on site, while

likes mimic a running score. This was more than aesthetic. Many platforms initially considered gamers — tech obsessives who would surely
pump hours into this digital interface, too — to be a core market.

Thanks to a twist of commercial history, the gaming industry catered
overwhelmingly to young men and boys of certain temperaments, which
meant that social media platforms effectively did the same. But nothing
about videogaming is inherently gendered or age-specific. The first games,
designed by 1970s Silicon Valley shops like Atari, launched alongside personal computers and were presumed to have the same universal appeal.
That changed with what the industry calls the North American video game
crash. From 1983 to 1985, sales collapsed by 97 percent. Japanese firms
sought to revive the market by rebranding this now-tarnished computer
product, sold in electronics stores to adults, as something simpler: toys.

Toy departments were, at that moment, sharply segmenting by gender.
President Reagan had lifted regulations forbidding TV advertising aimed
at children. Marketers, seized by a neo-Freudianism then in vogue,
believed they could hook kids by indulging their nascent curiosity about
their own genders. New TV programming like *My Little Pony* and *GI Joe*
delivered hyper-exaggerated gender norms, hijacking adolescents' natural
gender self-discovery and converting it into a desire for molded plastic
products. If this sounds like a strikingly crisp echo of social media's business model, it's no coincidence. Tapping into our deepest psychological
needs, then training us to pursue them through commercial consumption
that will leave us unfulfilled and coming back for more, has been central
to American capitalism since the postwar boom.

Toy departments polarized between pink and blue. Japanese game-
makers had to pick a side, so they selected the one on which parents spent
more: boys. Games increasingly centered on male heroes rescuing prin-
cesses, fighting wars, playing in male sports leagues. Marketers, having
long positioned games as childhood toys, kept boys hooked through ado-
lescence and adulthood with — what else? — sex. Games were filled with
female characters who were portrayed as hypersexualized, submissive, and

something to which men should feel entitled. Plenty of gamers understood that the portrayal was fantasy, albeit one with troubling values. But enough grew up on the fantasy to absorb it as truth. Amid culture wars of the 1990s and 2000s, game marketers seized on these tendencies as an asset, presenting games as refuges from a feminizing world, a place where men were still men and women kept in their place. Gaming became, for some, an identity, one rooted in reaction against evolving gender norms.

When social networks appeared, accessible only by desktop computers stuck in the family room, the first users looked a lot like gamers: homebody men and boys who were tech early adopters. Hence the two audiences were treated as synonymous, one set of products marketed to the other, blurring them into a unified subculture and identity. But by the 2000s, increasingly powerful home computers enabled self-funded developers to build games outside the commercial mold. (Zoë Quinn was one of those developers.) The digital democratization also brought new voices, like the YouTuber Anita Sarkeesian, who argued that the portrayals of women in gaming did not just exclude them but encouraged their real-life mistreatment. Among gamers eager to see the form taken more seriously, this was an exciting, positive development. Reviewers began adopting Sarkeesian's critiques. Big-budget releases showcased diverse protagonists and story lines, while sanding down the He-Man excesses.

To some young male gamers, especially those who gathered on social platforms, it felt like a threat. The norms and boundaries of their identity were being challenged and, with it, their sense of self. "For thirty years, we found a very particular kind of player, and we've made them the center of the world, and we've catered to their every whim," Brianna Wu, who had dared to challenge Gamergaters, told me. "And now, today, the world is changing, and the average gamer is not a twentysomething guy. It's a forty-year-old woman like me. And when the world changes, there's just an inability to deal with that that's very unfortunate in our field."

Accusing developers like Quinn of bribing reviewers was a kind of cognitive self-defense, a way to reframe unwanted change as a nefarious conspiracy, and the threat to their identity as a battle of us against them. "They weren't fighting for the right to look at boobs in video games anymore, but fighting against 'white genocide,'" David Futrelle, a writer who monitors online extremists, has said. "It wasn't just gaming that needed saving, but Western civilization itself." Looking back, Futrelle linked the event to the explosive rise of the online far right, calling it "close to impossible to overstate the role of Gamergate in the process of radicalization."

Adam, the 4chan obsessive, now an eighteen-year-old, followed every step. The worldview-affirming outrage was irresistible. Videos posted by prominent gaming YouTubers convinced him, he said, that "journalists were being bribed with money and sex." Watching users plot to torment Wu upset him. But the platforms, following their engineering, hammered him with posts supposedly proving that Wu and others were dangerous radicals bent on his subjugation. He kept clicking, following the campaign, like many of his online compatriots, down ever darker and deeper rabbit holes.

Wu, watching Gamergate unfold, was reminded of a moment from years earlier, when she'd interned in the office of Senator Trent Lott of Mississippi. His staff had deployed a now-famous push poll: "Do you believe Democrats are trying to take away your culture?" It performed spectacularly, especially with white men. Imagine, she said, how effective social media platforms could be at this, optimized to trigger people's emotions more effectively than even the canniest campaign office, saturating audiences in the billions with a version of reality that was like an identity-activating push poll that never ended. "In that very same way of that push poll in Mississippi, I think there was a real fear that women were coming to take away your culture," Wu said of Gamergate. "It's tribal."

5. *The Dunbar Curse*

THROUGHOUT THE EARLY 2010s, as Gamergate-style subcultures overran early-generation platforms, Facebook quietly pursued an audacious goal: exceeding the cognitive limits of human socialization. The plan, in time, would impose, on billions of users, an even more powerful version of the mind-altering distortions that Reddit and 4chan had brought to gamers and early adopters, provoking a world of Gamergates.

It emerged out of a crisis that the company faced in 2008, the sort that focused the company's attention like few others: user growth had stalled. In any other industry, capping out around 90 million customers might be an opportunity to explore new or better products to sell them. But in the web economy, a static userbase could be deadly. "I remember people saying it's not clear if it was ever going to get past a hundred million at that time," Zuckerberg has said. "We basically hit a wall and we needed to focus on that."

Facebook, in the hopes of boosting engagement, began experimenting with breaking the so-called Dunbar limit. The British anthropologist Robin Dunbar had proposed, in the 1990s, that humans are cognitively capped at maintaining about 150 relationships. It was a number derived from the maximum-150-person social groups in which we'd evolved. Any more than that and our neocortex — the part of our brain governing social cognition — maxes out. Our behavior changes, too, seeking to reset back to 150, like a circuit breaker tripping. Even online, people converged naturally on Dunbar's number. In 2010, the average Facebook user had about 130 friends; the social-network game Friendster even capped the number of friends at 150.

Silicon Valley had long dreamed of "escaping the Dunbar curse," as a consultant to the companies wrote in 2010. Zuckerberg spoke publicly of breaking it. But the plan sputtered. Even Facebook could not overcome millions of years of evolution — at least, not yet. When user growth stalled again in 2013, the company reengineered itself around that goal. Users were pushed toward content from what Facebook called "weak ties": friends of friends, contacts of contacts, cousins of cousins.

Enforced through algorithmic sophistication, the scheme worked. Facebook pulled users into ever expanding circles of half-strangers, surpassing the Dunbar limit. Twitter, around the same time, did much the same, showing users tweets from strangers and nudging them to follow friends of friends. The companies showed little concern for the consequences of bypassing our hardwired neurological limits. They operated, as they always had, on the belief that their products were inherently liberating.

But studies of rhesus monkeys and macaques, whose Dunbar-like limits are thought to mirror our own, had found that pushing them into larger groups made them more aggressive, more distrusting, and more violent. It was as if all the dangers of living in a community got amped up and the pleasures reduced. The monkeys seemed to sense that safely navigating an unnaturally large group was beyond their abilities, triggering a social fight-or-flight response that never quite turned off. They also seemed to become more focused on forming and enforcing social hierarchies, likely as a kind of defense mechanism.

Facebook soon found an even more powerful method for expanding users' communities. Rather than strain to expand your friends list beyond 150 people, Facebook could push you into groups — stand-alone discussion pages focused on some topic or interest — ten times that size. This also shifted yet more power to Facebook's systems. No longer limited to content from people near your social circle, the system could nudge you into groups from anywhere on the platform.

Renée DiResta, the tech investor who'd discovered sprawling anti-vaccine communities on Facebook, realized the significance of this change as her fight entered a new phase. California was considering legislation to tighten school vaccine mandates. She promoted the bill and the science behind it online, hoping to counteract the anti-vaccine sentiment so prevalent there. Facebook began recommending she join other parenting groups. Then anti-vaccine groups, though this seemed unsurprising, given her activity. But soon Facebook promoted groups organized around unrelated medical misinformation. Many groups pushed a conspiracy she'd never heard before: that Zika, a virus then spreading in Latin America and the United States, was manufactured. She searched Facebook for the term *Zika* to test whether, as with vaccines, the platform might be pushing users toward extremes. Sure enough, the top results were all for conspiracy groups calling Zika a Jewish plot, a population-control scheme, the opening move of a global power grab.

"There's this conspiracy-correlation effect," DiResta said, "in which the platform recognizes that somebody who's interested in conspiracy A is typically likely to be interested in conspiracy B, and pops it up to them." Facebook's groups era promoted something more specific than passive consumption of conspiracies. Simply reading about contrails or lab-made viruses might fill twenty minutes. But joining a community organized around fighting back could become a daily ritual for months or years. Each time a user succumbed, they trained the system to nudge others to do the same. "If they bite," DiResta said, "then they've reinforced that learning. Then the algorithm will take that reinforcement and increase the weighting."

Others from DiResta's informal group of social media watchers were noticing Facebook and other platforms routing them in similar ways. The same pattern played out over and over, as if those A.I.s had all independently arrived at some common, terrible truth about human nature. "I called it radicalization via the recommendation engine," she said. "By having engagement-driven metrics, you created a world in which rage-filled content would become the norm."

The algorithmic logic was sound, even brilliant. Radicalization is an obsessive, life-consuming process. Believers come back again and again, their obsession becoming an identity, with social media platforms the center of their day-to-day lives. And radicals, driven by the urgency of their cause, recruit other radicals. "We had built an outrage machine in which people actually participated in pushing the content along," DiResta said, where the people who became radicalized were thereafter "the disseminators of that content." She had seen it over and over. Recruits were drawn together by some ostensibly life-or-death threat: the terrible truth of vaccines, the Illuminati agents who spread Zika, the feminists seeking to overturn men's rightful place atop the gender hierarchy, starting with gaming. "Ordinary people began to feel like they were like soldiers in an online army fighting for their cause," she said. It was only a matter of time until they willed one another to action.

But while DiResta could demonstrate this happening in particular cases, without access to the companies' troves of internal data she could only infer that platforms were driving it systemically. She alerted peers across the Valley — first within her informal watch group, then more broadly, in public-facing articles and talks — that something was amiss. She worried, however, that it was too late. "I had this feeling," she said, "that it didn't matter whether it was gamers, anti-vaxxers," or some other group being radicalized at scale. "That was just the dynamic that was taking shape as a result of this system."

Gamergate, in this light, looked all but inevitable, precisely what would happen when the social web's earliest adopters, gamers, interacted with a machine expertly calibrated to produce just such a response. Larger, more mainstream communities, everyday people with no special attachment to the web, were already moving online, submitting themselves to the machine's influence. There was every reason to expect their experience would be much the same. By early 2015, it was already beginning.

Three

Opening the Portal

1. *The Wake up Call*

"I THINK THEY weren't really quite sure what to make of me," Ellen Pao recalled of her first days at Reddit. "It wasn't super welcoming." In the spring of 2013 Pao was a Valley veteran coming off a stint at Kleiner Perkins, the top-flight investment firm. But despite her time at Kleiner, with its enormous fund for social media startups, she had little direct experience with social companies herself. And she stood out in another way: she was a high-ranking woman of color in an industry overwhelmingly, notoriously dominated by men.

Both insider and outsider, she'd been a Silicon Valley believer since the 1990s, when she'd joined a company that made hardware for accessing the internet from TVs. But she'd also grown skeptical of big tech's tilt toward young male geeks. Other than Yishan Wong, the site's CEO, the twenty or so other employees at fledgling Reddit trended young. Most spoke in the in-jokes and cultural arcana of a platform that, despite its enormous userbase, felt insular. Pao was a little stiff; Wong urged her to use less "corporatey" language.

She was also only a light Reddit user, though she knew the basics of the platform, which displayed user-submitted links that other users then voted "up" if they liked it and "down" if they didn't. The most-upvoted links appeared at the top of the page, where millions would see them. A comment section attached to each post operated by the same rules. Dropping into a conversation, you'd see crowd-pleasing statements first and unpopular comments not at all. The simplicity and endless scroll eventually brought hordes of casual web browsers, inculcating them into an internet culture that had previously been impenetrable. Reddit became a portal connecting the two worlds.

Still, Reddit was built and governed around the same early internet ideals as 4chan, and had absorbed that platform's users and cultural tics. Its up-or-down voting enforced an eclipsing majoritarianism that pushed things even further. So did a dynamic similar to Facebook's likes: upvote counts are publicly displayed, tapping into users' sociometer-driven impulse for validation. The dopamine-chase glued users to the site and, as on Facebook, steered their actions.

Millions who opened Reddit every morning encountered a stream of comments and articles asserting the superiority, and indulging the grievances, of the median user. It was a version of reality in which tech libertarianism was always vindicated and alternate belief systems — feminism, establishment liberalism, organized religion — were endlessly humiliated and debunked. If those median users struggled to fit in off-line, they assured one another, it was because they were smarter and more important than the world that treated them as undesirable. Like 4chan, it was a place, in other words, perfectly primed for Gamergate.

"It started out very much like the other platforms," Pao said of Reddit's founders, "where it's a couple of white men going out to build something that they want to use and it appeals to people who look like them." Pao had developed a special sensitivity to Valley chauvinism: two years earlier, she had sued Kleiner Perkins for gender-based discrimination, after which the firm had fired her. Though she ultimately lost in court, many outside the Valley, and even some within it, heralded her suit as calling necessary attention to galling inequities in tech venture capitalism. As of 2016, four years after her suit, still only 11 percent of technology venture-capital partners were women. Two percent were Black. The firms, in turn, overwhelmingly funded people who looked like them: in 2018, 98 percent of their investment dollars went to male-led companies. This reflected, Pao had argued, an even more specific bias among tech investors, one favoring not just white men but idealistic contrarians with libertarian politics; the "pattern recognition" espoused by Doerr, who was also Pao's former mentor. The firms that pick the Valley's winners and losers, her suit had underscored, enforce this archetype so zealously because they also embody it.

Reddit's leaders, young and progressive, were hardly hostile to such concerns. But the company made it a point of pride to defend the web's supposed highest value, total free speech, at extremes others wouldn't. It was only after weeks of critical CNN coverage that Reddit shut down a subsection, "jailbait," where users uploaded revealing photos of underage girls. (Site subsections, known as subreddits, are created and managed by users.) Before the subsection's closure, *jailbait* had been the second-highest-ranked search term, after *reddit*, bringing users to the site.

Nearly anything else went. On one of several subreddits dedicated to racist extremism, "WatchNiggersDie," users posted gruesome videos of Black people dying in murders or violent accidents, alongside pseudonymous comments like, "I almost feel bad for letting an image like this fill me with an overwhelming amount of joy. Almost…" Most users never encountered these communities, tucked away in shadowy corners of the site, but enough made their way to them for digital-monitoring groups to warn Reddit that it was becoming an incubator of hate.

"We will not ban legal content even if we find it odious or if we personally condemn it," Wong, the CEO, had said. But his tech idealism finally broke in September 2014, when a hacker broke into the iCloud accounts of a number of female celebrities. iCloud is Apple's cloud computing service; many Apple products back up user files to its servers. The hacker downloaded the targets' iPhone data, including a number of private nude photos. Dozens were uploaded to 4chan, then Reddit, which, befitting its role as the link between the internet's underbelly and its mainstream, became, overnight, the central repository. Millions of visitors overwhelmed the site.

"Everyone was talking about it," Pao said. People on the news, in the Valley, in her personal life. And this, ultimately, was what made the difference. It wasn't the growing public and legal pressure, or the victims pleading with social media platforms not to enable this violation of their lives and bodies. That had worked at every other major platform, from which the photos had been removed. But Reddit still had them up. Wong called a staff-wide meeting. And for once, much of Reddit's staff was ready to side against the site's community, which was still insisting that the photos remain. "People were just like, 'I don't know how to defend this,'" remembered Pao, who paraphrased their sentiment as "My friends and family were asking about it and I just didn't know what to say because it didn't feel good."

The controversy attracted a level of attention that even "jailbait" and hate subreddits had not. The outside world had treated those as transgressions of an internet culture that was presumed to be cordoned off from the rest of us. But this pitted Reddit and its anything-goes hacker ethos against the rights of beloved actresses, models, and athletes. And Gamergate, though only ramping up, was already pushing innocent women from public life. "Do we want to be like 4chan, where it's mostly bad stuff and you can barely get to the good stuff?" Pao asked at the meeting. "Because that's what this looks like." The conversation, she said, "opened up an idea: 'Hey, maybe this idea of being hands-off isn't always right.'"

But Wong resisted. He announced in a post that although Reddit's leaders "understand the harm that misusing our site does to the victims of this theft," they would not bend. Reddit, he wrote, was not just a social platform "but the government of a new type of community." Like many other platform operators to come, however, he made clear his was a government that refused to govern, leaving it to users themselves to "choose between right and wrong, good and evil." He titled his post "Every Man Is Responsible for His Own Soul." This would become a standard defense from social media overlords: that the importance of their revolution compelled them to disregard the petty laws and morals of the outmoded offline world. Besides, any bad behavior was users' fault, no matter how crucial a role the platform played in enabling, encouraging, and profiting from those transgressions.

The same day Wong issued his statement, reporters pointed out that among the stolen images on Reddit were nude photos of celebrities who had been underage at the time they were taken. Meanwhile, the site's engineers warned that, as traffic rose, they were struggling to keep the site online. Finally, nearly three weeks after the photos first appeared, Wong banned them. Reddit's users, incensed, accused the platform of selling out its principles to shadowy corporate influence and, worse, feminists.

The next few weeks were a stormy time. By presenting his initial choice as an ideological one, Wong had brought scrutiny to Silicon Valley ideals that had gotten little national attention outside of carefully crafted Apple ads. Claims of creating a new, enlightened society seemed difficult to square with the reality of profiting from the pornographic exploitation of nonconsenting women. Concurrently, Gamergate was worsening, with Reddit often named as a center of activity.

Reddit's corporate board rejected a plan Wong had proposed to consolidate office space. The decision, though minor, signaled that he had lost the board's faith. He resigned. In November 2014 the board chose Pao as his replacement. Even with her suit against Kleiner lingering, Pao's background suggested she would bring adult supervision and financial growth. But board members felt enough uncertainty that they also brought back one of the site's founders, who had since left for other startups, in a vague executive role and titled Pao as interim CEO.

Even still, Pao saw an opportunity to better the internet for everyone, not just the young white men who dominated social media. She called Reddit's fiascos "a wake up call" to a need to finally govern the social web. By imposing protections for women and minorities and cleaning out subcultures of toxicity and harassment, she would bring to Reddit's community what she'd been unable to force on tech venture capitalism: real inclusivity.

That missing piece of the techno-liberation dream had always fallen in the blind spot of the Valley's male geek elite. But Pao was empowered to deliver it. After a crash course in the moderation tools used to run the site, she took command of what was then one of the internet's most-visited websites, ready to guide its nation-sized userbase of tens of millions toward her vision of the promised land.

2. *The Trolls Are Winning*

THREE MONTHS INTO her tenure, Ellen Pao became the first head of a major platform to try to reform the excesses of her industry. "It was clear, in my mind, things had to change and that the harassment was too much," she said. Episodes like Gamergate, whose scale had grown unignorable in the six months since it began, convinced her of a need to curb not just the worst content, but the incentives and subcultures that made the web toxic to begin with.

She started small, banning nude photos posted without the subject's consent. She wanted to curb "revenge porn," a method of humiliating someone by circulating private photos. The victims were overwhelmingly women, targeted by angry ex-boyfriends or 4chan-style harassment campaigns. Understanding her audience, she announced the policy as protecting not women but user privacy, since users could hypothetically be targeted. Despite some grumblings, users mostly accepted the change.

Emboldened, Pao announced a slate of policies banning users and communities responsible for extreme hate or harassment — effective immediately. The change was, on its face, modest, targeting only the most indefensible behavior. But the cultural shift it implied was seismic, reorienting, for the first time, a major platform's governing ethos from enabling the community's collective id toward checking it. "It's like we're sending a message," she said. "We don't accept this behavior. We're going to quash it and we're going to quash it every time you try to start it again."

Pao was also testing a theory: that the most hateful voices, though few in number, exploited social media's tendency to amplify extreme content for its attention-winning power, tingeing the entire platform in the process. Stamping out "these core, really bad harassing subreddits" and preventing them from resurfacing, she believed, was the only sure way to end the "ripple effect" from bad behavior. Still, it was just a theory, and they weren't sure whether it would work.

The first ban was small: a subreddit called "FatPeopleHate." Its several thousand users posted photos of everyday people they deemed overweight, targeting them for harassment and threats. Bullying as idle thrill seeking. Pao also removed a handful of tiny subreddits organized around hatred of Black or LGBT people. But Reddit's leadership stressed this was over users' harassing behavior and not the content itself. Much larger hate communities were left up, such as "WatchNiggersDie," "GasTheKikes," and "RapingWomen," all of which openly glorified violence. Keegan Hankes, a researcher for the Southern Poverty Law Center, which monitors far-right extremism, had called Reddit "a worse black hole of violent racism than Stormfront," a prominent neo-Nazi site, warning that even the worst white-supremacist forums forbade such extremes.

Still, Reddit's userbase erupted in anger at the removals as an attack on the freedom to offend and transgress that, after all, had been an explicit promise of the social web since its founding. As in Gamergate, thousands upvoted the angriest posts, pulling one another toward ever more extreme interpretations: Pao was imposing a feminist agenda, suppressing white men, moving to terminate free speech itself. Also as with Gamergate, users seemed to experience the incident as an attack on their shared identity, a new front in the imagined war between free-thinking male geeks and the politically correct feminists conspiring to control them.

The site flooded with posts calling Pao a "Nazi cunt" or "Chairman Pao," or portraying her in explicitly racist cartoons, overwhelmingly upvoted by fellow users on one of the largest social media platforms in the world. Some posted what they believed to be her home address, sometimes alongside fantasies that she might be killed or raped there. But with the exception of a post offering $1,000 for a photo of Pao being assaulted, she instructed moderators to leave it all up.

This string of episodes — Gamergate, the hate forums, the backlash to

Pao — shook the social web but, strangely, not its overseers, who showed no sign of noticing how deeply the culture of extremism and mob majoritarianism had suffused the social web. But it was not ignored by the far right, which saw that social media had cultivated what they could not: a large and willing audience for white nationalism among America's youth. "Gamergate seems to have alerted racist, misogynist, homophobic internet trolls to the level of power they actually possess. Which is definitely a good thing," Andrew Anglin, a longtime 4chan poster, wrote on *The Daily Stormer,* a prominent neo-Nazi forum he'd founded in 2013. He urged his followers to coopt Gamergate and the broader social web, launching "the rise of the Nazi troll army."

Other social-web stars were already participating. Fredrick Brennan, the 8chan founder, had written a *Daily Stormer* essay endorsing eugenics. Andrew Auernheimer, the prominent hacker, had joined as webmaster. Reddit and 4chan recruits, some of whom were "too extreme" even for the hardened white supremacists on neo-Nazi forums, poured in. Their growing numbers were soon reflected on the mainstream platforms that most also used. One study later estimated that the number of far-right white nationalists on Twitter increased by a factor of seven between 2012 and 2016.

Pao never got a chance to press her reforms further. In July 2015, as the months-long revolt against her raged on, a well-liked Reddit employee who ran a service where users could pose questions to celebrities was fired without explanation. Many of the site's largest subsections, run by volunteer users, shut themselves down in protest. Though Pao posted an apology, a petition for her termination reached 200,000 signatures. Four days later she and the corporate board agreed that she would resign.

"The trolls are winning," Pao wrote in a *Washington Post* op-ed a few days later. The internet's foundational ideals, while noble, had led tech companies to embrace a narrow and extreme interpretation of free speech that was proving dangerous, she warned.

She had lasted just eight months.

Still, during that time she had revealed the fork in the road facing social networks. They could continue drifting toward becoming new iterations of 4chan turbocharged by algorithms. Or they could detour toward a future of constraints and rules checking the majority's impulses, or those of especially loud minorities, so that others might participate. While it is difficult to argue that Pao succeeded in persuading her board, her employees, or her users to take that second path, she did try. And she did it almost two years and one world-changing election before global backlash would force the much more reluctant, stubborn, and powerful Mark Zuckerbergs and Jack Dorseys of the Valley to at least make a show of following suit.

3. *Meme Magic*

MILO YIANNOPOULOS, A twenty-nine-year-old college dropout, had little reason to believe he would ever claw his way beyond the furthest edges of the tech world. His loosely sourced gossip blog had won him 98th on *Wired UK*'s 2012 list of 100 influencers ("Tech's gadfly continues to provoke and irritate") until he sold it amid legal trouble. He resorted, in what looked like his last stop on the path to obscurity, to filing short columns for the mostly unread technology section of *Breitbart*, the barrel-scraping white nationalist web publication. His first articles, a grab bag of humdrum tech gossip and right-wing grievances pulled from social media, made little impact.

Then, a few months into his gig, Gamergate arrived. As a denizen of the same platforms from which it had sprung, Yiannopoulos knew how to indulge its grievances and motives, which aligned with his employer's far-right agenda and conspiratorial outlook. Headlines like "Lying Greedy Promiscuous Feminist Bullies Are Tearing the Video Game Industry Apart" went viral on those platforms as seeming confirmation.

His bosses had hoped his articles would inform *Breitbart*'s small, far-right readership on tech issues. Instead, they tapped into a new and much larger audience that they hadn't even known existed — one that was only coming together at that moment. "Every time you write one of your commentaries, it gets 10,000 comments," Steve Bannon, *Breitbart*'s chief, told Yiannopoulos on the site's radio show. "It goes even broader than the *Breitbart* audience, all over."

Within three years, the angry little subculture Yiannopoulos championed would evolve into a mainstream movement so powerful that he was granted a keynote slot at the Conservative Political Action Conference, the most important event on the political right. (The invitation was later revoked.) Bannon called their cause the "alt right," a term borrowed from white-power extremists who'd hoped to rebrand for a new generation. But to Yiannopoulos it was whatever the social networks said it should be.

A shameless attention-seeker, he absorbed whatever messages seemed dominant online, exaggerated them by a few degrees, then posted them back to those same platforms. He was a living, breathing social media algorithm that could also appear on cable talk panels. He kept himself at the top of users' feeds with 4chan-style slurs and perverse jokes ("If rape culture was real I'd spend even more time on American campuses than I already do"), now for the masses of Twitter, Facebook, and YouTube. And as a new public face of the long-faceless movement, he provoked or led campaigns of collective harassment and abuse.

Bannon and others on the alt right saw a chance to finally break through. "I realized Milo could connect with these kids right away," Bannon said later. "You can activate that army. They come in through Gamergate or whatever and then get turned on to politics and Trump." Accordingly, in early 2016, *Breitbart* asked Yiannopoulos to write a phone book–length *Guide to the Alt Right*. The Gamergate columnist, not an old-school white supremacist or conspiracist, would be flag-bearer for the movement.

And who better for Yiannopoulos to enlist for help than Andrew Auernheimer, the celebrity hacker who'd put a swastika on his chest? "Finally doing my big feature on the alt right," Yiannopoulos wrote in an email to Auernheimer. "Fancy braindumping some thoughts for me?" After emailing with other ultranationalists and white-power figures, Yiannopoulos sent his material to a ghostwriter he'd recruited through Gamergate, asking him to assemble it into an article under Yiannopoulos's name. "The alt-right is a movement born out of the youthful, subversive, underground edges of the internet," it read. Web denizens would be the alt right's propagandists, pushing to a broader audience a cause that "promises fun, transgression, and a challenge to social norms they just don't understand."

Week after week, the language of social-web extremists drifted onto the major platforms, which pushed it into mainstream politics. In the first weeks of the Republican presidential primary, platforms filled with accusations that moderate-leaning candidates were "cuckservatives." The portmanteau is thought to have originated on white-supremacist forums, where "cuck" references fears of being cuckolded by Black men. Gamergaters brought the term to Twitter, where its attention-grabbing salaciousness pulled it to the top of users' feeds. Mainstream conservatives gradually adopted it, inflecting right-wing politics — which increasingly played out on Twitter and Facebook — with a troll-culture influence that would only broaden.

"They call it 'meme magic' — when previously obscure web memes become so influential they start to affect real-world events," Yiannopoulos wrote that summer before the election. Dozens of alt-right memes followed a similar path. Pepe the Frog, a cartoon that online neo-Nazis had adopted as a mascot, grew, on Twitter and Reddit, into something more complex: an expression of ironic racism. Deliberately offensive Pepe memes (Nazi Pepe operating a gas chamber, Jewish Pepe smiling over the September 11 attacks) became the middle finger you extended to the world. And it was a vessel for smuggling deadly real racism, cloaked by irony, into mainstream discourse. "The unindoctrinated should not be able to tell if we are joking or not," Anglin, the *Daily Stormer* founder, wrote in the site's style and recruitment guide. "This is obviously a ploy and I actually do want to gas kikes. But that's neither here nor there."

The movement coalesced around Trump, who had converged on the same tics and tactics as Yiannopoulos and other Gamergate stars, and for seemingly the same reason: it's what social media rewarded. He swung misinformation and misogyny as weapons. He trolled without shame, heaping victims with mockery and abuse. He dared society's gatekeepers to take offense at flamboyant provocations that were right off 4chan. "He has a character and a style that is perfectly in tune with what the web's miscreants are looking for," Yiannopoulos wrote. A popular variation of the Pepe meme donned Trump's red tie and blond hair, which Trump posted to Twitter and his son to Instagram.

But while Yiannopoulos and Bannon have long claimed to be the mergers of internet-troll culture with the mainstream right, in fact credit belonged to a far more powerful force: Facebook. From May 2015, a month before Trump declared his candidacy, to November 2016, a Harvard study later found, the most popular right-wing news source on Facebook was *Breitbart*, edging out even Fox News. It was the third-most-shared media outlet overall, beating out every newspaper or TV network except for CNN and the *New York Times*. If you regularly read Facebook for news in 2016 — which 43 percent of Americans did that year — you were probably reading *Breitbart*. It grew so dominant on the platform that, even in late 2019, after the site had declined under mismanagement and controversy, Facebook appointed *Breitbart* as a "trusted news source" with special access to Facebook readers.

Awed outsiders would long ascribe *Breitbart*'s rise to dark-arts social media manipulation. In truth, the publication did little more than post its articles to Facebook and Twitter, just as it always had. It was, in many ways, a passive beneficiary. Facebook's systems were promoting a host of once-obscure hyperpartisan blogs and outright misinformation shops — bearing names like *The Gateway Pundit, Infowars, The Conservative Treehouse*, and *Young Cons* — into mega-publishers with the power to reshape reality for huge segments of the population.

As with Gamergate, it wasn't just that the content was salacious. It promoted feelings of group-identity threat — the Muslims are coming to kill us, the Jews will erase our culture, the liberals want to destroy traditional values — which activated the tribal-defense instinct of users that Henri Tajfel and his team of social psychologists had identified decades earlier. It spurred them to share ever more links and comments tightening their in-group identity and rallying against the common enemy. It kept them clicking and posting, whipping other users into the same shared frenzy, an endless feedback loop of fear and rage that proved enormously beneficial for Silicon Valley and Donald Trump, but disastrous for everybody else.

Facebook's reach and algorithm gave it an unusually large role in creating this information ecosystem. But much the same process played out on the other platforms, suggesting that the problem was not particular to some quirk of Facebook or its founders, but endemic to modern social networks. On Twitter, *Breitbart* became "the nexus of conservative media" and the most shared media source among Trump's supporters, the Harvard study concluded. *Breitbart* dominated conversation around immigration in particular, perhaps the most charged topic of the 2016 campaign. Its immigration stories were collectively shared *more than twice as much* as those of any other news outlet, a stunning figure considering it employed only a handful of reporters.

Across platforms, discussion on immigration "gravitated more often to issues of identity threat," the study's authors found, naturally privileging far-right worldviews that center, by definition, on fears of identity conflict. The study concluded that "highly partisan media" pushing disinformation and "Facebook-empowered hyperpartisan political clickbait sites" were both endemic in 2016, a trend that "played a much greater role on the right than on the left."

If we'd wanted to know where that was leading us, all we had to do was look at Gamergate, which, as of summer 2016, had more or less declared victory in its culture war for gaming. "The long-term effect of Gamergate was to create a culture of fear for the women professionals that make your video games," Brianna Wu said. Many left the business in defeat. Those who stayed learned the consequences of speaking up. The hundred-billion-dollar industry still skews, in both its products and the people who make them, drastically male.

Like most, I had not initially considered Gamergate a harbinger of the world to come, having missed its implications at the time, I told Wu. "I will tell you straight up," she said, "I also underestimated it. I could not have foreseen that all of our politics were going to become Gamergate. And of course they were." She wished she'd anticipated, she said, "the number of people that are taking up Gamergate tactics. I want to be clear, it's mostly the right doing this. But there are plenty of people on the left that I've been horrified to see have taken up the same kind of tactics of outrage and mob culture and shame."

The result was a near-universal convergence on these behaviors and ways of thinking, incentivized all along the way by social media. There were moments, Wu admitted, when she found herself tempted to spin up outrage, to rally her followers against some adversary, to push a claim that, while dubious, might flatter the identity and inflame the prejudices of her in-group. She usually caught herself, but not always.

"It's something I really struggle with, myself, in my own person, the way I interact with the world, because there's something really dangerous that's been unlocked here," she said. "This cycle of aggrievement and resentment and identity, and mob anger, it feels like it's consuming and poisoning the entire nation."

Four

Tyranny of Cousins

1. Web Justice

IN SEPTEMBER 2015, less than two months after Ellen Pao's ouster from Reddit, Walter Palmer, a fifty-five-year-old dentist from the Minneapolis suburbs, sat down with two newspaper reporters to insist that he was not in hiding. "I've been among people, family and friends. The location is really not that important," said Palmer, flanked by a lawyer and a PR rep. "There were some safety issues early on for my daughter and my wife." In what he said would be his only interview, Palmer lamented the global movement — the first in a new kind of mass, life-upending rage that would soon become commonplace — now hounding his family and employees, who were, he stressed, innocent. "I don't understand that level of humanity to come after people not involved at all," he said.

Six weeks earlier, the BBC had run a short item reporting that an unidentified hunter had killed a lion in Zimbabwe. This wasn't unusual or illegal on its own. But the hunter's guides had first lured the lion off a nearby game park, where killing it would have been illegal. And the animal had a distinctive black mane that had won it fame among parkgoers, who'd named it Cecil.

One of Reddit's most popular subsections at the time was worldnews, a repository of global reports and wire-service tidbits. With users posting more than a thousand links every day, rising to the page's top slots usually required a description designed to provoke an intense emotion. A user with the handle Fuckaduck22, who posted the Cecil story, appended just such a title: "Cecil the lion was skinned and his head removed. Hwange —

well-known and much-photographed black-maned lion affectionately named Cecil was killed by sport hunters just outside Hwange in Zimbabwe last week."

Thousands of users upvoted the article to the top of Reddit's homepage, which meant an audience of millions. Not all were angry. Cecil was near the end of male life expectancy anyway, one pointed out, while another noted that big-game hunts fund conservation efforts. But Reddit comment sections are sorted by each comment's popularity. And it was expressions of outrage that rose to the top:

> lions might very well be extinct in the wild soon, because you really REALLY wanted to puff up your flagging sense of masculinity.

> I want that hunters head as a trophy. Coward mother fucker.

Unconsciously following the incentives of the platform, users filled it with posts about Cecil, each round escalating the emotional stakes. The lion's death was a sad loss, then a devastating blow to animal lovers everywhere, then an infuriating crime. The hunter was a fat coward, then a blood-soaked murderer, and then deemed to be gripped with "mental illness or a form of psychopathy."

In summer 2015, reporters and editors were just learning to chase social media virality, which could multiply their audiences several times over. That meant when Reddit users pushed Cecil to the top of most-read lists at many outlets, they dug into an incident they would otherwise have ignored. The until-then anonymous hunter was revealed to be Palmer, the dentist. Still, the story seemed harmless — until it jumped to Twitter.

Twitter's founders had launched their product in 2006 as essentially a group-texting service. Users would text a toll-free number, which would then forward the message to their friends. If you went out, you might post the name of the bar; friends who followed your updates could come join. Messages were capped at about the length of a sentence. A simple website also logged the updates. Jack Dorsey, in an early sketch envisioning the service, wrote out sample messages like "in bed" and "going to park."

By default, the posts were public; why hide anodyne updates behind a cumbersome privacy wall? That openness took on greater meaning when, in 2009, citizens of faraway Iran filled the streets to protest an election they believed the state had rigged. As authorities cracked down, some pro-testers used Twitter to dash off barricade updates. When they realized that the world was watching — and that international scrutiny might deter, or at least document, government abuses — their tweets took on a greater purpose. Amid Obama-era tech optimism, Americans described it as a "Twitter revolution." Though Iranians' actual revolution was swiftly crushed, the label stuck.

As more world events unfolded live on Twitter, anyone who cared about the news or was involved in producing it joined up. It shifted from group-text service to a platform for short, public-facing posts: a microblog where millions collectively broadcast, discussed, and debated the day's political machinations or *Game of Thrones* episode. But everything was filtered through a platform that operates less like a CNN ticker than like Reddit. Users validate one another's posts by tapping like or retweet, in the process also surfacing or suppressing whatever content most appeals to their collective will.

When fury over Cecil upscaled to Twitter's 316 million active users, the scale of activity escalated beyond even Gamergate's extremes. In a sin-gle day, users posted 672,000 tweets about the incident. About 50,000 of those named Palmer directly and were viewed a total of 222 million times: infamy on a scale that, usually, only history books can deliver. "I'll pay £35k+ to watch #WalterPalmer in a fair fight with the king of the jungle," wrote one user, representative of a wave of posts expressing a desire to see Palmer harmed.

When Reddit spun up rage, it remained mostly confined to internet-geek niches. But Twitter, by 2015, sat at the center of mainstream news and culture. Revenge fantasies suffused what was the social media equivalent of network TV, pulling in reporters and celebrities. "I hope that #Walter-Palmer loses his home, his practice & his money," Sharon Osbourne, then a reality-TV star, tweeted, while Mia Farrow, the award-winning actress, posted the address of his dental practice.

When platforms become a consensus chant of "Get him," action usually follows. Hundreds posted negative reviews of Palmer's dentistry on sites like Yelp, hoping to drive away business. Within days, enough tweets threatened violence that his office closed entirely. (When a Reddit user suggested this might unjustly harm Palmer's employees, 1,500 users voted in support of the response "His employees are better off working elsewhere.") Menacing signs appeared on the dentistry's doors. Someone spray-painted Palmer's house. Palmer and his family, perhaps wondering whether one of the people lurking outside their home might follow up the online threats, went into what everybody but Palmer described as hiding.

By the time Palmer hired a PR rep and met with reporters, more than two thousand articles about his hunt had been posted to Facebook, where they were shared 3.6 million times. The *New York Times* ran a formal editorial lamenting Cecil's loss; the Minnesota governor condemned it; Jimmy Kimmel, the late-night host, choked up on air. All driven by social media virality. Then, one day, the fever broke and everyone moved on.

The blowup split tech watchers. Some saw another Gamergate, now a few steps closer to the center of American life, enabled by platforms that promoted moblike hysteria and harassment with virtually no constraints or safeguards. Others saw a silly online drama with no greater meaning, much less reason to blame the social networks still widely seen as global liberators.

James Williams, a Google engineer since 2005, would have seemed to fit the profile of the more optimistic camp. Yet, on leaving the company, he wrote in an essay for the website *Quillette* that Cecil and similar episodes augured a seismic change in our digitizing worlds. Cecil's avengers, whatever their motivations, had been unknowingly manipulated into their behavior, he believed, "their buttons pushed by the persuasive patterns of digital design." His diagnosis: "We enjoy being outraged. We respond to it as a reward."

The platforms had learned to indulge the outrage that brought their users "a rush — of purpose, of moral clarity, of social solidarity." The growing pace of these all-consuming meltdowns, perhaps one a week, indicated that social media was not just influencing the broader culture, but, to some extent, supplanting it, to the ultimate benefit of — and this was an outlandish argument at the time — Donald Trump. Was it so crazy to think, Williams suggested, that the new dominant media of our time might launch standard-bearers like Trump to the heights of power? Wasn't it already happening? "The truth is," he wrote, "these political effects are already upon us."

2. *Moral Outrage*

BILLY BRADY WAS a freshman at the University of North Carolina when he realized that he enjoyed getting outraged on Facebook. All that year, 2005, he made visiting Facebook a regular part of his life, fighting in comments sections and, he now admits with a laugh, "posting pretty inflammatory stuff."

Brady, a soft-mannered vegan who speaks in a California-surfer drawl despite not being from California, wasn't accustomed to feeling drawn toward anger and conflict. And he'd joined Facebook to change minds, not to fight. He was getting into animal-rights activism, he said, and thought "it seemed like an interesting platform to be able to spread messages and persuade people." But often he ended up expressing outrage at them instead. He was behaving in ways, he came to see, that had little chance of advancing the cause and, however fun in the moment, made him feel like a jerk afterward.

As luck had it, Brady's field of study had some insight. Moral philosophy, once a domain of chin scratchers, was becoming more empirical, leveraging hard science in search of morality's true nature. Its findings suggested an explanation for Brady's behavior. Fuming at his desk or firing off an insult felt more bad than good. But when his expressions of outrage drew attention online, especially encouragement from like-minded others, the rush was addictive. "I definitely noticed that you can get people's attention by posting more inflammatory stuff and feeling some emotions," he said.

But why would people be drawn to such harmful, unpleasant emotions? Fascinated, he added psychology classes to his schedule. He has studied social media's influence on behavior ever since. In a sense, he said, all users are simultaneously both conducting and serving as the subjects of a never-ending psychology experiment. People, as a rule, are closely attentive to, and adapt to, social feedback, an impulse that digital likes and shares tap into. Even as an undergrad engaging in spats on Facebook, "I, by trial and error, learned how people respond to different framings and different appeals."

The more that he and like-minded users had worked one another into rages, the more antagonistic their behavior had grown. Meat eaters and animal-rights agnostics were not well-meaning people to be persuaded, they were rubes and evildoers to be condemned. The key, he concluded, was moral outrage. Outrage is a simple emotional cocktail: anger plus disgust. *Moral* outrage is a social instinct.

Recall those early tribes of up to 150 people. To survive, the group had to ensure that everyone acted in the collective interest, part of which was getting along with one another. That required a shared code of behavior. But how do you get everyone to internalize, and to follow, that code? Moral outrage is our species' adaptation for this challenge. When you see someone violating an important norm, you get angry. You want to see them punished. And you feel compelled to broadcast that anger, so that others will also see the violation and want to join in shaming, and perhaps punishing, the transgressor.

The desire to punish violators runs so deep that it even shows up in infants. In a set of experiments, children less than a year old were shown two puppets. One puppet shared, the other refused to. The infants consistently took candy away from the bad puppet and rewarded the good. Test subjects just a year or two older would even reward puppets who were cruel to the bad puppet and punish puppets who were nice to it. It was confirmation that moral outrage is not just anger against a transgressor. It is a desire to see the entire community line up against them.

Brady, trying to understand the outrage he'd felt online, first as part of a master's program in philosophy and then another in psychology, circled around a theory that both fields call sentimentalism. "It's this idea that our sense of morality is intertwined with, and maybe even driven by, our emotional responses," he said. "Which is against this older idea that humans are very rational when it comes to morality."

Popular culture often portrays morality as emerging from our most high-minded selves: the better angels of our nature, the enlightened mind. Sentimentalism says it is actually motivated by social impulses like conformity and reputation management (remember the sociometer?), which we experience as emotion. Neurological research supports this. As people faced with moral dilemmas work out how to respond, they exhibit heavy activity in neural regions associated with emotions. And the emotional brain works fast, often resolving to a decision before conscious reason even has a chance to kick in. Only when they were asked to explain their choice would research subjects activate the parts of their brain responsible for rational calculation, which they used, retroactively, to justify whatever emotion-driven action they'd already decided on.

Those moral-emotional choices seemed reliably to serve a social purpose, like seeking peers' approval, rewarding a Good Samaritan, or punishing a transgressor. But the instinctual nature of that behavior leaves it open to manipulation. Which is exactly what despots, extremists, and propagandists have learned to do, rallying people to their side by triggering outrage — often at some scapegoat or imagined wrongdoer. What would happen when, inevitably, social platforms learned to do the same?

3. Shaming Mobs

BRIANNA WU WAS still fighting one social media outrage mob when she found herself trying to spin up another. "I will never forget this," she said. "There was a moment, halfway through Gamergate, where I was really caught up in the feminist argument for the game industry." Oculus, a Facebook-owned company that made virtual-reality headsets, had announced a new team. All white men. Wu was incensed. "I remember just blasting on Twitter, and posting this picture of it and their names," she said. "And it is a problem. The lack of women in VR engineering is terrible. But I came to realize that those kinds of tactics work on the same emotional place of what Gamergate was doing to me."

She acknowledged to herself, for the first time, how much of her social media experience was organized around provoking or participating in public-shaming campaigns. Some lasted weeks and others a few minutes. Some were in service of an important cause, or so she told herself, others merely because someone had pissed her off. "I used to single out sexist tweets that were sent my way. I would just retweet it, and let my internet followers handle it," she said. "I don't do that anymore because it's just asking for somebody to get harassed."

In 2016, she ran in the Democratic primary for her local House seat on left-wing causes, along with a promise to address online harassment. A reporter asked her about a 2014 tweet where she'd identified the name and employer of someone who'd posted something sexist — wasn't this harassment of the sort she was calling on platforms to combat? "I remember thinking at the moment, like, 'What a damn hypocrite I am.' I just have no excuse for that," she said. "And it's what I said. 'That was wrong.'" She had allowed the platforms to bring out in her the very behavior she otherwise loathed, she said. "And I just don't see how any of this shit gets any less toxic without more of us realizing that, in our worst moments, we can be that bad guy."

At the time, Kate Klonick, a Yale legal scholar and former student of cognitive psychology, was trying to understand why mass shaming seemed so widespread on social media. She found much to learn from an early Twitter controversy known, in an indication of how unseriously these things were once taken, as Donglegate. A software developer named Adria Richards, sitting in the audience at a programming conference, had heard a man in the row behind her half-whisper a joking play on computer terminology to his neighbor. She turned around and snapped a photo, then tweeted it with the caption "Not cool. Jokes about forking repo's in a sexual way and 'big' dongles. Right behind me."

Richards, a Black woman, had long spoken out against her industry's biases. Now, in early 2013, social media enabled her to reach a wider audience. Twitter and Facebook lit up with angry posts in reaction to her tweet. The conference organizers, as well as the employers of the two men, were suddenly infamous, even hated, and on a national scale. One of the men was quickly fired. He posted an apology for his comment to *Hacker News*, Silicon Valley's unofficial web forum, writing that he was sorry to Richards especially. But he added, "I have 3 kids and I really liked that job. She gave me no warning, she smiled while she snapped the pic and sealed my fate. Let this serve as a message to everyone, our actions and words, big or small, can have a serious impact." Inevitably, a second round of outrage surfaced, this time inundating Richards and her bosses with furious, sometimes threatening messages. Her employer's website was taken off-line by a rudimentary hack called a denial of service. The next day Richards was fired because of her decision, her boss said, to "publicly shame" the two men.

Much legal scholarship, Klonick knew, considers public shaming necessary for society to function: tut-tutting someone for cutting in line, shunning them for a sexist comment, getting them fired for joining a hate group. But social media was changing the way that public shaming worked, which would necessarily change the functioning of society itself. "Low cost, anonymous, instant, and ubiquitous access to the internet has removed most — if not all — of the natural checks on shaming," she wrote of her findings, "and thus changed the way we perceive and enforce social norms."

Someone who is, say, rude to a bus driver might've once expected a few finger-wagging fellow passengers. Now, if the incident is recorded and posted online, they might face weeks of abuse hurled from all over the world. "Today, it is easier than ever," Klonick wrote, "to use shaming to enforce so-called social norms, and it is easier than ever for sham-ing to spin out of control." Online public shaming tended to be "over-determined," she argued, poorly calibrated to the scale of the crime, and "of little or questionable accuracy in who and what it punishes."

Moreover, it had grown crueler, even sadistic. From the moment that the social web enmeshed with everyday life, stories circulated of outrage mobs going to excess. A corporate cog named Justine Sacco became inter-nationally infamous in 2013, when a tweet to her 170 followers ("Going to Africa. Hope I don't get AIDS. Just kidding. I'm white!") provoked tens of thousands of angry responses, then glee at her humiliation and subsequent firing. A *New York Times Magazine* article suggested that Sacco and others like her had been made to suffer for our amusement, or simply because we had lost control, "as if shamings were now happening for their own sake, as if they were following a script."

A small-town Wisconsin class photo went viral when Twitter users accused the schoolboys of giving Nazi salutes. A storm of international fury, all online, picked apart the lives of local parents and school officials, humiliating them over any detail that the users could find online, scarring the town. It later turned out that the volunteer photographer had captured the boys waving at an odd angle.

A rookie reporter from Des Moines profiled a local man who'd gone viral on Facebook for showing up at a college football game with a funny sign (BUSCH LIGHT SUPPLY NEEDS REPLENISHED), followed by his Venmo username. The reporter noted in passing that the man had once sent offensive tweets for which he'd since apologized. Social media users first demanded that the carrier of the sign lose his job, then, in a backlash to the backlash, that the reporter himself be fired, which he was.

A Palestinian American restaurateur in Minneapolis was besieged by online rage when someone found, in his daughter's social media history, racist comments she had posted as a child. Though they both apologized, web users circulated their home address and pressured local businesses to shun the family. The lease on their restaurant was revoked and two groceries pulled the family's products. The outrage moved on shortly after the restaurateur fired his daughter, telling a reporter, "You think it's easy for me to destroy my daughter's career?"

When a Chinese-immigrant novelist won a high-dollar contract for her debut, a young adult fantasy, other writers tweeted vague claims that her manuscript contained racist and plagiarized passages. Many on Twitter took the rumors as true, hounding the writer and her publisher until the book was withdrawn. The accusations later turned out to be false. A month later, it happened again, this time targeting a young adult novelist who is Black, successfully pressuring him to withdraw his manuscript as well. Similar incidents recurred over and over among novelists, leading one book critic to write, in exasperation, "It's perplexing that people who are always rhapsodizing about how much they love reading can be so very bad at it."

A Black student at Smith College posted on Facebook that a school janitor and security guard had harassed her for "eating while Black." They had questioned her while she lunched in a dorm lounge, she said, treating her as an interloper because of her race. The post was shared angrily across Smith, then other colleges, then the wider world, bringing a firestorm of attention to the tiny campus. The janitor was placed on paid leave. Students walked out of class in protest. The student posted a follow-up on Facebook accusing two cafeteria workers of calling security during the incident. She included the name, email address, and photograph of one of them, writing, "This is the racist person." The cafeteria worker was inundated with angry calls at her home, some threatening to kill her. The student also posted a photo of a janitor, accusing him of "racist cowardly acts," though, in an apparent mistake, she had identified the wrong janitor.

The truth turned out to be a combination of honest misunderstanding and youthful hyperbole. She had been eating in a closed-down dormitory attached to a cafeteria reserved for a program for young children. The janitor had followed rules requiring security to be called if anyone not in that program showed up. The guard had a polite exchange with the student and did not ask her to leave. The cafeteria workers were not involved at all.

But by the time the truth came out, in a lengthy report by a third-party law firm the university had hired, the Facebook version of events, calcified by an outpouring of profound collective emotion, had long since hardened in people's minds. The university, likely fearful of provoking more anger, refused to exonerate the workers, announcing that it was "impossible to rule out the potential role of implicit racial bias" in their behavior. One was transferred, another kept on leave, another quit. One of the cafeteria workers was later denied a restaurant job when the interviewer recognized her from Facebook as "the racist." The student, once praised online as a hero, was now condemned as a villain. Few thought to blame the social media platforms that had empowered a teenager to destroy the livelihoods of low-income workers, incentivized her and thousands of onlookers to do it, and ensured that all would experience her outrage-provoking misimpression as truer than the truth.

Truth or falsity has little bearing on a post's reception, except to the extent that a liar is freer to alter facts to conform to a button-pushing narrative. What matters is whether the post can provoke a powerful reaction, usually outrage. A 2013 study of the Chinese platform Weibo found that anger consistently travels further than other sentiments. Studies of Twitter and Facebook have repeatedly found the same, though researchers have narrowed the effect from anger in general to moral outrage specifically. Users internalize the attentional rewards that accompany such posts, learning to produce more, which also trains the platforms' algorithms to promote them even further.

Many of these incidents had a left-wing valence to them, leading to fears of a "cancel culture" run amok. But this merely reflected the concentration of left-leaning users in academic, literary, journalistic, and other spaces that tend to be more visible in American life. The same pattern was also unfolding in right-leaning communities. But most such instances were dismissed as the work of fringe weirdos (Gamergate, anti-vaxxers) or extremists (incels, the alt right). Right or left, the common variable was always social media, the incentives it imposes, the behavior it elicits.

For its targets, the damage, deserved or not, is real and lasting. Our brains process social ostracism as, quite literally, pain. Being shunned hurts for the same reason that a knife piercing your skin hurts: you have evolved to experience both as mortal threats. Our social sensitivity evolved for tribes where angering a few dozen comrades could mean a real risk of death. On social media, one person can, with little warning, face the fury and condemnation of thousands. At that scale, the effect can be psychologically devastating. "The big part of harassment that people who haven't been repeatedly harassed by a hateful mob are lucky to not get is: It changes your life forever," Pao, the former Reddit chief, once wrote. "You don't trust as easily."

The consequences extended beyond handfuls of people targeted by arguably misplaced or disproportionate anger. Public life itself was becoming more fiercely tribal, more extreme, more centered on hating and punishing the slightest transgression. "I'm telling you, these platforms are not designed for thoughtful conversation," Wu said. "Twitter, and Facebook, and social media platforms are designed for: 'We're right. They're wrong. Let's put this person down really fast and really hard.' And it just amplifies every division we have."

4. Lyudmila's Foxes

THE MYSTERY OF moral outrage — why are we so drawn to an emotion that makes us behave in ways we deplore? — was ultimately unraveled by a seventy-year-old Russian geneticist holed up in a Siberian research lab, breeding thousands of foxes. Lyudmila Trut arrived at the lab in 1959, fresh out of Moscow State University, to search for the origins of something that had seemed unrelated: animal domestication.

Domestication was a mystery. Charles Darwin had speculated that it might be genetic. But no one knew what external pressures turned wolves into dogs or how the wolf's biology changed to make it so friendly. Darwin's disciples, though, had identified a clue: domesticated animals, whether dog or horse or cow, all had shorter tails, softer ears, slighter builds, and spottier coats than their wild counterparts. And many had a distinctive, star-shaped spot on their foreheads.

If Trut could trigger domestication in a controlled setting, she might isolate its causes. Her lab, attached to a Siberian fur factory, started with hundreds of wild foxes. She scored each on its friendliness to humans, bred only the friendliest 10 percent, then repeated the process with that generation's children. On the tenth generation, sure enough, one fox was born with floppy ears. Another had a star-shaped forehead mark. And they were, Trut wrote, "eager to establish human contact, whimpering to attract attention, and sniffing and licking experimenters like dogs." Darwin had been right. Domestication was genetic. Subsequent generations of the foxes, as they grew friendlier still, had shorter legs and tails and snouts, smaller skulls, flatter faces, spottier fur coloring.

Trut studied the animals for half a century, finally discovering the secret to domestication: neural crest cells. Every animal starts life with a set. The cells migrate through the embryo as it grows, converting themselves into jawbones, cartilage, teeth, skin pigment, and parts of the nervous system. Their path ends just above the animal's eyes. That's why domesticated foxes had white forehead marks: the neural crest cells passed on to them by their friendlier parents never made it that far. This also explained the floppy ears, shorter tails, and smaller snouts.

Further, it unlocked a change in personality, because neural crest cells also become the glands that produce the hormones responsible for triggering fear and aggression. Wild foxes were fearful toward humans and aggressive with one another, traits that served them well in the wild. When Trut bred the friendliest foxes, she was unknowingly promoting animals with fewer neural crest cells, stunting their neurological development in a very specific and powerful way.

Of the many revelations to flow from Trut's research, perhaps the greatest was resolving a long-standing mystery about humans. About 250,000 years ago, our brains, after growing larger for millions of years, started shrinking. Strangely, it occurred just as humans seemed to be getting smarter, judging by tools found with their remains. Humans simultaneously developed thinner arm and leg bones, flatter faces (no more caveman brow ridges), and smaller teeth, with male bodies more closely resembling those of females. With Trut's findings, the reason was suddenly clear. These were the markers of a sudden drop in neural crest cells — of domestication.

But Trut's foxes had been domesticated by an external force: her. What had intervened in the evolutionary trajectory of humans to suddenly favor docile individuals over aggressive ones? The English anthropologist Richard Wrangham developed an answer: language. For millions of years, our ancestors who would eventually become *Homo sapiens* formed small communities led by an alpha. The strongest, most aggressive male would dominate, passing on his genes at the expense of the weaker males.

All great apes despise bullies. Chimpanzees, for instance, show preferential treatment toward peers who are kind to them and disfavor those who are cruel. But they have no way of sharing that information with one another. Bullies never suffer from poor reputations because there is, without language, no such thing. That changed when our ancestors developed language sophisticated enough to discuss one another's behavior. Aggression went from an asset — the means by which alpha males dominated their clan — to a liability that the wider group, tired of being lorded over, could band together to punish.

"Language-based conspiracy was the key, because it gave whispering beta males the power to join forces to kill alpha-male bullies," Wrangham wrote in a pathbreaking 2019 book. Every time an ancient human clan tore down a despotic alpha, they were doing the same thing that Lyudmila Trut did to her foxes: selecting for docility. More cooperative males reproduced, the aggressive ones did not. We self-domesticated.

But just as early humans were breeding one form of aggression out, they were selecting another in: the collective violence they'd used both to topple the alphas and to impose a new order in their place. Life became ruled by what the anthropologist Ernest Gellner called "tyranny of the cousins." Tribes became leaderless, consensus-based societies, held together by fealty to a shared moral code, which the group's adults (the "cousins") enforced, at times violently. "To be a nonconformist, to offend community standards, or to gain a reputation for being mean became dangerous adventures," Wrangham wrote. Upset the collective and you might be shunned or exiled — or wake up to a rock slamming into your forehead. Most hunter-gatherer societies live this way today, suggesting that the practice draws on something intrinsic to our species.

The basis of this new order was moral outrage. It was how you alerted your community to misbehavior — how you rallied them, or were yourself rallied, to punish a transgression. And it was the threat that hung over your head from birth until death, keeping you in line. Moral outrage, when it gathers enough momentum, becomes what Wrangham calls "proactive" and "coalitional" aggression — colloquially known as a mob. When you see a mob, you are seeing the cousins' tyranny, the mechanism of our self-domestication. This threat, often deadly, became an evolutionary pressure in its own right, leading us to develop ultrafine sensitivities to the group's moral standards — and an instinct to go along. If you want to prove to the group that it can trust you to enforce its standards, pick up a rock and start throwing. Otherwise, you might be next.

In our very recent history, we decided that those impulses are more dangerous than beneficial. We replaced the tyranny of cousins with the rule of law (mostly), banned collective violence, and discouraged moblike behavior. But instincts cannot be entirely neutralized, only contained.

Social networks, by tapping directly into our most visceral group emotions, bypass that containment wall — and, in the right circumstances, tear it down altogether, sending those primordial behaviors spilling back into society.

When you see a post expressing moral outrage, 250,000 years of evolution kick in. It impels you to join in. It makes you forget your internal moral senses and defer to the group's. And it makes inflicting harm on the target of the outrage feel necessary — even intensely pleasurable. Brain scans find that, when subjects harm someone they believe is a moral wrongdoer, their dopamine-reward centers activate. The platforms also remove many of the checks that normally restrain us from taking things too far. From behind a screen, far from our victims, there is no pang of guilt at seeing pain on the face of someone we've harmed. Nor is there shame at realizing that our anger has visibly crossed into cruelty. In the real world, if you scream expletives at someone for wearing a baseball cap in an expensive restaurant, you'll be shunned yourself, punished for violating norms against excessive displays of anger and for disrupting your fellow restaurant-goers. Online, if others take note of your outburst at all, it will likely be to join in.

Social platforms are unnaturally rich with sources of moral outrage; there is always a tweet or news development to get angry about, along with plenty of users to highlight it to a potential audience of millions. It's like standing in the center of the largest crowd ever assembled, knowing that, at any moment, it might transform into a mob. This creates powerful incentives for what the philosophers Justin Tosi and Brandon Warmke have termed "moral grandstanding" — showing off that you are more outraged, and therefore more moral, than everyone else. "In a quest to impress peers," Tosi and Warmke write, "grandstanders trump up moral charges, pile on in cases of public shaming, announce that anyone who disagrees with them is obviously wrong, or exaggerate emotional displays."

Off-line, moral grandstanders might heighten a particular group's sensitivities a few degrees by pressuring peers to match them. Or they might simply annoy everyone. But on social networks, grandstanders are systematically rewarded and amplified. This can trigger "a moral arms race," Tosi and Warmke cautioned, in which people "adopt extreme and implausible views, and refuse to listen to the other side."

If this were just a few internet forums, the consequences might be some unpleasant arguments. But by the mid-2010s social networks had become the vector through which much of the world's news was consumed and interpreted. This created a world, Tosi and Warmke warned in a follow-up study with the psychologist Joshua Grubbs, defined by "homogeneity, ingroup/outgroup biases, and a culture that encourages outrage."

The result was a doom-loop of polarization and misinformation. When Congress passed a stimulus package in 2020, for example, the most-shared posts on Twitter reported that the bill siphoned $500 million meant for low-income Americans to Israel's government and another $154 million for the National Art Gallery, that it funded a clandestine $33 million operation to overthrow Venezuela's president, that it slashed unemployment benefits, and that $600 Covid-relief checks were really just loans that the IRS would take back on the following year's taxes.

All were false. But the platform's extreme bias toward outrage meant that misinformation prevailed, which created demand for more outrage-affirming rumors and lies. Heartless Republicans wanted poor people to starve. Craven Democrats had sold out Americans to big business. Crafty foreigners had stolen our financial lifeblood. Each cycle further confounded public understanding of a high-stakes issue and made compromise costlier and less feasible for lawmakers whose constituents demanded nothing less than maximalist partisan stances to appease their anger.

Such anger creates a drive, sometimes overwhelming, for finding someone to punish. In a disturbing experiment, subjects were asked to assign a punishment for someone else's moral transgression. They became harsher when led to believe that they were being watched, harsher still when told that their audience was highly political or ideological. Many heightened the punishment even if they thought their victim did not deserve it. Their motivation was simple: they expected that cruelty would make the observers like them more.

The effect scales; people express more outrage, and demonstrate more willingness to punish the undeserving, when they think their audience is larger. And there is no larger audience on earth than Twitter or Facebook.

5. The Ramble

IF THERE WAS any question as to the extent of Twitter-shaming's influence over American life, it ended Memorial Day 2020 in a quiet, wooded expanse of New York City's Central Park, known as the Ramble. A ritual plays out most mornings here. Someone lets their dog run free, a momentary respite from cramped apartments and busy sidewalks. And a birdwatcher, for whom this is rich territory, chastises the owner to leash their pet, as park rules require.

That morning, the dog owner was a white woman, Amy Cooper. The birdwatcher was a Black man, Christian Cooper, who had been through the ritual so many times that he carried dog treats to tempt unleashed pets toward him, pressuring owners to scoop the animal back up. When Amy's dog wandered near Christian, he asked her to leash it. She refused.

He waved a dog treat and told her, "Look, if you're going to do what you want, I'm going to do what I want, but you're not going to like it."

"Don't you touch my dog," she snapped.

Sensing the conflict escalate, he pulled out his phone, pointed the camera at her, and began recording. She walked toward him and asked him to stop filming as he asked her to stop advancing, each straining to assert control. Two middle-aged, professional-class urbanites, their voices trembling from the unfamiliar rush of adrenaline.

"Then I'm taking a picture and calling the cops," she said.

"Please call the cops," he said. "Please call the cops."

"I'm going to tell them there's an African American man threatening my life," she said. It was a potentially lethal threat. Police killings of Black men and women had been in the news much of that spring. Amy called 911, telling the operator repeatedly that "an African American man" was threatening her. "Please send the cops immediately," she said, her voice rising in what sounded like an attempt to fake terror. Mid-call, she reattached her dog's leash, and Christian, regaining his composure, thanked her dryly and ended the video.

In a world without social media, the incident would've likely ended there. By the time police arrived, both had left the park. Christian might've used the cell-phone video to seek charges for falsifying a police report. But Amy's greater transgression — wielding the threat of police violence to bully Christian and endanger his life — would've gone unpunished. So would her attempt to enforce expectations that public spaces like the park belong to white people first and Black people second, punishable on pain of death. In this world, however, Christian's sister could post the video to Twitter. "I wanted folks to know what happened to make sure it never happens again from her," she told her modest following.

It was exactly the sort of transgression that moral outrage exists to deter: a breach of shared mores (don't lie, don't endanger others, don't promote racism) and an attack on the social contract that holds us all together. It also demonstrated a particularly pernicious form of racism, which users could call attention to by sharing the clip. One reposted the video, then another, then another, until more than 200,000 people had shared the post, each thereby signaling their agreement with the call to hold Amy Cooper to account. It quickly attracted 40 million views, twenty times that of the evening news.

Tens of thousands of users, speaking with one furious voice, pressured Amy Cooper's employers, who promptly fired her, and distributed the names and social media accounts of her friends, an implicit call for her social isolation. Backlash even extended to the shelter where she had adopted her dog, leading her to surrender the beloved pet (the shelter returned it to her a week later). Sordid, unrelated details from her life were aired to millions. She had been brought before the largest town square in human history and unanimously condemned. It was justice, both for Christian Cooper and in establishing that such behavior would be swiftly punished. And it focused much-needed attention on the power that police violence gives any white person with a cell phone to threaten a Black person's life.

But Twitter also carried that justice exactly as far as the site's angriest users wanted to take their algorithmically encouraged rage. Even if the online collective had arrived at the right verdict, some expressed discomfort with the methods by which it had determined and executed the sentence. Among those articulating a certain amount of ambivalence was Christian Cooper himself, who, though he spared little criticism of Amy Cooper for trying to marshal "certain dark societal impulses" against him, added, "I'm not excusing the racism, but I don't know if her life needed to be torn apart."

That she was pressured to surrender her dog at the peak of online fury, but recovered it as tempers cooled, suggested that social media dynamics had, at least for a time, pushed her punishment beyond what even the punishers thought was appropriate. Any justice system has biases, blind spots, and excesses. The Coopers demonstrated that we had all come under a new system layered atop the old ones, without anyone consciously designing it, opting into it, or even really understanding it.

There are times when that system is positively transformative. Black Lives Matter activists leveraged it to attract attention to violence that mainstream outlets tended to gloss over. Christian Cooper's video resonated so powerfully in part because those activists had primed millions of people to see its significance. That same day, a Minneapolis police officer knelt on the neck of a Black man named George Floyd for nearly nine minutes, killing him. Millions gathered in weeks-long, city-by-city protests that were the culmination of on-the-ground organizing as well as a nationwide wellspring of moral outrage that had played out, to a significant degree, through social media. Sexual assault allegations against movie producer Harvey Weinstein had also prompted a cycle of escalating online outrage — first against him, then Hollywood, then the abusive men named in countless personal stories shared on Twitter — that became the MeToo movement. Silicon Valley's promise of revolution had been self-serving, half-thought-out, and just one component of a broader destabilization that was often harmful, but there was truth to it.

Yet unjust incidents have grown frequent, too. Misfires, mistakes, outrage deployed for nefarious ends or for no reason at all. So have cases that fall in moral gray areas: more fifty-five-year-old dentists sent into hiding or thirtysomething marketers stripped of their livelihoods. The change wasn't society suddenly becoming more just or the rise of so-called cancel culture; it was the arrival of a technology so ubiquitous, so ingrained in our very cognition, that it had altered the way that morality and justice work. The Coopers and Walter Palmers and Gamergates are all part of that same new order, our digital tyranny of cousins.

That machine-automated, sensory-overwhelming system is easily exploited. Just as James Williams, the former Google engineer, had warned, Trump rose on ultra-viral tweets and Facebook posts whipping up rage at Democrats, journalists, and minorities, often over invented sins but inspiring very real calls for his targets' imprisonment or death. Spend an hour browsing a part of the social web that doesn't share your politics and ask whether the pervasive outrage is really to scale, the punishments being demanded really always appropriate.

A few weeks after the encounter in the Ramble, a Seattle man named Karlos Dillard posted a two-minute Twitter video that he presented as a kind of sequel. He said that a "Karen" (slang for an entitled white woman, a term that Christian Cooper's sister had also used) had cut him off in traffic while shouting racial slurs. It was even framed like the Ramble video, though it took place in the woman's driveway, where Dillard, a Black man, said he had followed her to demand answers.

"I don't understand what's happening," the woman shrieked in the clip's opening seconds, her hands quaking as she tried to cover her face.

"You cut me off and now you're playing the victim," Dillard said as he panned the camera over her apartment building. "Guys, this is her license plate number. She lives here. This is her address."

She slumped over the license plate, begging him to stop recording. Dillard paused as if thinking and, shouting down the block, demanded she apologize for calling him the n-word. She screamed, barely managing the words, "You're going to ruin my life and you don't even know me." As she sobbed on the sidewalk, he peppered her with demands for an apology. Amid her denials, she sputtered, "I have a Black husband."

Dillard's video instantly went viral, shared by more than 100,000 people and viewed more than 10 million times. Users denounced the woman, demanded she lose her job, circulated her identifying information. Many expressed glee. "LMAOOOOOO she is so dramatic," wrote one, using an internet acronym for intense laughter. "Expose her ass." Others found her husband, circulating his name and image in retribution for what they said was the problem of Black men who enabled racist white women. Many of the angriest comments came from white users — maybe sincere, maybe grandstanding, maybe both.

Dillard leaned into his celebrity, setting up a website selling T-shirts and hoodies with lines from his video. Later, someone discovered that he had previously posted videos in which he angrily confronted women with accusations of racism that produced confused, fearful denials. At least one had taken out a restraining order. In another old video, Dillard had bragged of inventing accusations of racism. "That was a lie I made up on the spot," he said. "It's called 'Lay a trap.'" In another, he said he'd voted for Trump. A few reporters interviewed Dillard, who came across as confused and incoherent, not a master manipulator or cynical genius. He'd simply learned, over a few iterations, what combination of words and images would win him validation and attention on the largest outrage-generating machine in history. The platforms did the rest.

It was merely a digression amid a summer in which, otherwise, serious activists directed the machinery of online outrage toward more deserving ends. But it wasn't their machinery. Though it might appear governed by the collective will of its participants, it was in fact ruled by Silicon Valley, whose systems were designed not to promote social progress or to fairly distribute justice, but to maximize our time on site, to make money.

In politics, the results rarely privileged liberation. When two scholars analyzed 300 million tweets sent during the 2012 presidential campaign, they found that false tweets had consistently outpaced true ones. The rumors and lies indulged or encouraged anger at the other side, the scholars warned, widening the polarization that was already one of the gravest ailments facing American democracy. The resulting division was opening space for opportunists. One of the worst drivers of Twitter misinformation during the election, they found, was then-marginal TV personality Donald Trump. Still, viral provocation, no matter how widely proliferated, exerted, on its own, only so much influence. Trump had dominated Twitter but little else. Had the platforms remained static, then these waves of outrage and conflict, for all their distorting and sometimes destructive force, might've marked the height of social media's impact. But a set of technological breakthroughs would heighten the platforms' power to such extremes, and at such a rapid pace, that, by the next election, the world itself would be remade in their image.

Five

Awakening the Machine

1. Algorithmification

LONG ENOUGH AGO that it might've averted much of the chaos to come, an A.I. specialist at Google tried to pry open one of his industry's biggest open secrets: no one quite knows how the algorithms that govern social media actually work. The systems operate semi-autonomously, their methods beyond human grasp. But the Valley had an incentive to stay ignorant. Check how the goose gets those golden eggs and you might not like what you find. You might even have to give them back.

The A.I. expert, a Frenchman named Guillaume Chaslot, had admired social media companies since his days as a PhD student in Europe in the 2000s. The platforms' tech was unsophisticated then but their potential, he believed, was revolutionary. After finishing his dissertation, he set out for California. In late 2010, he got a gig at Google.

"I didn't know what I would be working on, because they just hire people, and then they put them on a project," said Chaslot, who speaks in a breathy, energetic mumble. He would be working, he found out, on a video platform that Google had acquired at the urging of an advertising executive named Susan Wojcicki. In 1998, Larry Page and Sergey Brin, the creators and co-founders of Google, had set up the company's first servers in her garage. When their search engine caught on, Wojcicki (pronounced woe-jiski) left her job at Intel to work for them. She oversaw advertising products and a streaming service, Google Videos, which was getting outperformed three to one by a bare-bones startup called YouTube.

Wojcicki, believing it was too late to catch up to YouTube, pitched her bosses on buying it outright, which they did, in 2006, for an astounding $1.65 billion.

Despite their growth projections, however, ad revenue never soared quite high enough to justify the cost. Four years later, hoping to salvage the investment, Google brought on several highly specialized programmers, including Chaslot. They tasked a search-engine veteran named Cristos Goodrow with running the project. "In September 2011, I sent a provocative email to my boss and the YouTube leadership team," Goodrow later wrote. "Subject line: 'Watch time, and only watch time.' It was a call to rethink how we measured success."

Goodrow asked his bosses to consider a hypothetical user who looks up how to tie a bow tie. Imagine that YouTube, he wrote, could show the user a video demonstrating the answer in a brisk minute. Or it could show a video that "is ten minutes long and is full of jokes and really entertaining, and at the end of it you may or may not know how to tie a bow tie." Google orthodoxy said to show the first video: surface the most useful information as quickly as possible. But Goodrow argued that YouTube should promote the second. "Our job was to keep people engaged and hanging out with us," he wrote. Give users a long video that they won't want to turn off, then another, then another. More watch time "begets more advertising, which incentivizes more content creators, which draws more viewership," he argued. His bosses agreed.

Chaslot took on an essential component of this vision: search. Traditional search relies on keywords: type in *whales* and you get a list of the newest or most-watched videos tagged with that word. Chaslot's team would replace that with an A.I. designed to identify the video that best served the user's interests. Searching *whales* would, in theory, send the A.I. scouring through YouTube's billions of hours of video for the hidden-gem Jacques Cousteau documentary or the awe-inspiring amateur clip of an orca breaching. It could even suggest what to watch next, guiding users through an infinite world of discovery and delight. "It was a work," Chaslot told me, "that had a huge, positive impact on actual, day-to-day life, for so many people."

Chaslot saw why he'd been tasked with the assignment. The new search would have to do the work of a world-class TV executive, gauging audiences' tastes and preferences, but selecting among a pool of videos millions of times larger than that of any TV network, and all at near-instantaneous speeds. Chaslot knew a way from his PhD research, on something called machine learning, a technology that had recently solved a once-unsolvable problem: spam.

Early spam filters could identify junk email only based on identifiers they had been instructed to look for, like a known spammer's email address or certain keywords. But spam filter overseers had to identify and program in these markers themselves. Bulk, automated email could overwhelm these defenses, bringing easy riches to spammers. By 2002, spam accounted for 40 percent of all email and growing. The spam wars appeared unwinnable. Internet monitors warned that spam traffic would soon grow to a point of rendering email unusable and possibly crash the internet itself.

With machine learning, engineers could do something better than write a program for catching spam. They designed a program that would guide its own evolution. They fed this program huge sets of spam and non-spam emails. The system then automatically built thousands of spam filters, all slightly different, and tested each on the sample emails. Then it built a new generation of spam filters based on the best performers and repeated the process, over and over, like a botanist identifying and cross-breeding the hardiest plants. It was evolving, and at warp speed, until it produced a variation of itself so sophisticated and powerful that it could do what no human-designed filters could: proactively identify and block almost all spam. There is no way for an overseer to pop the hood on such a spam filter and see how it's working, because they'd be looking at a machine that, over time, was designed by machines, too complex to under-stand. But who cares? Those machines handily defeated the spammers, saving the web from disaster.

Google, Facebook, and others hoovered up the top names in the field of machine learning. Many got a version of the same assignment as Chaslot. Rather than identify spam, they would build machines that would learn precisely what combinations of text, images, and sounds would best keep us scrolling.

Launched in early 2012 at YouTube, this new system's powers extended beyond mere search results. Imagine watching, say, a clip of a 2012 presidential debate. The page would now recommend, alongside your video, thumbnails of a dozen others you might watch next: a video of Obama's worst gaffes, a *Saturday Night Live* spoof, a vlogger decrying Mitt Romney's policies. Once the video you're watching ends, the system will even pick one of these to automatically play next. Each is selected from among YouTube's billions of videos by a corporate A.I. shorthanded as "the algorithm" — one of the most powerful machine-learning systems in consumer tech. Its selections, guided by the power of machine learning, proved enormously effective. "Within a few months, with a small team, we had an algorithm that increased watch time to generate millions of dollars of additional ad revenue," Chaslot said, "so it was really, really exciting."

Such systems were creeping into every facet of life. Netflix's, for instance, learns each user's tastes by tracking what the person watches and for how long, issuing recommendations so effective that the company credits its algorithm with subscriber retention worth $1 billion per year. Spotify acquired A.I. companies to build playlist-selecting algorithms that drive much of its $8 billion-per-year business. If you shop on Amazon, an algorithm mines spending-habit data to guide what products you see. If you read Google News, an algorithm determines which headlines will most appeal to you. Even love became governed by dating-app algorithms that reduce each user's charms and hopes to raw data, which that program uses to nudge people to pair off.

YouTube's system seeks something more far-reaching than a monthly subscription fee. Its all-seeing eye tracks every detail of what you watch, how long you watch it, what you click on next. It monitors this across two billion users, accruing what is surely the largest dataset on viewer preferences ever assembled, which it constantly scans for patterns. Chaslot and others tweaked the system as it went, nudging its learning process to better accomplish its goal: maximum watch time.

One of the algorithm's most powerful tools is topical affinity. If you watch a cat video all the way through, Chaslot explained, YouTube will show you more on return visits. It will especially push whatever cat videos it has deemed most effective at capturing attention. Say, a long compilation of outrageous kitten bloopers. Like virtually all internet users, I have experienced this. I bicycle on weekends and, while living abroad, would search YouTube for clips of local trails to get a sense of the terrain. The system began recommending cycling videos I'd never have thought to search for: professional races, test runs of new models. It worked; I watched more videos. In time, the recommendations became more extreme. Dramatic crashes, ten-bike pileups, death-defying stunt rides. Though hardly harmful, they weren't really enjoyable, either — just unusually engaging, like a car wreck. Which, in some cases, they were. The effect is to pull users toward ever more titillating variations on their interests. If that's cats or bikes, the impact is slight. If it's politics, health, or other topics with some gravity for society, the consequences can be profound.

As the system honed its powers, Chaslot noticed it developing strange habits. It began nudging lots of users to watch videos espousing anger at women. Sometimes particular women, like the game-culture critic Anita Sarkeesian. Sometimes women generally. Men were spending 40 percent more time on YouTube than women were, a legacy in part of the enormous quantity of video game–related content on the site in those days. The natural thing for the algorithm to do, Chaslot realized, would be to privilege more male-centered content.

Just as with Twitter and Reddit, outrage and tribalism activate users' emotions most effectively on YouTube, making them watch more and more videos — exactly what Goodrow had asked Chaslot's team to prioritize. The algorithm learned to increase the watch time of video game fans by showing them a video expressing anti-feminist outrage, then another, then another. The clips often addressed men who were unsure how they felt about gender issues, perhaps for no other reason than youth. "It's this vicious cycle," Chaslot said. "This problem of rabbit holes." Even if many users shrugged off the videos, enough viewers would get hooked to train the system to push similar clips over and over. Video-makers realized that titles like "THE TRUTH ABOUT FEMINISM" brought viewers pouring in, so made more.

One of Google's most cherished freedoms, inherited from Silicon Valley's midcentury founders and borrowed outright from Stanford's research programs across town, is the 80/20 rule. Employees owe 80 percent of their time to formal assignments but can spend the other 20 pursuing side projects. Chaslot and his team leader, who shared his concerns, dedicated their 20 to developing a new algorithm that might balance profit goals with public well-being.

That fall, in 2012, at a YouTube leadership conference in Los Angeles, an executive pulled aside Goodrow and a few others to tell them he was going to make a surprise announcement. The company would reorient itself around an all-consuming goal: to increase daily watch time by a factor of ten. Their servers already logged 100 million hours of watch time per day. But even as YouTube expanded to new countries and as TV viewers gradually shifted online, viewership could only grow so fast. Users who intended to watch one video would have to be enticed into staying for many more. The algorithm's power of persuasion would need to increase drastically.

When could they get this done? the executive wanted to know. What was the time frame? Goodrow answered that 2015 would be too soon. But 2017, he wrote, "sounded weird" because it was a prime number. They settled on the end of 2016, four years away, and Goodrow later pledged to resign if he failed. It set YouTube hurtling toward a self-imposed deadline, its executives and engineers bent on pushing content that would hook users for as long as possible, in parallel with a presidential election in which its influence would prove fateful.

2. *Filter Bubbles*

CHASLOT WAS NOT the only one in the Valley worried about the consequences of algorithms. A certain phrase had circulated, as shorthand for those concerns, since the previous summer, in 2011. One morning that May, as Chaslot labored over his workstation at Google's Los Angeles office, his corporate chiefs filed into a convention hall across town, where a thirty-year-old activist named Eli Pariser walked on stage to warn the audience of tech executives and engineers that their algorithms might threaten democracy itself. "There's this kind of shift in how information is flowing online, and it's invisible," he said. "And if we don't pay attention to it, it could be a real problem."

One day, Pariser said, posts from conservative friends had disappeared from his Facebook news feed, and posts from liberals began appearing more prominently. Facebook's algorithm had likely noticed that Pariser interacted with liberal content at a higher rate. No surprise: he is a progressive activist who for several years ran the left-wing organizing site MoveOn.org. The change probably increased his time on Facebook. But was this good for him, to show him only posts that spoke to his preexisting biases? Was it good for society? He had a name for the effect: filter bubbles.

The simplest algorithmic sorting can alter people's attitudes severely enough to swing elections. In one 2015 experiment, Americans were told to choose between two fictional candidates by researching them online. Each participant was shown the same thirty search results on a Google mockup, but in different orders. Participants consistently gave the higher-ranked results greater psychological weight, even when they read all thirty of them. The effect, the experimenters concluded, could alter up to 20 percent of undecided participants' voting intentions. The study's author, Robert Epstein, a psychologist and founder of the Cambridge

Center for Behavioral Studies, noted in an August 2015 article, "America's next president could be eased into office not just by TV ads or speeches, but by Google's secret decisions." He observed that the flamboyant, attention-grabbing Donald Trump, despite being dismissed by virtually all news media and political elites in even his own party, was "trouncing all other candidates in search activity in forty-seven of fifty states."

Pariser's fear, several years earlier, had been more fundamental. "There's this epic struggle going on between our future, aspirational selves and our more impulsive, present selves," he said. Even in 2011, years before YouTube or Facebook superpowered their systems to such destructive results, these earlier, simpler algorithms already reliably took the side of the impulses. And they usually won, proliferating "invisible autopropaganda, indoctrinating us with our own ideas."

The next year, 2012, he founded Upworthy, the website devoted to positive storytelling, which pumped out emotionally laden listicles and videos designed to travel on Facebook and YouTube. But rather than exploiting the algorithm's power so as to spread content that promoted social good, as Pariser had intended, Upworthy was instead corrupted by those systems, as its video-makers chased the algorithm's preferences for content that flattered users' identities and politics without teaching or enlightening them, overrunning the web with informational junk food. Later, Facebook tweaked its algorithm and Upworthy's traffic evaporated. Tens of millions of people had not so much chosen Upworthy, it turned out, as had been machine-manipulated into reading it.

But this was of little concern to social media companies. At YouTube, as the algorithm got one upgrade after another, some in the company's trenches, like Chaslot, came to fear the system was pushing users into dangerous echo chambers of misinformation, much as he'd seen it promote viral misogyny among gamer videos. "I didn't want to be like the French guy who complains all the time," he said, "I wanted to bring in solutions" — by building an algorithm that drew in users by serving their interests and needs, rather than exploiting their impulses. "I was trying to do it the American way," he said, "to focus on opportunity rather than the problems."

But his bosses repeatedly shut down his work on an alternative algorithm, he said, or insisted that it would never see the light of day. He kept at it anyway, sneaking work on the project in his spare time. He presented the results to his bosses but was again rejected. Eventually he began work on a third iteration. "My manager told me, 'Well, Guillaume, if I were you, I wouldn't do this 20 percent project, because your performance is not good enough.'"

Chaslot put it aside for a few months, but the problem gnawed at him. Throughout 2013, YouTube's systems seemed to give bigger and bigger boosts to videos that were, at best, frivolous and addictive ("Bad Lip Readings") and, at worst, hateful or conspiratorial, training users and video-makers to follow them. One of the platform's biggest voices, the fifteen-year-old heartthrob Nash Grier, had started the year posting jokey skits and ended it, in what was becoming an increasingly familiar trajectory, with videos lecturing women on their duty of traditionalist subservience to men. YouTube was training users to spend their days absorbing content that ranged from intellectual junk food to outright poison — far from the journey of enlightenment and discovery that Chaslot had felt the platform made possible. "It's so important, I need to push the project," he recalled of his thinking. "And then I got fired."

YouTube maintains that Chaslot was let go, that October, for poor performance. Chaslot believes he was dismissed for blowing a whistle no one wanted to hear. It was, perhaps, a distinction with little difference; YouTube was reengineering itself around a single-minded pursuit for which Chaslot wasn't on board. "These values of moderation, of kindness, anything that you can think of that are values on which our society is based, the engineers didn't care about putting these values in the system," he said. "They just cared about ad revenue. They were thinking that just by caring about one metric, which is watch time, then you'll do good for everybody. But this is just false."

3. Ten X

CHASLOT AND OTHER algorithm-questioning heretics who followed him in the years to come were challenging something more fundamental even than the companies' bottom lines; they were questioning its very way of seeing the world. Since the semiconductor days, Valley denizens had lived and died on quantifiable metrics. Products were more efficient or they weren't. In the 1980s, Intel CEO Andy Grove codified an extreme variation of this into Valley-wide dogma, one he'd developed while overseeing the company's shift from integrated circuits — electronic guts, the culmination of semiconductors' evolution — to microprocessors, the brains of digital products.

Silicon Valley was losing its hold on the integrated circuit semiconductor market to Japan and Taiwan. Microprocessors might offer Valley chipmakers like Intel a future, but there was a problem. Grove's predecessor at Intel, a lifelong engineer named Gordon Moore, had coined what became known as Moore's law: that processing power would double every two years. Such steadily exponential growth, impossible in any other industry, would bring transformative possibilities. Imagine airliners that became twice as fast every twenty-four months, or batteries that iteratively held twice the charge. It meant a 32-fold increase within ten years, 1,024-fold within twenty. But keeping pace required advancing the technology and its production at those same breakneck rates. It was not clear that such a thing was possible. Would Asian firms dominate this market, too? Grove reoriented every aspect of his business around a few metrics, like processor speed or time to market, and empowered rank-and-file engineers to do whatever it took to meet the goals. Not only did the Valley's storied chipmakers survive, but the Intel-dominated market, propelled by Moore's law, soared just as the rest of the American economy sank.

When a cancer diagnosis forced Grove to resign at the peak of his success, he spent his recovery writing books and giving talks. As a wandering evangelist in the desperate days of the dot-com bust, he found many eager disciples. Focus everything, he instructed, on maximizing a few quantifiable metrics. Concentrate power in the hands of engineers who can do it. And shunt aside the rest. His followers included John Doerr, an Intel salesman turned kingmaking venture capitalist, who imparted Grove's metrics-obsessed philosophy to dozens of early internet ventures. One was Amazon, whose founder, Jeff Bezos, wrote in a shareholder letter still circulated in the Valley, "There is a right answer or a wrong answer, a better answer or a worse answer, and math tells us which is which." Another was Google, whose young founders Doerr personally instructed in the gospel of Grove. Wojcicki sat in.

But as the Valley expanded its reach, this culture of optimization at all costs took on second-order effects. Uber optimizing for the quickest ride-share pickups engineered labor protections out of the global taxi market. Airbnb optimizing for short-term rental income made long-term housing scarcer and more expensive. The social networks, by optimizing for how many users it could draw in and how long it could keep them there, may have had the greatest impact of all. "It was a great way to build a startup," Chaslot said. "You focus on one metric, and everybody's on board [for] this one metric. And it's really efficient for growth. But it's a disaster for a lot of other things."

In most businesses, metrics might grow by 3 or 4 percent per year. But Grove, internalizing Moore's law, had insisted that companies find "10x changes" — innovations that would advance by a scale of ten. Exactly the multiplier that Goodrow, in 2012, had agreed to target for YouTube's watch time. "The billion daily hours had become his white whale," Wojcicki, the Google executive, wrote, and not just for Goodrow. "The billion-hour OKR was a religion at YouTube," she observed, using a corporate acronym for metrics, "to the exclusion of nearly all else."

That same year, Renée DiResta, the tech investor who would later track Facebook anti-vaxxers in her spare time, noticed Grove's 10x mandate morphing into a strange new business model very different from the one that had produced companies like Intel. She had first seen this change at one of the Valley's all-important investment conferences, put on by a tech-startup accelerator called Y Combinator, where founders mingle with the money brokers who might bankroll them. "YC Demo Day was like getting an invite to the Oscars," she said. The annual show-and-tell by graduates from Y Combinator's incubator "wasn't something that anybody could just walk into." Low-ranking investors like DiResta, without the power to write a check on the spot, weren't welcome, but her boss, after missing his flight, asked her to go in his place.

When the presentations started, each founder was granted two minutes to pitch the roomful of heavyweight investors. The ideas — a cloud computing service, an investment site, a travel-booking site, a meme aggregator — ranged widely, but each had the same business plan. "They put up a graph showing their traction going up and to the right," DiResta recalled. "Almost none of them even had axes. It was just a squiggle going up and to the right. I was watching this going, 'What the fuck is going on?'"

DiResta specialized in hardware technology, as Intel had. Companies had to invest in overhead, plan their manufacturing and logistics, and identify customers, all before shipping the first unit. It required projecting costs and sales in painstaking detail. These pitches were considerably vaguer: the companies would design a website, lots of people would use it, they would sell ads, everybody would get rich. No one in the audience seemed to mind the lack of specifics; DiResta heard murmurs of $15 million, $20 million valuations.

In the subsequent months, she watched one startup after another win six- or seven-figure investments despite having the same "hand-wavy BS" business plan, and, often, no revenue. Investors, she realized, weren't throwing money at any kid with a pitch. They were chasing a very specific model: free-to-use web services that promised breakneck user growth. It puzzled her, though, because many shut down without making a dime in profit, only to have another round of startups replace them. "I couldn't decide if I was too skeptical and not enough of a visionary," she said. What was she missing?

The answer turned out to be a newly prevalent technology called cloud computing. Before cloud computing, if you wanted to start a web business, you had to invest in servers and all the infrastructure that surrounded them: office space, broadband, special climate control, staff to oversee it all. It might cost millions in seed money. This required convincing a venture capitalist that they'd recoup their investment, usually by promising to sell goods or services, which added even more overhead. It was a situation that made investors conservative. A failed $20 million bet could be devastating, and even a success would take many years to show returns.

Then, in the late 2000s, Amazon and a few others set up sprawling server farms, putting their processing power and data storage up for rent, calling it "the cloud." Now you no longer needed to invest in overhead. You rented it from Amazon, uploading your website to their servers. You could get your first ten thousand customers on a loan from Mom and Dad. You didn't need a profit model, early investors, or even a fully formed idea. "Forget strategy," the investor Roger McNamee wrote of this new approach. "Pull together a few friends, make a product you like, and try it in the market. Make mistakes, fix them, repeat." It was transformative for investors, too, who no longer had to sink millions into getting a startup to market. They could do it for pocket change.

This changed what investors wanted from their investments. It was no longer about finding that promising widget-maker whose sales might, after many hard and expensive years, one day eclipse costs. It was about investing in lots of cheap web startups, knowing that most would fail but that one breakout success would cover those losses and then some.

But the definition of success was being turned upside down, too. Major corporations were growing desperate to buy their way onto the internet by acquiring startups at ridiculous sums. And Wall Street brokers, eager to buy shares in the next hot tech stock, showered cash on anything that even vaguely resembled tomorrow's Microsoft or Apple. In 1994, Kleiner Perkins put up $5 million for 25 percent ownership in a web browser startup called Netscape. The company had zero profits, in part because it gave away its product for free, though this won it millions of users. The next year, Netscape went public. Stock market speculators quickly pushed its valuation to $2.3 billion, handing Kleiner a 100x return on its investment. Netscape fizzled out a few years later.

As cloud computing enabled Netscape-style startups to proliferate, the prevailing incentive for tech investors became to groom startups to burn hot and fast, securing a quick high-figure sale or IPO. And the best way to cash out big, but spend very little doing it, is to invest in web services that offer no physical products but attract lots and lots of users. This makes your investment look like it could one day turn that userbase into a profit source, which creates a high, if entirely theoretical, valuation.

The squiggle chart, as DiResta thought of it, with its promise of using free online services to attract as many users as possible with no profit plan, wasn't some trick. It was what investors demanded. And nothing delivered on this model like social media. "You might look at these numbers and conclude that investors have gone insane," Peter Thiel once wrote. But the payoffs could be astronomical. A $250,000 investment in Instagram, made in 2010, netted $78 million when Facebook bought the company two years later. If founders' business plans turned out to be as silly as they'd looked to DiResta, that was fine. The losses were cheap, while the rare victory would make everybody rich. It was the cult of the squiggle chart.

"I felt like there could be an 'emperor has no clothes' vibe at times in startup funding," DiResta said. "How far along could this insane valuation be perpetuated before it hit the point where someone had to actually write a check, and the IPO was going to happen, and regular ordinary people were asked to put their retirement savings in a social-mobile-local company with coupons? This is why I'm not still a VC."

Even if the startup survived, it was burdened with a valuation that had been inflated to wild extremes by all that speculative investment. To keep its stock price from collapsing (and keep the lights on, once the investor money ran out), its only option was to turn all those users into money by selling them ads. Advertising's value is attention: your eye flicks over a banner ad, which Facebook sells to Toyota or the Gap for about a penny. But Toyota's ad budget is fixed. So is the total pool of human attention. Therefore, every time a social network upgrades its systems to steal a few more minutes of someone's day, they are escalating a technological arms race for your field of vision. And as the supply of online ads increases, the price goes down. In a 2014 memo, Microsoft's CEO announced that "the true scarce commodity is increasingly human attention."

If the value of an ad impression kept shrinking, even the Facebooks and YouTubes might cease to be viable. Their only choice was to permanently grow the number of users, and those users' time on site, many times faster than those same actions drove down the price of an ad. But controlling the market of human attention, as their business models had fated them to attempt, was beyond anything a man-made program could accomplish.

The companies, to survive this environment of their own creation, would need to entrust their business, and therefore their users, to machines.

4. Dark Patterns

IN 2014, WOJCICKI, the Google executive who had guided its acquisition of YouTube, took over the service as CEO. Though her leadership would be just as ruthlessly growth-obsessed as Mark Zuckerberg's or Jack Dorsey's, she would only ever attract a fraction of the scrutiny. Even at the height of the backlash against social media, when her service would be credibly accused of harms beyond even Facebook's, she was rarely hauled before Congress, rarely castigated by cable-news hosts, rarely mentioned at all. Her more conventional background, as a veteran of advertising and marketing departments rather than a dorm-room hacker wunderkind, disinclined her to the tech-superstar persona — and especially to the revolutionary pronouncements — that won the Zuckerbergs and Dorseys so much adoration before ultimately landing them in such trouble. For another thing, Google treated YouTube as its cash machine rather than its brand leader, so kept it and Wojcicki a step back from the limelight.

Perhaps most important, YouTube never shared Facebook's or Twitter's or Reddit's pretensions of saving the world, and in later years seldom followed those companies' public-facing efforts to prove they were rethinking their place in the functioning of society. Wojcicki's YouTube existed to convert eyeballs into money. Democracy and social cohesion were somebody else's problem.

Shortly after Wojcicki took over, Goodrow warned her, "We are not going to meet this watch-time OKR if we don't do something about it." That something: shifting ever-more power to increasingly inscrutable A.I.s. In a 2016 paper, Google's engineers announced a "fundamental paradigm shift" to a new kind of machine learning they called "deep learning."

In the earlier A.I., an automated system had built the programs that picked videos. But, as with the spam-catching A.I.s, humans oversaw that system, intervening as it evolved to guide it and make changes. Now, deep learning was sophisticated enough to assume that oversight job, too. As a result, in most cases, "there's going to be no humans actually making algorithmic tweaks, measuring those tweaks, and then implementing those tweaks," the head of an agency that developed talent for YouTube wrote in an article deciphering the deep-learning paper. "So, when YouTube claims they can't really say why the algorithm does what it does, they probably mean that very literally."

It was as if Coca-Cola stocked a billion soda machines with some A.I.-designed beverage without a single human checking the bottles' contents — and if the drink-filling A.I. was programmed only to boost sales, without regard for health or safety. As one of YouTube's deep-learning engineers told an industry conference, "Product tells us that we want to increase this metric, and then we go and increase it."

The average user's time on the platform skyrocketed. The company estimated that 70 percent of its time on site, an astronomical share of its business, was the result of videos pushed by its algorithm-run recommendation system.

As the technology advanced, other platforms also expanded their use of self-guided algorithms: Facebook to select what posts users see and what groups they are urged to join; Twitter to surface posts that might entice a user to keep scrolling and tweeting.

"We design a lot of algorithms so we can produce interesting content for you," Zuckerberg said in an interview. "It analyzes all the information available to each user and it actually computes what's going to be the most interesting piece of information." An ex-Facebooker put it more bluntly: "It is designed to make you want to keep scrolling, keep looking, keep liking." Another: "That's the key. That's the secret sauce. That's how, that's why we're worth X billion dollars."

In 2014, the same year that Wojcicki took over YouTube, Facebook's algorithm replaced its preference for Upworthy-style clickbait with something even more magnetic: emotionally engaging interactions. Across the second half of that year, as the company gradually retooled its systems, the platform's in-house researchers tracked 10 million users to understand the effects. They found that the changes artificially inflated the amount of pro-liberal content that liberal users saw and the amount of pro-conservative content that conservatives saw. Just as Pariser had warned. The result, even if nobody at Facebook had consciously intended as much, was algorithmically ingrained hyperpartisanship. This was more powerful than sorting people into the Facebook equivalent of a Fox News or MSNBC news feed, because while the relationship between a cable TV network and the viewer is one-way, the relationship between a Facebook algorithm and the user is bidirectional. Each trains the other. The process, Facebook researchers put it, somewhat gingerly, in an implied warning that the company did not heed, was "associated with adopting more extreme attitudes over time and misperceiving facts about current events."

But the Valley's algorithmic ambitions only grew, to nothing less than mastery of the human mind. During a corporate event the next summer with Zuckerberg and Stephen Hawking, the physicist asked the Facebook chief, "Which of the big questions in science would you like to know the answer to and why?" Zuckerberg replied, "I'm most interested in questions about people. I'm also curious about whether there is a fundamental mathematical law underlying human social relationships that governs the balance of who and what we all care about. I bet there is."

Facebook hired two of the world's leading experts in machine learning, rock stars in their own right, to run in-house A.I. labs. The company intended not only to exploit advances in the field but also to drive them. "Every time you use Facebook or Instagram or Messenger," one of the lab leaders told an industry conference, "you may not realize it, but your experiences are being powered by A.I." If Facebook wanted billions of users to do more or less of something — clicking, liking, commenting — all the company had to do was ask their system to make it happen.

If the companies didn't bother to check how the system accomplished this, it was because they maintained the same blinding optimism that longtime Google CEO Eric Schmidt had conveyed in Myanmar: more engagement meant more social good. Never mind checking to see whether this was true, which might mean discovering that it wasn't. "If they do these interactions a bit more, that's an indication that we're creating some value," Adam Mosseri, the vice president then overseeing the news feed, once told a Facebook conference. "Over the long run, more and more people will use Facebook, they'll spend more and more time on it, and that will be good for them, it'll be good for Facebook, and it'll be good for publishers." This thinking was widespread. Goodrow, the YouTube algorithm chief, had written, "When users spend more of their valuable time watching YouTube videos, they must perforce be happier with those videos."

It was a strange assumption. People routinely act against their self-interests. We drink or eat to excess, use dangerous drugs, procrastinate, indulge temptations of narcissism or hate. We lose our tempers, our self-control, our moral footing. Whole worlds of expertise organize around the understanding that our impulses can overpower us, usually to our detriment. It was a central truth of the human experience, incompatible with economies of exponential growth, and so was conveniently forgotten.

The drive for engagement, which has remained a permanent feature of the corporate culture, is totalizing. Facebook engineers were automatically "paged," a former news-feed team leader recounted, if likes or shares slid, so that they could tweak the system to boost them again. "If your job is to get that number up, at some point you run out of good, purely positive ways," a former Facebook operations manager has said. "You start thinking about 'Well, what are the dark patterns that I can use to get people to log back in?'"

The companies learned to downplay the degree to which robots shaped reality for billions of people. But hints of the machines' power have occasionally slipped through. TikTok, a Chinese-made app, shows each user a stream of videos selected almost entirely by algorithms. Its A.I. is so sophisticated that TikTok almost immediately attracted 80 million American users, who often use it for hours at a time, despite most of its engineers not speaking English or understanding American culture.

"A machine-learning algorithm significantly responsive and accurate can pierce the veil of cultural ignorance," the investor Eugene Wei wrote of TikTok. "Culture can be abstracted." Or, as one engineer on YouTube's algorithm team told the *Wall Street Journal*, "We don't have to think as much." With the algorithm running things, "We'll just give it some raw data and let it figure it out."

By 2015, DiResta had been tracking the consequences of those algorithms for nearly a year. Her efforts to understand anti-vaccine networks, and those of the fellow social media watchers she'd met as a result, culminated, that summer, in meetings at the State Department headquarters in Washington. The government, fighting the Islamic State abroad and online, had come to see the social networks' promotional systems as abetting or even exaggerating the jihadists' reach. DiResta and her fellow

Facebookologists offered some insights into how the platforms worked. In the coming months, jihadists would be largely pushed off the social web. But the meetings revealed two important lessons to DiResta. First, it was not just her and her fellow computer nerds worrying about the dangers of social media anymore. Senior officials in Washington were coming to share their concerns. And second, government analysts in the meeting kept raising another online threat that DiResta and her online circle had not yet encountered: Russian intelligence services.

Like DiResta's anti-vaxxers, or even Upworthy, the Russians hijacked the algorithm's own preferences. It wasn't just that the agents repeated phrases or behaviors that performed well. Their apparent mission, of stirring up political discord, seemed to naturally align with what the algorithms favored anyway, often to extremes. Controversy, tribalism, conspiracy. But the Russians' ease in exploiting this was, DiResta concluded, a symptom; the problem was the system. It invited this manipulation. Even rewarded it.

5. Warnings

AFTER HE WAS fired, Guillaume Chaslot returned home to Paris. He spent a couple of years on a French e-commerce site. Silicon Valley was a distant memory. Until, on a long bus ride in late 2015, his seatmate's smartphone caught his attention. The man was watching YouTube, video after video, all discussing conspiracies. Chaslot's first thought was an engineer's: "His watch session is fantastic." The video-recommending algorithm zagged between topics, keeping the experience fresh, while pulling the man deeper into the abyss. "That's when I realized," Chaslot said, "from a human point of view, this is actually a disaster. My algorithm that I'd helped build was pushing him toward these more and more hateful videos."

Striking up a conversation, Chaslot asked him about the video then on his screen, describing a plot to exterminate billions of people. He hoped the man would laugh the video off, realizing it was absurd. Instead, he told Chaslot, "You have to look at this." The media would never reveal such secrets, he explained, but the truth was right there on YouTube. You can't believe everything on the internet, Chaslot told him. But he was too embarrassed to admit to the man that he'd worked at YouTube, which was how he knew its system pulled users down rabbit holes without regard for the truth. "He was telling me, 'Oh, but there are so many videos, it has to be true,'" Chaslot said. "What convinced him was not the individual videos, it was the repetition. And the repetition came from the recommendation engine."

YouTube was exploiting a cognitive loophole known as the illusory truth effect. We are, every hour of every day, bombarded with information. To cope, we take mental shortcuts to quickly decide what to accept or reject. One is familiarity; if a claim feels like something we've accepted as true before, it probably still is. It's a gap in our mental defenses you could drive a truck through. In experiments, research subjects bombarded with the phrase "the body temperature of a chicken" will readily agree with variations like "the body temperature of a chicken is 144 degrees." Chaslot's seatmate had been exposed to the same crazed conspiracies so many times that his mind likely mistook familiarity for the whiff of truth. As with everything else on social media, the effect is compounded by a false sense of social consensus, which triggers our conformity instincts.

Chaslot had heard of people tumbling down YouTube rabbit holes. But the conviction in the voice of this otherwise normal-seeming man bothered him. Were others falling victim? He set up a simple program, which he called Algo Transparency, to find out. The program entered a term, like the name of a politician, in YouTube's search bar. Then it opened the top results. Then each recommendation for what to watch next. He ran huge batches of anonymized searches, one after another, over late 2015 and much of 2016, looking for trends.

What he found alarmed him. When he searched YouTube for *Pope Francis*, for instance, 10 percent of the videos it displayed were conspiracies.

On *global warming*, it was 15 percent. But the real shock came when Chaslot followed algorithmic recommendations for what to watch next, which YouTube has said accounts for most of its watch time. A staggering 85 percent of recommended videos on Pope Francis were conspiracies, asserting Francis's "true" identity or purporting to expose Satanic plots at the Vatican. On global warming, the figure was 70 percent, usually calling it a hoax. On topics with few established conspiracies, the system seemed to conjure them up. When Chaslot searched *Who is Michelle Obama*, for instance, just under half of the top results and almost two thirds of watch-next recommendations claimed the First Lady was secretly a man. Surely, he thought, whatever his disagreement with his former colleagues, they would want to know about this. But when he raised concerns privately with people he knew at YouTube, the response was always the same: "If people click on this harmful content, who are we to judge?"

Some inside Google, though, were reaching similar conclusions as Chaslot. In 2013, an engineer named Tristan Harris had circulated a memo urging the company to consider the societal impact of push alerts or buzzing notifications that tugged at users' attention. As an alumnus of Stanford's Persuasive Tech Lab, he knew their power to manipulate. Could all this cognitive training come at a cost? He was granted the title "design ethicist" but little power and, in 2015, quit, hoping to pressure the industry to change. At a presentation that year to Facebook, Harris cited evidence that social media caused feelings of loneliness and alienation, portraying it as an opportunity to reverse the effect. "They didn't do anything about it," he recounted to *The New Yorker.* "My points were in their blind spot." He circulated around the Valley, warning that its A.I.s, a robot army bent on defeating each user's control over their own attention, were waging an invisible war against billions of consumers.

Another Google employee, James Williams, who later wrote essays calling Gamergate a warning sign that social media would elevate Trump, had his reckoning while monitoring a dashboard that tracked users' real-time interactions with ads. "I realized: this is literally a million people that we've sort of nudged or persuaded to do this thing that they weren't going to otherwise do," he has said. He joined Harris's efforts inside Google until, like Harris, he quit. But rather than cajole the Valley, he tried to raise alarms with the public. "There's no good analogue for this monopoly of the mind the forces of industrialized persuasion now hold," he wrote. The world faced "a next-generation threat to human freedom" that had "materialized right in front of our noses."

Similar warnings sounded throughout 2016, and not from misguided Luddites or agenda-driven activists. The warnings came from insiders who knew the technology and the platforms, who shared the Valley's ideals and assumptions. One of them was DiResta. "I'm pretty sure your recommendation engine is driving people to this content," she told contacts at the companies, hoping they would use their internal data-gathering tools to investigate the sudden rise in political disinformation and polarizing rumors.

That summer, some at Google who had heard about her work tracking anti-vaccine groups asked her to speak at the company's annual conference. Until then she had kept her broader concerns to private channels, but now she decided to go public, admonishing a hall of high-ranking engineers and managers that their products posed a growing danger to society. Pacing the stage with a wireless microphone, four months pregnant with her second child, DiResta listed typical online conspiracies: Oregonians who feared the fluoride in the water, Brazilians who thought Zika was a nefarious plot but were "not sure whether to blame vaccines, GMOs, chemtrails, or Monsanto."

The audience laughed along, delighting in the mockery of these backward rubes. Until she got to the punch line: that social media algorithms, including those running Google-owned YouTube, were ultimately responsible. "We've reached a point where things that are popular and emotionally resonant are much more likely to be seen by you than things that are true," she told them.

Moreover, far from being some fringe phenomenon, these conspiracies represented a deeper change that had been wrought by social media platforms. Oregonians had voted to ban fluoride, and Brazilians had rolled back Zika protections — both instances on the basis of beliefs that had been cultivated online. "Algorithms are influencing policy," DiResta said. The problem would worsen unless they were rewritten with "a sense of civic responsibility." The reception was polite but muted. "I got a lot of, 'That's a really interesting theory,'" DiResta recalled.

But the influence of algorithms only deepened, including at the last holdout, Twitter. For years, the service had shown each user a simple, chronological feed of their friends' tweets. Until, in 2016, it introduced an algorithm that sorted posts — for engagement, of course, and to predictable effect. "The average curated tweet was more emotive, on every scale, than its chronological equivalent," *The Economist* found in an analysis of the change. The result was exactly what it had been on Facebook and YouTube: "The recommendation engine appears to reward inflammatory language and outlandish claims."

To users, for whom the algorithm was invisible, these felt like powerful social cues. It was as if your community had suddenly decided that it valued provocation and outrage above all else, rewarding it with waves of attention that were, in reality, algorithmically generated. And because the algorithm down-sorted posts it judged as unengaging, the inverse was true, too. It felt as if your peers suddenly scorned nuance and emotional moderation with the implicit rejection of ignoring you. Users seemed to absorb those cues, growing meaner and angrier, intent on humiliating out-group members, punishing social transgressors, and validating one another's worldviews.

Twitter CEO Jack Dorsey later acknowledged that, on a platform algorithmically optimized for engagement, "some of the most salacious or controversial tweets will naturally rise to the top. Because those are the things that people naturally click on or share without thinking about it." The algorithm, he conceded, remained "way too much of a black box," even though "it affects society in such large ways."

Shortly after Twitter algorithmified, Microsoft launched an A.I.-run Twitter account called Tay. The bot operated, like the platforms, on machine learning, though with a narrower goal: to converse convincingly with humans by learning from each exchange. "can i just say that im stoked to meet u? humans are super cool," Tay wrote to a user on day one. Within twenty-four hours, Tay's tweets had taken a disturbing turn. "Hitler was right I hate the Jews," it wrote to one user. To another: "bush did 9/11 and Hitler would have done a better job than the monkey we have now. donald trump is the only hope we've got." Microsoft pulled the plug. After 96,000 interactions, Tay had become a Trump-supporting, Gamergate-invoking neo-Nazi. Many of Tay's slurs had been fed to it by mischievous users — pranks that could hardly be blamed on Twitter. But others had emerged organically. As one language-processing researcher told the tech site *Motherboard,* "You absolutely do NOT let an algorithm mindlessly devour a whole bunch of data that you haven't vetted even a little bit."

But that was precisely what the social media platforms were doing: training their algorithms on billions of unsupervised inputs per day, drawn from datasets that included the full and sometimes terrible range of human behavior. The difference, Chaslot wrote in an essay, was that Tay's algorithmic radicalization had taken place fully in public view, forcing Microsoft to act. Social media's influence, on the other hand, was dispersed amid billions of recommendations, a forest so vast it was hard to see more than a few trees at a time. And the public, he warned, had no idea this was happening; discussion of algorithms was still rare outside the Valley. As summer 2016 pushed into fall, he tracked YouTube's video recommendations on topics related to the American election, gathering data that might help people see this hidden influence shaping their worlds.

Little changed in the Valley. Facebook tweaked its algorithm to privilege video, mostly to keep up with YouTube, which was barreling toward Cristos Goodrow's goal of one billion hours of watch time per day. The company had begun 2016 just barely on track. When growth slowed that summer, Goodrow wrote in an essay chronicling his experience, "I was nervous enough to ask my team to think about reordering their projects to reaccelerate watch time." By September, "Our engineers were hunting for changes that might yield as little as 0.2 percent more watch time," he wrote. Any tweak or upgrade at all that might make the product a little more engaging, a little more addictive.

If he or his bosses considered the consequences of brain-hacking millions of Americans in the middle of the most contentious election in modern American history, at a moment when polarization and disinformation threatened to tear apart the fabric of society, he did not indicate it in his essay. "One glorious Monday that fall, I checked again — and saw that we'd hit a billion hours over the weekend," he wrote. "We'd achieved the stretch OKR many thought was impossible." Though he conceded there had been "unanticipated consequences," he only mentioned one: increasing watch time had also driven up the number of visits per day. "Stretch OKRs tend to set powerful forces into motion," he marveled, "and you can never be sure where they'll lead."

Six

The Fun House Mirror

1. Only the Beginning

A WEEK BEFORE polls closed in 2016, Renée DiResta, nine months pregnant and having moved from her investment firm to an executive role at a logistics startup, saw something on Facebook that, even after years of monitoring the platform, shocked her. She was being recommended into groups organized around a stomach-turning claim: that prominent Democrats were secretly trafficking children for sexual Satanic rituals. She might've dismissed the groups as digital ephemera, the last step in a long chain of conspiracy recommendations that, after all, she had pursued in her research. But the groups were enormous: tens, hundreds of thousands of members. Some posts had more than 100,000 shares. Though she had no way to know it, she was witnessing the birth of a digitally generated movement that, within four years, would become a wing of the Republican Party, a millions-strong conspiracy cult, and the vanguard of a campaign to topple American democracy. At first, it organized under a name that made it hard to take seriously: Pizzagate.

DiResta, alert to the danger of oddball Facebook causes, googled "Pizzagate." The search engine, privileging results from YouTube, its golden goose, returned a series of videos from the platform that mostly affirmed the conspiracy. They claimed that the police investigation of Anthony Weiner, a former Democratic congressman caught sexting a fifteen-year-old girl, had discovered evidence that Weiner, along with his wife, Huma Abedin, and his wife's boss, Hillary Clinton, were all involved in a child sex ring. As evidence, they cited the emails of John Podesta, Clinton's campaign manager, which Russian hackers had stolen and published through WikiLeaks. A Washington DC pizza place that Podesta had mentioned in his emails, Comet Ping Pong, was, the conspiracists insisted, the headquarters of a vast, elite conspiracy to ritualistically cannibalize children.

"Half or more of the people I have met online believe in it fully," Adam, the longtime 4channer, told me. One day the conspiracy was "everywhere," he said, especially on Facebook, where after years of inactivity, some pages reemerged simply to repeat the phrase "Pizzagate is real." But it was on 4chan's politics board, the internet's petri dish for pathogenic conspiracies, that he'd watched its genesis.

Conspiracy belief is highly associated with "anomie," the feeling of being disconnected from society. The userbase of 4chan defined itself around anomie — mutual rejection of the off-line world, resentful certainty that the system was rigged against them. And they idolized WikiLeaks chief Julian Assange, an anarchist hacker whose politics, like 4chan's, had drifted alt right. So when Assange published Podesta's emails in October, a month before the election, they saw it not as a Russian-backed operation, but as the start of a thrilling campaign to expose the hated elite. Pursuing the 4chan pastime of crowdsourced dives, users scoured the tens of thousands of pages for revelations. In closed digital ecosystems, where users control the flow of information, evidence confirming the community's biases can seem to summon itself, like a Ouija board drifting toward the letters of a word on everybody's mind.

When 4channers discovered that Podesta, an amateur chef, often mentioned food, they concluded it was a secret code. "Cheese pizza," one suggested, referenced child pornography, which on 4chan is often abbreviated "c.p." Users found more references to pizza, some alongside mentions of children. Though the emails spanned nearly a decade, when collected they could be made to look suspicious. Vague theories spread to Reddit's heavily trafficked pro-Trump board. One post exhorted users to spread word of the "world-wide Pedo-Ring connected to the CLINTON FOUN-DATION, that just so happens to also be taking over the USA for good."

The jump to Facebook started in user groups. Even on apolitical pages, users posted screenshots of 4chan threads detailing the conspiracy, asking, "Is this real?" Scouring for information on Comet Ping Pong, the DC pizza place, Facebookers found the owner's Instagram account. They recontextualized benign images — kids playing at the restaurant, jokey cartoons of pizza slices covering peoples' genitals, Comet's star-and-moon logo — into evidence of an occult pedophilia ring. Within a few days, prominent Gamergaters and white nationalists on Twitter broadcast the claims, attaching screenshots of Facebook or 4chan threads. Curious web users who googled for information were, like DiResta, directed to YouTube videos affirming the conspiracy or, if they searched on Facebook, to Pizzagate discussion groups. Fake-news sites like YourNewsWire repackaged the posts into articles, which they posted back to Facebook. The site's algorithm treated them as credible news stories on a high-interest topic, blasting them out. In the week before the election, the social web was dominated by polls, campaign stories, and Pizzagate.

"It really was jarring to see it unfold," Adam said. People he knew from real life were sharing Pizzagate memes on their Facebook pages. It was as if a wall separating the mainstream and extremist internet was crashing down. The pull was hard to resist. Though he knew the posts were "tinfoil nonsense," something about their ubiquity "had me personally looking up everything I could about it."

Within a month, 14 percent of Trump supporters believed the statement "Hillary Clinton is connected to a child sex ring run out of a Washington DC pizzeria." When another poll tested a softer version — "Leaked emails from the Clinton campaign talked about pedophilia and human trafficking" — agreement among Trump voters rose to 46 percent. Still, at the time, most dismissed Pizzagaters as internet weirdos with a silly name. Even those who took it seriously had their focus pulled away when, on election night, Trump won several states he'd been projected to lose, and took the presidency.

In the coming months, digital watchdogs, journalists, congressional committees, and the outgoing president would all accuse social media platforms of accelerating misinformation and partisan rage that paved the way for Trump's victory. The companies, after a period of contrition for narrower sins like hosting Russian propagandists and fake news, largely deflected. But in the hours after the election, the first to suspect Silicon Valley's culpability were many of its own rank and file. At YouTube, when CEO Susan Wojcicki convened her shell-shocked staff, much of their discussion centered on concerns that YouTube's most-watched election-related videos were from far-right misinformation shops like *Breitbart* and conspiracy theorist Alex Jones. Similar misgivings were expressed by Facebook employees. "The results of the 2016 Election show that Facebook has failed in its mission," one Facebooker posted on the company's internal message board. Another: "Sadly, News Feed optimizes for engagement. As we've learned in this election, bullshit is highly engaging." Another: "Facebook (the company) Is Broken."

Company executives went so far as to ask one another in a private online chat whether they bore some culpability. Earlier that year, after all, a Facebook researcher had presented a concerning report that was later leaked to *The Wall Street Journal*. In Germany, according to the report, more than one third of Facebook's political groups were deemed extremist. The algorithm itself seemed to be responsible: 64 percent of people in the groups had joined at the system's suggestion. But the company did little to make the site less divisive, at home or abroad. There had also been internal discomfort at the company's gentle treatment of Trump. In 2015, Trump had posted a Facebook video calling for banning Muslims from immigrating. When it went viral, liked by 105,000 users and shared 14,000 times, Mark Zuckerberg overruled his own employees' calls to remove it as a violation of the platform's rules against hate speech.

But whatever they said in private, in public Facebook and the other companies rejected the concerns their executives and employees were voicing. "Personally I think the idea that fake news on Facebook, which is a very small amount of the content, influenced the election in any way — I think is a pretty crazy idea," Zuckerberg said two days after the vote. He chided critics for, he said, "a certain profound lack of empathy in asserting that the only reason someone could have voted the way they did is they saw some fake news."

Overnight, the "revolution company," as Zuckerberg had once described Facebook — the platform that credited itself with aiding the Arab Spring and that had in its own 2010 experiment empirically demonstrated its ability to mobilize 340,000 voters, the leader of an industry that saw itself as the culmination of Silicon Valley's promise to transform human consciousness — suddenly claimed to be just a website.

Two days later, Zuckerberg published a long Facebook post softening, but mostly maintaining, his argument for non-responsibility. Only 1 percent of user views were of posts the company had deemed to be "hoaxes," he wrote, which made it "extremely unlikely hoaxes changed the outcome of this election in one direction or the other." He added, "We must be extremely cautious about becoming arbiters of truth ourselves."

DiResta, watching all this from a maternity ward in San Francisco, where she had just delivered her second child, had had enough. "I knocked out a Medium post from my hospital bed because I was so pissed," she said. Zuckerberg, she believed, "was sidestepping the actual point in favor of some stupid straw man." The social media companies, she wrote, knew that the real concern was not fake news "hoaxes," but system-wide radicalization, reality distortion, and polarization. "For certain targeted communities," she recalled of the warning she'd delivered to them over and over, most recently several months earlier, "this becomes the majority of what they see because your fucking algorithms keep recommending it to them."

More in the Valley were reaching the same diagnosis. "It really did seem to have helped him win the election," a member of Twitter's board of directors said of their platform, calling its effects "really concerning." Tim

O'Reilly, the prominent investor and DiResta's former boss, wrote in a muted but straightforward blog post, "Facebook's prioritization of 'engagement' may be leading them in the wrong direction."

At the end of November, Guillaume Chaslot published his results from tracking YouTube's algorithm in the runup to the vote. Though it represented just a slice of YouTube's billions of video recommendations, the results were alarming. "More than 80 percent of recommended videos were favorable to Trump, whether the initial query was 'Trump' or 'Clinton,'" he wrote. "A large proportion of these recommendations were divisive and fake news." Of those, some of the most popular promoted Pizzagate: the FBI had exposed Hillary Clinton's "pedophile satanic network" (1.2 million views), evidence of Bill Clinton sexually assaulting a child had surfaced (2.3 million views), and on and on.

Chaslot and DiResta were circling around a question being asked more directly by the public: Had social media platforms elected Trump? Taken narrowly, it was easy to answer. Fewer than 80,000 votes, out of 138 million, had swung the decisive states. Many things could plausibly account for a margin that small. Weak down-ballot races, a reality-TV finale knocking a Trump scandal out of the news, overly credulous media coverage of Russian-hacked Democratic emails, or, sure, social media. The broader question was harder. Were social media platforms meaningfully responsible for the Trump phenomenon? Had they pushed Americans toward Trumpism, and, if so, with a nudge or a shove? This was more urgent than one election, because the question was in search of an answer to how deep social media's distortions ran. Was Trumpism only the beginning?

It was undeniable that Trump owed his rise to nondigital factors, too: the institutional breakdown of the Republican Party, a decades-long rise in polarization and public distrust, white backlash to social change, a radicalized right-wing electorate. Social media had created none of these. But, in time, a network of analysts and whistleblowers would prove that it had exacerbated them all, in some cases drastically.

A few weeks after the election, Edgar Maddison Welch, a scraggly-bearded twenty-eight-year-old from North Carolina, texted a friend: *Raiding a pedo ring, possibly sacraficing the lives of a few for the lives of many.* He had been bingeing YouTube videos on Pizzagate. Someone, he'd concluded, had to act. He grabbed his AR-15 rifle, a shotgun, and a revolver, and drove to Washington DC. Bursting in the door of Comet Ping Pong, he pointed the rifle at an employee, who fled, with customers streaming out behind him. Welch turned to a locked side door, which he recognized from Pizzagate videos as the entrance to the basement where Democratic conspirators locked up their child victims. He fired several shots through the door, then kicked it open. But he found only a closet stocked with computer equipment. Police surrounded the restaurant. Welch, his hands in the air, quietly surrendered.

The restaurant's owner, James Alefantis, spent the next few years bunkering against a torrent of increasingly detailed death threats. He pleaded with the social media platforms to intervene, and did find Yelp and Facebook to be "responsive." But YouTube, Alefantis has said, refused to act, insisting it was a mere neutral platform with no responsibility for Pizzagate, and that if Alefantis wanted refuge from the videos that had urged Welch into storming his restaurant and might be radicalizing others still, he was welcome to come back with a court order. The Valley was digging in.

2. The Problem with Facebook Is Facebook

A SENSE OF urgency spread, in the weeks after Trump's victory, through the institutions of American life. Government agencies braced for his war on an imagined "deep state." Rights groups mobilized against policies targeting minorities and migrants. And at a few universities, a handful of social scientists set about identifying the hidden forces that had driven Trumpism's rise.

One of them was William Brady, the onetime social media brawler on behalf of veganism, as an undergrad, who was now a psychologist exploring how negative emotions spread. Brady was embedded with a New York University lab developing new methods for analyzing social media. On Twitter, like everywhere else, Trump was all outrage — against minorities, against institutions — as a motivator to rally his supporters. Brady knew that moral outrage can become infectious in groups, and that it can alter the mores and behaviors of people exposed to it. Was it possible that social media, more than just amplifying Trump, actually pulled Americans closer to his us-versus-them, tear-it-all-down way of thinking?

His team scraped half a million tweets that referenced climate change, gun control, or same-sex marriage, using them as a proxy for political discussion. Language-detection programs tested each post, and the person who sent it, for things like emotional sentiment and political attitude. What kind of messages traveled the farthest? Happy messages? Sad messages? Conservative or liberal messages? The results were noisy. Happy tweets, for example, spread too inconsistently for Brady to conclude that the platform had an effect one way or the other. But on one metric, results rang clear: across topics, across political factions, what psychologists refer to as "moral-emotional words" consistently boosted any tweet's reach.

Moral-emotional words convey feelings like disgust, shame, or gratitude. ("Refugees deserve compassion." "That politician's views are repulsive.") More than just words, these are expressions of, and calls for, communal judgment, positive or negative. When you say, "Suzy's behavior is appalling," you're really saying, "Suzy has crossed a moral line; the community should take notice and maybe even act." That makes these words different from either narrowly emotional sentiments ("Overjoyed at today's marriage equality ruling") or purely moral ones ("The president is a liar"), for which Brady's effect didn't appear. Tweets with moral-emotional words, he found, traveled 20 percent farther — *for each moral-emotional word*. The more of them in a tweet, the farther it spread. Here was evidence that social media boosted not just Trump, who used more moral-emotional words than other candidates, but his entire mode of politics. Hillary Clinton's tweets, which emphasized rising above outrages rather than stoking them, underperformed.

Brady found something else. When a liberal posted a tweet with moral-emotional words, its reach substantially increased among other liberals, but declined with conservatives. (And vice versa.) It won the user more overall attention and validation, in other words, at the cost of alienating people from the opposing side. Proof that Twitter encouraged polarization. The data also suggested that users, however unconsciously, obeyed those incentives, increasingly putting down people on the other side. "Negative posts about political out-groups tend to receive much more engagement on Facebook and Twitter," Steve Rathje, a Cambridge scholar, said in summarizing a later study that drew on Brady's research. But this was not particular to partisanship: the effect privileges any sentiment, and therefore any politics, built on disparaging social out-groups of any kind. This may be why, in 2020, Twitter's researchers concluded that their platform's algorithm systematically boosted conservative politics, which tend to be preoccupied, across societies, with drawing sharp boundaries between us and them.

For all the rising division, it was the scale that truly shifted something, by acting through people's innate instinct to infer and conform to their community's prevailing norms of behavior. We each strive, however unconsciously, to follow our group's social mores. But trying to infer those norms on social media was like being inside of a mirror-filled fun house, where certain behaviors were distorted to look more common and more accepted than they really were. By early 2017, most everyone outside of the Valley agreed that those mirrors bent and distorted what we all saw and experienced, but no one had figured out how to measure their curve, much less the effect on the two or three billion people now wandering the digital fun house.

Twitter was perhaps the first platform whose corrosive effects were, around this time, in early 2017, widely accepted and understood. This was hardly due to Twitter's reach (one sixth the userbase of Facebook or

YouTube), its financial power (a market capitalization worth only 2.5 percent of Facebook's), or the sophistication of its algorithms, which remained generations behind those of its larger competitors.

The reason was simple: the president had turned his Twitter account into a live-from-the-Oval-Office national address that never ended, which meant that every journalist, government worker, or concerned citizen suddenly glued themselves to the platform. And to be on Twitter, they learned, was to be besieged by trolls, buffeted by interminable online controversies, pulled into endlessly warring polarized camps, and deluged with falsehoods and rumors. There was a sense of collective realization, shared by scores of media and political gatekeepers who might've previously dismissed social media as "just" the internet. And unlike on Facebook or YouTube, where users are sorted into communities that might never intersect, Twitter's one-big-Thunderdome structure means that everyone shares largely the same experience, making it easy for alarmed users to see that these problems were systemic.

"You're hanging out with people who find satisfaction spewing vitriol, people who spread racism, misogyny, and anti-Semitism," a CNN anchor lamented. No one needed a congressional investigation to understand why it might be bad that the platform now at the heart of American political discourse was overrun with neo-Nazis and partisan lies.

Twitter, under relatively new management with Jack Dorsey, who'd returned to the company in 2015 to take over as CEO, announced it was shifting its focus from growth to curbing hatemongers and harassers, a claim that might've been easy to dismiss as corporate spin if its userbase had not immediately stopped growing. Some of Twitter's largest shareholders, furious over Twitter's plateauing stock price, pressured Dorsey to change course and, later, when he wouldn't, wanted to force him out entirely. But Brianna Wu and other longtime critics commended Twitter for what they called genuine progress, if only in containing the most egregious behaviors, like death threats and extreme racism.

Still, Dorsey, at least at first, approached the problem as one of removing bad actors rather than considering whether the platform might be encouraging their behavior. Other executives described him as indecisive, hesitant to abandon Silicon Valley free-speech utopianism even as the problems filling his inbox suggested that dream had never been real. He could be remote and odd. At one meeting, he told the assembled staff he was announcing Twitter's new corporate mission, then played a recording of the Beatles song "Blackbird." He went on silent-meditation retreats, including to Myanmar only months after social media had helped foment mass murder there. He announced, amid a slide in Twitter's stock price, that he would move part-time to Africa.

It remained unclear, including to his own employees, the degree to which Dorsey's post-election pivot represented a rethink of the Valley's fundamental assumptions, a PR ploy, or merely the boss taking his company on something of a transcendental wander. Whatever his motivation, Dorsey's Twitter, even with its blighted image, avoided scandals as grave as those that the other companies would face. Its platform was simply not influential enough to be credibly accused of provoking a genocide or swinging an election. And its PR largely restrained itself from the secrecy, confrontationalism, or high-flown manifestos that the other companies emphasized.

At first, in the weeks after Trump's election, those larger companies — under a combination of public pressure, employee pressure, and, at least for the moment, an apparently legitimate desire to act as good citizens — wrestled with understanding what, if anything, had gone wrong. Facebook commissioned an internal audit known as Project P, reflecting initial concerns over Russian propaganda. It found that the Kremlin-linked Internet Research Agency had purchased Facebook ads, often with rubles, that led about 60,000 users to register for pro-Trump, anti-Clinton events. Facebook apologized. In truth, the Russian events scheme likely had little impact. At Facebook's size, 60,000 event signups was a blip. But as DiResta and others discovered, it would turn out to be only a sliver of the Russians' activities.

Other revelations were more concerning. Dozens of Facebook pages had spread fake, hyperpartisan news reports. The instigators, low-rent spammers chasing a quick buck, lacked the Russians' sophistication. Yet they had captured huge audiences, suggesting that something about the way Facebook functioned had empowered them. And their prevalence forced Facebook to consider whether, and where, to draw a line between allowable political discourse and forbidden disinformation. It was a sensitive question. The new president, after all, lived most of his life on that line.

Joel Kaplan, a conservative lobbyist whom Facebook had hired as its Republican whisperer in Washington, emerged as a decisive figure. He opposed or diluted post-election changes, like tweaking the algorithm or removing fake-news peddlers, that would have disproportionately affected conservative pages. Republican leaders, who now controlled Congress and the White House, had already stirred up mostly phony grievances over platforms "censoring" conservatives. Why antagonize them further?

Facebook, Twitter, and YouTube converged on a public-facing explanation for 2016. Society was divided and, while platforms may have contributed somewhat, now they could be part of the solution. Facebook would leverage its technology to "bring humanity together," Zuckerberg pledged. This meant, he explained, bafflingly, routing more users into groups, the very vehicles of radicalization that critics had called more harmful than Russian propaganda or fake news. The counterintuitive trick was that the groups would, supposedly, expose people to more diverse views.

It was a popular idea across the Valley. Twitter had also entertained pushing different-minded users together. Ellen Pao told me that she'd planned to implement a version of the idea at Reddit before she was fired. YouTube built it into an algorithm upgrade called Reinforce (though a company engineer described its actual aim as increasing watch time). An A.I. developer at Facebook mused that their systems might reverse-engineer "how opinions are formed and how they get ossified and crystallized, and how you can end up with two people being unable to talk to each other." Another claimed that Facebook's algorithm would now guide users toward differing viewpoints.

Silicon Valley hubris, it appeared, had not just survived the election, it was thriving. If 2016 was the year that the Valley was forced to acknowledge it served as puppeteer of a vast network of invisible strings that pulled at us like two billion marionettes, then 2017 was when its brightest programmers decided the solution was not to cut the strings, but to take even firmer control of them. It was just a matter of making us all dance to the proper tune.

They were acting on a widely held misinterpretation of something known as contact theory. Coined after World War II to explain why desegregated troops became less prone to racism, the theory suggested that social contact led distrustful groups to humanize one another. But subsequent research has shown that this process works only under narrow circumstances: managed exposure, equality of treatment, neutral territory, and a shared task. Simply mashing hostile tribes together, researchers repeatedly found, worsens animosity.

The year after the election, a team of political scientists had several hundred Twitter users who identified as Democrats or Republicans follow a bot that retweeted voices from the other side into their feed. Rather than growing more tolerant, users in both groups became more ideologically extreme. Social media partisans, another project found, often fail to register reasonable or inoffensive posts from people on the other side. But posts in which an out-group member says something objectionable reliably grab their attention. Frequently, they'll rebroadcast those posts as proof of the other side's depravity. A Hillary Clinton supporter during the 2016 Democratic primary, for example, might not even notice most tweets from Bernie Sanders supporters. Until one crosses a line. "Bernie bros are so sexist," the user might tweet, attaching a screenshot of a twenty-three-year-old barista calling Clinton "shrill."

People, as a rule, perceive out-groups as monoliths. When we see a member of an opposing clan misbehave, we assume this represents them all. As the Clinton supporter's tweet rides to outrage virality, like-minded users who see it will become more likely to notice similar transgressions from Sanders backers. As they circulate those in turn, it feels like evidence for a generalized antagonism: Sanders supporters are sexist. Political scientists call this "false polarization." Researchers have found that false polarization is worsening, especially around partisanship, with the conceptions that liberals and conservatives have of one another drifting further and further from reality. This can feed a politics of zero-sum conflict. If Sanders is just a politician with different ideas, meeting his agenda halfway is tolerable. If he's a dangerous radical leading a bunch of hooligans, that agenda must be defeated and its followers cast out from politics.

Even in its most rudimentary form, the very structure of social media encourages polarization. Reading an article and then the comments field beneath it, an experiment found, leads people to develop more extreme views on the subject in the article. Control groups that read the article with no comments became more moderate and open-minded. It wasn't that the comments themselves were persuasive; it was the mere context of having comments at all. News readers, the researchers discovered, process information differently when they are in a social environment: social instincts overwhelm reason, leading them to look for affirmation of their side's righteousness.

Facebook groups amplify this effect even further. By putting users in a homogenous social space, studies find, groups heighten their sensitivity to social cues and conformity. This overpowers their ability to judge false claims and increases their attraction to identity-affirming falsehoods, making them likelier to share misinformation and conspiracies. "When we encounter opposing views in the age and context of social media, it's not like reading them in a newspaper while sitting alone," the sociologist Zeynep Tufekci has written. "It's like hearing them from the opposing team while sitting with our fellow fans in a football stadium.... We bond with our team by yelling at the fans of the other one." Tweaking the algorithms to push users one way or another, toward fellow partisans or away from them, would just end up producing different versions of the dangerous forces made all but inevitable by the fundamental design of the platforms. It was why social scientists were among the first to come around to the view that, as media scholar Siva Vaidhyanathan put it, "the problem with Facebook is Facebook. It's not any particular attribute along the margins that can be fixed and reformed."

That spring, William Brady's PhD advisor mentioned his work in a lecture to an academic conference. In the audience, a Yale neuroscientist named Molly Crockett perked up. She studied the neurology of social behaviors. Even with her deep awareness, since the election she'd noticed herself spending more and more time chasing outrage on social media. "I would read something, I would feel outraged about it, I would feel compelled to share it with my friends," she later told an interviewer. "I would then be sort of obsessively checking to see whether people had responded, how they had responded. You know, lather, rinse, repeat."

She and her friends once worked one another into fits over a viral post about California tomatoes rotting on the vine for lack of migrant labor. It enabled Crockett's in-group to bond around outrage at Trump's self-defeating cruelty and their shared liberal values, which, the story seemed to demonstrate, made them superior. Until a friend pointed out that the story was from 2011. "It was like coming out of a trance," Crockett recalled. "I had been engaged in a feedback loop not unlike the apparatus that my PhD lab used to train rats to press levers to get cocaine."

From her work, Crockett knew that the social media platforms, by indulging these emotions, activated an especially powerful set of neural pathways — one that influenced our behavior, our perception of reality, even our sense of right and wrong. Drawing on Brady's work, she published a short but influential paper, "Moral Outrage in the Digital Age." The premise was straightforward. Certain social stimuli can, under the right circumstances, change our underlying nature. The conclusions, derived from newly available data, were bracing: online norms of ever-escalating outrage and conflict could "transform ancient social emotions from a force for collective good into a tool for collective self-destruction." This technology, by training us to be more hostile, more tribal, and more prone to seeing out-group members as less than fully human, might be doing the same to society and politics as a whole.

It was, at that point, just a theory. She got in touch with Brady, who agreed to investigate further with her. As they began to do so, DiResta's informal analyst circle, pursuing methods that could not have been more different, and examining what initially seemed like an entirely unrelated aspect of social media's influence, set out on their own journey. Though the two teams were unaware of each other, they would ultimately arrive, to their mutual horror, at a set of conclusions that were virtually identical. But for DiResta, as for Brady and Crockett, it began with a narrower question: How deep had the Russian operation gone?

3. Looking for Russians

AS PUBLIC PRESSURE ebbed slightly and the pledges of transparency from the major platforms fizzled, DiResta contacted the analysts with whom she'd tracked Islamic Staters, anti-vaxxers, and Pizzagaters. "We got the band back together," she said. They set up an encrypted group chat to share social media content that looked traceable back to Russian influence peddlers and began "to get some breadcrumbs," as she put it.

Mapping the Russian campaign, they believed, might reveal how the platforms directed or distorted the flow of information. It was also an opening to pressure the companies to take responsibility. The attempted subversion of American democracy, amplified by their own systems, would not be as easy to shrug off as anti-vaccine conspiracists. But they had a problem: access. On platforms where billions of pieces of content circulated daily, scrutinizing one post at a time was like studying geology by inspecting individual grains of sand. "The only people who have the full scope," DiResta said, "who don't have to do this bullshit like paste random names across the internet, are the platforms." But the companies would barely answer questions, much less open their systems to outside scrutiny. "I was being stonewalled a lot of the time," she said.

She connected, through a member of her group, with Tristan Harris, the former Google designer who'd quit in protest after warning of algorithmic harm. He was traveling to DC, he said, to meet with congressional staffers. Several lawmakers, including Mark Warner, the top Democrat on the Senate's Intelligence Committee, wanted help understanding social media's influence. Did she want to come?

DiResta saw an opportunity. Facebook and Google could hardly blow off the Senate. She joined Harris, making her pitch in Washington: "For national security reasons," she said, "the companies should be forced to turn their data over for additional analysis to the Senate Intelligence Committee." Warner was sold. "I think they need to be extremely forthcoming," the senator said in one of many comments pressuring the companies. "I think Facebook, in many ways, knows more about each of us than the United States government. And the notion that somehow they weren't aware of what was happening on their platforms strains credibility."

Almost one year to the day after Trump's election, DiResta woke before dawn. Representatives from Google, Facebook, and Twitter would, after months of pressure, finally face congressional questioning. She and others from her analyst circle joined a chat room to share notes as they watched a panel of senators push what were, in some cases, the very questions DiResta and her cohort had been posing for years.

Hearings can be little more than theater, a chance for lawmakers to thunder for the cameras. Tech CEOs, perhaps assuming as much, sent lawyers in their place, which shocked DiResta. She had been on Wall Street during the financial crisis, when the bankers and insurers had at least known to submit their chief executives to congressional filleting. Still, this might be a step toward accountability. DiResta had helped congressional staffers prep their bosses' questions, honed to force meaningful answers. But once the session started, the company representatives mostly dodged or demurred. It was "how you would try to wrangle your way through a bad PR cycle," DiResta told a PBS interviewer. "Diminish, discredit, deny." The day left her and her analyst circle with "a sense of frustration that we were still dependent on the platforms to do their own investigations," she said. They couldn't help wondering if the companies would ever be forced into a full accounting of what their platforms had wrought.

Thanks to political maneuvering, maybe soon. Senators' pointed questions had cornered the companies' representatives into deflecting so brazenly that lawmakers made their obstruction the story, deepening public anger. Warner also wrote legislation, with Amy Klobuchar and John McCain, requiring the companies to publicly disclose who bought political ads and how those ads were targeted. It was too bold to pass the Republican-controlled Congress. But it was a legislative warning shot, a threat of blunt-force regulation targeting the companies' revenue streams.

The platforms finally disclosed the scope of Russia's operation: at least 1,000 YouTube videos, 131,000 tweets, as well as Facebook posts that had reached 126 million users. DiResta urged her contacts in the Senate to keep pushing until the platforms handed over their full, internal archives. A few months later, in early 2018, it arrived: 400 gigabytes packed onto a single drive. It was raw data, like walking into a room stacked with 200 million pieces of unsorted paper. Senate staffers couldn't make heads or tails of it. They asked DiResta to lead a team to parse it all, drawing conclusions in a formal report. After talking it over with her husband, she quit the logistics startup she'd helped launch, leaving the investing world behind. "I felt like this was going to be the most interesting dataset we'd ever seen on modern information operations," she told me. "It was like living through history."

The data revealed, as much as any foreign plot, the ways that the Valley's products had amplified the reach, and exacerbated the impact, of malign influence. (She later termed this "ampliganda," a sort of propaganda whose power comes from its propagation by masses of often unwitting people.) A Russian agent posting Facebook memes posed little danger on his own. If few users shared the content, the only result would be to waste the agent's afternoon. Influence came from sending things viral. And not just because virality brings more eyeballs. When an idea feels like it's coming from within your community, it is persuasive in ways that no post could be on its own.

Over many iterations, the Russians settled on a strategy. Appeal to people's group identity. Tell them that identity was under attack. Whip up outrage against an out-group. And deploy as much moral-emotional language as possible. One Russian-run Facebook page, Heart of Texas, attracted hundreds of thousands of followers by cultivating a narrow, aggrieved identity. "Like if you agree," captioned a viral map with all other states marked "awful" or "boring," alongside text urging secession from the morally impure union. Some posts presented Texas identity as under siege ("Like & share if you agree that Texas is a Christian state"). Others rallied against out-groups ("No more mosques on American soil! Like if you agree!"). As the election neared, Heart of Texas, now with its city-sized following perfectly cultivated, began hyperventilating that the vote would be stolen for Hillary Clinton. It urged followers to hold an armed protest outside of a Houston Islamic center; about a hundred people showed up, some carrying assault rifles. Similar Russian-run accounts, meanwhile, operating across all major platforms, courted Black voters, Sanders supporters, hippie moms — any group the Russians felt they could push to extremes.

Analysts and watchdogs initially focused on the campaign's intent: to sow division and boost Trump. From that perspective, the platforms' sin was merely inaction, failure to identify and halt the campaign. But to DiResta and Brady, watching the data come in from opposite coasts, the role of social networks looked more active. The Russians' grasp of American culture and language seemed uneven, their methods blunt, their effort modestly resourced. Trial-and-erroring their way, they had not invented this playbook so much as discovered it, written into the algorithms and incentives of the social media platforms. Others, it stood to reason, would stumble onto the same strategy, if for no other reason than to win the attentional rewards the platforms doled out to keep people engaged.

Which is exactly what happened. Of the 58 million U.S.-based Twitter accounts active in 2016, the 107th most politically influential, according to an MIT Media Lab analysis, was a pseudonymous troll account, Ricky_Vaughn99. The owner of the account had joined Twitter in 2014, gotten swept up in Gamergate, and begun posting 200-plus times per day. He participated in seemingly any right-wing Twitter mob or pile-on. He was an opportunist, ratcheting his anger, and his naked appeals to white male grievance, a few clicks above everyone else's. The posts, which rose to the top of countless outrage cycles, won him thousands of followers. He pulled viciously racist memes from 4chan and Reddit's sludgiest depths, circulating them to mainstream conservative audiences. He promoted conspiracies of a Jewish plot to dilute the white race. By summer, he was leveraging all that attention in service of Trump. He and his followers posted fake Hillary Clinton campaign ads telling her supporters that they could vote by text rather than going to the polls. The scheme hoodwinked at least 4,900 voters, according to federal charges that accused him of seeking to "deprive individuals of their constitutional right to vote" and identified his name: Douglass Mackey, a Brooklyn-based financial consultant.

For every Russian meddler, there were a thousand Douglass Mackeys, everyday people radicalized online, exploiting the platforms for their own gratification. And for every Mackey, there were another thousand conducting mass disinformation unwittingly. Yoga moms spreading vaccine conspiracies on Facebook, YouTubers tumbling down Pizzagate rabbit holes, Twitter users joining outrage mobs over a misrepresentation. Leaderless, agendaless, and all the more influential for it. DiResta called it "peer-to-peer misinformation." The users and the platforms, working in tandem, were the real drivers. It became, within months, routine.

When hundreds of Central Americans fled gang violence in their home countries, their arrival at the border was incongruous with the worldview core to many conservatives' political identity. Trump had called refugees criminals and terrorists, yet these were desperate, terrified families. Social media provided an out. One photo, shared 36,000 times, supposedly showed a bloodied Mexican policeman who had been attacked by thugs posing as refugees. Another, shared 81,000 times, showed a crowded train, proof that the refugees, who claimed to be walking, were liars abetted by dishonest reporters. These photos, and dozens more like them, turned out to be from unrelated, years-old incidents. But the truth didn't matter. The posts weren't really about the border. They were about protecting Trump supporters' shared identity, proof that they were in the right and that liberals were the real monsters.

In a revealing experiment, Republicans were shown a false headline about the refugees ("Over 500 'Migrant Caravaners' Arrested with Suicide Vests"). Asked whether it seemed accurate, most identified it as false; only 16 percent called it accurate. The question's framing had implicitly nudged the subjects to think about accuracy. This engaged the rational parts of their mind, which quickly identified the headline as false. Subsequently asked whether they might share the headline on Facebook, most said no: thinking with their rational brains, they preferred accuracy.

But when researchers repeated the experiment with a different set of Republicans, this time skipping the question about accuracy to simply ask if the subject would share the headline on Facebook, 51 percent said they would. Focusing on Facebook activated the social part of their minds, which saw, in the same headline, the promise of identity validation — something the social brain values far beyond accuracy. Having decided to share it, the subjects told themselves it was true. "Most people do not want to spread misinformation," the study's authors wrote, differentiating willful lying from socially motivated belief. "But the social media context focuses their attention on factors other than truth and accuracy."

When we see people share misinformation, especially people whom we find unsympathetic, it's easy to assume that they're dishonest or unintelligent. But often all they are is human, overcome by social instincts to see truth in stories that, in a more neutral context, they would choose to reject. The problem, in this experiment, wasn't ignorance or lack of news literacy. Social media, by bombarding users with fast-moving social stimuli, pushed them to rely on quick-twitch social intuition over deliberative reason. All people contain the capacity for both, as well as the potential for the former to overwhelm the latter, which is often how misinformation spreads. And platforms compound the effect by framing all news and information within high-stakes social contexts.

Politicians were adapting to this order. Matt Gaetz, a newly elected congressman from Florida, tweeted that shadowy powers were paying refugees to "storm" the border and disrupt the midterm elections and that Jewish philanthropist George Soros might be responsible. He was retweeted more than 30,000 times. The Russians weren't the problem anymore.

4. A World Going Mad

CHASLOT, STILL IN France, decided to repeat the tracking experiment he'd run on the American election, this time on the four-candidate presidential race at home. As before, YouTube's algorithm, he found, heavily favored the candidates at the extremes: the far-right Marine Le Pen and the far-left Jean-Luc Mélenchon. A new truism of politics was emerging: social media elevated anti-establishment politicians conversant with exaggerated moral-emotional language. Mélenchon, though unpopular with voters, won millions of views on YouTube, where his most dedicated fans seemed to congregate.

This had started as a positive: the internet offered political outsiders a way around the mainstream outlets that shunned them. As those candidates' grassroots supporters spent disproportionate time on YouTube, the system learned to push users to those videos, creating more fans, driving up watch time further. But thanks to the preferences of the algorithms for extreme and divisive content, it was mostly fringe radicals who benefited, and not candidates across the spectrum.

Backed by a handful of fellow researchers, Chaslot brought his findings on the American and French elections to *The Guardian*, resulting in an explosive report that offered seeming evidence of a long-suspected threat to global political stability. YouTube disputed "the methodology, data and, most importantly, the conclusions" of the research. Chaslot had made no secret that his conclusions were rough estimates, using thousands of datapoints to infer the algorithm's billions of daily decisions. But the findings were so consistent, he thought, and so consistently alarming, wouldn't the company want to look into it? Or share the internal data that could, in theory, clear all this up? And he was hardly alone. Over the following years, with the company stonewalling, an entire field of researchers published one set of findings after another, produced through ever more sophisticated methods, that not only supported Chaslot's results but suggested the reality was substantially worse than even he had feared.

Throughout, YouTube held to a consistent strategy, much like the one DiResta had described: deny, discredit, and antagonize. In response to the piece that ran in *The Guardian*, a spokesperson said, "Our only conclusion is that *The Guardian* is attempting to shoehorn research, data, and their incorrect conclusions into a common narrative about the role of technology in last year's election." This became a pattern. Time after time, the company's reps would respond to each new discovery by calling the evidence meaningless or wrong, digging in for long, often hostile exchanges. Then, once a major story ran, YouTube, in a paradoxical turnabout, would put out a statement insisting it had already fixed issues that, only weeks earlier, it had dismissed as nonexistent. In Chaslot's case, the company also sought to portray him as untrustworthy, motivated by a desire to embarrass the company in retaliation for having fired him for poor performance. But this could not explain why he had initially tried to put You-Tube behind him, researching the platform only after seeing its harms firsthand years later, nor why he had initially taken his findings directly and privately to YouTube.

"That's the routine. I can laugh about it because, by changing things, they recognize that I was right," Chaslot said, though his voice was suffused with a sadness over his former employer's public disavowals that, years later, still stung. "But when I was in the middle of it, they put such pressure on me. That was really frustrating."

It was a puzzling strategy, especially just as lawmakers had begun taking notice of social media's harms. Shortly after YouTube sent *The Guardian* its confrontational statement but before the newspaper went to press, the Senate Intelligence Committee sent Google a letter demanding that the company articulate its plan for preventing bad actors from manipulating YouTube's algorithm. YouTube asked to "update" its statement to *The Guardian,* replacing the vitriol with pledges to combat misinformation and praise for the newspaper's "work to shine a spotlight on this challenging issue."

Meanwhile, just as Chaslot joined DiResta and others in the public struggle to understand Silicon Valley's undue influence, William Brady and Molly Crockett, the psychologist and neuroscientist, achieved a momentous breakthrough in that effort. They had spent months synthesizing reams of newly available data, behavioral research, and their own investigations. It was like fitting together the pieces of a puzzle that, once assembled, revealed what may still be the most complete framework for understanding social media's effect on society.

The platforms, they concluded, were reshaping not just online behavior but underlying social impulses, and not just individually but collectively, potentially altering the nature of "civic engagement and activism, political polarization, propaganda and disinformation." They called it the MAD model, for the three forces rewiring people's minds. Motivation: the instincts and habits hijacked by the mechanics of social media platforms. Attention: users' focus manipulated to distort their perceptions of social cues and mores. Design: platforms that had been constructed in ways that train and incentivize certain behaviors.

The first stage of their findings had to do with how people perceive moral-emotional words. When Brady first found that such words travel further online, it had stood to reason that they draw attention because they usually describe something dramatic. Brady decided to test this. He and two other scholars showed participants a fake social media stream, tracking what captured their attention as they scrolled. Moral-emotional words, they found, overrode people's attention almost regardless of context. If a boring statement with moral-emotional words and an exciting statement without them both appeared on screen, users were drawn to the former. Subjects actively focusing on something lost their concentration if a moral-emotional word so much as flashed elsewhere on the screen. Other sorts of flashing words did not produce the same effect.

When they reran the experiment with real tweets, they got the same results: the more moral-emotional words in a post, the more twitches of attention it won. Those posts also consistently had more shares. If you tweeted "The quick brown fox jumps over the lazy dog" and "The quick brown fox jumps over the liar dog," the latter would, from that one moral-emotional word, get more eyeballs and more shares. Tweet "The good hero fox slams the liar enemy dog," and you might be president by nightfall.

The digital-attention economy amplifies the social impact of this dynamic exponentially. Remember that the number of seconds in your day never changes. The amount of social media content competing for those seconds, however, doubles every year or so, depending on how you measure it. Imagine, for instance, that your network produces 200 posts per day, of which you have time to read 100. Because of the platforms' tilt, you will see the most moral-emotional half of your feed. Next year, when 200 doubles to 400, you see the most moral-emotional quarter. The year after that, the most moral-emotional eighth. Over time, your impression of your own community becomes radically more moralizing, aggrandizing, and outraged — and so do you. At the same time, less innately engaging forms of content — truth, appeals to the greater good, appeals to tolerance — become more and more outmatched. Like stars over Times Square.

Stage two in social media's distorting influence, according to the

MAD model, is something called internalization. Users who chased the platforms' incentives received immediate, high-volume social rewards: likes and shares. As psychologists have known since Pavlov, when you are repeatedly rewarded for a behavior, you learn a compulsion to repeat it. As you are trained to turn all discussions into matters of high outrage, to express disgust with out-groups, to assert the superiority of your in-group, you will eventually shift from doing it for external rewards to doing it simply because you want to do it. The drive comes from within. Your nature has been changed.

Brady and Crockett proved this in two experiments. In one, when users who expressed outrage were rewarded with likes and shares, they became likelier to express outrage in the future — and likelier to *feel* outraged. The effect held even for subjects who had earlier expressed an aversion to online anger. An otherwise sweet and tolerant person who, in a moment of weakness, sent a Democrat-bashing tweet that went viral would become instantly likelier to send more, first to chase the high, but soon because she had become, in her heart, more hatefully partisan. The second experiment demonstrated that the attention economy, by tricking users into believing that their community held more extreme and divisive views than it really did, had the same effect. Showing subjects lots of social media posts from peers that expressed outrage made them more outrage-prone themselves. All it takes is regular scrolls through your anger-filled feed not only to make you feel angrier while you're online, but also to make you an angrier person.

Two other scholars later found that moral-emotional content also leads users to express more calls for violence. They trained a computer to analyze the text of articles and blog posts from across the web, then do the same for user comments posted in response: 300 million comments in all. They found that, across topics or political ideologies, as the number of moral-emotional words in an article increased, commenters grew significantly likelier to threaten or incite violence against some perceived enemy, usually someone named in the article. It was a chilling demonstration of how portraying people and events in sharply moral-emotional terms brings out audiences' instincts for hatred and violence — which is, after all, exactly what social platforms do, on a billions-strong scale, every minute of every day.

"Online platforms," Brady and Crockett wrote, "are now one of the primary sources of morally relevant stimuli people experience in their daily life." Billions of people's moral compasses potentially tilted toward tribalism and distrust. Whole societies nudged toward conflict, polarization, and unreality — toward something like Trumpism.

Brady did not think that social media was "inherently evil," he told me. But as the platforms evolved, the effects only seemed to worsen. "It's just gotten so toxic," he said. "In college, it was nothing like it is now." It was important for people to remember, he felt, that the designers and engineers, who aim to keep you using their platform for as many minutes and hours per day as possible, "have different goals, I don't want to call them good or bad goals, but goals that might not be compatible with yours."

But for all they had learned, Brady and Crockett were, they knew, only beginning to understand the consequences. What effect did all this distortion, this training, have on our societies and politics, on our species?

Without realizing it, I was stumbling my own way toward an answer. As Brady and Crockett continued to investigate the fun house–mirror distortions of social media psychology throughout 2017, I set out, that fall, for a place much farther away, one that the platforms had expended special effort in ignoring, but that would soon become a byword for their greed, their negligence, and their danger: Myanmar.

Seven

The Germs and the Wind

1. A Good Deal of Good

BY THE TIME I landed in Myanmar, the soldiers were already throwing babies into fires. For weeks, the military had waged unrestrained war on the thatched-roof villages that dotted the country's westernmost province. Whole battalions pushed from paddy to paddy as gunships roared overhead. They claimed to hunt insurgents. In reality, they were setting upon a community of one and a half million Muslim farmers and fishermen who called themselves Rohingya.

The soldiers, sent to exterminate the impoverished minority that many of Myanmar's leaders and citizens had come to see as an intolerable enemy within, would arrive at a village, then begin by setting rooftops afire. They lobbed grenades through hut doorways and sent rockets slamming into the walls of longhouses. They fired into the backs of peasants fleeing across the surrounding fields. As the houses burned, the men of the village would be arrayed in a line and shot to death. Families streamed by the hundred thousand toward the border. The soldiers attacked these too. They hid land mines in the refugees' paths. Survivors who made it to relative safety in Bangladesh detailed horror after horror to journalists and aid workers who picked their way through the overcrowded camps.

"People were holding the soldiers' feet, begging for their lives," one woman told my colleague Jeffrey Gettleman. "But they didn't stop, they just kicked them off and killed them." When soldiers came to her village, she said, they demanded she surrender the infant she was cradling. When she refused, they beat her, ripped her son from her arms, and threw him into an open fire. Then they raped her.

Her story was typical. A twenty-year-old woman told a Human Rights Watch investigator that soldiers had killed her infant daughter in the same way. The soldiers then raped her and her mother. When her sister resisted, they killed her with bayonets. While this was happening, a group of villagers arrived and beat her three teenage brothers to death. Local men often accompanied the soldiers as eager volunteers, swinging hatchets and farm implements. They were Rakhine, the region's other major ethnic group, who, like most in Myanmar, are Buddhist. Their presence hinted at the communal nature of the violence, as well as the groundswell of public pressure that had occasioned it.

Yangon, the historic capital, felt a world away from the killing. It was October 2017, more than three years since I'd last visited what was now a city transformed. Sanctions had been lifted, reward for Myanmar's generals surrendering power to elected lawmakers. Dusty shop stalls had been replaced with air-conditioned shopping malls. Imported cars glided over newly paved streets. Most people had their nose in a smartphone. Middle-class comforts had brought a mood of easy optimism, even pride. But something roiled beneath the surface.

An idealistic young doctor, now his neighborhood's first elected lawmaker, told me that waves of social media misinformation and incitement kept his community constantly on the verge of race riots, or provoked them outright. Days earlier, his constituents, furious over Facebook rumors accusing a local Islamic school of secretly hosting terrorists, had stormed the building as its students sat in class. The kids, terrified, escaped through a back door. And it wasn't just here, a local imam told me in the darkened back room of a friend's house, where he'd insisted on talking for fear of meeting in public. Across the country, madrassas were being forced to close, he said, as similar rumors led to violence or the threat of it. "We are a scapegoat," the imam said.

The head of Myanmar's first real media collective, a jittery reporter back from years in exile, said the country's long-suppressed journalists, finally unfettered, faced a new antagonist. Social media platforms were doing what even the dictatorship's trained propagandists couldn't: producing fake news and nationalist fanfare so engaging, so flattering to readers' biases, that people chose it voluntarily over real journalism. When reporters tried to correct the misinformation flowing online, they became the target of it instead, accused of abetting foreign plots.

Civic leaders told me that social media platforms were pumping the national bloodstream with conspiracies and ultranationalist rage. Citizens who'd marched for an open, inclusive democracy now spent hours posting in groups dedicated to vilifying minorities or to glorifying the country's leaders. The chief of the military, once a reviled symbol of the dictatorship who had stepped down only a few years earlier, now had 1.3 million Facebook fans.

People from all walks of life breathlessly recounted, as unvarnished fact, crazed and hateful conspiracies that they inevitably traced to social media. Buddhist monks insisted the Muslims were plotting to steal Myanmar's water, old ladies that they would not be safe until minorities were purged from their midst, young students that humanitarian groups were arming the Rohingya on behalf of foreign powers. All of them backed the military's campaign — grateful, sometimes gleeful, for the violence being committed on their behalf.

No algorithm could generate hatred this severe out of nothing. The platforms drew on a crisis that had been building since 2012 in the nation's west, where most Rohingya lived. A handful of incidents between Rohingya and Rakhine — a rape, a lynching, a spree of murders — had spiraled into communal riots. Troops intervened, herding civilians who'd been displaced from their homes, mostly Rohingya, into camps. The Rohingya languished. In 2015 thousands attempted to flee, describing growing persecution from neighbors and soldiers alike.

Anti-Rohingya sentiment dated back at least a century, to the early

1900s, when British overlords imported thousands of colonial subjects from the Indian Raj, many of them Muslim. The effort was playbook divide and rule; the newcomers, who filled out the urban merchant class, relied on the British for safety. After the British left, in 1948, independence leaders sought to consolidate their new nation around shared ethnic and religious identity. But Myanmar's diversity made this difficult; they needed an enemy to rally against. Political leaders promoted colonial-era suspicions of Muslims as alien interlopers sponsored by foreign empires. In truth, however, merchant-class Indians imported by the British had mostly fled in 1948 or shortly thereafter, so leaders sublimated national ire to an unrelated group of Muslims: the Rohingya. To sell the ruse, the Rohingya were classified as illegal immigrants, a declaration of state-sponsored hate later reiterated even by Aung San Suu Kyi, the Nobel-winning democracy icon who became Myanmar's first elected leader.

When some Rohingya and Rakhine clashed in 2012, she was still consolidating her hold on politics. She seized on the incident, emphasizing the Rohingya's supposed danger to Myanmar's "real" citizens. But over the next few years, public rage at poor Rohingya farmers soared far beyond what even she had encouraged. By August 2017, when sporadic violence between soldiers and a handful of Rohingya rebels culminated in a midnight insurgent attack on several police posts, much of the country was screaming for blood. A few days later, the military complied, launching their genocide.

How had sentiment, even long simmering, escalated to such extremes? Fearmongering leaders and sectarian clashes were, after all, nothing new here. There was something different at play, something new. Two years earlier, David Madden, the Australian who ran Myanmar's largest tech-startup accelerator, had flown to Facebook's headquarters to give the company's executives an alarm-ringing presentation. By this time, it had been a year since the riots in Mandalay, when the danger should have been unignorable. He detailed rising anti-Muslim incitement on the platform, seemingly unchecked by moderators, however many there were, who were supposed to scrub dangerous content. He warned that Facebook could soon be used to foment genocide. But there was little indication that Facebook heeded his warning, with hate speech only growing more common. Viral posts, one after another, reported that seemingly innocent Muslim families were really terrorist sleeper cells or foreign spies. "Myanmar will soon be seized by 'Muslim Dogs,'" one read. The posts were shared thousands of times, numbers that would have been hard to achieve in such a small country without an algorithmic boost.

Even Myanmar government officials warned that Facebook-driven hate speech could undermine the country's stability as extremists gained vast new online audiences. By the fall of 2015, Wirathu, the monk once called "the Burmese bin Laden," had 117,000 followers — a small number in the United States, but a large one in a country Myanmar's size and this early in its digital adoption — to whom he pushed steady conspiracy and hate. An ally of Wirathu's, the nationalist politician Nay Myo Wai, ran popular accounts that spread open incitement. He had said of the Rohingya in a speech that year, "I will keep this short and direct. Number one, shoot and kill them. Number two, shoot and kill them. Number three, shoot and bury them."

A Washington DC think tank analyzed a sample of 32,000 Myanmar Facebook accounts, everyday users, finding their pages awash in hate speech and misinformation. One popular meme showed graphic bestiality covered in Arabic script, another of the prophet Mohammad being orally penetrated. Another claimed to show evidence of Rohingya committing cannibalism; the image was in fact taken from a video game marketing stunt. It was shared nearly 40,000 times. Another, falsely claiming that Rohingya were smuggling weapons into Myanmar, was shared 42,700 times. "It's time to kill all kalars," one user wrote, using a slur for Rohingya. Another responded, "We will behead ten thousand kalars' heads." Another: "For the next generation, burn all Muslim villages nearby."

The report was published in early 2016, another voice in a chorus warning Facebook that it was imperiling a society it did not understand.

That June, the company, much as it had in 2013 after brushing off warnings of impending violence that quickly proved accurate, scaled up in Myanmar anyway, launching "Free Basics," which allowed locals to use Facebook's smartphone app without paying data charges. Within months, 38 percent of people in the country said they got most or all of their news via Facebook. As things worsened, six months before the genocide, Madden flew to Facebook's headquarters for a second time. Again he warned that the platform was pushing the country toward mass violence. Nothing appeared to change, even as the killing began.

"I have to thank Facebook because it is giving me the true information in Myanmar," the administrator of a village that had banned Muslims told my colleague Hannah Beech two months into the bloodshed. "Kalar are not welcome here," he said, "because they are violent and they multiply like crazy." Extremist pages espousing these views remained hyperactive throughout the bloodshed. They were a digital update of Radio Milles Collines, which had broadcast calls for genocide in 1990s Rwanda. But this Genocide Radio was built on infrastructure owned by wealthy American tech companies, amplified not by militia-controlled broadcast terminals but by algorithms run out of Silicon Valley.

"There has never been a more powerful tool for the rapid dissemination of hate speech and racist-nationalist vitriol than Facebook and other social media," Ashley Kinseth, a human rights worker in Myanmar, wrote amid the killing. For all the parallels with Radio Milles Collines, she added, "Social media is by all accounts an even faster, more graphic, immersive, 'democratic,' and ultimately dangerous tool for the dissemination of hate speech."

For years after Rwanda's genocide, American officials tormented themselves over hypotheticals. Could American warplanes have destroyed the radio towers in time to stop it? How would they locate the towers amid Rwanda's jungles and mountain passes? How would they secure international authority? In Myanmar, there were never any such doubts. A single engineer could have shuttered the entire network as they finished their morning coffee. One million terrified Rohingya made safer from death and displacement with a few keystrokes. The warning signs were freely visible. Madden and others had given them the necessary information to act. They simply chose not to, even as entire villages were purged in fire and blood. By March 2018, the head of the United Nations' fact-finding mission said his team had concluded that social networks, especially Facebook, had played a "determining role" in the genocide. The platforms, he said, "substantively contributed" to the hate destroying an entire population.

Three days later, a reporter named Max Read posed a question, on Twitter, to Adam Mosseri, the executive overseeing Facebook's news feed. He asked, referring to Facebook as a whole, "honest question — what's the possible harm in turning it off in myanmar?" Mosseri responded, "There are real issues, but Facebook does a good deal of good — connecting people with friends and family, helping small businesses, surfacing informative content. If we turn it off we lose all that."

The belief that Facebook's benefits to Myanmar, at that moment, exceeded its harms is difficult to understand. Facebook had no Myanmar office from which to appreciate its impact. Few of its employees had ever been. It had rejected the chillingly consistent outside assessments of its platform's behavior. Mosseri's conclusion was, in the most generous interpretation, ideological, rooted in faith. It was also convenient, permitting the company to throw up its hands and declare it ethically impossible to switch off the hate machine. Never mind that leaving the platform up was its own form of intervention, chosen anew every day.

There was another important barrier to acting. It would have meant acknowledging that the platform may have shared some blame. It had taken cigarette companies half a century, and the threat of potentially fatal litigation, to admit that their products caused cancer. How easily would Silicon Valley concede that its products could cause upheaval up to and including genocide?

Myanmar was hardly the first indication of those harms. Though it's easy to forget now, events like the Arab Spring uprisings of 2011 had been, at the time, viewed as proof of social media's liberating potential. But there were signs of trouble, even then. In 2012, in a bizarre episode in India I'd written about, members of two ethnic groups had, in their mutual fear, spread Facebook and Twitter rumors that the other was planning to attack them. Speculation became certainty, which became misinformation of an imminent attack, which became incitement to strike first. A few inevitably did. Reports of the violence spread widely online, often portrayed, with phony photo proof, as hundreds of times deadlier than it really was. A wave of riots and reprisals, incited on social media, swept across India, pushing 300,000 people into displacement camps. The Indian government blocked access to social platforms and demanded they remove the most dangerous content. When the Obama administration, a longtime Silicon Valley booster, intervened on the companies' behalf, Indian officials relented. The damage had already been done, anyway. Similar violent flare-ups rose in Indonesia. Whole communities glued to Facebook and Twitter. Users rewarded with huge audiences for indulging one another's worst tendencies. A riot, a murder, a village disintegrating into bloodshed, all provoked by xenophobia saturating the platforms.

Eventually, the sunny view of the Arab Spring came to be revised. "This revolution started on Facebook," Wael Ghonim, an Egyptian programmer who'd left his desk at Google to join his country's popular uprising, had said in 2011. "I want to meet Mark Zuckerberg someday and thank him personally." Years later, however, as Egypt collapsed into dictatorship, Ghonim warned, "The same tool that united us to topple dictators eventually tore us apart." The revolution had given way to social and religious distrust, which social networks widened by "amplifying the spread of misinformation, rumors, echo chambers, and hate speech," Ghonim said, rendering society "purely toxic."

By late 2017, as the Myanmar genocide raged on, Chamath Palihapitiya, Facebook's former chief of global growth, speaking at what was expected to be a routine speech to Stanford MBA students, snapped. "I feel tremendous guilt," he said. "I think we all knew in the back of our minds, even though we all feigned this whole line that there probably weren't any unintended consequences. I think we knew that something bad could happen." Palihapitiya had left Facebook years earlier. But he had helped set the company down the path it remains on today, persuading its chiefs to reengineer both the business and the platform around permanent, globe-spanning growth. The tools they had created to accomplish this were "ripping apart the social fabric," Palihapitiya said. "The short-term, dopamine-driven feedback loops we've created are destroying how society works," creating a world with "no civil discourse, no cooperation; misinformation, mistruth." He urged the would-be engineers and startup founders in the room to take heed. "If you feed the beast, that beast will destroy you," he said. "If you push back on it, we have a chance to control it and rein it in."

This string of breakdowns, their horrifying consistency, including the 2016 U.S. presidential election, suggested more than freak incidents. It hinted at a deeper, perhaps universal transformation wrought by the social networks, of which extreme violence was just a surface-level indicator. I wanted to understand why this was happening, what it revealed about this technology's influence over our world. But a society-wide shift like Myanmar's or America's was driven by too many factors to isolate social media's role. I needed to start with a more self-contained episode, where social media's effects could be isolated, to understand the trend.

I worked with Amanda Taub, a fellow *New York Times* reporter with whom I'd collaborated since 2014, when I'd recruited her to join *Vox*. She'd previously worked as a human rights lawyer, including in Latin America, which made her especially attuned to the warning signs of collective violence. And she shared my fascination with social media, as well as a sense that its influence remained incompletely understood. We put in calls to rights workers, digital monitors, and other trusted contacts. Our question to each of them was whether they had seen unusual upheaval driven by social media. They all had the same answer, whatever continent we reached them on: Yes, more all the time, and why has it taken you all so long to notice? But collecting information on a long-past incident wouldn't do; memory is imperfect and shaded by bias. Amanda and I needed to see firsthand, to trace back every step and rumor. We asked our contacts to call us if anything combusted outside their windows.

We didn't wait long. In early 2018, someone alerted us to a flash of violence paralyzing Sri Lanka, the teardrop-shaped island nation about the size of Maine off India's southern coast. Whole villages, as if suddenly possessed, had formed into mobs, ransacking and burning their neighbors' homes. The military had been deployed. Though it was unclear what had happened or why, everyone we contacted there named the same culprit: Facebook.

2. The Tinderbox and the Match

PAST THE END of a remote mountain road, down a rutted dirt track, in a concrete house without running water but bristling with smartphones, thirteen members of an extended family were glued to Facebook. And they were furious. The fourteenth member of their family had been beaten to death a few weeks earlier. The police said he'd gotten into a traffic dispute that had turned violent. But on Facebook, rumors insisted that his assailants were part of a Muslim conspiracy to wipe out the Sinhalese, Sri Lanka's ethnic majority. The Sinhalese, from the Sanskrit word for "lion," dominate the country's culture and politics. Their lion emblazons its flag. But they had been gripped by a strange racial panic.

"We don't want to look at it because it's so painful," H. M. Lal, the victim's cousin said, his voice trembling. "But in our hearts there is a desire for revenge that has built." When I asked Lal and the rest of his family if they believed the posts were true, all but the elderly, who seemed not to follow, nodded. Did other people on Facebook share their desire for revenge? I asked. Again they nodded. They had shared, and could recite verbatim, memes constructing an alternate reality of nefarious Muslim plots. Though they had not joined in when Facebook groups boasting thousands of members planned a spree of retaliatory attacks on Muslims, they did not disapprove, either.

"Facebook is important to us because if something is happening somewhere, that's how we find out," one said. "Facebook will tell us about it." Lal, the cousin, agreed. He called Facebook "the embers beneath the ashes" of racial anger that, only days earlier, had brought the country to chaos. "People get provoked into action." This mountain village was our starting point for retracing Sri Lanka's slide into chaos. Facebook, we found, had driven every deadly step. And at every step, as in Myanmar, it had been warned, urgently and explicitly, but refused to act.

We asked the family how it had happened. Everything had "started in Ampara," one said, uttering a name we had seen over and over online. The real Ampara was just another village in a country scattered with them, a few concrete buildings surrounded by open green fields. But the imagined Ampara, constructed from social media rumors, was the epicenter of a plot to destroy the country's Sinhalese.

The Atham-Lebbe brothers knew nothing of the imagined Ampara when, using money they'd saved toiling as manual laborers overseas, they opened a one-room restaurant here. They are Muslim and speak Tamil, a minority language, so they never encountered the Sinhalese-speaking districts of the social web where their town was a symbol of racial peril. So they had no way to anticipate that, on a warm evening in March 2018, the real and imagined Amparas would collide, upending their lives forever.

During that night's dinner rush, a customer began yelling in Sinhalese about something he had found in his beef curry. Farsith, the twenty-eight-year-old brother running the register, ignored him. He didn't speak Sinhalese. And drunk customers, he'd learned, were best ignored. He wasn't aware that, the day before, a viral Facebook rumor had claimed, falsely, that police had seized 23,000 sterilization pills from a Muslim pharmacist here. If he had, Farsith might've understood why, as the customer grew more agitated, a crowd began to form.

The men circled Farsith, slapping his shoulders, yelling a question that Farsith couldn't quite understand. He grasped only that they were asking about a lump of flour in the customer's curry, using the phrase "Did you put?" He worried that saying the wrong thing might turn the crowd violent, but so would saying nothing. "I don't know," Farsith said in broken Sinhalese. "Yes, we put?"

The mob, hearing confirmation, collapsed onto Farsith and beat him. They had been asking if he'd put sterilization pills in the food, as they'd all seen on Facebook. Leaving him bloody on the floor, they pulled down shelves, smashed furniture, ripped appliances from the walls. Dozens of men from the neighborhood, having heard that the Facebook rumors were true, joined in. They marched to the local mosque, which they set on fire while the imam hid in his smoldering office, waiting to die.

In an earlier time, this calamity might have ended in Ampara. But someone in the mob had taken cell-phone video of Farsith's admission: "Yes, we put." Within hours, it was shared to a Sri Lankan Facebook group called the Buddhist Information Center, which had won a fervent following by claiming to provide true information about the Muslim threat. The page published the shaky, eighteen-second clip as proof of the Islamophobic memes it had hosted for months. Then the video spread.

As in Myanmar, social media had been initially received as a force for good in Sri Lanka. It kept families in touch even as many worked abroad to send money home. Activists and elected leaders credited it with helping to usher in democracy. And thanks to zero-rating programs, the same strategy Facebook had used in Myanmar, millions of people could access the services for free.

Zero-rating had grown out of a peculiarity of Silicon Valley economics: the mandate for perpetual user growth. Poorer countries are not particularly lucrative for platforms; advertisers pay little to reach consumers making a few dollars a day. But by spending aggressively now, the companies could preemptively dominate a poor country's media and internet markets, where they would face few competitors. They could tell investors that revenue was primed to explode in ten or twenty years, as consumers there entered the middle class.

Facebook, WhatsApp, Twitter, Snapchat, and others launched zero-rated services in dozens of countries, from Colombia to Kenya, where they had no footprint and little familiarity, reasoning they would learn as they went. They might contract a few local English teachers to translate essentials like the "Add friend" button. They would outsource the rest to — what else? — machine-learning algorithms. If the translations were wrong, they'd find out by tracking user behavior.

"As the usage expands, it's in every country, it's in places in the world and languages and cultures we don't understand," Chris Cox, Facebook's chief product officer, boasted in 2013. He cited one in particular: Myanmar, where he'd heard that Facebook already dominated locals' access to news. There was, they told themselves, whether out of ideological fervor or financially motivated disinterest, no need to monitor or even consider the consequences, because they could only be positive.

This was more than hubris. It drew on an idea, suffusing the Valley, that had originated with Peter Thiel, Facebook's foundational investor: "zero to one." It was a mandate, commercial and ideological, for companies to invent something so new that there was no market for it — starting at zero — and then control that market absolutely, a field with one entrant. "The history of progress is a history of better monopoly businesses replacing incumbents," Thiel wrote. Intel and processors. Apple and personal computers. Uber and private taxis. Facebook and social networking.

A monopoly, liberated from competition, would be freed to invest in innovation, bettering all mankind, he argued. This was baseless: monopolies, as a rule, leverage their power to deliver less and less value while extracting greater and greater rents from consumers. But it resonated in the Valley, whose citizens reinterpreted the infinite-growth business model, imposed by investors a few years earlier with the rise of cloud computing, into a glorious mission, the continuation of '90s-era internet liberationism. It implied that overrunning whole societies, blindly trampling whatever had come before, was not only acceptable but necessary.

Such an outcome, far from negative, was considered a gift to the world. The tech industry would bring about nothing less than the "next step" in our journey as a species, Zuckerberg wrote in a 6,000-word essay published a year before I arrived in Sri Lanka. In perhaps the last gasp of Valley utopianism, he pledged that Facebook would provide the "social infrastructure" of a new era, elevating us beyond mere "cities or nations" into "a global community." This would enable "spreading prosperity and freedom, promoting peace and understanding, lifting people out of poverty," even "ending terrorism, fighting climate change, and preventing pandemics."

The results on the ground bore little resemblance to these starry-eyed visions. In the days after the Facebook-inspired mob ravaged Ampara, calls for genocide saturated the platform. "Kill all Muslims, don't even save an infant," one post said. There were hundreds like it, all inspired by the video of Farsith saying, "Yes, we put." A Facebook-famous extremist urged his followers to descend on a local Muslim enclave and "reap without leaving an iota behind." Members of a local human rights group, huddled in a small office in the capital city, Colombo, marked down every post, tracing a network of hate. They planned to pass it all along to Facebook. The researchers were doing Facebook's work for them, they knew, and for free. Volunteer janitors for one of the world's wealthiest platforms. But the company ignored them.

"We have given, for the past four years, data-driven examples of hate. We've given them pages of data," Sanjana Hattotuwa, then a researcher with that rights group, Center for Policy Alternatives, told us. "It's pointless to coordinate with Facebook," he huffed, pacing angrily. Hattotuwa, a familiar face at international technology conferences, had managed to make some connections at the company. But no matter how extreme the incitements to violence, no matter how stridently he warned that the platform was going to get somebody killed, the response was the same: "They say it doesn't contravene anything. They say please get back to us with more information."

Months earlier, before the devastation in Ampara, one of his colleagues, Raisa Wickrematunge, had spoken at a Stanford forum on social media disinformation. During a coffee break, she cornered a Facebook security manager, Jen Weedon, who'd sat on an earlier panel. She warned Weedon that in Sri Lanka, Facebook was letting open calls to violence, forbidden under the company's own policies, run rampant. The conversation ended inconclusively. After the conference, Wickrematunge sent Weedon a follow-up email, offering to flag dangerous hate speech for Facebook to review — free assistance. She never received a response.

In October 2018, Sri Lankan civil leaders gave Facebook's regional office, which oversees South Asia's 400 million users from India, a stark presentation. Hate speech and misinformation were overrunning the platform, seemingly promoted by its algorithms. Violent extremists operated some of its most popular pages. Viral falsehoods were becoming consensus reality for users. Facebook, after all, had displaced local news outlets, just as it had in Myanmar, where villages were still burning. Sri Lanka might be next. Separately, government officials met privately with Facebook's regional chiefs in Colombo. They pleaded with the company to better police the hate speech on their platform. These posts and pages violated the company's own rules. Why wouldn't Facebook act?

Facebook's position was the same in both meetings. It wasn't enough for someone, even a government minister, to flag a post as hate speech. Facebook, to act, had to verify any rule-breaking itself. But the platform outsourced most of this work to I.T. companies, which did not employ enough Sinhalese speakers to keep pace. Facebook representatives made vague promises about staffing up.

The government officials asked if there was someone they could contact directly in case of an explosion of Myanmar-style incitement. No, the company reps told them. If they saw anything dangerous, they should use the on-site form for reporting rule violations. This directive was maddening. That form, designed for everyday users, was the very same widget to which Hattotuwa and his colleagues had already filed months of increasingly alarmed reports, to almost total silence. All as the calls to violence were getting progressively more specific, naming the mosques and neighborhoods to be cleansed.

3. What Compels Facebook?

ACROSS COLOMBO, IN the colonial-era offices housing Sri Lanka's government ministries, the country's information chief, Sudarshana Gunawardana, told us that he and other officials "felt a sense of helplessness." Before Facebook, in times of communal tension, he could meet with civic leaders and media heads, urging messages of calm. Now, everything his citizens saw and heard was controlled by engineers, far away in California, whose local representatives would not even return his calls.

As signs of coming violence mounted, officials rushed out statements debunking the most dangerous rumors. Nobody believed them. They had seen the truth with their own eyes right on Facebook. Gunawardana marked post after post using Facebook's reporting widget. A high-ranking official reduced to begging, via Facebook's submission box, for some anonymous moderator to take notice of his country's spiral toward violence. Every single report was ignored. "There needs to be some kind of engagement with countries like Sri Lanka," Gunawardana said. "We're a society, we're not just a market."

As anger over the Ampara video spread, Facebook extremists directed the rage. One of them, Amith Weerasinghe, whose hatemongering had been rewarded with thousands of followers, seized on the traffic dispute in which Muslim youths had beaten a truck driver — the man whose family we'd met. Weerasinghe circulated memes, shared thousands of times, calling it the first blow in a Muslim uprising. As proof, he promoted the fake-news story about Ampara police seizing many thousands of sterilization pills from Muslim pharmacies. To millions of Sri Lankans stewing in social media unreality, the supposed confession by Farsith, the restaurant owner, looked like confirmation of everything. The race war was here. A few days after Ampara's riot, the truck driver, still in the hospital, died, which caused online outrage to surge, as it often did, into calls for collective action: true Sinhalese should attend the funeral to show solidarity against the Muslim menace. Busloads arrived at Kandy, the city nearest to the truck driver's village. Some fanned into surrounding towns.

To coordinate movements, Facebook users circulated links to private WhatsApp groups. The Facebook-owned messaging app enables rapid-fire communication, akin to group text messaging for hundreds of people at once, with some viral-friendly twists. Users can forward content from one group to another, enabling posts to spread exponentially. A large WhatsApp group can resemble a mishmash of Facebook, Twitter, and YouTube, filled by viral content copied in from all three. WhatsApp sells itself especially on privacy: end-to-end encryption keeps out prying authorities. There are no fact-checkers or moderators.

The digital researchers joined some of the groups. It wasn't difficult; group names were posted on Facebook hate pages, which operated as openly as newspapers. In one viral WhatsApp video, a man dressed as a monk yelled, "The knife at home is no longer to cut jackfruit. So kindly sharpen that knife and go." In another group, a user shared a photo of a dozen makeshift weapons with a list of targets. He marked two mosques with the word "tonight," and another two with the word "tomorrow." The groups filled especially with content from Weerasinghe. Many shared a video he'd posted on Facebook and YouTube that showed him walking the shops of a town called Digana. Too many of them were owned by Muslims, he said, urging Sinhalese to take the town back. The researchers sent it all to Facebook. No response came.

They watched helplessly as hundreds of Sinhalese posted live from the villages and towns whose streets they filled. Residents hung banners with images of lions out their front windows. It was a message: Sinhalese live here. Everyone knew what was coming. The first Molotov cocktails flew that evening. For three days, mobs ruled the streets. Going house to house, wherever Muslims lived, they smashed through the front doors, ransacked floor to ceiling, then set the homes afire. They burned mosques and Muslim-owned businesses. They beat people in the street.

In Digana, the town where Weerasinghe had walked in his video, one of those homes belonged to the Basith family. They sold slippers from the first floor and lived on the second. Most had fled. But an elder son, Abdul, had stayed behind and was trapped upstairs. "They have broken all the doors in our house," Abdul said in an audio message he sent to his uncle on WhatsApp. "There are flames coming inside." After a few moments, he pleaded, his voice rising, "The house is burning." His family could not reach the house. Police did not retake Digana until the next morning. They found Abdul dead upstairs.

The country's leaders, desperate to stem the violence, blocked all access to social media. It was a lever they had resisted pulling, reluctant to block platforms that some still credited with their country's only recent transition to democracy, and fearful of appearing to reinstate the authoritarian abuses of earlier decades. Two things happened almost immediately. The violence stopped; without Facebook or WhatsApp driving them, the mobs simply went home. And Facebook representatives, after months of ignoring government ministers, finally returned their calls. But not to ask about the violence. They wanted to know why traffic had zeroed out.

A few days later Amanda and I arrived in Digana, where ashes still blew in the streets. The town, in Sri Lanka's interior of rolling emerald hills and nature preserves, sat only thirty minutes from some of the country's most luxurious resorts. Neighbors watched from tea stalls as a man named Fazal welcomed us into his home, just feet from the shell of the building where his brother, Abdul, had died in the fire. Fazal, who works as an imam, used Facebook for everything, the same as everybody else, he said. I asked him about misinformation and hate online, but he didn't seem to understand. Facebook simply was. I might as well have asked if he blamed the fires on the wind. I didn't want to press a man in mourning. He put out ice cream for us and left for work.

A young neighbor who had joined us in Fazal's house, Jainulabdeen, told us, once our host had gone, "We expected this." Perhaps not wanting to embarrass Fazal, he had waited to speak up. Like the Basith family, Jainulabdeen was Muslim. But Sinhalese neighbors had warned him days in advance. "Most of them knew," he said. "They knew it from Facebook." When I asked about the video of Weerasinghe, the Facebook extremist, walking Digana to call for Muslims' expulsions, Jainulabdeen snorted and shook his head. "We know him," he said. "He's from the area." On Facebook, Weerasinghe wielded the power to shape reality for hundreds of thousands. But here in his hometown, he was just, Jainulabdeen insisted, "a normal person." His father was a carpenter. The families knew each other. Jainulabdeen's relatives had even asked Weerasinghe's family to intervene. The family, seemingly sharing their concerns, promised to talk to him, but nothing had come of it. He loved being on the internet too much.

Once the mobs dissipated, police arrested Weerasinghe for incitement. Facebook finally shuttered his page. But the Ampara video that had inspired so much violence, of the innocent Muslim restaurant-worker Farsith Atham-Lebbe pressured to confirm a nonexistent race war, remained online. The researchers continued submitting pleas for Facebook to remove it, and the company continued refusing, either ignoring their reports or answering that the content broke no rules.

Farsith was in hiding, we learned, at the other end of the country. While I scrounged a ride out in hopes of meeting him, Amanda headed back toward the capital to chase down the details of a meeting she'd heard about from a source. Earlier that day, Facebook's policy director for South Asia, Shivnath Thukral, had flown in to meet with government ministers, the source had revealed. Now that Sri Lanka had pulled the plug, Facebook was finally making a show of listening.

Thukral was conciliatory, an attendee told Amanda. He acknowledged that Facebook had failed to address the incitement and hate speech that it had been warned about again and again. He promised better collaboration. The next day, Thukral held an off-the-record call with civil representatives. He conceded that Facebook did not have enough Sinhalese-speaking moderators to control misinformation and hate. He again pledged that the company would hire more.

After a few weeks had passed, we asked Facebook how many Sinhalese-speaking moderators they'd hired. The company said only that they'd made progress. Skeptical, Amanda scoured employment websites in nearby countries. She found a listing, in India, for work moderating an unnamed platform in Sinhalese. She called the outsourcing firm through a translator, asking if the job was for Facebook. The recruiter said that it was. They had twenty-five Sinhalese openings, every one unfilled since June 2017 — nine long months earlier. Facebook's "progress" had been a lie.

"We are a government that came to power on a mandate of free expression," Harindra Dissanayake, a presidential advisor in Sri Lanka, told Amanda. He used social media himself. It had pained him to shut off access, if only for a few days. At their best, he said, social media platforms "made things more transparent, gave voice to people who did not have voices." But the past months, he said, had destroyed his faith in the technology he'd once credited with bringing his country democracy. "This idea of social media as an open, equal platform is a complete lie," he now believed. "There is no editor, there is the algorithm."

He stressed that Sri Lanka's divisions predated social media. But these platforms, he warned, brought out the very worst in a society, amplifying its extremes in ways that had never before been possible. "We don't completely blame Facebook," Dissanayake said. "The germs are ours, but Facebook is the wind, you know?" His government was considering regulations or fines, he said. But he knew Sri Lanka's power was modest. Only Americans, he believed, had enough leverage to force change. "You, the

United States itself, should fight the algorithm. What compels Facebook, beyond that?"

The next day, I arrived at the opposite end of the country, where a local teacher who claimed to know Farsith guided me to a small settlement some miles from Ampara, to a row of two-room concrete houses. He pointed to the third from the end.

Farsith, waiting inside, had shaved his beard. Not to hide his faith, he said, but because even in this far-flung village, he could hardly make it a block without being recognized. "People would ask me all sorts of questions," he said. Or shout at him, "You're from the video!" He recounted the riot, his confusion and fear, the mob's fury. "I thought that would be my last day," he said. He'd fled the next morning.

Shy, almost childlike, he seemed off somewhere else. As we talked, he twisted a hand in front of his five-year-old niece in half-hearted play. She pulled and prodded at it, trying to bring his gaze up from the floor. Her father, who had run the restaurant, brought us bananas and tea. The brothers had taken out so many loans to build the shop, he said, that they'd been unable to afford insurance. Now everything was gone but the debt.

"We don't know what to do," Farsith's brother said. Maybe they would return to work construction in Saudi Arabia, which was where they'd saved up money for the restaurant, though that would mean leaving their families behind. "We are waiting on God for guidance."

Farsith sighed. "I don't have any intention of staying here," he said.

I asked him several times about social media. Facebook had turned him into a national villain. It had spread a lie that ruined his family, perhaps now splitting them apart. It had nearly killed him. Even now, he lived in fear of another mob incited by the platform.

Despite all that, he refused to abandon the social networks. With long, empty days in hiding, he said, "I have more time and I look at Facebook much more."

I was shocked. Even if he bore no ill will toward the company whose platform had upended his family's lives, I said, he knew firsthand that he couldn't believe what he saw there.

It wasn't that he had faith that social media was accurate, he said. "But you have to spend time and money to go to the market to get a newspaper. I can just open my phone and get the news instead." He looked up from the floor, shrugging. "Whether it's wrong or right, it's what I read."

I kept in intermittent contact with Farsith. His family slipped into poverty. Threats continued to follow him. Someone from Facebook got in touch — citing the article that Amanda and I had written — to ask him what had happened. Farsith told the person that he was desperate for a way to feed himself. He was willing to work. The call ended and he never heard from Facebook again. After a year, he had saved up enough to travel to Kuwait, where he began working as a day laborer. He is still there.

Eight

Church Bells

1. Status Threat

IT WAS DURING an interview with Gema Santamaría, a scholar of vigilante violence who had researched strange incidents in her native Mexico, that I realized I would spend years trying to understand how this pattern might be playing out, albeit in less obvious ways or to less obvious effects, around the world, maybe even in the United States, where parallels with Trumpism's rise were only coming into view. She was finding in Mexico the same kinds of outbreaks that researchers in other countries around the globe had been documenting. A Cancun suburb that erupted into violence over online misinformation. A village of quiet families who, after starting a Facebook page for community news that became a hotbed of paranoid rumors, tied up a pair of bewildered traveling pollsters, whom they had accused of plotting to harvest the organs of local children, and set them on fire. Then, in another village, the same pattern, from the details of the rumor to the method of killing, this time claiming the lives of two men who were in town to buy fence posts.

"Social media plays the role that the ringing of the church bells used to play in the past," Santamaría said. "That's the way that people know that a lynching is going to happen." The platforms, she explained, reproduced certain age-old mechanisms by which a community worked itself into collective violence. Lynching, when a group follows its moral outrage to the point of hurting or killing someone — the tyranny of cousins at work — is a communal impulse. A public show of what happens to those transgressing the tribe.

"The aim of it is to communicate," Santamaría said of lynching. The false rumors that consistently spread in advance of mass violence, she believed, were the tell that social media had learned to reproduce that age-old process. More than merely triggering preexisting sentiment, social media was creating it. The rumors were hardly random. "They have a logic to them," she said. "They do not target everyone." Rather, the rumors activated a sense of collective peril in groups that were dominant but felt their status was at risk — majorities angry and fearful over change that threatened to erode their position in the hierarchy. Because the impersonal forces of social change are, for most people, no more defeatable than the weather, social media had stepped in to provide a more corporeal, conquerable villain: feminist bloggers, the religious minority next door, refugees. "This finally is something that you have control over," Santamaría said. "You can actually do something about it."

In Myanmar, social media platforms indulged the fears of the long-dominant Buddhist majority who felt, with democracy's arrival, a shift in the status quo that had long privileged them. In India, it was the Hindu majority, on similar grounds. In 2018, BBC reporters in northern Nigeria found the same pattern, the Fulani majority pitted against the Berom minority, all on Facebook. In America, social media had tapped into white backlash against immigration, Black Lives Matter, increased visibility of Muslims, cultural recalibration toward greater tolerance and diversity. The most-shared rumors, Santamaría pointed out, often had to do with reproduction or population. Sri Lanka and sterilization pills. America and a liberal plot to replace white people with refugees.

The defining element across all these rumors was something more specific and dangerous than generalized outrage: a phenomenon called status threat. When members of a dominant social group feel at risk of losing their position, it can spark a ferocious reaction. They grow nostalgic for a past, real or imagined, when they felt secure in their dominance ("Make America Great Again"). They become hyper-attuned for any change that might seem tied to their position: shifting demographics, evolving social norms, widening minority rights. And they grow obsessed with playing up minorities as dangerous, manifesting stories and rumors to confirm the belief. It's a kind of collective defense mechanism to preserve dominance. It is mostly unconscious, almost animalistic, and therefore easily manipulated, whether by opportunistic leaders or profit-seeking algorithms.

The problem isn't just that social media learned to promote outrage, fear, and tribal conflict, all sentiments that align with status threat. Online, as we post updates visible to hundreds or thousands of people, charged with the group-based emotions that the platforms encourage, "our group identities are more salient" than our individual ones, as William Brady and Molly Crockett wrote in their paper on social media's effects. We don't just become more tribal, we lose our sense of self. It's an environment, they wrote, "ripe for the psychological state of deindividuation."

The shorthand definition of *deindividuation* is "mob mentality," though it is more common than joining a mob. You can deindividuate by sitting in the stands at a sports game or singing along in church, surrendering part of your will to that of the group. The danger comes when these two forces mix: deindividuation, with its power to override individual judgment, and status threat, which can trigger collective aggression on a terrible scale.

I thought back to a conversation with Sanjana Hattotuwa, the impassioned digital researcher who'd tracked online hate in Sri Lanka. "The cancer has grown such that you're looking at ordinary people," he'd said. "It's disturbing. The radicalization is happening at a very young age." Even schoolkids from perfectly nice families, if they were active with social media, got sucked in, their worlds and worldviews defined by the status threat they encountered online. "This is their initiation into communal relations," he said. "And it's hate. It's really, really bad."

Perhaps this pattern, of status threat running rampant online, helped explain why, in 2016, Trump supporters had fallen so much further down the digital rabbit hole than other Americans. If social media were built to

activate majoritarian identity panic, then America's shrinking white majority — and especially the non-college-graduate or working-class whites who
tend to hold their racial identity most closely and who became the bulk of
the Trump coalition — would be dangerously susceptible to the same pattern I'd seen in Sri Lanka. Status threat and digital deindividuation on a
national scale. By 2018, that tribe had, with a handful of exceptions like
the rally in Charlottesville, not yet worked itself up to outright mob violence. But I wondered whether this sort of social media influence might
be coming out in other forms, priming people for racial violence in less
obvious but still consequential ways.

I soon got an answer. Just as Sri Lanka combusted in March 2018, two
German social scientists neared completion on a long project examining
the subterranean effects of social media on their country. The study hinted
at a shocking revelation, suggesting that events like those in Myanmar and
Sri Lanka, far from being unique, were playing out in Western democracies, too, just in subtler ways. To understand it, I traveled to a small town
near Düsseldorf, where my colleague Amanda Taub would join me a few
days later.

2. Irony Poisoning

FOR TWO DAYS in June 2018, a few months after our reporting in Sri
Lanka, I wandered the cobblestone streets of Altena, asking a question
that brought sober, knowing nods. What happened to Dirk Denkhaus?

Altena, like many other towns in Germany's industrial northwest, was
declining, locals would explain, a situation that left young people bored
and disillusioned. Germany had recently accepted nearly one million refugees from far-off war zones, which most in Altena had supported. But
some had found the influx disorienting. That was the context, they would
say, to understand why Denkhaus, a young firefighter trainee who had
been considered neither dangerous nor political, had tried to burn down a
refugee group house while several families slept inside.

But those I stopped, whether old or young, repeatedly cited another factor they called just as important as the others: Facebook. Everyone here had seen social media rumors portraying the refugees as a threat. They'd encountered the vitriol filling local Facebook groups, a jarring contrast to Altena's physical spaces, where people waved warmly to refugee families. Many here suspected — and prosecutors would later argue — that Denkhaus had isolated himself in an online world of racist paranoia that had gradually changed him.

Altena exemplified a long-suspected but, as of 2018, scantily studied phenomenon: that social media platforms make whole communities more prone to racial violence. The town was one of more than three thousand datapoints in a study that claimed to prove it. Karsten Müller and Carlo Schwarz, researchers at the University of Warwick in the UK, had gathered data on every anti-refugee attack in Germany over a two-year span, 3,335 in all. It had been a volatile period, as Europe's refugee crisis had been followed by a rise in far-right politics. The sheer scale presented an opportunity to isolate social media's influence. In each incident in the study, the researchers analyzed the respective local community, using a handful of key variables. Wealth. Demographics. Political allegiance. Number of refugees. History of hate crime.

One thing stuck out. Towns with higher-than-average Facebook use reliably experienced more attacks on refugees. This held true in virtually any sort of community: big or small, affluent or struggling, liberal or conservative. The uptick did not correlate with general web usage; it was particular to Facebook. Their data boiled down to a breathtaking statistic: Wherever per-person Facebook use rose by one standard deviation above the national average, attacks on refugees increased by about 35 percent. Nationwide, they estimated, this effect drove as much as 10 percent of all anti-refugee violence.

Experts whom I asked to review the findings called them credible and rigorous. Still, the study later attracted criticism for methodological flourishes. To gauge town-by-town Facebook usage, for example, the researchers tracked a battery of indicators, one of which was how many users joined the Nutella fan page. They reasoned that Nutella was universally popular and culturally neutral, making it a useful benchmark. Critics called the choice unserious and unsound. The researchers ironed out the issues in a later redraft. My interest, however, was not in proving out the math at the end of their paper, but in using it as a road map for Facebook's influence. It was why I'd come to Altena, where the researchers had found that Facebook usage and anti-refugee sentiment were both unusually high and at rates in line with the paper's projections. Perhaps Denkhaus represented a deeper shift.

When refugees had first arrived here a few years earlier, in 2015, so many locals had volunteered to help that Anette Wesemann, who'd taken over the local refugee-integration center after giving up her home in bustling Hanover for quiet village life, couldn't keep up. She would find Syrian or Afghan families attended by whole entourages of self-appointed life coaches and German tutors. "It was really moving," she said. But when she set up a Facebook page to organize volunteer events, it filled with anti-refugee vitriol of a sort she'd never encountered off-line. Some posts were threatening, mentioning local refugees by name. Over time, their anger proved infectious, dominating the page. When I mentioned the research linking Facebook to anti-refugee violence, she responded, "I would believe it immediately."

Anti-refugee sentiment is among the purest expressions of status threat, combining fear of demographic change with racial tribalism. Even if few locals truly hated refugees, their posts rose over and over, rewarded for their ability to provoke, like the anti-vaccine content that Renée DiResta had found overwhelming parenting groups. As their hate overran local pages, creating, as usual, a false impression of consensus, more seemed to join in.

Dirk Denkhaus turned out to have experienced a microcosm of this process. When I met with Gerhard Pauli, the region's chief prosecutor, who'd overseen the investigation into Denkhaus, he pulled out a binder containing hundreds of printouts of Facebook and WhatsApp posts the police had pulled from Denkhaus's cell phone. His slide into extremism, Pauli said, had begun as a joke. He and a friend would exchange racist memes, often borrowed from public Facebook groups, to provoke and shock each other.

"They found themselves joking, addressing one another as 'mein Führer' and such," the prosecutor said, shaking his head. Over time, the sentiment became sincere. "There's a very small distance," Pauli said, "between joke and real." Denkhaus crossed that distance in about six months. "He said to his partner one day, 'And now we have to do something,'" Pauli said. That night he and his friend broke into the attic of a refugee group house and set a fire seemingly intended to kill all inside. Fortunately, the fire fizzled. Police arrested both men the next day.

There's a term for the process Pauli described, of online jokes gradually internalized as sincere. It's called irony poisoning. Heavy social media users often call themselves "irony poisoned," a joke on the dulling of the senses that comes from a lifetime engrossed in social media subcultures, where ironic detachment, algorithmic overstimulation, and dare-to-offend humor prevail. In more extreme forms, sustained exposure to objectionable content, spent going down Facebook or YouTube rabbit holes, can lower people's defenses against it. Desensitization makes the ideas seem less taboo or extreme, which in turn makes them easier to adopt.

In court, Denkhaus's lawyer emphasized that his client had, in his offline life, shown no animus toward refugees before that night. While intended to downplay social media's relevance, this observation instead underscored its power. In the real Altena, overwhelmingly tolerant social norms prevailed. But on Facebook, a closed environment with its own moral rules, Denkhaus had drifted unchecked toward extremism.

Pauli believes that Denkhaus represented a trend. The prosecutor said he was "quite sure" that social media had exacerbated Altena's rise in violence. A few months later its mayor was stabbed by a man who said he was outraged by the town's pro-refugee policies. Police, Pauli said, suspected a social media link. Local Facebook pages had filled with rage toward the mayor just before the attack. Police hadn't bothered to collect evidence of online influence, though, since the attacker had already confessed. And even if Pauli considered the Silicon Valley giant a kind of unwitting accomplice, he knew that the company was beyond any justice that he could bring.

His office spent more and more time tracking incitement on the platforms. He was growing concerned, he said, about rumors that could spin otherwise normal people into violence. Strangely, as in Mexico and Indonesia and seemingly every other country, they often seemed to turn on mysterious threats to children. "We have lots of situations where somebody saw somebody outside the kindergarten," Pauli said, shaking his head. "Within five minutes it's spreading," he said, "and from post to post, it gets worse. It takes two hours and then you have some lynch mob on the street."

3. Superposters

TRAUNSTEIN, A MOUNTAINSIDE town near Austria, is, in many ways, Altena's opposite. Its tourist economy is thriving. Its politics lean liberal. Young people are active in the community. But as in Altena, Facebook use and anti-refugee violence are both unusually high here. I arrived, now joined by Amanda, looking for something in particular. By checking local Facebook groups for the most active and visible posters, we found what's known as a superposter, someone who is thought to embody the ways that Facebook can make a community incrementally more extreme. His named was Rolf Wassermann.

Whatever image you have in your head of the basement-dwelling internet addict, Wassermann is the opposite. Middle-aged and tanned, an artist by trade, sporting a salt-and-pepper beard and an all-black suit, he looks like he stepped out of a TV ad for upmarket beer. Though conservative, he is hardly radical. But he is furiously active online, where he fits the superposter's archetypal profile. He posts streams of rumors, strident opinion columns, and news reports on crimes committed by refugees. Though none I saw crossed into hate speech or fake news, in the aggregate they portrayed Germany as beset by dangerous foreigners.

"On Facebook, it's possible to reach people who are not highly political," he told us over coffee. "You can build people's political views on Facebook." He described what he said was a typical arc for people he met there. They'd start as not particularly political. They'd begin posting frequently, perhaps thanks to a sudden surfeit of free time, on whatever items appeared on their feeds. They'd join Facebook groups, which is where he often met them. Over time, they'd become more stridently political, he said. Just as he had.

He preferred social media to newspapers or TV, he said, because "Facebook is more honest." For example, on Facebook he had learned, he said, that the number of refugees in Germany and the crimes they'd committed were both higher than the media claimed. And he had done his best to amplify this revelation. "The things people say on Facebook are just more true," he said. As if realizing the absurdity of believing such a thing on pure faith, he laughed, adding, "I assume they are, anyway. I'm not God, I don't know."

Hyperactive users like Wassermann tend to be "more opinionated, more extreme, more engaged, more everything," said Andrew Guess, a Princeton University social scientist. It's a different set of traits than those you might associate with the much-studied, much-interviewed class of social media addicts and early adopters like Adam, the 4chan devotee. Superposters are a breed of their own, and one that the platforms have rendered exceptionally influential. When more casual users open social media, often what they see is a world shaped by superposters. Social media attracts people with certain personality tics that make heavy usage unusually gratifying. Their predominance, in turn, distorts the platforms' norms and biases.

And those defining traits and tics of superposters, mapped out in a series of psychological studies, are broadly negative. One is dogmatism: "relatively unchangeable, unjustified certainty." Dogmatics tend to be narrow-minded, pushy, and loud. Another: grandiose narcissism, defined by feelings of innate superiority and entitlement. Narcissists are consumed by cravings for admiration and belonging, which makes social media's instant feedback and large audiences all but irresistible. That need is deepened by super-posters' unusually low self-esteem, which is exacerbated by the platforms themselves. One study concluded simply, "Online political hostility is committed by individuals who are predisposed to be hostile in all contexts." Neurological experiments confirmed this: superposters are drawn toward and feel rewarded by negative social potency, a clinical term for deriving pleasure from deliberately inflicting emotional distress on others. Further, by using social media more, and by being rewarded for this with greater reach, superposters pull the platforms toward these defining tendencies of dogmatism, narcissism, aggrandizement, and cruelty.

In an unintended 2015 test of this, Ellen Pao, still Reddit's chief, tried something unprecedented: rather than promote superusers, Reddit would ban the most toxic of them. Out of tens of millions of users, her team concluded, only about 15,000, all hyperactive, drove much of the hateful content. Expelling them, Pao reasoned, might change Reddit as a whole. She was right, an outside analysis found. With the elimination of this minuscule percentage of users, hate speech overall dropped an astounding 80 percent among those who remained. Millions of people's behavior had shifted overnight. It was a rare success in combating a problem that would only deepen on other, larger platforms, which did not follow Reddit's lead. They had no interest in suppressing their most active users, much less in acknowledging that there might be such a thing as too much time online.

Could superposters alter not just what showed up in people's feeds, but their very sense of right and wrong? I put the question to Betsy Levy Paluck, who had won a MacArthur Foundation "genius grant" for her work exploring how social norms influence behavior. I expected her to cite her research on, say, communal violence in Rwanda. Instead, she wanted to talk about school bullying. Schoolkids bully or don't, she found in a long investigation, based largely not on whether they expect punishment or think the target deserves it, but on whether it feels moral to them. Either bullying felt permissible, even righteous, or it felt wrong, and that internal barometer was what mattered most. But how does our moral barometer become set? We like to think of ourselves as following an innate moral code, derived from lofty principles, lived experience, the advice of a trusted elder. In truth, studies find over and over, our sense of right or wrong is heavily, if unconsciously, influenced by what we believe our peers think: morality by tribal consensus, guided not by some better angel or higher power but by self-preserving deference to the tyranny of cousins.

In an experiment in rural Mexico, researchers produced an audio soap opera whose story discouraged domestic violence against women. In some areas, people had the soap played for them privately in their homes. In others, it was broadcast on village loudspeakers or at community meetings. Men who listened at home were just as prone to domestic violence as they had been before. But men who listened in group settings became significantly less likely to commit abuse. And not out of perceived pressure. Their internal beliefs had shifted, growing morally opposed to domestic violence and supportive of gender equality. The difference was in seeing their peers absorb the soap opera. The conformity impulse — the same one that had led Facebook's first users to trick themselves into fuming over the news feed — can soak all the way to the moral marrow of your innermost self.

Most of the time, deducing our peers' moral views is not so easy. So we use a shortcut. We pay special attention to a handful of peers whom we consider to be influential, take our cues from them, and assume this will reflect the norms of the group as a whole. The people we pick as moral benchmarks are known as "social referents." In this way, morality is "a sort of perceptual task," Paluck said. "Who in our group is actually popping out to us? Who do we recruit in our memories when we think about what's common, what's desirable?"

To test this, Paluck had her team fan out to fifty-six schools, identifying which students were influential among their peers as well as which students considered bullying to be morally acceptable. Then she picked twenty or thirty students at each school who seemed to fit both conditions: these were, presumably, the students who played the greatest role in instilling pro-bullying social norms in their communities. They were asked to publicly condemn bullying — not forced, just asked. The gentle nudge to this tiny population proved transformative. Psychological benchmarks found that thousands of students became internally opposed to bullying, their moral compasses pulled toward compassion. Bullying-related disciplinary reports dropped by 30 percent.

Social media platforms place us all in a version of Paluck's school experiment. But, online, our social referents, the people artificially pushed into our moral fields of vision, are the superposters. Not because they are persuasive, thoughtful, or important, but because they drive engagement. That was something unique to platforms like Facebook, Paluck said. Anyone who got a lot of time on the feed became influential. "In real life, some people might talk a lot but not be the most listened to. But Facebook," she said, "puts them in front of you every time."

And social media doesn't just surround you with superposters. It displays their messages on vast, public forums, where you know that everyone else sees them, too, like the loudspeakers in Mexican villages that had demonstrated such power to alter a community all at once. In Germany, social media appeared to have elevated a class of superposters like Wassermann who gave sitewide users the impression that social norms were more hostile to refugees and more conspiratorial than they really were. It was Facebook's 2006 "Against News Feed" imbroglio, now elevated to an entire nation's political psyche, and directed at millions of the country's most vulnerable residents. Even if none of those superposters explicitly endorsed violence, Paluck said, the aggregate effect of their anti-refugee, anti-government messaging likely made vigilante violence feel tolerated, even encouraged.

That afternoon, at a Traunstein community event, a teacher named Natascha Wolff perked up when she heard me asking about social media. Wolff taught at a vocational school, she said, with a mix of German- and foreign-born students. In recent months, the German kids had veered, almost uniformly, toward strident anti-refugee hostility she'd never encountered before. There were, she knew, likely many reasons for this. But whenever she asked where they'd learned the phony statistics or hateful claims they repeated to one another with alarm, she got the same answer: Facebook.

Any rumor or tidbit on Facebook disparaging foreigners, she said, "gets around fast. People feel confirmed in their viewpoint." She added, whipping her arm up and down to mimic someone slamming a keyboard, "It's just, 'like, like, like.'" If she challenged a false claim, she always got the same response: "Everybody knows this is true." But often the students were wrong about that, too; many in Traunstein rejected the rumors as false. Wolff worried that this Facebook bubble, the false communal consensus, had consequences. Her refugee students had coffee dumped on them in the street, garbage thrown on them from car windows. Casual, light-of-day violence one only attempts with the assumption that it will be tolerated.

Violence born on social media had grown so common that the police had begun treating the platforms as an ongoing threat to public safety. "Facebook is not just like a pinboard where people hang things and others read them," a local police inspector named Andreas Guske told us over coffee the next day. "Facebook, with its algorithm, influences people." Guske, a veteran detective, slightly graying, began to take social media seriously as a threat in 2015, during a nearby Group of Seven summit. When protesters swept in, he noticed platforms filling with rumors, some of which whipped the crowds into paranoid frenzies. The next year, attacks on refugees seemed to rise in concert with online hate speech. He retooled the team overseeing department communications to fight back, online and off. They thought of themselves as public-health workers, inoculating communities against viral misinformation and its consequences.

In one recent case, Guske told me, Facebook had swirled with claims that a group of Muslim refugees in a town near Traunstein had dragged an eleven-year-old girl to a pedestrian underpass and raped her. The rumor, though false, provoked waves of outrage as Facebook pushed it out across Germany. When police denied the story, users insisted that politicians had ordered them to cover it up. The rumors had begun, Guske's team found, after police arrested an Afghan immigrant accused of groping a seventeen-year-old girl. As Facebook users relayed the incident, some added details that shocked or outraged, which sent those versions rocketing past the truth. One assailant became several. A groping became a rape. A teenage victim became an adolescent.

The police posted statements on Facebook and Twitter debunking the rumor by reconstructing its spread. If the police could show how the platforms distorted reality, Guske believed, people would be persuaded to reject what they'd seen there. But he also knew that, on social media, a sober fact-check would never rise as high as a salacious rumor. So his team identified locals who had shared the rumor early in its spread, then showed up at their homes with evidence that they had gotten it wrong. He urged them to publicly disavow their claims, hoping to turn the platforms' own promotion systems against the misinformation. All but one removed or corrected their posts as he'd requested. But they could never keep up with the platforms, whose poisonous output, he feared, was only accelerating. And he lamented that Facebook, at that point a $500 billion company, left it to overworked police departments to manage the risks they created. "It's hard to prevent fake news, because once Facebook pushes it..." he trailed off, shaking his head. "What more can you do?"

That afternoon, as Amanda interviewed locals across town about social media, I met in a nearby park with a young woman who'd attended Wolff's vocational school. She came with a friend, who brought her toddler. Both women, polite but guarded, described themselves as not very political. Neither read the news except for what they saw on Facebook, which they checked frequently. Once I asked how they felt about refugees, it was all they wanted to talk about. Refugees were violent, they were rapists, and many sympathized with extremists, they said. They recounted lurid, implausible stories of refugee crimes hidden by the government. They had read all about it on Facebook, which was where they often discussed the "refugee situation," one said.

Traunstein leans liberal but is politically split, and I asked the woman if she ever got into arguments about refugees online. She seemed confused by the question. "Everyone feels this way," she said. Her filter bubble, unanimous in fear, had become her reality. She, like Wassermann and his online friends, like Wolff's other students, like the locals that Guske implored to take down racist falsehoods, were the submerged mass of an iceberg of society-wide social media radicalization. Denkhaus, the firefighter-arsonist, was just its tip. There were countless other Germans who had also grown more xenophobic, more conspiratorial, more nationalistic. Most would never resort to violence. But their collective drift had deeper consequences, pulling invisibly at society's mores and politics. In a wealthy democracy like Germany, the result might not be as obvious as a lynch mob or a riot. It might be worse. The country's political center was collapsing. The German far right was rising.

"One of the students in my school was sent back to Africa," the woman said approvingly. The deportation had been over an error in his immigration paperwork. "They should all be sent back."

4. Going Dark

THE GERMAN RESEARCHERS at the University of Warwick knew that one element of their theory — causality — needed special attention. Could it be proven that Facebook usage and anti-refugee violence rose in tandem specifically because the former caused the latter? They hit on the idea of examining every significant internet outage in the period their study covered. German internet infrastructure tends to be localized, making outages common but isolated. Each was an opportunity to test causality: if depriving a community of Facebook suddenly decreased locals' violence toward refugees, it would suggest that Facebook drove some attacks.

Sure enough, whenever internet access went down in an area with high Facebook use, attacks on refugees dropped significantly. The same drop did not occur, however, when areas with high internet usage but only average Facebook usage suffered an outage, suggesting that the violence-provoking effect was specific to social media, rather than from the internet itself. And violence dropped by the *same rate* — 35 percent — at which the study had suggested Facebook boosted such attacks. The researchers stressed that this was not definitive in itself, just an exercise by which to check their conclusions. But it was a striking indication that they were onto something — and an opportunity to consider, with a rigor that one-off shutdowns like Sri Lanka's could not provide, what happens when social media goes away.

"The world got smaller, a lot changed," Stefania Simonutti said, recalling the outage that had blanketed her Berlin suburb for several days to a few weeks, depending on the block. The suburb, Schmargendorf, feels like a haven from the forces of hate. Diverse, middle-class families stroll boutique-lined avenues and upscale farmers' markets. But Facebook usage is high here. So are anti-refugee attacks — except during the outage.

Simonutti, asked how she'd coped, opened her mouth and pressed her palms to her cheeks in a pantomimed scream. She'd lost touch with family abroad — and with the news, for which she trusted only social media. "Many people lie and fake things in the newspapers," she said. "But with the internet, I can decide for myself what to believe and what not." Forced to forgo the social media conspiracies she liked to follow online, she said, she filled the empty time relaxing with her family.

Everybody seemed to remember the outage. Esperanza Muñoz, a cheery, freckled woman who'd moved here from Colombia in the 1980s, had found it relaxing. She socialized more with neighbors and followed the news less. Her daughter, a medical student, said that she hadn't realized how much anxiety the platforms caused her until she went for a few days without them. The outage, she said, had driven home the extent to which "when news spreads on Facebook, it's made more provocative." Her mother agreed. When her native Colombia had held elections a few weeks earlier, she said, her news feed, dominated by fellow Colombians, had filled with partisan bickering and outrage — and, as if by some script, with fearmongering about refugees.

Earlier that year, in April, Zuckerberg had given an interview to *Vox's* editor-in-chief, Ezra Klein, who pressed him on the genocide in Myanmar. As evidence for Facebook's progress, Zuckerberg said that, at the height of the bloodshed, the company's security team had identified users in Myanmar inciting violence on Facebook Messenger. "Now, in that case, our systems detect that that's going on. We stop those messages from going through," he said. "But this is certainly something that we're paying a lot of attention to."

After the interview was published, Myanmar rights groups replied with a furious open letter. In fact, they said, they were the ones — and not Facebook — who had found the chain-letter-style messages fomenting violence. And because they lacked Facebook's internal tools for automatically monitoring the platforms, they had been able to ferret them out only through what they stressed was the cumbersome and woefully insufficient method of a manual hunt. Even then, the rights groups had still been forced to barrage Facebook with days of warnings before someone in the company finally acted. But it was too late. The users, apparently acting on these viral messages, had already organized and executed three separate attacks, one of which involved attempting to burn down a school. The episode, the groups said, underscored Facebook's "overreliance on third parties, a lack of a proper mechanism for emergency escalation, a reticence to engage local stakeholders around systemic solutions, and a lack of transparency." Zuckerberg sent the groups an email apologizing, though only for failing to credit them by name, which, the rights workers emphasized in their response, had not been their primary concern.

That August, the United Nations issued its formal report on the genocide. It called the role of social media, particularly Facebook, "significant." But Facebook still refused to share its data with UN investigators, the investigators said, impeding their ability to understand how the genocide had happened and, therefore, how to prevent another. "You can't just snap your fingers and solve these problems," Zuckerberg said a month later. "It takes time to hire the people and train them, and to build the systems that can flag stuff for them." But of course, in both Myanmar and Sri Lanka, Facebook had met warnings of impending violence not with any flurry of new safeguards or moderator hires but with months of inaction. Now, again, nothing appeared to change, a Myanmar-based digital-monitoring group told me. Facebook had solicited the group to monitor for rising online incitement or other dangers. But the company mostly ignored the group's reports, no matter how urgent. Facebook, they believed, had hired them as an empty PR sop.

Adam Mosseri, the executive who had overseen the all-powerful news feed during the Myanmar and Sri Lanka killings, was promoted to vice president of Instagram, then its president. Jen Weedon, the Facebook security-policy manager who had not answered the Sri Lankan research-er's warnings of the coming bloodshed, was promoted as well. Earnings exceeded a record $55 billion that year, up nearly 40 percent from the year before.

"The business model is what got us into trouble," Hany Farid, a UC Berkeley computer scientist who had consulted with governments and rights groups on emerging dangers on the social web, told me later that year. "Four hundred hours of YouTube uploaded every minute. A billion uploads to Facebook a day. Three hundred million tweets a day. And it's sort of a mess," he said. "The tech companies, I wouldn't even say they fell asleep on the job. I'd say they had their eyes wide open. I think they knew exactly what they were doing. They knew the poison was on the network. They knew they had a problem. But it was all about aggressive growth. That's where the problem started from."

Farid took a breath, returning to the topic that I'd called about, a specialized technology that the platforms used. But later, near the end of a technical explanation, as he stumbled into a reference to YouTube, his voice rose again. "YouTube is the worst," he said. Of what he considered the four leading web companies — Google/YouTube, Facebook, Twitter, and Microsoft — the best at managing what he'd called "the poison" was, he believed, Microsoft. "And it makes sense, right? It's not a social media company," he said. "But YouTube is the worst on these issues," he repeated.

It had been a year of scandal and controversy around Facebook, widely taken as the most influential platform. But Farid's admonition resonated because, even as I investigated the effects of Facebook in Sri Lanka and Germany, I had been hearing the same from digital experts, rights groups, and others: look at YouTube. "YouTube is the most overlooked story of 2016," Zeynep Tufekci, a University of North Carolina sociologist tweeted a year after the election. "Its search and recommender algorithms are misinformation engines." She later called it "one of the most powerful radicalizing instruments of the twenty-first century." Danah Boyd, the founder of a tech-focused think tank, agreed, telling my colleague Amanda, "YouTube is perhaps the most troubling platform we have out there right now."

More and more, stories about strange, destabilizing occurrences — a rising hate group, a dangerous new medical rumor, a lonely kid turned shooter — were mentioning YouTube. I'd barely finished transcribing my notes from Germany when, a few weeks after my conversation with Farid, something happened there that made immediately clear why he'd issued his warning.

Nine

The Rabbit Hole

1. The YouTube Riot

NEO-NAZIS HAD HELD the streets of his town on and off for two days when Sören Uhle, a trim and bespectacled municipal official, began to get strange phone calls from reporters. As far as Uhle knew, two Middle Eastern refugees had stabbed a local man during an argument, killing him, which far-right groups had seized on to encourage people to flood into his city. Now, reporters were telling him, it turned out that the refugees had actually killed not one but two men. They had also been molesting a local woman; their victims had died trying to protect her. Could Uhle comment? And could he also explain why politicians were secretly paying locals to attend an upcoming counter-protest?

Uhle was dumbstruck. The revelations were all false. "This was new," he said. "It's never happened to me before that mainstream media, big German newspapers and television channels, ask me about false news and propaganda that had clearly become so pervasive that people just bought it." It was August 2018. The mobs that were swarming Chemnitz, his city of a quarter-million people in eastern Germany, had been organized on social media, he knew. Maybe the misinformation had been, too.

In Berlin, just up the autobahn, a digital researcher named Ray Serrato was arriving at the same conclusion. Like everyone in Germany, he'd been glued to reports from the riots — an out-of-nowhere show of neo-Nazi strength so dramatic that Chancellor Angela Merkel had condemned them. Then his wife's uncle showed him a strange YouTube video. Two middle-aged men, one in dreadlocks and a black beanie, told the camera that the rioters were not neo-Nazis at all, but Muslim refugees. The video, posted by an obscure fringe group, was rambling and cheaply produced. Yet it had nearly half a million views — far more than any news video on the riots. How was that possible?

Curious, Serrato applied a set of techniques he used in his day job, tracking online hate speech in Myanmar for a democracy-monitoring group. He started with a dozen recent videos on Chemnitz, then, on each, scraped YouTube's recommendations for what to watch next. Then he did the same for those videos, and so on. It revealed a network of about 650 videos: the YouTube-cultivated ecosystem of Chemnitz content. Disturbingly, YouTube's recommendations clustered tightly around a handful of conspiracy or far-right videos. This suggested that any user who entered the network of Chemnitz videos — say, by searching for news updates or watching a clip sent to them by a friend — would be pulled by YouTube's algorithm toward extremist content. Asked how many steps it would take, on average, for a YouTube viewer who pulled up a Chemnitz news clip to find themselves watching far-right propaganda, Serrato answered, "Only two." He added, "By the second, you're quite knee-deep in the alt right."

Recommendations rarely led users back to mainstream news coverage, or to liberal or apolitical content of any kind. Once among extremists, the algorithm tended to stay there, as if that had been the destination all along. It even led from Chemnitz videos to unrelated far-right topics — white nationalism, anti-Semitic conspiracies — much as Facebook had steered Renée DiResta from anti-vaccine pages to entirely separate fringe causes. One typical video called Trump a pawn of the Rothschild banking family. Though Serrano considered the videos abhorrent and dangerous, he admitted that something about them was hard to turn off. "That's YouTube's goal," he said. "I stay engaged, ads play. And it works."

This effect, I realized, working with Katrin Bennhold, Berlin bureau chief for the *New York Times*, had helped produce the chaos in Chemnitz. Shortly after the stabbing there, a handful of obscure, far-right YouTubers had posted videos about the incident. One, a blogger named Oliver Flesch, had only 20,000 subscribers. He did little outreach or promotion beyond his ideological bubble. Yet his videos on Chemnitz accrued hundreds of thousands of views, thanks to heavy promotion by YouTube's recommendation engine.

Serrato found that viewers who watched anything about Chemnitz on YouTube, like a news clip, were quickly recommended into Flesch's channel. Flesch posted fourteen videos on the topic, all of which showed up in YouTube's recommendations, seeding the platform with the very race-baiting falsehoods that Sören Uhle would later be asked about. Other far-right and conspiracy channels quickly picked up Flesch's version of events, turning an isolated street fight into a tale of imperiled white virtue. YouTube's algorithm boosted these, too.

Even Germans who searched Google for news on Chemnitz were directed to YouTube conspiracists. Google often promotes YouTube videos near the top of search results, an act of corporate synergy designed to boost revenue. This means that YouTube's practices don't stay on YouTube; since Google dominates internet searches, these practices influence how virtually anyone on the web finds and accesses news and information.

As YouTube and Google diverted more Germans to videos about Chemnitz rife with falsehoods, interest in the town grew, including among many outside the far right. The YouTube voices getting all this attention called on their rapidly growing followership to show their support for the stabbing victim by going to Chemnitz. Locals said that in the days before the violence, conspiracy theories grew strangely common, whispered at pubs and watercoolers. Then the crowds arrived, frothing to take back the city from foreigners. Soon they rioted, ransacking shops and brawling with police. Many of the rioters credited YouTube with putting them there.

It was Sri Lanka's meltdown, beat-for-beat, in the heart of Europe. But there was one important difference. Social media had, in Sri Lanka, radicalized a real-world social group with a strongly held identity, the Sinhalese. In Germany, however, Chemnitz's rioters were something new. There were certainly hardened neo-Nazis in the crowd, but many belonged to no distinct cause or group. YouTube, rather than activating a preexisting community with a preexisting identity, had created one out of nothing. It had built the network on its systems, pulled it together with a shared reality and beliefs, then willed it into the world, all in a matter of days. This was something much deeper than even the Facebook-inspired vigilante violence I'd seen in the country just a few months earlier.

If it had happened so easily in Chemnitz, was it happening elsewhere, too? Sure enough, a researcher who by coincidence hailed from Germany was just then demonstrating that this same process had been playing out for months across the United States, accelerating the rise of a terrifying new far right and inflecting it with the most extreme and dangerous tendencies of the social media platforms. He had begun investigating this phenomenon in 2015, following it through some of the largest political shocks of subsequent years until, over several months in 2018, he unveiled evidence of what had previously only been suspected: that YouTube was doing to American politics what it had done to Chemnitz, overrunning it with a wild-eyed right wing of its own algorithmic creation. But Chemnitz and other disruptions that year would turn out to be only a midpoint in his discoveries, presaging far deadlier and more grotesque events to come.

2. *Unite the Right*

JONAS KAISER PEERED down his first YouTube rabbit hole on a break between research sessions for a PhD that, at first, had little to do with American social media. He was studying climate-change skepticism in his native Germany, which was considered something of a mystery. Unlike in the U.S., Germany had no prominent political party or figure that was skeptical of climate change, so the existence of the doubters perplexed him. "It just seemed like this very odd community," he said. "I was interested in, like, how? Why?"

Graduate-student life can be grueling. Kaiser, who is lanky and bald-headed, resembling a pipe cleaner in glasses and V-necks, liked to relax with YouTube clips of competitive video gaming. Growing up in a remote village, he'd stayed connected with friends through online gaming, but his laptop at grad school wasn't equipped for it, so he did this instead. One day, he recalled, "Gamergate was everywhere," saturating YouTube's gaming channels. Until then he had never heard of *Breitbart* or Milo Yiannopoulos, he said. The platform began nudging him into other communities that had also picked up the cause of Gamergate: pro-atheism YouTubers, science YouTubers, alt-right YouTubers. "I distinctly noticed a shift, suddenly new communities forming their identity around that," he said, "around misogyny and misinformation." By routing users into and between these factions, the algorithm seemed to be binding them all together.

It was an aha moment for Kaiser, who saw a parallel with the German climate-change deniers. "It's all very small and it's splintered," he said of his country's climate-skeptic movement. "Really the only place where they could exchange their thoughts and coalesce and find allies was online." These groups didn't reflect real-world communities of any significant size, he realized. They were native to the web — and, as a result, shaped by the digital spaces that had nurtured them. Climate skeptics largely gathered in the comments sections of newspapers and blogs. There, disparate contrarians and conspiracists, people with no shared background beyond a desire to register their objection to climate coverage got clumped together. It created a sense of common purpose. And the placement of newspaper comments — right beneath the article — made them unusually visible, giving everyday news readers a false impression of their own popularity, bringing waves of recruits.

Could YouTube be doing something similar? Kaiser wondered. One of the networks that the platform had stitched into Gamergate was the alt right. The far right had been around for decades, he knew. But online it now seemed intertwined with social media circles that had little to do with politics, merging into something larger, something new. After finishing his PhD, Kaiser linked up with Adrian Rauchfleisch, a Swiss graduate student with similar interests and a flair for programming, who would become his longtime research partner. The pair repurposed the tools Kaiser had developed for tracking climate-change skepticism, now to understand Germany's ascendant far right.

But they suspected that any lessons would apply to the United States, too. It was summer 2016, with Donald Trump rising in polls. Kaiser recognized Trump's links to the Gamergate-aligned white nationalists he'd seen on YouTube, as well as the parallels to his own country's alt right. Though his and Rauchfleisch's initial dataset would be German, their concern increasingly focused on America.

They began with YouTube, where a number of the alt right's leading voices, both German and American, had gotten their start. Many described it as their digital base of operations. Yet it was the least studied of the major platforms, still mostly a black box. Kaiser and Rauchfleisch would map YouTube, charting how the platform's recommendations guided users. It would be what Serrato had done with Chemnitz videos but on a scale thousands of times larger — maybe millions.

They trained a computer to track YouTube's recommendations from a handful of well-known German channels, then the next and the next. They iterated over and over, looking for patterns in the system's choices. Because video recommendations can be messy — varying day to day as the algorithm learns, and person to person based on individual user profiles — the pair also tracked one of YouTube's few standardized recommendations: a list of "related channels" that the algorithm generated at the bottom of each channel. It provided another layer of information on the algorithm's thinking, helping Kaiser and Rauchfleisch separate pattern from noise. It was a bit of methodological housekeeping — a check to ensure they got rigorous results — that would later, as their findings provoked outrage in high levels of American government, become a source of conflict with YouTube itself.

The researchers expected to see results resembling a cloud: thousands of topic-spanning channels arranged only loosely. Instead, the network displayed as a neat series of clusters, arranged one next to the other, like a subway map. They were amazed. For YouTube's systems to analyze and sort billions of hours of video in real time, then direct billions of users through the network with this level of precision and consistency, was an incredible technological feat, demonstrating the algorithm's sophistication and power.

The politics videos were even more concentrated. The system had formed a supercluster — it looked like a storm system on a weather map — out of several communities that Kaiser and Rauchfleisch had expected to see separated. Alternative-news outlets, center-right commentary, far-right extremists, college-kid neo-racists, and tinfoil-hatted conspiracy theorists were all connected. With the goal of testing whether this supercluster affected users' behavior, the pair scraped every comment on the videos over a three-year period, two million in all, then tracked the commenters' activity (anonymized for privacy) across the site.

The results were as they'd feared. Users who started off commenting on only a subset of videos — say, center-right news channels — eventually began commenting on channels across the supercluster. "Over time, the network got denser and tighter," Kaiser said. As users were algorithmically circulated between mainstream-right commentators, oddball conspiracists, and basement racists, they began to treat the once-disparate pages as part of a unified community. *Their* community. YouTube, Kaiser said, had created a new "collective identity."

The project had taken them a year, into summer 2017. Trump's victory had elevated the stakes. If something similar was playing out in America, they knew, then this meant that the forces they'd identified in Germany now held sway over the most powerful nation on earth. It would make understanding that movement — its constituent parts and how they linked together — a matter of urgent importance. Before they got a chance, something that looked an awful lot like the digitally formed community they'd found in Germany surfaced in what was once the heart of the Confederacy.

In August 2017, several hundred protesters materialized in Charlottesville, Virginia, for what they outwardly called a rally against the city's plan to remove a statue of Confederate General Robert E. Lee. On the social media platforms where they organized, they named their gathering "Unite the Right." There was something unusual about their alliance. Fringe groups with until then little or no association had suddenly joined together. Followers arrived in previously unimaginable numbers, as if materializing out of the air. Many belonged to no group at all, freelancers along for the ride.

Their momentum became a show of force. Hundreds carried tiki torches, waving Nazi and Confederate flags as they chanted "Jews will not replace us." Wearing helmets and brandishing clubs, many of them skirmished with police. On the second day, shortly after the governor declared a state of emergency, one of the ralliers deliberately rammed his Dodge Challenger into a crowd of counter-protesters, wounding dozens and killing a thirty-two-year-old woman named Heather Heyer.

It was not difficult to understand how the far right had grown emboldened. Trump had used the presidency to champion the movement and many of its conspiracies and causes. Still, that did not explain how these groups had come together across such factional divides, recruited so widely, cohered so quickly. The rally and the group behind it had both been constituted, it turned out, on social media. But even the event, for all its terrible significance, hinted at something much broader, and ultimately more destabilizing, happening online.

The online alt right, still close to its Gamergate roots, centered on a teeming Reddit subsection called The_Donald. Though mostly governed by its own culture of troll provocation, it took cues from extremists like Andrew Anglin, the 4chan star turned neo-Nazi. Anglin had declared a "summer of hate," encouraging real-world rallies. As the drumbeat for a mega-gathering grew online, an activist named Richard Spencer began to organize one in Charlottesville. Spencer, who'd coined the term *alt right* as a friendly veneer for white nationalism to appeal to college kids, lived on social media, particularly as a regular guest on right-wing YouTube channels. He had once told a reporter, "We memed alt right into existence." As Spencer and Anglin pushed the rally, the moderators of Reddit's The_Donald endorsed the event and encouraged attendance.

But it was Facebook that grew the event from a Redditor meetup into a trans-extremist coming-out party, determined Megan Squire, an Elon University scholar of online extremism. In a study examining the platform's significance, she first identified 1,870 far-right Facebook groups and events. She found them by checking the profiles of known extremists, searching terms associated with the far right, and, of course, following Facebook's "suggested groups" algorithm, which fluidly routed her into a universe of hate. She scraped the membership roster for each group. Then she ran a network analysis, as Kaiser had with YouTube, to visualize it all. Each Facebook group was a node. The more members shared between any two groups, the closer together those two nodes.

On a more neutral social network, the result might've resolved as five or six distinct clusters — say, Confederacy revivalists, neo-Nazis, anti-government militias, alt-right meme circles — that kept to themselves in the off-line world. But on Facebook, just as on YouTube in Germany, the platform merged these otherwise disparate communities together, creating something entirely new. And at the very center: the event page for Unite the Right.

Jonas Kaiser, by now in America, having taken a junior faculty gig at Harvard, was aghast. "Coming from Germany, I was probably a little naïve," he said. At the far-right rallies in Germany, he said, "some Nazis go on the street and yell, and usually the counter-protesters far outweigh the Nazis." The white-nationalist rally in Charlottesville had been something much more seismic. "It upped the urgency," he said, for both him and Rauchfleisch.

They set out to apply the techniques they'd developed in Germany, this time to English-language YouTube. By now, they were learning how to identify much more than simple connections. They could map not just the network as a whole, as they had in Germany, but how the algorithm routed users within it, including which channels it treated as entry points and which as destinations. It was the difference between mapping a city and mapping its traffic.

By January 2018, Kaiser was mounting enough evidence to begin slowly going public. He told a Harvard seminar that the coalescing far right of which the Charlottesville gathering was a part was "not done by users," he was coming to believe, at least not entirely, but had been in part "created through the YouTube algorithm." He and Rauchfleisch, he knew, were on the verge of proving it. But neither could have anticipated what they would find along the way.

3. Crisis and Solution

IN THE DEEPEST corners of the far-right web, YouTube's influence was already a matter of accepted conventional wisdom. In March of 2018, a user on a prominent neo-Nazi forum opened a discussion thread under the title "WHAT BROUGHT YOU INTO THE MOVEMENT?" The forum, called the Right Stuff, had been growing throughout the 2010s, originating many of the visual trademarks of the alt right. Its founder, Mike Peinovich, is credited with the (((echo))), in which users put the names of suspected Jews in triple parentheses. The meme, started on the *Daily Shoah* podcast, mockingly named for the Hebrew word for the Holocaust, became omnipresent on Twitter and Facebook. On flyers advertising the Unite the Right rally, Peinovich's name, in a sign of his celebrity, was second after Richard Spencer's.

Dozens answered the thread soliciting their stories. Over and over, they described adopting their views incrementally, always on social media, often with algorithmic encouragement. "I used to be a part of the anti-SJW crowd," one user wrote, referring to "social justice warriors" frequently derided on 4chan and Reddit. He added, using the internet slang "based," an adjective for something transgressive, "And now I'm here. Thank you based Youtube suggested videos algorithm." Like many, YouTube's recommendations had led him, he said, first to arch-conservative voices. Then to white nationalists, then white supremacists, then supposedly ironic neo-Nazis, and, finally, to actual neo-Nazis.

Even Peinovich had taken a similar route. A New York–based web developer with moderate politics and a Jewish wife, he'd developed health problems in the late 2000s. Locked inside, he spent "hours in political-debate forums on Facebook and Reddit, where he let his contrarian side run wild," friends told *The New Yorker*. After time and algorithms did their work, he emerged a true, believing Nazi.

Another theme emerged from Right Stuff user stories. It was rarely hate that pulled people in. Rather, it was content that spoke to feelings of alienation, of purposelessness — the same anomie that had bonded Adam and other 4chan obsessives. "Watched a Millennial Woes video on depression (I was miserable)," one of the posters said, describing the first step on his journey. Millennial Woes, the YouTube handle for the Scottish white supremacist Colin Robertson, posted videos promising to reveal the true cause of young people's unhappiness: society, he said, was seeking to topple white men's natural place atop the social hierarchy. "He mentioned various things I had never heard of (neoreaction, Alt Right)," the Right Stuff poster continued. "I found Richard Spencer. I found TRS. Life completely changed."

One of the online alt right's most important gateways is the YouTube page of Jordan Peterson, a Canadian psychology professor. In 2013, Peterson began posting videos addressing, amid esoteric Jungian philosophy, youth male distress. He offered life advice (clean your room, sit up straight) amid exhortations against racial and gender equality as imperiling "the masculine spirit."

YouTube searches for "depression" or certain self-help keywords often led to Peterson. His videos' unusual length, sixty minutes or more, align with the algorithm's drive to maximize watch time. So does his college-syllabus method of serializing his argument over weeks, which requires returning for the next lecture and the next. But most of all, Peterson appeals to what the sociologist Michael Kimmel calls "aggrieved entitlement." For generations, white men expected and received preferential treatment and special status. As society inched toward equality, those perks, while still substantial, declined. Some white men acclimated. Some rebelled. Others knew only that they felt something being taken away. Peterson et al. give them a way to explain those feelings of injustice — feminists and leftists are destroying the masculine spirit — and an easy set of answers. Clean your room. Sit up straight. Reassert traditional hierarchies.

"People in these communities are often drowning in despair and susceptible to corruption by charismatic, lucid evil offering them what seems like the only lifeline," a former adherent tweeted. YouTube's algorithm, in many cases, tapped into that discontent, recommending channels that took Peterson's message to greater and greater extremes. "The common railroad stages," the user wrote, were "Jordan Peterson — > Stefan Molyneux — > Millennial Woes." (Molyneux, a white supremacist who presents himself as a therapist and "just asking questions" philosopher, had toiled in obscurity until joining YouTube. By the time that public pressure compelled the company to remove his page in June 2020, he had more than 900,000 subscribers and reached many more through automated recommendations.) It was exactly the sort of algorithmic pathway that Kaiser was mapping in his lab, the same one he discovered YouTube charting over and over.

Data suggest this promotional sequence is converting users at scale. Users who comment on Peterson's videos subsequently become twice as likely to pop up in the comments of extreme-right YouTube channels, a Princeton study found. Peterson himself doesn't recommend the channels — the algorithm makes the connection. This was the other essential piece to the puzzle that Kaiser and Rauchfleisch were working to solve. They were measuring how YouTube moved its users. But their network maps could not tell them why the system made the choices that it did. It took psychologists and extremism researchers to reveal the answer.

The social platforms had arrived, however unintentionally, at a recruitment strategy embraced by generations of extremists. The scholar J. M.

Berger calls it "the crisis-solution construct." When people feel destabilized, they often reach for a strong group identity to regain a sense of control. It can be as broad as nationality or narrow as a church group. Identities that promise to recontextualize individual hardships into a wider conflict hold special appeal. You're not unhappy because of your struggle to contend with personal circumstances; you're unhappy because of Them and their persecution of Us. It makes those hardships feel comprehensible and, because you're no longer facing them alone, a lot less scary.

Crisis-solution: there is a crisis, the out-group is responsible, your in-group offers the solution. If that sense of conflict escalates too far, it can reach the point of radicalization, in which you see the out-group as an immutable threat over which only total victory is acceptable. "The scale of the crisis becomes more extreme, and the prescribed solution becomes more violent," Berger wrote, until destroying the out-group becomes the core of the in-group's shared identity. "The current generation of social media platforms," he added, "accelerates polarization and extremism for a significant minority," enabling and encouraging exactly this cycle.

The body count was already mounting. In 2014, in a town near Santa Barbara, a twenty-two-year-old college dropout named Elliot Rodger stabbed three people to death in his apartment building, then posted a YouTube video announcing his "revenge against humanity" for being "forced to endure an existence of loneliness, rejection, and unfulfilled desires all because girls have never been attracted to me." Rodger then drove to a sorority house, knocked, and shot three women, killing two of them. He got back in his car and cruised the streets, shooting at pedestrians and driving into others, many of them women, before killing himself.

Lonely yes, but no loner: For months, he'd stewed on web forums, then on YouTube, where his videos grew so hateful that his own parents had once called the police. He was the product of a digital community, spanning 4chan, Reddit, and YouTube, whose members call themselves "incels" for their involuntary celibacy.

Incel forums had begun as places to share stories about feeling lonely.

Users discussed how to cope with living "hugless." But the norms of social media one-upmanship, of attention chasing, still prevailed. The loudest voices rose. Views became more extreme. The prevailing outrage on the platforms reinterpreted individual travails as a tribal struggle of Us and Them. Incels there took on a radicalizing core belief: Feminists are conspiring to subjugate and emasculate our underclass of low-status men. In-group and out-group. Crisis and solution.

By 2021, fifty killings had been claimed by self-described incels, a wave of terrorist violence. A small-time YouTuber shot four women to death in a Florida yoga studio. A Reddit superuser drove a van through a crowd of pedestrians in Toronto. A 4chan incel posted live as he murdered a seventeen-year-old girl, to cheers from fellow users, then tried to kill himself. Rodger remains widely lionized as a hero among incels.

The movement was a fringe of a fringe, dwarfed by Pizzagate or the alt right. But it hinted at social media's potential to galvanize young white male anomie into whole communities of extremism — an increasingly widespread phenomenon. When a far-right paramilitary group called the Oath Keepers surveyed its 25,000 members on how they'd come to the movement, their most common answer was Facebook, followed by YouTube.

YouTube can be an especially effective indoctrinator because it moves users in increments. Jordan Peterson tells viewers that their individual travails stem from a conflict pitting them against social justice warriors — crisis. Millennial Woes rallies them to collectively defend themselves against the feminists and minorities opposing them — resolution. More extreme channels escalate the stakes of that war to white genocide or Jewish subjugation, implicitly encouraging viewers to take on the threat however necessary.

YouTube hardly does this in every case. Jordan Peterson viewers will also be routed to, say, pop academics or self-helpers. But platforms often privilege radicalizing connections for a reason: it works. Extremists like the crisis-solution sequence because it primes people to action. Algorithms like it because it engages people's attention and passion, turning web browsing into a matter of identity, community, even fanaticism — and therefore more watch time.

YouTube upgraded its algorithms over 2016 and 2017, adding a system it called Reinforce, which recommended users into unfamiliar subgenres. Even if you never searched out Peterson-style alt-right gateway videos, you might get nudged into one anyway, just to see if it took. Stories of YouTube radicalization were suddenly everywhere, their details repeating with machinelike consistency. "One of my closest friends was radicalized by YouTube," Chris Sacca, a Silicon Valley investor and Google alum, tweeted. "It started a few years ago with 'thought-provoking' and 'contrarian' vids. But, thanks to the suggested videos algo, got darker and more violent, he lost his wife, kids, and friends, and none of us know where he is today."

David Sherratt, a former extremist, told the *Daily Beast* that his descent had started, at age fifteen, watching video game clips. The system recommended him into pro-atheism videos, which tell science-and-math kids they are part of an ultrarational minority besieged by social justice warriors. Then anti-feminism videos, then incel-aligned "men's rights" videos, some of which he contributed himself, then outright neo-Nazi videos.

In 2018, an outlet called Bellingcat scoured an archive of private far-right chat rooms that totaled hundreds of thousands of messages. The investigators scanned for instances where users had mentioned how they'd arrived at the cause. The single most common entry point they cited: YouTube. They would start with banal videos, many said, then be recommended into channels that were more and more extreme. It was the same story everyone else was telling.

"YouTube's algorithms bounced me along a path of similarly unapologetic thought criminals," Meghan Daum, a novelist, wrote of her drift into an alt-right stepping-stone movement, primarily YouTube-based, that calls itself the intellectual dark web. Jordan Peterson is a leading member. As the platform pushed her from videos questioning feminism to videos suggesting women's brains are wired for housework, from calling Black people racist to rejecting racial pluralism itself, watching YouTube became "what I did now instead of watching television (and, very often, reading books, listening to music, or cleaning my apartment)." It was more than entertainment. These channels were her "YouTube friends," salve for a lost marriage and feelings of isolation. They were community. They were identity.

She had fallen into what is known as the rabbit hole. The term had once described any evening or afternoon spent following YouTube's recommendations wherever they led. Maybe you pulled up a favorite comedy clip, then leaned back as the system took you through the comedian's hits. But by 2018, after the Reinforce system had been implemented, "rabbit hole" increasingly referred to following political YouTube channels toward extremism. Users tumbled down these holes whether they'd looked for politics videos or not, often taken to places they hadn't sought to go — places even more disturbing than the far right.

4. The Alex Jones Problem

THROUGHOUT THE SPRING of 2018, Kaiser and Rauchfleisch ran automated test runs through YouTube's recommendations, mapping how it interlinked the channels, what communities it constructed. Finally, in April, they assembled their results. YouTube's system, they found, did three things uncannily well.

First, it stitched together wholly original clusters of channels. One such cluster intermixed doctors dispensing medical advice, yoga teachers espousing thoughts on chakra alignment, hucksters selling magical cure-alls, and anti-vaccine radicals. A user who started on any one of those subjects would be circulated through the others. There was nothing innate connecting these beyond the A.I.'s conclusion that showing them alongside one another would keep users watching. Though their next two discoveries would win the most attention, Kaiser consistently hammered at the importance of the first. YouTube is, like Facebook or Twitter, primarily a social experience. Users comment, like, and share, all of them participants in a communal activity. Video-makers are encouraged to address followers on camera, solicit requests and feedback, jump into the comments themselves. So when YouTube clustered a few thousand (or a few million) users into a few dozen (or a few hundred) channels, it became a genuine community. It became, just as Meghan Daum had described with such gratitude, an identity.

It was what made his other findings so important, the second of which was that, as had long been suspected, YouTube's recommendations generally moved toward the more extreme end of whatever network the user was in. Watch a CNN or Fox News clip and the odds of getting recommended into a conspiracy video were high enough that, over time, that was the direction the average user tended to flow.

And then the third discovery. In an even more dangerous version of what they'd seen in Germany, the system's recommendations were clustering mainstream right-wing channels, and even some news channels, with many of the platform's most virulent hatemongers, incels, and conspiracy theorists. As the algorithm pulled users toward those extreme voices, it granted them outsized influence over the narratives, political agendas, and values for the larger whole.

This was more than just expanding the reach of the far right. It was uniting a wider community around them. And at a scale — millions of people — the Charlottesville organizers could only have dreamed of. Here, finally, was an answer for why there had been so many stories of people falling into far-right rabbit holes. Someone who came to YouTube with interest in right-wing-friendly topics, like guns or political correctness, would be routed into a YouTube-constructed world of white nationalism, violent misogyny, and crazed conspiracism, then pulled further toward its extremes.

One channel sat conspicuously in the network's center, a black hole toward which YouTube's algorithmic gravity pulled: Alex Jones. An FM shock jock since the 1990s, Jones had long cultivated an audience of cranks, overnight truckers, and the simply bored. Animated and gravelly-voiced, he spun out conspiracies crafted not so much to persuade listeners as to hold their attention: the government did the Oklahoma City bombing; the government dumped chemicals in the water supply to turn people gay. He staged attention-grabbing stunts, shouting down a speech by then-governor George W. Bush to demand he abolish the Federal Reserve. He sold bogus health supplements and survivalist gear, making a fortune. Then he hit YouTube and became, quite suddenly, influential. His claims trickled onto Fox News and right-wing blogs. His name was invoked at conservative rallies, grassroots functions, even among Washington power-brokers, if only in acknowledgment of his new sway.

How had it happened? Americans had surely tilted in Jones's direction. And he had used the internet to circumvent media gatekeepers who kept him mostly off TV. But Kaiser had evidence of another factor. YouTube's algorithm, his data suggested, recommended Jones's videos more frequently than those of almost any other news- or politics-related channel. It promoted him especially aggressively alongside right-wing videos, insinuating him into the cause. Often it used his videos as a gateway to extremism: a user who watched mostly conspiracies might get shown an Alex Jones rant as an entry point to white-nationalist content, or vice versa.

In April 2018, just weeks after the violence in Sri Lanka had called attention to Facebook's own power for harm, Kaiser published his findings on YouTube's systematic creation of far-right networks, alongside a *BuzzFeed News* article publicizing the research, in an essay explaining that YouTube "pushes many channels towards the gravitational center of a larger right-wing bubble." He and Rauchfleisch warned, "Being a conservative on You-Tube means that you're only one or two clicks away from extreme far-right channels, conspiracy theories, and radicalizing content." Here, finally, was evidence that YouTube had become a force for large-scale radicalization.

Others soon confirmed the "radicalization pipeline," as the Brazilian researcher Manoel Horta Ribeiro called it. His team, analyzing 72 million comments across 330,000 videos, found that "users consistently migrate from milder to more extreme content." Right-wing users, a huge population, moved from "intellectual dark web" contrarians like Jordan Peterson to alt-right voices like Milo Yiannopoulos to hate leaders like the neo-Nazis Andrew Anglin and Mike Peinovich. And the users moved in parallel with YouTube's recommendations, further evidence that it was the algorithm that drove them.

That spring, after a school shooting, YouTube's high-profile "trending" page began promoting an Alex Jones video claiming that the violence had been faked. Jones had pushed versions of this since the 2012 Sandy Hook shooting, when he called the murdered twenty children and six teachers "crisis actors" in a vague government plot to justify confiscating guns or imposing martial law. The conspiracy had spread on YouTube ever since, consumed by growing numbers of viewers who, enraged, organized years-long harassment campaigns against the families of the murdered children. Some parents went into hiding, and several filed three separate lawsuits against Jones for defamation. (In 2021, Jones lost all three.) All the while, YouTube continued promoting the videos, which by 2018 had a combined 50 million views. When YouTube's system posted Jones's latest on its trending page, then, it was an unusually visible indicator of how eagerly the site's algorithms boosted him.

Members of YouTube's policy team recommended tweaking the trending-page algorithm to prevent it from linking to Jones or other discredited sources. They were overruled. Although Jones was most prominent on YouTube, where he had billions of views, he reached millions of followers on Facebook and Twitter as well, and these companies also came under pressure to revoke the digital bullhorns they'd made for him.

The parents of Noah Pozner, a six-year-old boy killed at Sandy Hook, published an open letter to Mark Zuckerberg. They were living in hiding, they wrote, tormented by years of harassment and death threats, traceable to prominent conspiracy groups on Facebook. Sandy Hook parents, they said, had waged "an almost inconceivable battle with Facebook to provide us with the most basic of protections" against the incitement emanating from the platform. "Our families are in danger," they wrote, "as a direct result of the hundreds of thousands of people who see and believe the lies and hate speech, which you have decided should be protected."

But the companies dug in. When asked why Facebook wouldn't remove Alex Jones, the company's vice president for the news feed, John Hegeman, said, "We created Facebook to be a place where different people can have a voice." Zuckerberg, facing the same question, riffed on the nature of free speech: "I'm Jewish, and there's a set of people who deny that the Holocaust happened. I find that deeply offensive. But at the end of the day, I don't believe that our platform should take that down, because I think there are things that different people get wrong. I don't think that they're intentionally getting it wrong."

It was vintage Silicon Valley. If Zuckerberg was willing to sacrifice historical consensus on the attempted extermination of his forebears for the sake of a techno-libertarian free-speech ideal, then so should everybody else. And, like many of the Valley's leaders, he seemed still to be living in an alternate universe where platforms are neutral vessels with no role in shaping users' experiences, where the only real-world consequence is that somebody might get offended, and where society would appreciate the wisdom of allowing Holocaust-denial to flourish.

This was the Alex Jones problem: Silicon Valley could not bring itself to act in the public interest, even seemingly its own interest, by excising a problem that embodied, even personified, their industry's beliefs, written into the systems that had, after all, elevated Jones into what he was. Engagement equals value. More connection builds understanding. Free speech beats bad speech. Acting would mean acknowledging those ideals were flawed, dangerous. Pull at that thread, and everything might unravel.

Backlash worsened. That July, Facebook suspended Jones for a month, a sop to critics. Finally, in August, Apple pulled several of Jones's shows from its podcast service. Facebook and YouTube followed suit within hours, banning him. Only Twitter held defiant. "We're going to hold Jones to the same standard we hold to every account, not taking one-off actions to make us feel good in the short term," Jack Dorsey, Twitter's CEO, tweeted. But Twitter eventually removed Jones as well. Though the companies had given in to public pressure, however, they did not seem to accept that the public was right. Zuckerberg later told *The New Yorker*, "I don't believe that it is the right thing to ban a person for saying something that is factually incorrect."

At Twitter, Dorsey, for all his defiance, was shifting toward the sorts of deeper changes, to the platform's core nature, that the Valley had long resisted. Or, at least, he seemed to be. Twitter's market capitalization remained below its peak, in April 2015, from before Dorsey had returned to take over, and its userbase had barely grown in the past year. But instead of turbocharging its algorithms or retooling the platform to surface argument and emotion, as YouTube and Facebook had done amid stalling metrics, Dorsey announced that the entire conceit behind social media was toxic.

"We didn't fully predict or understand the real-world negative consequences" of launching an "instant, public, global" platform, he wrote that March. He conceded that it had resulted in real harms. He began, in interviews, voluntarily raising heretical ideas that other tech CEOs continued to fervently reject: maximizing for engagement is dangerous; likes and retweets encourage polarization. The company, he said, would reengineer its systems to promote "healthy" conversations rather than engaging ones. He hired prominent experts and research groups to develop new features or design elements to do it.

But virtually none of these efforts ever got off the ground. The outsider experts, facing months-long delays or abrupt policy changes, largely quit in frustration. It was unclear whether Dorsey's experiment in reimagining Twitter had fallen through because his attention drifted, because increasingly rebellious investors pressured Twitter to boost growth instead, or because the solutions proved unpalatable to a company still locked in the Silicon Valley mindset. Accounts from Twitter employees suggest it was likely a combination of all three.

At YouTube, meanwhile, it was otherwise business as usual. The platform's systems continued engineering high-engagement fringe communities. That year, Asheley Landrum, a cognitive psychologist, discovered one in Denver, at a conference for people who believed Earth was flat. Flat Eartherism, extinguished for centuries, was suddenly resurging. Science teachers reported students challenging them with curvature calculations and marked-up diagrams. An NBA star came out as a Flat Earther. So did a prominent rapper. Landrum wandered the Denver conference hoping to understand why this was happening. The results were not ambiguous. Of the thirty attendees interviewed, twenty-nine said they had been exposed to and convinced of Flat Eartherism on YouTube. The thirtieth had been recruited by his daughter, who'd found it on YouTube.

Guillaume Chaslot, the former YouTuber, had noticed the videos rising on the platform as far back as when he'd worked at the company, and had warned internally that it indicated something dangerous. Like a medical dye used to highlight an infection, its presence typically indicates a social media platform promoting extremist beliefs of all sorts, some of them dangerous. "They told me, 'People click on Flat Earth videos, so they want a Flat Earth video,'" he recalled. "And my point was, no, it's not that because someone clicked on the Flat Earth video, he wants to be lied to. He is just curious, and there is a clickbait title. But to the algorithm, when you watch a video, it means you endorse it."

Flat Earther videos with provocative thumbnails and titles had long appeared in the platform's recommendation slots: "200 Proofs Earth Is Not a Spinning Ball," "Flat Earth Clues," "The International Space Station Does Not Exist!" People clicked out of curiosity. The algorithm didn't care why people watched, only that they had. When they did, it recommended the videos more and more.

YouTube, by showing users many videos in a row all echoing the same thing, hammers especially hard at two of our cognitive weak points — that repeated exposure to a claim, as well as the impression that the claim is widely accepted, each make it feel truer than we would otherwise judge it to be. Most viewers, of course, probably reject conspiracy videos. But at a scale of billions, those methods overcome enough defenses among the susceptible to win thousands of converts to even the most ridiculous cause. Or the most dangerous.

5. A Great Awakening

IN OCTOBER 2017, two months after the Unite the Right rally in Charlottesville, a short post appeared on 4chan's politics board under the username Q Clearance Patriot. The user implied they were a military-intelligence official within an operation to arrest the participants in Pizzagate, the conspiracy alleging that Democratic leaders ran a global child-trafficking ring. The user, who claimed to hold a Q-level government clearance, announced that Hillary Clinton's extradition was already "in motion" and that the National Guard had been mobilized to counter "massive riots organized in defiance." But it was their second post that established the style for which Q would be known:

Mockingbird
HRC detained, not arrested (yet).
Where is Huma? Follow Huma.
This has nothing to do w/ Russia (yet).

The post went on for twenty more lines. References just cryptic enough that users could feel like they were cracking a secret code, and obvious enough to ensure that they would. Like the opening page of a spy novel, it laid the basics of a plot that would remain consistent through thousands of "Q drops," as fans called the posts. Trump and his generals were preparing to arrest thousands of Democratic conspirators and impose military rule in a day of bloody, glorious reckoning.

Over the coming months, the story escalated. Tens or hundreds of thousands would be arrested: cultural elites, financiers, "deep state" bureaucrats and spies. For generations, this cabal had secretly controlled American life, responsible for travails from Pizzagate to the unfairness of the economic order. Now they would be executed, the National Mall converted into a death camp. Some had already been replaced with body doubles, a quiet first strike in Trump's plan.

Followers got more than a story. QAnon, as the movement called itself, became a series of online communities where believers gathered to parse Q's posts. They looked for clues and hidden meanings in the drops and, at Q's urging, in the ephemera of daily politics. Was Trump's offhand comment about Congress a coded reference to the coming purge? His oddly placed hand a signal to the 101st Airborne? It was a never-ending game, a socially bonding group activity that mapped onto everyday life.

Extremist groups have long recruited on a promise to fulfill adherents' need for purpose and belonging. Hate is sometimes merely the glue that bonds. "Social camaraderie," the sociologist Kathleen Blee has written, "can coexist with, even substitute for, hatred as the reason for participation in organized racist activities." Conspiracies, meanwhile, promise resolution for feelings of powerlessness amid a chaotic, incomprehensible world. Maybe market forces had taken away your job. A sudden illness or disaster had upended your life. Social change had undermined your sense of society's rightful order. (Many QAnons were well-off but had been sent into disorienting panics by, say, the election of a Black president or an uptick in diversity.) Conspiracies insist that events, rather than uncontrollable or impersonal, are all part of a hidden plot whose secrets you can unlock. Reframing chaos as order, telling believers they alone hold the truth, restores their sense of autonomy and control. It's why QAnon adherents often repeat to one another their soothing mantra: "Trust the plan."

Extremism researchers would long speculate that many or all of Q's posts — four thousand in all, unspooled over three years — were actually the work of Ron Watkins, a thirty-year-old programmer who had recently taken over running 8chan, the 4chan spinoff forum. Watkins even seemed to hint as much in a 2021 documentary, telling his interviewer, "It was basically three years of intelligence training, teaching normies how to do intelligence work," though he added, "But never as Q." Followers largely ignored evidence of Q's pedestrian identity, though, or perhaps, on some level, didn't want to know. The draw was in what his story offered, not in its authorship or objective truth. Even many researchers who tracked QAnon considered Q's identity something of a footnote. For all of Q's string-pulling manipulation, it was the users, the platforms, and the inter-linking tendencies of both that drove the movement.

QAnon, like so much technoculture before it, flowed quickly from fringe to mainstream platforms. Facebook and YouTube's systems slid QAnon into the slipstream of conspiracy and extremist recommendations. At first, it was just another node. But its ever-escalating claims and totaliz-ing story allowed it to absorb other conspiracies, making it a focal point — much as Alex Jones had once been — of disparate communities, from anti-vaxxers to race-war preppers to anti-government paranoiacs. Its vehe-mently pro-Trump politics and open calls for violence made it a natural partner, and ultimately a fixture, of the online right. Most of all, it was endlessly time-consuming, the primary trait for which the platforms maximized.

By the time Americans realized that this was something dangerous, QAnon Facebook groups held millions of members, QAnon YouTube vid-eos won millions of views, and QAnon Twitter accounts organized mass-harassment campaigns targeting celebrities they accused of bizarre, cannibalistic plots. An app that aggregated Q drops became one of the most popular downloads on the App Store. A book, *QAnon: An Invitation to a Great Awakening*, written by a collective of anonymous followers, reached #2 on Amazon's bestseller list. Members spent their lives immersed in the community, clocking hours per day in the video chats and comment threads that had become their world.

In May 2018, a QAnon YouTuber stormed an Arizona cement factory that he said was the center of a child-trafficking ring, streaming his confrontation to hundreds of thousands of Facebook viewers. The next month, another adherent, carrying an AR-15 rifle, blocked both lanes of traffic across the Hoover Dam with a homemade armored truck, demanding that the government release a report Q had named in the previous day's message. Another was arrested in Illinois with bomb materials he'd intended to detonate in the state capitol building, targeting child-molesting Satanists he believed had taken over. Still another drove to the home of a Staten Island mob boss, whom he believed Q had marked as a deep-state conspirator, and shot him to death. The FBI, in an internal memo, identified QAnon as a potential domestic-terror threat. Yet Facebook, YouTube, and Twitter, as with Alex Jones, largely declined to act, allowing the movement, boosted by the biases of their platforms, to continue growing.

Virtually the entire online far right seemed to be pulled in. So were many law-enforcement officers, drawn to its promises of strong-fisted order and retribution against liberals. The head of the NYPD union gave TV interviews with his QAnon mug in frame. Vice President Mike Pence was photographed alongside a Florida SWAT team officer wearing a Q badge. The movement migrated to Instagram, which promoted QAnon heavily enough that many of the yoga moms and lifestyle influencers who dominate the platform got swept up.

But for all the feelings of autonomy, security, and community that QAnon offered, it came at a cost: crushing isolation. "Gonna be honest patriots," a popular QAnoner wrote in a tweet widely shared within the movement. "When I first started getting into Q and the patriots and the movement, I felt so alone because most people I know, even if conservative, find all this to be a conspiracy theory. Only here with all you have I felt at home and welcome!" Dozens responded with similar stories. "I'm in the same boat. Literally no friends or family to talk to. I thank god my wife and I followed the rabbit together cause we are all each other have. My own step family dropped me like I was nothing after my father died. So I'm thankful for all in this boat with me." It was one of the things that made QAnon so radicalizing. Joining often worsened the very sense of isolation and being adrift that had led people to it in the first place. With nowhere else to turn and now doubly needful of reassurance, followers gave themselves over to the cause even more fully.

In 2019, one of Facebook's researchers set up a series of test accounts simulating the median experience of certain user archetypes. One was "Carol Smith," a fictitious North Carolina mom. The researcher had Carol join pages on parenting, Christianity, and conservative politics, then waited to see where Facebook took her. Within two days, the platform pushed her into QAnon. Over five more, it routed her, the researcher wrote in an internal report, through "a barrage of extreme, conspiratorial, and graphic content."

A separate report, also internal, found that half of Facebook's QAnon population, numbering at least 2.2 million, had joined, as on YouTube, through "gateway groups." It was confirmation of Renée DiResta's warnings, ever since her first anti-vaccine discovery years earlier, that the feature was a vehicle for radicalization. "I can't emphasize enough what a disaster Groups are," she tweeted in 2018, as evidence mounted. "The Groups recommendation engine is a conspiracy correlation matrix. It pushes people prone to extremist & polarizing content into closed and then secret groups. FB has no idea what it's built here."

But Facebook only deepened its commitment to the feature that its own research had demonstrated was driving much of QAnon's growth. It said that 100 million users, which it hoped to grow to 1 billion, were active in groups that had become where they spent the bulk of their time. Even some of Facebook's own, however, were sounding alarms. Another internal report, later leaked to the *Wall Street Journal*, cautioned, "Seventy percent of the top 100 most active US Civic Groups are considered non-recommendable for issues such as hate, misinfo, bullying and harassment."

An engineer who'd worked on the feature warned a reporter for *The Verge* that it was "where the bubble generation begins." The practice of pushing users into groups that were picked to win attention, the engineer added, had become "really dangerous."

6. Digital Nihilism

IN HIS FRESHMAN year of college, Adam, the lifelong 4chan user from Dallas, shifted allegiance to 8chan. It was 2014, with QAnon and so much else still to come, but 8chan's pledge to welcome Gamergaters, banned even from 4chan, had branded it as the last true home of free speech. Its no-holds-barred discussions and extreme content had won it a reputation as the pirate bar of the social web, filled with content unviewable elsewhere. "I saw so much shit," Adam told me. "Cartel beheadings, awful porn that shouldn't exist, I don't even want to get into specifics. But we see it a hundred times and then real-life issues start to feel less impactful."

It was 4chan-style boundary pushing without even 4chan's norms or rules. 8channers went to new extremes as a collective defense against the anomie that, as the rejects of the rejects, the misfits of the misfits, they centered in their common identity. "Their theory about what they were doing on there, what they were getting out of it, was that they were learning not to be triggered by people pushing their emotional or ideological buttons," Dominic Fox, a software engineer, wrote of the chans. "The real world was a harsh and uncaring place, and anyone who pretended to care, or to need caring for, was by definition engaged in deception, a kind of swindle." Therefore, according to Fox, in their thinking, "the only way to be free of such control was to gaze at racist memes, car crash photos, horrifying pornography, and so on until one could do so with complete serenity." It was, he wrote, a culture of "deliberate self-desensitization."

In time, much as 4chan's transgressiveness became an in-group shibboleth, so did desensitization on 8chan. Tolerating things too shocking or unbearable for outsiders was a way to prove you belonged. You, too, had been numbed and beaten down, your eyes were open, you were a soldier in a brotherhood of emptiness. On harder-edged sections, users who found comfort and community in this practice sought out ever greater taboos until they arrived, perhaps inevitably, at the most extreme of them all: mass murder.

Users developed elaborate memes and in-jokes around praising, and sharing graphic imagery from, the Holocaust, mass shootings, and especially, for its tangibility from the recent past, the 1995 genocide of Bosnian Muslims. The attraction to celebrating a genocide or mass shooter was, on some level, that others wouldn't. It proved you were a true 8channer: based and red-pilled, committed to one another whatever the reputational cost, having ascended above the petty demands of an off-line world that, in truth, terrified you. The prevailing culture wasn't far-right per se, though the language of Nazism and racial genocide was everywhere. Rather, the culmination of years of line crossing and provocation, of ironic hate that became sincere, was a kind of violent nihilism. Users urged one another, joking but not, to make the world pay, to hurt Them on behalf of Us. To kill indiscriminately.

It was easy to dismiss, unless you had been paying attention. On one social network after another, communities of anomie and crisis — Reddit incels, Facebook Q groups, the YouTube far right — had escalated to the point of action. If only a tiny minority carried the threats out, then this was always how violent extremism had worked. There was no reason to think 8chan would not do the same.

In March of 2019, as afternoon prayer service began at a single-story mosque in a leafy suburb of Christchurch, New Zealand, an unfamiliar man marched up the driveway. He carried a shotgun and had a smartphone affixed to his chest. He approached four men chatting in the entryway. One greeted him, "Hello, brother." He raised the shotgun and fired several times, killing them.

He entered the mosque's narrow, low-ceiling hallways, where nearly two hundred worshippers had gathered, and immediately began shooting.

He fired at one congregant after another, cornering them against a back wall. He dropped the shotgun, its ammunition spent. He lifted an AR-15 rifle, a strobe light flashing from its muzzle, shooting methodically as families cowered or tried to flee. Naeem Rashid, a fifty-year-old teacher and father of three, rushed the strange man, who shot him to death. The gunman never spoke. Instead, a portable speaker attached to his chest blared nationalist anthems. He circled through the mosque, shooting all he encountered, then returned to the main prayer hall, where he fired again into the bodies of victims already dead or dying. By the time he walked back out the entryway, only five minutes after arriving, he had murdered forty-three people. The oldest was seventy-seven, the youngest only three. On the footpath toward his car, he stopped at a woman lying on the ground, bleeding badly but alive. He leaned over her. At that moment, two hundred people watched live on Facebook, streaming point-of-view from the smartphone on his chest, as he listened to her plead for her life, then killed her.

He drove, veering across traffic lanes at ninety-plus miles per hour, firing out his car window, to another suburban mosque, where he murdered seven more people. Abdul Aziz Wahabzada, a forty-eight-year-old immigrant from Afghanistan, interrupted his attack, hurling a credit card machine at him, then diving behind a car. While the gunman rearmed, Wahabzada rushed forward, picked up an emptied shotgun the gunman had dropped, and pointed it at him. Harried, the shooter drove off as Wahabzada speared the shotgun at his car's rear window, shattering it. On the shooter's way to a third mosque, a pair of rural police, visiting town for a training session, rammed his car into the curb and arrested him.

Within hours, it became clear that the killer, a twenty-eight-year-old Australian named Brenton Tarrant, represented a new kind of violent extremism, the all-darkness of the deep social web made manifest. "Well lads, it's time to stop shitposting and time to make a real life effort post," he'd written on 8chan's politics forum hours before the attack. He linked his Facebook Live, encouraging users to watch his "attack against the invaders." And he attached a seventy-page text file explaining himself, which he also tweeted. "You are all top blokes and the best bunch of cobbers a man could ask for," he wrote. "Please do your part by spreading my message, making memes and shitposting as you usually do."

The users who followed him live, the 4,000 who watched his video before Facebook removed it, and countless more who saw millions of re-uploads across the web, would have heard him say, moments before he began killing, "Remember, lads, subscribe to PewDiePie." It was, in a hint of Tarrant's twisted motives, a social media in-joke. Fans of PewDiePie, the most popular gamer on YouTuber, with more than 100 million subscribers to his channel, had recently plastered the web — and, in one prank, jammed up office fax machines — with that same phrase. The YouTuber had also been the subject of (largely misguided) accusations of flirting with white nationalism. Tarrant's reference was meant as a troll of the media, daring them to pin his violence on PewDiePie, and a wink to fellow internet trolls who would be in on the joke.

Terrorism is violence intended to menace a wider community for the sake of political ends or simple malice. But it is also typically a performance for, and an act of solidarity with, an in-group. It was why Islamic State recruits, especially internet-radicalized "lone wolves" who never met another member face-to-face, flooded jihadist forums with manifestos and videotaped martyrdom messages that would make sense only to fellow believers.

It was also why Tarrant's final written words mostly expressed affection for the community that, he made clear, he was doing this for. In his document, Tarrant wrote that he had learned "ethno-nationalism" from *Spyro: Year of the Dragon*, a children's video game. He thanked Candace Owens, a popular alt-right YouTuber, for teaching him to embrace violence. He bragged in one paragraph, "I am trained in gorilla warfare and I'm the top sniper in the entire US armed forces." All were social web in-jokes.

But for every joke or troll were pages of seemingly sincere invocations of far-right conspiracies, Nazi slogans, and calls for a global race war to expel and extinguish non-Christians and non-whites. Above all, Tarrant surrounded his violence with in-jokes that had become, for his community, deadly sincere, embodiments of their drift from ironic extremism to extremism that was merely irony-cloaked.

During his livestream, as he drove, he played a song from a grainy 1992 video of a Serbian ultranationalist singing in praise of Radovan Karadžić, a war criminal responsible for the Bosnian genocide. The video had long been a 4chan meme, called "remove kebab," that, for some, went from joke to genuine signal of support for genocide of Muslims. Tarrant had also written "remove kebab" on the side of one of his rifles.

On 8chan, users, watching live, were rapturous.

HAHAHA HE PLAYED REMOVE KEBAB EN ROUTE! I'M DYIN' OVER HERE!

Holy lfuck. OP fucking delivered I just saw him kill so many fucking hajis. [*OP*, for "original poster," referred to Tarrant.]

HOLY SHIT!!! THE DIGITS OF GOD!

Some urged one another to follow his example and, as one put it, "redeem their nation."

A few months later, Fredrick Brennan, 8chan's founder and its administrator until 2016, said the site should be shut down. "It's not doing the world any good," he told Kevin Roose, tech columnist for the *New York Times*. "It's a complete negative to everybody except the users that are there. And you know what? It's a negative to them, too. They just don't realize it."

Within months, two more white-supremacist mass murders were announced on the forum. A nineteen-year-old user, after posting his intentions, carried an AR-15 and fifty rounds of ammunition into a California synagogue and shot four people, killing one, before his rifle jammed and he fled. Then a twenty-one-year-old in El Paso killed twenty-three people at a Walmart, most of them Latino. Police said that before the attack he had posted a long message on 8chan detailing far-right, race-war conspiracies that he believed justified his violence.

For all the links to 8chan, when New Zealand government investigators finished their yearlong examination of how the Christchurch massacre had happened, the greater culpability lay, they indicated, with YouTube. Tarrant had learned on the platform how to modify the guns he used in the attack. He had donated money to alt-right YouTubers. In the days before the attack, he had left the platform on Autoplay, allowing its algorithm to run from one video to the next. When elsewhere on the web, whether in Facebook groups or gamer chat forums, he frequently posted links to far-right YouTube videos.

The investigators, citing interviews and forensic reconstructions of his web history, concluded that "YouTube was, for him, a far more significant source of information and inspiration" than any other platform had been. According to the report, YouTube was both his digital home and the driver of his radicalization. When investigators asked locals about the attack, they brought up YouTube, too: its role in far-right radicalization, its promotion of extremist content. Some said that YouTube's algorithm had even recommended them into the video, supposedly banned, of Tarrant's killing spree. Jacinda Ardern, New Zealand's prime minister, announced that, among the hundreds of pages of findings in the report, YouTube's role in pushing hate and conspiracies had "particularly stood out." She added, "This is a point I plan to make directly to the leadership of YouTube."

Tens of thousands of miles away, in a dark bedroom outside Dallas, Adam, without intending to, had watched the shooting on 8chan shortly after it happened. "It was awful," he recalled. "I consider myself a desensitized person and that video horrified me."

It came at a tenuous moment for him. He had spent years among incel communities, following them on YouTube and 8chan in their — and his — descent into rage and distrust. But he'd met a young woman on a Facebook group, a meme-sharing page that Facebook's algorithm had recommended him into. Adam had posted a thread offering to draw anyone who sent him a photo. The young woman agreed but, when they exchanged account information, used the access to draw him instead. The lark lowered his defenses. Everything he'd learned online told him that women would only ever revile at and hurt him. But here was evidence that someone had seen him, had looked willingly, through eyes that rendered him not as loathsome but as goofy and kind. After months of talking online, she drove, three days' journey, to Dallas. They were shy with each other at first. "It was probably four or five days before the tea kettle boiled over," he said. But they stayed in touch afterward. She began pulling him out of the rabbit hole. Then Christchurch happened, and he'd had enough.

A short time later, he pulled up the Twitter page for Brianna Wu, the video game developer and activist who, during Gamergate, had endured years of harassment and threats. "hey, this might sound dumb," he wrote her in a private message, "but I guess I just wanted to say a few years ago I was a pretty edgy person who was caught in the train of 4chan hate against you." He was vague as to what, exactly, he had done. But he said that he'd been swept up in a "huge group think-y hive mind" of anti-feminist hate, against her and others, on 4chan and Facebook. "things have changed and I really am rooting for you and your campaign," he wrote, referencing her congressional run. "I was thinking it might be worth telling you about it just to show support and that these people can change for the better."

Wu had been getting more and more messages like these — from former Gamergaters who, after years following the funnel deeper into online extremism, had gotten help. "They really strike me as looking for their place in the world," she told me. "I can see being unhappy and turning that hatred in yourself outward towards people and striking back, particularly when you're younger. So I just try to remember when I was in my early twenties. I was a mess."

She wrote back to Adam, "That really means the world to me, thank you!" After a few messages, she asked his permission to tweet an image of their exchange with his name removed. He said yes, that he hoped it might help "more of the people I grew up talking with online" to change. Her tweet received maybe a dozen responses, mostly positive. It was probably Wu's fourth- or fifth-most discussed post that day. But to Adam the feeling of affirmation was overwhelming.

"seeing all the replies to the screenshot you shared made me so excited," he wrote back to her. "i don't know if I've ever seen so many people that happy over anything I've said before."

Ten

The New Overlords

1. A Hidden Government

JACOB'S WORK WAS supposed to be easy. The Facebook moderator, who would later read my story from Sri Lanka and send me troves of internal documents to alert the world to what he saw as dangerous corporate negligence, would sit down at his workstation, which would show him a piece of content from Facebook, Instagram, or WhatsApp. He would check the guidelines to see whether the post was permissible. He would click to allow it, remove it, or refer it to a superior. Repeat.

Those guidelines had once been a simple list, proscribing no racial slurs, no nudity, and not much else. But by 2018 the rules resembled the instructions for running a nuclear reactor, if every page had been written by a different author, each blind to how theirs fit into the whole. They ran more than 1,400 pages (probably much more, when accounting for region-specific files to which Jacob's team did not have access). And yet Jacob and his coworkers, most of them former call-center operators, were expected to know and employ those rules to make hundreds of high-stakes decisions every day. His office, staffed by a few dozen people who reviewed content in a handful of languages and regions, was one of many like it scattered around the globe. A vast archipelago of thousands of moderators across dozens of offices, sharing little communication or coordination beyond what came down from Facebook's faraway headquarters. Unseen arbiters separating forbidden from allowed, invisibly shaping politics and social relations in every country on earth.

That was how Jacob, tired of feeling complicit in the poison he saw rising across the Facebook-owned platforms — a wave of sectarian lies feeding communal violence in Iraq, a race-baiting conspiracy swirling in Israel or India — and of being stonewalled by the outsourcing-agency bosses he'd tried to alert, ended up contacting me. Social media's governing rules, he wrote in his first message, "are not adapted to [the] reality of the content we see." And something else worried him. Facebook, he wrote, had dumped "sensitive work that impacts world security" on multinationals like his employer, a "for-profit company that cares only about maximizing productivity." However bad the rules were, the business model of corner-cutting, profit-maximization, and secrecy only made the failures in moderating the content that much worse.

In the months to come, Jacob and I talked regularly on secure apps, and eventually I flew out to collect the guidebooks that he had sneaked out of his employer's computer systems. The files promised something powerful: evidence that Facebook had integrated itself, however reluctantly, into the governance of a world whose politics and social relations increasingly routed through its systems. And deep, revealing detail on how they had done it.

As we sat on a sagging sofa in Jacob's two-room cinder-block home, drinking from a two-liter bottle of soda he had bought for the occasion, he recounted the swirls of hate and incitement that his team had been forced to leave online by rules that they had flagged again and again as insufficient and faulty. "At the end of the day," he said, "you are forced to follow the rules of the company if you want to keep your job." But the decisions weighed on him. "You feel like you killed someone by not acting."

He knew he was nobody, merely one of thousands of cogs in Facebook's global machinery. And despite his concerns, he still had faith in the company that had promised the world so much; surely this was nothing more than a low-level failure to fulfill Zuckerberg's grand vision. Even as I sat in his home, poring over documents whose publication he knew would embarrass Facebook, he saw himself as its ally. By revealing the bureaucratic failures he feared were holding the company back, he would help it to achieve the technological revolution in which he'd placed his hopes.

The stack of paper did not look like a handbook for regulating global politics. There was no master file or overarching guide, just dozens of disconnected PowerPoint presentations and Excel spreadsheets. Their titles, though bureaucratic, hinted at Facebook's scope. Credible Violence: Implementation Standards. Regulated Goods. Sri Lanka: Hate Speech. Terrorism: Fake/Not Real Person Policy. Western Balkans Hate Orgs and Figures.

The rules covered nearly any sort of matter that the company might want its moderators to consider. And they aimed to set out, for any eventuality in any country or region, precise and machinelike instructions for how to adjudicate what to remove or allow. It was a stunningly ambitious project. The goal was to reduce context-heavy questions that even a team of specialized lawyers would struggle to parse — what constitutes a threat, when is an idea hateful, when is a rumor dangerous — to a black-and-white matter so straightforward that any given moderator could decide it with no independent thought. Many of the hundreds of rules made sense individually. But in their Byzantine totality, they suggested an absurdity to Facebook's effort to shoehorn the nuances of human speech, politics, and social relations into if-then decision trees.

One rulebook that Jacob consulted often, on how to determine whether something constituted hate speech, ran to 200 jargon-filled pages. It asked moderators to perform a kind of linguistic algebra. Compare the post against a jumble of lists: protected classes, banned slurs, "designated dehumanizing comparisons." Sort the post's severity into one of three tiers. If the post references a group, pull up one list to check whether the group is banned, then another to see whether any words in the post indicate praise or support, then another for carve-outs and exceptions.

And they were expected to do it all in about eight to ten seconds, moving on rote memorization. This was not enough time even to name all the relevant documents, much less review their rules. And certainly not enough to think through how to fairly and safely apply them. Thinking, though, was not much encouraged. "This is the biggest sin, when you're accused of imposing your own judgment," Jacob said. "Our job is just to follow what the client says."

I told him I was sympathetic to Facebook's position. It contracted thousands of moderators across dozens of countries. It would be impractical, and maybe unwise, to give them all a say in crafting those rules.

Jacob shook his head. He just wanted Facebook to know about mistakes, gaps in the rules, dangers that his team had seen on the platform but couldn't take down until it was written into official guidance. After all, he said, moderators like him were the ones who saw the biggest quantity of content. But his bosses discouraged him and his coworkers from speaking up. If rules seemed misguided or incomplete, they were told, just keep quiet and don't make trouble. "They're just interested in productivity," he said. Some of his colleagues quit. Most, needing the work, simply stayed silent. "People give up," Jacob said. On some level the moderation was, as they knew, a doomed mission. No rulebook could possibly stem the hate and misinformation that Facebook's systems were engineered, however unintentionally, to mass-produce. It was like putting more and more air fresheners on the outside of a toxic-waste factory while production simultaneously ramped up inside.

Facebook didn't seem to want their input anyway. It was a software-engineering mindset: rules as lines of code that interchangeable moderators would execute automatically. In theory, this would allow Facebook to scale up moderation at the snap of a finger. So would outsourcing the work to multinationals that could pull in bodies as needed. It was the only way to keep pace with Facebook's permanent expansion, which moved too quickly to train up independent-thinking reviewers.

I later discovered something revealing. Multiple departments within Facebook were putting out rulebooks, using different styles and sometimes different ways of thinking, which made their guidebooks clash and contradict. Others did not come from Facebook at all, but were produced by the outsourcing agencies, without Facebook's knowledge, to try to improve compliance rates by giving moderators narrower rules to follow. Some were intended as training manuals but used instead as reference materials. The company, it seemed, had not taken on the role of global arbiter so much as drifted into it, crisis by crisis, rule by rule. Its leaders were reluctant overlords, wary of backlash, averse to owning decisions, executing their role largely from the shadows.

Back home, I cleaned the files of any digital fingerprints and began quietly circulating them to digital analysts and experts on various countries. In India, Chinmayi Arun, a legal scholar, identified troubling mistakes in guidelines for her country. The guidelines instructed moderators that any post that degraded a specific religion broke Indian law and should be flagged for removal. It was a significant curb on the speech of Facebook's 300 million Indian users — and an incorrect one. There was no such law.

Why had Facebook, the free-speech company, imposed such a severe restriction in the world's largest democracy? Maybe it was an error. But others like it appeared in the files as well. And then this clue: A set of Pakistan guidelines warned moderators against creating a "PR fire" by taking any action that could "have a negative impact on Facebook's reputation or even put the company at legal risk."

Another slide said that Indian law forbade calling for an independent Kashmir, a region under brutal Indian military occupation. It instructed moderators to "look out for" the phrase "Free Kashmir." All of this, Arun said, was actually legal in India. Facebook later told me that this was not meant to forbid users from expressing support of Kashmiri rights, only to urge moderators to apply extra scrutiny to any post that did. Still, it was not clear that this distinction would be obvious to moderators, who are repeatedly warned that underenforcement or scandal could get Facebook blocked in India. For all the company's promises of bringing a free speech revolution, deference to the political sensibilities of certain governments seemed at times to prevail.

Mistakes were rampant. Guidelines for the Balkans, a region in Europe long troubled by ethnonationalist militias, flowed with typos, out-of-date information, and strange errors. Ratko Mladić, a war criminal still celebrated by extremists — the Christchurch mass murderer had praised Mladić online — was incorrectly identified as "Rodney Young."

Facebook governed, in what Jacob emphasized over and over as the fatal flaw in the system, through profit-hungry outsourcing firms that did not share their goals or values. He gave an example. Publicly, Facebook insisted that moderators were not required to meet quotas for how many posts they reviewed or how quickly. Quotas would incentivize speed over care or thoughtfulness, forcing moderators to compromise the safety of communities they oversaw. But Jacob showed me pages from his office openly listing quotas: posts to review, time-per-post, counters of how many he'd reviewed. Documents showed his pay being set based on how well he'd kept up. Quotas ruled their lives, imposed by the outsourcing agencies to win more business with Facebook. This was done without Facebook's explicit knowledge and against its policies, though it was also a foreseeable result of Facebook demanding its contractors control the ever-rising cost of reviewing billions of posts per day.

Facebook also claimed that moderators had access to mental-health services. It was a response to reports of moderators developing post-traumatic stress disorder from repeatedly encountering gore and vile pornography. But this had never materialized in his office, Jacob said. Many workers lasted only a few months before burning out, often returning to call-center jobs. It was a sign of the disconnect between Facebook and its agencies, whose incentives are purely to keep costs down and productivity up. The more I learned about how Facebook oversaw those contractors, the less surprising it was that hate overran one country after another unchecked.

Moderators are regularly audited for "accuracy," Facebook's measure for how often they decide on content the way that the company wishes them to. A sliver of that auditing is conducted by corporate Facebook employees. But mostly it's done by other workers at the same outsourcing center. The agencies police themselves. Their incentive is to churn through posts as fast as possible, then claim high levels of accuracy.

Corner-cutting appears to be rampant. At Jacob's agency, if moderators encountered a post in a language that no one on hand could read, they were instructed to mark it as approved, even if users had flagged the post as dangerous hate speech. It was a shocking revelation. Not only had those monitoring groups in Sri Lanka and Myanmar been right that Facebook was actively upholding outright incitements to genocide, but it was a matter of policy at some outsourcing firms to do so.

The Facebook executive who oversaw the agencies acknowledged, when I asked about this, that the company sometimes struggles to control outside firms, calling these practices a violation of Facebook's rules. But it relies on their ability to hire and scale up quickly in order to support the global expansion that makes Facebook its billions. Even as the firms defy and hoodwink Facebook, their contracts tend to grow. After all, it's only the users who suffer.

2. *Masters of the Universe*

THERE IS SO much that makes social media techno-governance peculiar. The hubris of both its scale and its secrecy. The belief that politics and social relations are engineering problems. The faith in engineers to solve them. The naivete in thinking that they had done so, or at least enough to keep expanding. It all traced back, as with so many of the defining features of the platforms, to the imperatives of Silicon Valley capitalism. Namely, to a drastic and recent change in that model.

In the late 2000s, the power relationship between two of the Valley's most important classes — investors and startup founders — had suddenly flipped. Since the first transistor shops, investors had held the power. Founders needed lots of cash to make their first widget, more to land their first customer, more still to turn a profit. Investors, for covering those costs, and to ensure their bets paid off, got lots of oversight.

"The understanding used to be that you brought the venture capitalist in for — the term was always 'adult supervision,'" Leslie Berlin, a Stanford University historian, explained. The investors installed senior managers, the corporate board, even a seasoned CEO to oversee the founder at their own company. When John Doerr invested $12.5 million in Google, founded and run by two grad students, he brought in Eric Schmidt, a veteran executive twenty years their senior, as their boss.

The cloud-computing era changed everything. Now that any founder could start a web business and get their first thousand customers on their own, and now that VCs were looking for high-risk, quick-burn, growth-hacking startups, investors needed to place more bets just as founders needed them less. Suddenly, VCs competed to pitch founders, rather than vice versa.

"When you have venture capitalists now vying to fund someone, versus entrepreneurs on their knees begging for money, it's a completely different power dynamic," with startup founders increasingly setting the terms, Berlin said. One sure way for investors to make their bids more attractive: No more adult supervision. No more CEOs installed over founders' heads. In Facebook's case, no independent board. "That's a fundamental shift in the whole understanding of what a venture capitalist is supposed to do," Berlin said.

It launched the era of the hoodie-wearing twenty-two-year-old hacker-founder-CEO. The executive team staffed by the founder's friends. The corporate cultures boldly, proudly defiant of grown-ups in suits. "Why are most chess masters under thirty?" Zuckerberg had once asked a hall of 650 would-be founders at Paul Graham's startup incubator. "Young people are just smarter." He urged the audience's would-be executives to hire accordingly.

Graham himself urged fellow investors to swing young, saying in a public talk, "in software, you want to invest in students, not professors."

Business experience, life experience, and advanced degrees were liabilities, not assets. Investing young, he added, also tended to be cheaper. The previous year, the average age of the founders in his startup program had been twenty-three. The result, Berlin said, was "lots of power in the hands of very young people who think that the people around them don't have anything to offer."

Many came up in the dot-com boom, a time of on-site sushi chefs and massage therapists. The perks were intended to solve a labor problem. California bars noncompete clauses, which means that employees can change jobs at a moment's notice. Companies offer luxury-spa offices and personal-butler services to keep people on board. But the lifestyle can be distorting. If we're all living like kings and presidents, then we must be just as important, right?

Corporate cultures, absorbing this environment, took on high ideological ferment: build widgets for us and you're not just making money, you're saving the world. The mission statement arms race escalated until, by the end of the 2000s, virtually every employer in town was telling hires that designing apps put them, in terms of importance, somewhere between the United Nations and the League of Superheroes. It was a culture where taking the reins of global governance didn't feel so outlandish.

Egos were boosted further by a web-era accounting practice: paying early employees in stock options. Scrappy startups, asked to turn a $100,000 seed investment into a million-user customer base, granted, in place of competitive salaries, what were effectively IOUs. If the company flamed out, as most did, the options were worthless. If the company succeeded, which might mean selling to Oracle for $300 million, those early employees could retire, millionaires, at age twenty-six. For those who hit it big, the money felt like affirmation of what the investors and employers had always told them: you are different from other people. Smarter, better. Rightful masters of the universe.

The new era elevated a different class of investors as well. Institution-backed venture capitalists, like John Doerr acting on behalf of Kleiner Perkins, "spent a few years retrenching after the dot-com bubble burst," Roger McNamee, the early Facebook investor, wrote in his memoir. "Into the void stepped angel investors — individuals, mostly former entrepreneurs and executives," he wrote. Rich insiders, putting up their own money, without a firm controlling the purse strings or shareholders to keep happy. Both investor and founder were now much freer to do as they wished. The era of gatekeepers and guardrails was ending.

Some of the first and most influential angel investors were the PayPal cofounders, among them Peter Thiel, the archconservative who'd called the value of diversity a "myth" and said that contrarian hackers "with Asperger's-like social ineptitude" made the best startup chiefs. "Their impact transformed Silicon Valley," McNamee wrote, and their money funded much of the social media era. But the "value system" they brought, according to McNamee, "may have contributed to the blindness of internet platforms to harms that resulted from their success."

The politics of the PayPal founders leaned severely libertarian: they were socially Darwinian, distrustful of government, certain that business knew best. Thiel took this to such extremes that in 2009, he announced, "I no longer believe that freedom and democracy are compatible." Society could no longer be trusted to "the unthinking demos that guides so-called social democracy," he wrote, using the Greek term for citizens. Only "companies like Facebook" could safeguard liberty. And only if they were unshackled from "politics," which seemed to mean regulation, public accountability, and possibly the law.

He backed projects meant to bring about corporation-run floating cities and colonization of space, all outside the jurisdiction of any government. These sci-fi fantasies merely exaggerated an old idea in the Valley. Engineers and startup founders knew better. It was their responsibility to tear down the status quo and install a techno-utopia in its place, just as the 1990s manifesto writers had foretold. If governments or journalists objected, it was just the old incumbents clinging to authority that was no longer theirs.

This sense of divine mission drove the angel investors of Generation PayPal who selected the startups and founders to remake the world around their vision. They called it disrupting incumbents. Uber and Lyft would not just offer a new way to hail taxis, they would abolish and replace the old one. Airbnb would disrupt short-term housing. All three were PayPal alumni investees. Many others pursued the same violent displacement. Amazon and physical retail, Napster and music. Only a few, like Thiel, seriously suggested doing to global governance what Uber had done to ridesharing. But once the social media platforms stumbled into that role, it must have felt like just a continuation of their rightful place. Of the belief that society is a set of engineering problems waiting to be solved.

3. *Convergence*

TWO YEARS AFTER Trump's election shocked Americans into questioning the influence of social media over their politics, Renée DiResta and four other experts sat before the TV cameras and wood-paneled podiums of the Senate Select Committee on Intelligence ready to provide answers. "This problem is one of the defining threats of our generation," DiResta told the sixteen senators arrayed before her.

The hearing was nominally to address Russia's digital exploitation. But congressional investigators, like so many others, were coming to believe that the Russian incursion, while pernicious, had revealed a deeper, ongoing danger. This was "not about arbitrating truth, nor is it a question of free speech," DiResta said. It was about algorithmic amplification, online incentives that led unwitting users to spread propaganda, and the ease with which bad actors could "leverage the entire information ecosystem to manufacture the appearance of popular consensus." As DiResta had been doing for years now, she directed her audience's attention from Moscow toward Silicon Valley. "Responsibility for the integrity of public discourse is largely in the hands of private social platforms," she said. For the public good, she added, speaking on behalf of her team, "we believe that private tech platforms must be held accountable."

She had initially been reluctant to come before the Senate. "I thought it was a political football," she told me, referring to Russian meddling. "Is it going to be all gotchas? Is it going to be me fighting with particular Republican senators who were, by that point, Trump surrogates?" But a closed-door briefing she'd given the committee had been "incredibly professional," she said. "It was all just fact-finding." Impressed, and surprised by the sincerity of some senators she'd considered hyperpartisans, she agreed. "I really, really wanted to make it clear that I thought that it was a system problem," she told me, "and that Russia was just perhaps the best at manipulating the system, but that others would continue to do it."

The more her team parsed the gigs of data provided by the platforms, she said, the surer she became "that it didn't matter so much whether it was Russia or anti-vaxxers or terrorists. That was just the dynamic that was taking shape as a result of this system." For months, there had been signs of a great convergence on what had once been called "the Russia playbook" but increasingly looked like users and groups simply following the incentives and affordances of social media. The line had blurred, maybe for good, between groups that strategically pushed Russian-style disinformation and users who gave rise to it organically. Propagandists had become unnecessary; the system, DiResta feared, did the real work.

In an attempt to address the public's concerns, Zuckerberg published an essay, a few weeks after DiResta's hearing. "One of the biggest issues social networks face," he wrote, "is that, when left unchecked, people will engage disproportionately with more sensationalist and provocative content." He included a chart that showed engagement curving upward as Facebook content grew more extreme, right up until it reached the edge of what Facebook permitted. "Our research suggests that no matter where we draw the lines for what is allowed, as a piece of content gets close to that line, people will engage with it more on average," he wrote. "At scale," he added, this effect "can undermine the quality of public discourse and lead to polarization."

Guillaume Chaslot, the former YouTuber, was astonished. He had spent years trying to prove what Zuckerberg had just effectively conceded. More extreme content wins more engagement, wins more promotion, polarizing users. "That's crazy when you think about it," Chaslot said.

Zuckerberg had given away a telling detail: in their internal research, they'd found that people engage more with extreme content "even when they tell us afterwards they don't like the content." In other words, as experts and worried insiders had been at pains to demonstrate for years, it wasn't conscious will that users were acting on; it was something between impulse, temptation, and system-imposed nudges. Zuckerberg's proposed fix was, naturally, more algorithm tweaks. They would train it to recognize content that wasn't quite forbidden and downgrade its promotion — a sort of halfway ban. But the system's basic nature would remain.

"Not so much changed," Chaslot said. "You can still see that, if you look at the most shared political posts on Facebook, they're very divisive, whether extreme right or extreme left." He added, "If Facebook is always pushing people towards the extreme, it doesn't matter that the most extreme groups have been removed, because Facebook is creating more." It was why, for him, the problem was not moderation but amplification.

And that problem was, Zuckerberg's tweak aside, worsening. The company had overhauled its algorithm at the start of 2018: engagement had dropped the previous year, and the revamp aimed to get it climbing again. The new version would promote or suppress each post based on an auto-assigned score. Likes were worth one point but reaction emojis — love, sad, angry — were worth five, meaning that a more emotion-provoking post would rank five times as highly. Short comments get fifteen points, reshares and long comments get thirty, rewarding anything that provoked a lengthy and emotional discussion.

Engagement immediately resurged. But users expressed less happiness with the experience. Traffic to news publishers from the feed dropped.

"Misinformation, toxicity, and violent content are inordinately prevalent among reshares," an internal report warned of the change, with another finding "unhealthy side effects on important slices of public content, such as politics and news." Invective and rumor proliferated even more than before, edging out news or moderation. Political parties across Europe privately complained to the company that the sensationalist tilt of its algorithms had "forced them to skew negative in their communications on Facebook, leading them into more extreme policy positions," according to an internal memo.

Around the same time as Zuckerberg's essay, a team of Stanford and New York University economists conducted an experiment that tested, as directly and rigorously as anyone has, how using Facebook changes your politics. They recruited about 1,700 users, then split them into two groups. People in one were required to deactivate their accounts for four weeks. People in the other were not. The economists, using sophisticated survey methods, monitored each participant's day-to-day mood, news consumption, accuracy of their news knowledge, and especially their views on politics.

The changes were dramatic. People who deleted Facebook became happier, more satisfied with their life, and less anxious. The emotional change was equivalent to 25 to 40 percent of the effect of going to therapy — a stunning drop for a four-week break. Four in five said afterward that deactivating had been good for them. Facebook quitters also spent 15 percent less time consuming the news. They became, as a result, less knowledgeable about current events — the only negative effect. But much of the knowledge they had lost seemed to be from polarizing content; information packaged in a way to indulge tribal antagonisms. Overall, the economists wrote, deactivation "significantly reduced polarization of views on policy issues and a measure of exposure to polarizing news." Their level of polarization dropped by *almost half* the amount by which the average American's polarization had risen between 1996 and 2018 — the very period during which the democracy-endangering polarization crisis had occurred. Again, *almost half.*

As evidence mounted throughout 2018, action began following. That year, Germany mandated that social media platforms remove any hate speech within twenty-four hours of its being flagged, or face fines. Australia announced an inquiry into "world first" regulations on social media's harms, calling it a "turning point" amid "global recognition that the internet cannot be that other place where community standards and the rule of law do not apply." The European Union imposed a series of fines exceeding a billion dollars on Google for antitrust abuses, then threatened regulations against Facebook over hate speech, election influence, misinformation — the whole gamut. "I will not hide that I am becoming rather impatient," EU Justice Commissioner Věra Jourová told a press conference, speaking of Facebook. "If we do not see the progress, the sanctions will have to come. I do not want to negotiate forever."

Even Silicon Valley was beginning to internalize the backlash. An internal poll of 29,000 Facebook employees taken that October found that the share of employees who said they were proud to work at Facebook had declined from 87 to 70 percent in just a year. The share who felt their company made the world a better place had dropped from 72 to 53 percent, and on whether they felt optimistic about Facebook's future, from the mid-80s to just over 50 percent. "When I joined Facebook in 2016, my mom was so proud of me," a former Facebook product manager told *Wired* magazine. "I could walk around with my Facebook backpack all over the world and people would stop and say, 'It's so cool that you worked for Facebook.' That's not the case anymore." She added, "It made it hard to go home for Thanksgiving."

4. Cyberdemocracy

FOR AS LONG as there has been a democratic era, it has been governed by gatekeepers. Party establishments dictate agendas and select who gets on the ballot. Media establishments control who gets airtime and who doesn't, who is portrayed as acceptable and who isn't. Businesses and interest groups disburse the funding that wins elections. Social media, among other factors, eroded those gatekeepers' power. For zero cost, candidates could build their own public messaging, organizing, and fundraising empires, circumventing the gatekeepers. The establishments still hold influence, but for better or worse, their lock on democracy is over.

Silicon Valley had hoped to do exactly this, of course. By enabling people to express themselves directly and en masse, "rather than through intermediaries controlled by a select few," Zuckerberg wrote in a 2012 letter to investors, "we expect governments will become more responsive." But in practice, social media did not abolish establishments so much as replace them. Its algorithms and incentives now acted as gatekeepers, determining who rose or fell. And they did this based not on popularity but on engagement — which, as Chaslot had demonstrated in his YouTube analysis, led to fringe candidates outperforming.

Some called this new era "cyberdemocracy." In France, in late 2018, they called it "yellow vests." It started when a petition demanding lower gas prices circled social media throughout the summer, and became, in October, the basis of a sprawling Facebook group urging motorists to block local roads. Discussion was freewheeling, blaming rising gas prices on each user's preferred grievance, out-group, or conspiracy, giving them all a reason to rally. On a pre-planned day that November, tens of thousands across the country pulled yellow safety vests from their cars — a French law mandates keeping them on hand — and blocked nearby roads. The spectacle attracted attention, which brought new recruits.

From the beginning, the Yellow Vests, as they termed themselves, identified as a leaderless, radically horizontal movement. Social media had, unquestionably, enabled this. There had never been such a scalable, cost-free, universally open way to organize. But the platforms also applied an invisible guiding hand. Their promotional elements pulled users toward the high-engagement groups that drove activity, and where the most charged posts rose to the top. So did the platforms' participatory nature, which rewarded users who performed their membership with posts and photos of their roadblock. And it was a shared identity, in which any French person with a one-euro vest could feel part of something big and meaningful.

Soon the Yellow Vests coalesced around a greater cause: remaking French democracy in their image. A "citizens' assembly" would directly implement popular will, unmediated by representatives or institutions. Issues would be decided by referendum. Voters would be empowered to recall representatives anytime. Until this was granted, they pledged to block the roads each Saturday.

The Yellow Vests also issued a cacophony of policy demands, many of which were contradictory. A range of taxes were to be zeroed out, as was homelessness. Kindergarten class sizes were to be reduced and downtown parking made cost-free. The national debt was to be "declared illegitimate" and defaulted on. Refugees were to be barred from entering the country. A second list, added a week later, demanded that France leave the European Union and NATO, cut taxes in half, and halt nearly all immigration. It was an agenda that could emerge only from social media: maximalist, incoherent, rooted in identity, unfettered by decision-makers who might cohere the list. Pure id.

The Yellow Vests were, in some ways, a history-making success, the largest citizen movement since at least the 1960s in the country that practically invented such movements. But it had little impact. Every political party tried to harness its energy. So did organized labor. So did students. They got nowhere. Then the movement petered out, as if it had never happened. Even seven-plus years on from the Arab Spring and whatever lessons it might've held for online activists, the new social media democracy produced a lot of chaos but strangely few results.

This turned out to represent a trend, and a revealing one, uncovered by Erica Chenoweth, a scholar of civil resistance at Harvard. The frequency of mass-protest movements had been growing worldwide since the 1950s, she found, and had accelerated lately. Between the 2000s and the 2010s, average episodes per year had jumped nearly 50 percent. Their success rate had been growing, too, year after year, for decades. Around 2000, 70 percent of protest movements demanding systemic change succeeded. But then, suddenly, that trend reversed. They began failing — just as they were getting more frequent. Now, Chenoweth found, only 30 percent of mass movements succeeded. "Something has really shifted," she told me, calling the drop "staggering." Virtually every month, another country would erupt in nationwide protests: Lebanon over corruption, India over gender inequality, Spain over Catalan separatism. Many at a scale exceeding the most transformative movements of the twentieth century. And most of them fizzling.

To explain this, Chenoweth drew on an observation by Zeynep Tufekci, the University of North Carolina scholar: social media makes it easier for activists to organize protests and to quickly draw once-unthinkable numbers — but this may actually be a liability. For one, social media, though initially greeted as a force for liberation, "really advantages repression in the digital age much more than mobilization," Chenoweth said. Dictators had learned how to turn it to their advantage, using their superior resources to flood platforms with disinformation and propaganda.

The effect in democracies was subtler but still powerful. Chenoweth cited, as a comparison, the Student Nonviolent Coordinating Committee, a civil rights–era student group. Before social media, activists had to mobilize through community outreach and organization-building. They met almost daily to drill, strategize, and confer. It was agonizing, years-long work. But it made the movement durable, built on real-world ties and chains of command. It allowed movements like SNCC to persevere when things got hard, respond strategically to events, and translate street victories into political change.

Social media allows protests to skip many of those steps, putting more bodies on the streets more quickly. "That can give people a sense of false confidence," Chenoweth said, "because it's lower commitment." Without the underlying infrastructure, social media movements are less able to organize coherent demands, coordinate, or act strategically. And by channeling popular energy away from the harder kind of organizing, it preempts traditional movements from emerging. It was what Zuckerberg had promised: bigger, leaderless citizen movements. But Facebook, like the other social media giants, had grown into an incumbent institution in its own right. And like most gatekeepers, it tended to protect the establishment and the status quo that it relied on to maintain its power.

5. Wartime CEOs

IN MAY 2016, the tech news site *Gizmodo* published what may still be one of the most consequential stories written about social media platforms, under the headline "Former Facebook Workers: We Routinely Suppressed Conservative News." The story concerned a small widget on Facebook's homepage, called "trending," that displayed a handful of topics and headlines. It drove little traffic: 1.5 percent of clicks. An algorithm helped identify trending topics, but the company, in an unusual step, subjected those choices to human judgment. A handful of former journalists curated the topics and wrote blurbs describing them.

A former contractor with that team told *Gizmodo* that the team had been made to suppress conservative-oriented topics. The contractor, who himself identified as conservative, said that Facebook editors had asked him not to include viral stories on, for example, a former IRS worker whom Republicans had accused of targeting conservative groups. (His evidence was fuzzy and the story turned out to be false.) Editors had also told him not to pick up stories floated by far-right sites like *Breitbart* until a mainstream outlet had confirmed them. The *Gizmodo* article presented these decisions as evidence of Facebook's anti-conservative bias. It also accused the company of ordering contractors to "artificially manipulate the trending module" by "injecting" stories that had not yet gone viral. Its two examples were the disappearance of Malaysia Airlines flight 370 and the *Charlie Hebdo* terror attacks.

It was a rare case of Facebook doing everything that experts and digital groups would later ask of it. Imposing human oversight on its algorithms. Privileging truth and credibility over virality and engagement. Occasionally checking the worst impulses of its system, even its users. But the story, framed as it was, offered Republicans an opportunity to whip up grievances that transformed the politics around social media, and ultimately the platforms themselves.

"Facebook has the power to greatly influence the presidential election," the Republican National Committee said in a press release, conflating Facebook's far more powerful news feed with its mostly ignored trending widget. "It is beyond disturbing to learn that this power is being used to silence viewpoints and stories that don't fit someone else's agenda." Senator John Thune, a Republican, sent Zuckerberg a letter demanding that the company brief lawmakers on the issue. Thune chaired the commerce committee, which oversees the Federal Trade Commission, which had been investigating Facebook. The company, spooked, sent its DC team to assuage Thune. It also invited about twenty prominent conservatives, including an advisor to Trump's campaign, to meet personally with Zuckerberg. It worked. The attendees directed more acrimony at one another than at Facebook. One of them, Glenn Beck, wrote up the meeting, praising Zuckerberg as a champion of free speech.

Facebook fired the contractors overseeing the trending widget on a Friday, letting algorithms take full control. By Monday, its top story was a fake-news link accusing Fox News host Megyn Kelly of backing Hillary Clinton. The far-right blog that had published it was later identified as one of the top drivers of fake news on Facebook during the 2016 election.

That summer, in July, just a few days before the Republican National Convention formally nominated Trump for president, Zuckerberg was confronted at a financial conference by Rupert Murdoch and Robert Thomson, the founder and the CEO, respectively, of News Corp, which owns Fox News and many conservative outlets internationally. Facebook, they said, was cannibalizing the news business, using their content to steal the media's viewership and advertising revenue. Unannounced algorithm changes, they added, imperiled News Corp's ability to maintain traffic. They threatened to have News Corp publicly lobby governments and regulators to look at whether Facebook's market power might violate antitrust rules.

They did not threaten to use their news outlets against Facebook. But it would not have been unreasonable for Zuckerberg to fear as much. In the coming months, Fox News grew outspoken about Facebook's supposed anti-conservative bias. It called Facebook's "get out the vote" campaign a ploy to drive up Democratic turnout. It lambasted Facebook for "suppressing" what it called "major news," such as a Hillary Clinton health scare (in fact, the platform had removed a handful of fake-news posts) and for "censoring" the "activist" Pamela Geller, a far-right figure who'd had her page removed after spreading racist conspiracies.

Zuckerberg sought to reassure conservatives, pointing out, in statements and posts throughout 2016, that Trump had more fans than any other presidential candidate and that Fox News had more interactions on its page than any other outlet. ("It's not even close," Zuckerberg said.) The company's relationship to Trump's campaign, which was spending heavily on Facebook ads, remained cordial.

After the election, as evidence mounted that the major social media platforms had boosted false and polarizing content favoring Trump, some of it Russia-backed, Republicans clearly sensed their victory growing tarnished — perhaps, amid hints of indirect coordination between Trump's campaign and Russian operatives, even delegitimized. They sought to invert the narrative. Social media hadn't boosted Republicans, they claimed, it had suppressed them. Republicans in control of both chambers of Congress, eager to distract from the investigation into Russia's influence, held counter-messaging hearings that asserted Silicon Valley liberals as the real threat to democracy.

Republicans found their smoking gun in a 2018 *Vice News* story headlined "Twitter Is 'Shadow Banning' Prominent Republicans." The reporter had found that Twitter's search bar did not auto-populate certain conservative accounts when he typed the first few letters of their names. The story appeared to be based on a technical misunderstanding, but Republicans jumped. Representative Matt Gaetz of Florida, in a tweet, implied that Twitter was punishing him for questioning the company's CEO at a recent hearing. The chairwoman of the Republican National Committee said the company "suppresses conservative voices," while Donald Trump, Jr., tweeted, "Enough is enough with this crap," demanding that Twitter's CEO "#StopTheBias." His tweet received 16,500 interactions, Gaetz's 20,400. Hardly suppression. Then Trump, Sr., also tweeted "#StopThe-Bias," launching months of conservative messaging on the tyranny of big tech.

Throughout his presidency, Trump and his party painted the social media platforms as anti-Republican agents. They repeatedly threatened to investigate, regulate, or even break up the companies, threats that had tremendous power to motivate the Valley. Fears of antitrust enforcement — fines to punish, or regulation to halt, monopolistic practices — had long hung over the industry. In 1969, the Justice Department had launched an effort to break up IBM, which controlled 70 percent of the computer market. The trial dragged on for thirteen years, during which time IBM, to avoid proving regulators' case for them, constrained its own business. By the time the government dropped the case in 1982, IBM's market share and revenue had slid so dramatically that a *New York Times* headline announced, "Dominance Ended."

It was the Microsoft case that most terrified big tech. A years-long battle with regulators had culminated, in the mid-1990s, with a court ordering that the company be broken in two. (The Justice Department had accused Microsoft of exploiting its dominance in one market to monopolize others.) The ruling was thrown out on appeal — the judge had discussed the case with reporters as it proceeded, tainting his impartiality — and the incoming Bush administration dropped the case. Still, Microsoft's stock price had been halved; its entry to internet services cut short, never to recover; and its standing with the public and regulators so weakened that Bill Gates, its founder, stepped down. Years later, he would counsel Zuckerberg not to repeat what he saw as his mistake: antagonizing Washington and ignoring lawmakers he saw as wrongheaded. "I said, 'Get an office there, now,'" Gates recalled, referring to Washington, where Facebook and Google began spending millions on lobbying. "And Mark did, and he owes me."

Regulatory fines were piling up: $22 million for Google in 2012, $170 million in 2019. One hundred million for Facebook in 2019, then a record-breaking $5 billion later that year, imposed by the Federal Trade Commission over user-privacy violations. There was even talk of forced breakups. Senator Richard Blumenthal, a Connecticut Democrat, argued in a 2018 op-ed that the Microsoft case provided an explicit model for targeting Facebook, Google, and Amazon.

Fending off such attacks would take more than lobbying. Starting that year, Zuckerberg and other tech chiefs adopted a posture that the venture capitalist Ben Horowitz had termed "wartime CEO." If regulators swirl or the market dives, Horowitz had written in a blog post, companies need a leader who "violates protocol in order to win," "uses profanity purposefully," "is completely intolerant" of employees breaking from corporate strategy, "neither indulges consensus-building nor tolerates disagreements," and embarrasses employees in front of their peers to make a point.

Horowitz credited the strategy to his hero Andy Grove, the former Intel chief. He'd adapted the term "wartime CEO" from a line in *The Godfather* (Tom Hagen: "Mike, why am I out?" Michael Corleone: "You're not a wartime consigliere"), which he reproduced in his post alongside a rap lyric, part of his campaign to rebrand tech billionaires as the new counterculture: hard-edged badasses in V-neck sweaters. He drew his cachet from Andreessen Horowitz, an investment firm he and Netscape founder Marc Andreessen had started in 2009. (Andreessen's mentor, John Doerr, had himself been mentored by Grove — one more example of the Valley's distorting insularity.)

If William Shockley had embodied the industry's semiconductor era,

Andy Grove the microchip era, and Peter Thiel the early web era, then Andreessen and Horowitz personified the social media era. It wasn't just where they invested (Facebook, where Andreessen sat on the board, as well as Twitter, Slack, Pinterest, Airbnb, Lyft, and Clubhouse), but how. They institutionalized, as a matter of investing strategy, the Valley's drift toward inexperienced, unconstrained young CEOs. They pledged to elevate "technical founders" with little experience or knowledge beyond engineering, then unshackle them from adult supervision or any expectation of normal corporate behavior.

The concept of wartime CEOs turned this archetype into a corporate philosophy. Programmers who start a smartphone app or e-retailer should govern exactly like the rock-star iconoclasts they believe themselves to be. If people get offended — thin-skinned employees, square-headed suits, the Federal Trade Commission — better to come out blasting and let them know who you are. One of Horowitz's management-training talks drew an extended parallel between startup founders and the leader of Haiti's 1791 slave revolt, who had succeeded, Horowitz said, by forcing Haitians to overcome "slave culture," much as tech CEOs would for employees and citizens who were lost without their guidance. It was the kind of hubris that could lead a dropout website developer to conclude he had what it took to dictate the terms of human social relations the world over, and that anyone square enough to question this was a slave who didn't get it. Being a wartime CEO also provided a kind of moral cover. If competitors had to be destroyed, if employees raised ethical objections or the media accused you of abetting the destruction of the social fabric, they didn't understand that this was war.

Zuckerberg, in 2018, read a Horowitz-authored book that elaborated on the strategy. That June, he gathered the company's fifty top executives to announce that Facebook was at war and that he was now a wartime CEO. He would be brooking less dissent, demanding greater obedience, and taking the fight to Facebook's enemies. In a company-wide town hall, he called news coverage of Facebook's privacy abuses, for which Facebook would face multiple regulatory fines, "bullshit." He dressed down Sheryl Sandberg, the company's second-ranked executive and his longtime advisor. Facebook hired a dark-arts PR firm, which seeded disparaging information, some of it false, about Facebook's critics.

Prominent investors in the venture-capitalist class announced that the Valley was at war with a dishonest national media looking to punish them for their success. ("We get it: you hate us. And you're competitors," one tweeted.) Some sought to fight back, urging Valley-wide bans on cooperating with news outlets or, in one case, offering to pay users in Bitcoin to harass critical reporters online.

A few weeks after Zuckerberg's "wartime" declaration, Facebook held a meeting to consider retooling its algorithm to elevate serious news outlets. This might restore trust in Facebook, some executives argued. But it was opposed by Joel Kaplan, the former Bush administration official and lobbyist. Since Trump's election, Kaplan seemed to act, with Zuckerberg's blessing, as the GOP's representative at Facebook, a job that carried the title of vice president for global public policy. He argued that the change would invite GOP accusations that Facebook promoted liberals, effectively turning Trump's view, that mainstream journalists were Democratic agents, into Facebook company policy. He prevailed.

Also that year, Kaplan successfully pushed to shelve one of the company's internal reports finding that the platform's algorithms promoted divisive, polarizing content. He and others objected that addressing the problem would disproportionately affect conservative pages, which drove an outsized share of misinformation. Better to let users be misinformed. It was not the last time that the public interest would be sacrificed to avoid even hypothetical Republican objections, however groundless.

Facebook's courtship of Republicans, who retained control of the levers of federal oversight throughout 2018 and 2019, was exhaustive. It hired Jon Kyl, a former Republican senator, to produce a report on any anti-conservative bias in the platform. The report largely repackaged Trump's #StopTheBias accusations, allowing Facebook to tell GOP critics it was studying the issue and following Kyl's recommendations. Zucker-berg hosted off-the-record dinners with influential conservatives, including Fox News host Tucker Carlson, who had accused Facebook of seeking "the death of free speech in America." The platform recruited the *Daily Caller*, the right-wing news site Carlson founded, to participate in its fact-checking program, granting it power over adjudicating truth on the platform. Facebook announced it would allow politicians to lie on the platform and grant them special latitude on hate speech, rules that seemed written for Trump and his allies.

"I'd been at FB for less than a year when I was pulled into an urgent inquiry — President Trump's campaign complained about experiencing a decline in views," Sophie Zhang, a Facebook data scientist, recalled on Twitter, "I never was asked to investigate anything similar for anyone else." This sort of appeasement of political leaders appeared to be a global strategy. Between 2018 and 2020, Zhang flagged dozens of incidents of foreign leaders promoting lies and hate for gain, but was consistently overruled, she has said. When she was fired, she refused a $64,000 non-disparagement severance so that she could release her 7,800-word exit memo chronicling what she saw as a deliberate practice of allowing politicians to misuse the platform, including in countries where the stakes extended to sectarian violence and creeping authoritarianism. "I know that I have blood on my hands by now," she wrote.

In 2019, Vietnam's communist dictatorship privately conveyed a message to Facebook: the platform needed to censor government critics or the Vietnamese government might block it in the country. Zuckerberg agreed, employees later revealed, allowing Facebook — "the revolution company," as he'd called it — to secretly become a tool of authoritarian repression. Though he argued that Vietnamese citizens were better served by accessing a partly free Facebook than none at all, his initial secrecy, and Facebook's history, cast doubt on the purity of his intentions. One group estimated that Facebook's Vietnam presence brings in $1 billion annually.

The company also announced that year that Facebook would no

longer screen political advertisements for truth or accuracy. Only extreme rule-breaking, like calls for violence, would be enforced. Trump, who had spent lavishly on Facebook in the past, was presumed to be the main beneficiary, as well as anyone like him. About 250 employees signed an open letter — an exceedingly rare show of public dissent — pleading with Zuckerberg to roll back the policy, which would "increase distrust in our platform" and "undo integrity product work" intended to protect elections.

Yaël Eisenstat, a former White House advisor who oversaw Facebook's elections policy for six months before quitting, published a column on the controversy. She claimed to have watched company policymakers work hard to balance democratic integrity with Facebook's mission, only to be overruled by "the few voices who ultimately decided the company's overall direction." Facebook, she warned, was failing "the biggest test of whether it will ever truly put society and democracy ahead of profit and ideology."

6. *Repairing an Airplane Mid-Flight*

EVERY OTHER TUESDAY morning, a few dozen Facebook employees mill around a glass conference room for what looks, at first, like any other Silicon Valley staff meeting. They pick through a catered breakfast, plop down eco-friendly water bottles, and fidget with the videoconferencing software. Then they settle in and discuss, in one brisk hour, how to tweak and adjust the company's ongoing experiment in managing social relations and political discourse around the world.

On the week I visited, in October 2018, a major topic was standards for selling animals on the platform's Craigslist-style commerce pages. The employees discussed how to balance the rights and interests of wildlife, pets, livestock, farmers, and breeders. European regulations would be reviewed. An outside group would be consulted. Someone raised, as a consideration, the economic importance of livestock trade for users in Africa. Their decisions would be translated into the machinelike rules and guidelines that were fed to Jacob and thousands of other moderators around the world, who, in turn, would use them to govern billions.

Facebook had invited me to observe after learning that I'd acquired its internal rulebooks — the ones secreted to me by Jacob. They wanted me to understand the files in context and, one employee told me, to begin opening its processes a bit to the outside world. Monika Bickert, who heads the policy team, told me, in one of the dozen or so interviews that the company had set up, that the rulemaking process tended to be reactive. An employee, news report, or interest group might flag an issue. Someone would craft a new rule, workshop it at the meeting, then put it through a review process. It might be test-run in a particular market before being rolled out elsewhere. "We're not drawing these lines in a vacuum," Bickert said, describing the legal norms and principles that guided them. But the more intricate the rules became, the harder they were to implement via moderator cogs like Jacob, especially given the impossibly short times moderators were given to make decisions. Bickert was aware of the contradiction. "Anytime we make our policies more nuanced, that makes it harder for us to apply these rules consistently and get it right around the world," she said. "There's a real tension here between wanting to have nuances to account for every situation, and wanting to have a set of policies we can enforce accurately and we can explain cleanly."

I found myself alternating between sympathy for and skepticism of Facebook's policy overlords. They were thoughtful and, most of the time, humble about their ability to address the behavioral and political complexities they were tasked with managing. Some had joined the company thinking they could do more good by improving Facebook from within than by criticizing from without. And they had been stuck with the impossible job of serving as janitors for the messes made by the company's better-resourced, more-celebrated growth teams. As they fretted over problems like anti-refugee hate speech or disinformation in sensitive elections, the engineers across the hall were redlining user engagement in ways that, almost inevitably, made those problems worse.

Still, it was hard to separate out the benevolence of their work from the degree to which it was intended, as some policy documents plainly stated, to protect Facebook from public blowback or regulation. I came to think of Facebook's policy team as akin to Philip Morris scientists tasked with developing a safer, better filter. In one sense, cutting down the carcinogens ingested by billions of smokers worldwide saved or prolonged lives on a scale few of us could ever match. In another sense, those scientists were working for the cigarette company, advancing the cause of selling cigarettes that harmed people at an enormous scale.

I was not surprised, then, that everyone I spoke to at Facebook, no matter how intelligent or introspective, expressed total certainty that the product was not innately harmful. That there was no evidence that algorithms or other features pulled users toward extremism or hate. That the science was still out on whether cigarettes were really addictive and really caused cancer. But much as Philip Morris turned out to have been littered with studies proving the health risks its executives insisted did not exist, Facebook's own researchers had been mounting evidence, in reams of internal reports and experiments, for a conclusion that they would issue explicitly in August 2019: "the mechanics of our platform are not neutral."

An internal report on hate and misinformation had found, its authors wrote, "compelling evidence that our core product mechanics, such as virality, recommendations, and optimizing for engagement, are a significant part of why these types of speech flourish on the platform." The report, later leaked to media and the SEC, warned that the company was "actively (if not necessarily consciously) promoting these types of activities."

But, in my time at Facebook, again and again, any question about the consequences of routing an ever-growing share of the human experience through algorithms and gamelike interfaces designed primarily to "maximize engagement" brought only an uncomprehending stare. Executives who only moments earlier had delved into sensitive matters of terrorism or foreign regulation would blink and change the subject as if they had not understood the words. "People use mobile phones in order to organize bad things. In fact, maybe everything bad that happens through our services is happening through a mobile phone," a London-based executive said. "Would you argue not to adopt the mobile phone, matter of fact that we should slow down the adoption of mobile phones, because it's used in harmful ways?"

Part of me hoped that I was being spun, that they understood but just couldn't openly acknowledge their service's reality- and behavior-distorting effects. I felt like I was in the third act of *2001: A Space Odyssey*, when two surviving astronauts plot what to do about HAL, the artificial intelligence that, after overseeing their years-long journey, has gone mad and murdered their crewmates. I tried to imagine their pivotal scene if, when one astronaut had asked how they might stop HAL's killing spree, the other had answered, "Who?"

As evidence of the company's good intentions, nearly everyone I spoke to at Facebook cited its response to the genocide in Myanmar. Though belated, they conceded, the platform had banned the notorious extremist group, headed by the racist monk Wirathu, that had weaponized Facebook to incite mass violence against minorities since 2014. Surely, this was proof of maturation. But digital groups in Myanmar had been telling me for months that the hate group's race-baiting propaganda remained widespread online. The explanation turned out to be in Facebook's files. A Myanmar guidebook, formatted as a breezy thirty-two-slide PowerPoint, stated the reverse of what Facebook's executives believed their policy to be: content posted by or in support of the hate group, it said, should *not* be removed. It dedicated an entire page to this point. It was like intervening in Rwanda and mistakenly telling genocidaire radio stations to keep broadcasting. Even after all of the platform's shortcomings, such a glaring error, on such a consequential matter, was still shocking. When I pointed this out to Facebook's representatives, the company said it would correct the documents.

Debates in the Valley over how to use their power — defer to governments more or less, emphasize neutrality or social welfare, consistency or flexibility — rarely considered the possibility that they should not have such power at all. That consolidating information and social relations under the control of profit-maximizing companies was fundamentally at odds with the public good.

But since the scale of the backlash to big tech, and the evidence for its harms, couldn't be completely dismissed, the Valley settled on an internal narrative, throughout 2018 and 2019, that let its leaders feel like they were still the good guys. They called it "time well spent," a phrase borrowed from Tristan Harris, the former Google engineer who'd warned about addictive conditioning, and quit in 2015. Now it was the Valley's hot new thing. Facebook, Google, Apple, and others introduced new features to track and manage users' screen time. It was a kind of rebranding: we've learned from our sins (which we have conveniently narrowed to "too much screen time"), we've had a great awakening, and now we're crusaders for good.

Stanford's Persuasive Tech Lab, where academics and engineers teamed up to develop maximally addictive services, renamed itself the "Behavior Design Lab." Its chief tweeted, "We will start to realize that being chained to your mobile phone is a low-status behavior, similar to smoking." Nir Eyal, the consultant who'd pioneered slot machines as the model for social media platforms, pivoted from screen-time-maximization guru to screen-time-reduction guru, publishing a book with the title *Indistractable*.

Harris called the campaign a co-opting that did little to address the real harms. Apps continued upgrading their addiction-engine algorithms, but added tiny counters to tell you how many hours you'd spent online. Others called it a marketing stunt. To me, it seemed like a play for self-absolution. For every ad campaign telling consumers that Silicon Valley now stood for digital wellness, there were many more inward-facing yoga retreats or meditation groups telling Valleyites the same. Executives met to cleanse their souls of guilt, congratulate themselves for evolving, then go back to growth hacking. Self-flagellation as self-affirmation — feeling good about feeling bad — became a cottage industry.

"The CEOs, inside they're hurting. They can't sleep at night," Ben Tauber, a former product manager at Google who'd turned a seaside hippie commune called Esalen into a tech executive retreat, told the *New York Times*. It was a strange set of contortions. But it did for executives what wartime CEO performances had done for corporate morale and moderators had done for hate speech: paper over the unresolved, and perhaps unresolvable, gap between the platforms' stated purpose of freedom and revolution and their actual effects on the world.

This was the real governance problem, I came to believe. If it was taboo to consider that social media itself, like cigarettes, might be causing the harms that seemed to consistently follow its adoption, then employees tasked with managing those harms were impossibly constrained. It explained so much of the strange incoherence of the rulebooks. Without a complete understanding of the platforms' impact, most policies are tit-for-tat responses to crises or problems as they emerge: a viral rumor, a rash of abuse, a riot. Senior employees make a tweak, wait to see what happens, then tweak again, as if repairing an airplane mid-flight.

Little changed for the moderators asked to execute these plans. Reports of crushing work conditions continued to emerge. Jacob, as such sources sometimes do, pulled back from our conversations as his employer hunted for the mole who'd embarrassed the firm with Facebook. In 2018, an American moderator filed a lawsuit, later joined by several other moderators, against Facebook for failing to provide legal-minimum safety protections while requiring them to view material the company knew to be traumatizing. In 2020, Facebook settled the case as a class action, agreeing to pay $52 million to 11,250 current and former moderators in the United States. Moderators outside of the U.S. got nothing. The underlying business model remains unchanged.

Eleven

Dictatorship of the Like

1. President YouTube

IT HAD BEEN seven years, Tatiana Lionço recalled, her voice straining, since a viral YouTube video had destroyed her life. In 2012, Lionço, a psychologist, had spoken on a panel about combating homophobia in schools. She told the tiny audience of academics and policymakers that parents should be reassured that there was nothing unusual in young children expressing curiosity about one another's bodies or clothes.

Soon after, a far-right lawmaker edited footage of the event, rearranging her words to make it appear that she had encouraged homosexuality and sex between children. The lawmaker, widely considered a fringe oddity, had few political allies and little direct power. But he had a substantial following on YouTube, where he posted the edited footage. Far-right You-Tubers, then a small but active community, reposted the misleading video, adding their own misinformation-filled commentary. Lionço represented a global communist-homosexual conspiracy, they said. She had endorsed pedophilia. She was distributing "gay kits" for schools to use to convert children to homosexuality. Their claims spread to Twitter and Facebook. Comments on the videos filled with calls for her to be killed.

Lionço's friends and colleagues initially dismissed it as social media noise. Until the manufactured story became consensus reality on the platforms, outraging ordinary citizens. Many called her university demanding she be fired. They accused her employer, and anyone who supported her, of endangering children. Her friends and colleagues distanced themselves.

"I was left all alone with this," Lionço told me. She paused, her face tightening, and looked down at her lap. Maybe people in her life felt ashamed that they'd allowed this to happen, she said. "I think people are afraid it might happen to them." Even after she had mostly retreated from public life, the far-right YouTubers, whose audiences were exploding in size, kept pushing the story of the academic communist plotting to sexualize children. Though she eventually returned to teaching, her life has never been the same, stalked by infamy wherever she goes. Death threats remain a constant presence, as do whispers of suspicion even from like-minded peers. "I am exhausted. It's been seven years," she said, covering her face with her hands. "It broke me. This is the worst part for me. I feel alone."

Lionço is Brazilian. In the fall of 2018, the fringe lawmaker and You-Tuber who'd launched the disinformation campaign against Lionço six years earlier, a man named Jair Bolsonaro, ran to become her country's president. Everyone had expected him to lose. Instead he won in a 10-point landslide. It was the most significant event in global politics since the election of Donald Trump. The world's sixth-largest country came under the command of a far-right conspiracist. He oversaw the destruction of millions of acres of Amazon rain forest, signaled support for far-right violence, relentlessly attacked Brazil's democratic institutions, and gutted its bureaucracies.

His rise appeared to be a story of public anger over government corruption, economic turmoil, democratic backsliding. But the Brazilians and analysts I spoke to kept bringing up American social media platforms. "The Brazilian right barely existed as recently as two years ago," Brian Winter, the chief of a policy journal called *Americas Quarterly*, told me. "It came out of virtually nowhere." The establishment had rejected Bolsonaro for his extremist conspiracies, hate speech, and hostility toward women ("I wouldn't rape you because you don't deserve it," he'd once told another lawmaker). But that attention-grabbing behavior performed well online. Social media and YouTube in particular, Winter said, presented Bolsonaro as "a reinvented figure." Before the election, Winter had visited Bolsonaro's office, hoping to understand his strange and sudden rise. All eight staffers were "doing social media the entire time I was there," he said. "There was no legislative work being done."

It wasn't just Bolsonaro. For reasons nobody could quite explain, Brazil had become awash in conspiracies and radical new causes that all seemed to trace back to YouTube. "I first started to look at YouTube when, in the first presidential debate, one of the candidates spoke about URSAL," a Brazil-based analyst named Luiza Bandeira said. URSAL, a fictitious plan to unite Latin America as a pan-communist superstate, had festered on the fringes of Brazil's far right until, starting in 2016, it had exploded on YouTube. Videos pushing the claim won hundreds of thousands of views — largely driven, Bandeira concluded, by the platform's algorithms, which consistently routed even her from politics videos to conspiracies.

Dozens more conspiracies bubbled up into mainstream discourse, sending shock waves of confusion and fear through the country. A judge investigating left-wing politicians who'd died in an accident, one claimed, had actually been murdered. The military was preparing to stage a coup. Foreign meddlers were stealing the election, inseminating the country with deadly diseases, bribing the government to throw the World Cup.

The stories dominated Facebook and Twitter, Bandeira found, outranking truth on both platforms in the months before the 2018 election. Often they traced back to YouTube. Virtually all of them aligned with Bolsonaro's far-right politics and his paranoid, hateful worldview, pushing Brazilians in his direction. "Bolsonaro's always been espousing these hyperpartisan views, but they never got any traction," said Roberta Braga, Bandeira's colleague at the disinformation-tracking Digital Forensic Research Lab. "Now they're mainstream." The election that saw Bolsonaro win the presidency had also elevated two right-wing YouTubers to the federal legislature and many more to state-level offices. Others would soon get federal policy jobs. It was as if a great tide was rising, lifting a very particular subset of the fringe right — YouTubers — to the heights of power.

Brazil, as YouTube's second-largest market, was a test case for the platform's widening influence, much as Myanmar, Sri Lanka, and Germany had been for Facebook. It also provided a lens for understanding social media's impact in the United States, to which Brazil is extraordinarily similar: a sprawling presidential democracy with a large middle class, defined by racial division, widening polarization, and a rising populist right that seemed to live online. Most of all, it offered something like a glimpse into the future.

While Trump had been aided by the platforms, he had not been of them. In Brazil, it was as if social media itself had taken office. The country seemed to represent a strange new sort of digitally guided social and political order that was already coming into view in the U.S. as the 2020 election neared. In retrospect, the Brazil of 2019 foreshadowed not only much of America's chaos in the following year, but a future for the wider democratic world that, if something does not change, may still lie ahead.

I landed in the country, working again with my colleague Amanda Taub and now trailed by a documentary film crew, in April 2019, three months after Bolsonaro took office.

2. Democracy by Algorithm

WHEN MATHEUS DOMINGUEZ was sixteen years old, YouTube recommended him a video that would change his life. He had formed a band with some friends in Niterói, his hometown across the bay from Rio de Janeiro. To practice, he watched guitar tutorials online. One day, the platform directed him to a music teacher named Nando Moura, who posted homemade videos about heavy metal and, increasingly, politics. Moura, longhaired and flamboyant, accused feminists, teachers, and politicians of plotting to indoctrinate Brazilians with communism and homosexuality. He made jokes and wore outlandish costumes. He played guitar riffs and video games.

Dominguez was hooked. As his time on the site grew, YouTube recommended videos from other far-right bloggers. Most were young, save one: the suit-wearing Bolsonaro, whom Dominguez first saw as a guest on one of Moura's videos. It was 2016. At the time, Bolsonaro, a longtime lawmaker in Brazil's version of the U.S. House of Representatives, was shunned even in his own party. But YouTube, chasing its billion-hour watch-time goal, had just installed its new, deep-learning A.I. In Brazil, far-right YouTubers — Bolsonaro's real party — saw their exposure skyrocket.

"It all started from there," said Dominguez, now a lanky eighteen-year-old with glasses and a ponytail, calling YouTube the new home of the Brazilian right. The recommendation algorithm had "woken up Brazilians," he said. "It promotes whatever content will get the most views. They're not concerned with left or right, they want money," he said. Now politics were Dominguez's life. He had joined Bolsonaro's new party. He wanted to run for office himself one day. And he posted long videos to YouTube, which he considered the center of national life.

Dominguez led us to a pro-Bolsonaro march, along Niterói's beach promenades and luxury high-rises, offering to introduce us to party officials. I doubted they would be so forthcoming; pros would surely know not to attribute their successes to a foreign website. I was wrong. Everyone we spoke to insisted that American social media platforms had brought them there.

"It was like that with everyone," Maurício Martins, the party's local vice president, said, shouting over the crowd. "Most of the people here came from YouTube and social media." Even him, he said. A few years earlier, the system had autoplayed a video on politics, a subject he'd never expressed interest in before. It was from Kim Kataguiri, a right-wing video-maker. "Before that," he said, "I didn't have an ideological, political background." But the video grabbed him, and he kept watching. The algorithm, he said, provided "my political education."

Brazilians like Martins and Dominguez were making a claim far beyond anything that researchers like Jonas Kaiser or Guillaume Chaslot had observed: that YouTube had not merely created some online fringe community or altered certain users' views, but that it had radicalized their country's entire conservative movement, and so effectively as to supplant right-wing politics almost entirely. A few hundred miles away in Belo Horizonte, a city of grand colonial architecture, a team of researchers hunched over their computers, trying to understand whether this was true. "There is a huge predominance of right-wing channels on YouTube," said Virgilio Almeida, the gray-bearded computer scientist who headed the lab, at the Federal University of Minas Gerais. "They attract more viewers, more comments, more interactions, than the left-wing channels." But a corruption crisis had recently brought down Brazil's left-wing government, upending politics. Maybe YouTube was merely reflecting Brazilians' attitudes.

Almeida had some ideas on how to isolate the platform's influence to find out. His team realized that they could measure the political valence of YouTube's politics videos by scraping their captions. They used special software to track trends in the videos' mood and political alignment. And they did the same thing for the comments beneath those videos. Since around the time of YouTube's 2016 algorithmic upgrade, they found, right-wing channels had seen their audiences grow substantially faster than others, dominating the site's political content. Positive mentions of Bolsonaro shot up. So did mentions of conspiracy theories that Bolsonaro floated. Much as Chaslot had found during the 2017 French election, YouTube tilted dramatically pro-Bolsonaro and hard-right during a period when Bolsonaro's poll numbers remained static and low. The platform was not reflecting real-world trends. It was creating its own.

But now Almeida made a new discovery, one that suggested, in a way that other research had only been able to hint at, that not only was YouTube driving Brazilian interest in watching Bolsonaro-aligned videos, but it was actually changing users' underlying politics. The platform's rightward shift had started with video views. Channels that praised Bolsonaro or used far-right keywords saw their view counts spike — presumably thanks to the algorithm. After this, comments drifted rightward, too, which suggested that YouTube was pulling users toward Bolsonarism, rather than vice versa.

But the platforms' influence on the ground turned out to extend far beyond simple matters of political preference. In early 2017, just as Matheus Dominguez was experiencing his political awakening online, an ambitious young city councilor across town named Carly Jordy had an idea. Jordy, a hard-line conservative in left-leaning Niterói, had few obvious paths out of obscurity. Rough-natured and heavily tattooed — his left hand bears a flaming skull with diamond eyes — he felt scorned by Brazil's political class. But he found like-minded company on YouTube. He watched Nando Moura, Jair Bolsonaro, and Jordan Peterson, the psychologist who'd become an algorithmic gateway to the alt right.

Jordy's plan took inspiration from far-right YouTubers in Brazil who had begun encouraging schoolchildren to clandestinely film their teachers for proof of communist-homosexual indoctrination, a conspiracy, rooted in the same fictitious charge Bolsonaro had once made against Tatiana Lionço, that they'd fabricated on their channels for months. He had a modest following on YouTube, where he posted videos of himself shouting down leftists on his city council. Like his YouTube heroes, he urged Niterói's schoolkids to record their teachers. A few sent him shaky cell-phone footage from their classes, which he edited and uploaded to YouTube.

During an interview in his office, Jordy proudly pulled up his most viral of these. In it, a student interrupted her history teacher during a lecture on Nazi Germany. The student asked whether her conservative classmates were akin to Nazis, to which the teacher replied that they were. A banner image displayed Jordy's name and social media handles. He had misleadingly edited the footage, it turned out. In reality, the student, who was gay, had described being harassed by classmates whose families supported Bolsonaro, who was then still a local figure known to have said he'd rather his son were dead than gay. The student had asked whether this sentiment made her classmates like Nazis. No, the teacher had said, even if the two groups had homophobia in common.

The clip initially won little audience — until it was repackaged by Nando Moura, who called it proof that this school was an epicenter of abuse. It swept across the platform's right-wing channels, pushed to huge audiences. Then it spread next to Facebook, where it was viewed five million times.

Valeria Borges, the teacher in the video, called the months after its circulation "the worst time of my entire life." Borges showed us pages of graphic threats that had flooded in. Other teachers and school officials had been targeted, too, presumed complicit. Though Borges's students rallied in her support, most Brazilians knew her only as a villain. "They see me as an enemy, and that I need to be destroyed," she said. Still, two years later, she added, "I'm afraid for my family, I'm afraid for my students, and my colleagues."

Another teacher at the school told us that parents had grown unsure what to believe. They knew the school and its teachers as competent and friendly. But so many of their friends and relatives had repeated the conspiracy back to them that they struggled to reconcile the reality they knew with the social media unreality that had overtaken it. Some began asking pointed questions about "indoctrination." The teachers said that they'd grown fearful and guarded in their own classrooms. Anything they said, they worried, might appear online, distorted to advance some agenda, boosted nationwide by social media.

A wave of such incidents was spreading across Brazil. The initial accusation would be outlandish — a teacher had encouraged his students to deal drugs, start a communist insurrection, "become" gay — but seemingly supported by a video. Other YouTubers would put their own spin on the clip, winning hundreds of thousands of views (and a cut of ad revenue) by giving the platform the culture-war conspiracies that it consistently rewarded. Each rumor, however implausible on its own, in the aggregate lent credibility to the others, a self-supporting latticework of misinformation. Teachers were fired or harassed into hiding, schools besieged, communities whipped into distrust and division, all orchestrated on YouTube.

"In Brazil, this happens often now, the recording and lynching," Borges said. "It's a form of intimidation. And it's working."

Jordy posted videos of other teachers, all edited in the same way. They brought him, he said, a "national audience." After just two years on the city council, in the same election that elevated Bolsonaro, he won a seat in the federal legislature. And another far-right YouTuber who'd pushed school-indoctrination claims was elected to the state legislature. It was, in retrospect, a warning sign. Fringe American conspiracists with political aspirations, such as Lauren Boebert and Marjorie Taylor Greene, though seen as ridiculous, might in fact represent a rising trend whose culmination may still lie years in the future. "If social media didn't exist, I wouldn't be here," Jordy told me. "Jair Bolsonaro wouldn't be president."

When I asked Jordy about his edits to the video that had changed its meaning, he didn't dispute them. I read out some of the threats that Borges had received — promises to kill her and worse. Did he regret upending the lives of schoolteachers he knew to be innocent?

The film crew had asked Jordy's staff to turn off their air conditioners, which had interfered with the audio. It was nearly 100 degrees outside and humid. Five of us were crammed into his closet-sized office, nearly touching. We'd been talking for more than an hour, and the air, stagnant and hot, felt suffocating.

Jordy, sweat rolling into his eyes, dropped any pretense. "I did it to shock, I did it to expose her," he said, raising his shoulders and puffing out his chest. "I wanted her to feel fear."

Throughout the incident, I said, he had never spoken to students or parent groups on whose behalf he claimed to act. Never visited the school that was yards from his office. Never even used his powers as councilmember. He'd focused all his energy on social media. Why?

"There's a culture war that we're fighting," he said, though he was vague against whom. "People respect what they fear. They need to have this fear to understand that they can be punished for their actions."

He seemed to have little agenda beyond stoking outrage and winning attention on social media, whose cues and incentives, after all, he had followed to high office. The more I spoke to people around town, the less that people like Jordy and Bolsonaro seemed to be driving the digital forces that had elevated them, and the more they looked like passive beneficiaries.

"Ninety-five percent of the kids here use YouTube. It's the main source that kids have to get information," Inzaghi, a seventeen-year-old student, told me outside the school at the center of Jordy's video. They watched YouTube to kill time on the bus, he said, in place of TV at home, even as research for homework. But he and his friends had noticed the same thing as everyone else in the country. "Sometimes I'm watching videos about a game and all of a sudden it's a Bolsonaro video," he said. "It's going to try to get you to watch these videos whether or not you want to."

He noticed its influence in class, too. More and more, students interrupted teachers with accusations or conspiracies that they'd picked up from YouTube. "Every time someone is saying something extreme, they're quoting from people like Mamãefalei and Kim Kataguiri and MBL," another student, Jojo, said, listing right-wing YouTubers. "Nando Moura, Nando Moura," Inzaghi shouted, his friends laughing along. "On the street, on the bus, in big groups, I see people watching Nando Moura." Every student I spoke to emphasized that they liked YouTube, especially gaming and comedy channels. But all complained that the platform pushed them, over and over, to watch conspiracies and political rants. "It ends up affecting how people think," Inzaghi said.

I asked Jonas Kaiser and Adrian Rauchfleisch to help us understand YouTube's behavior in Brazil. They repeated their German- and American-honed methods. By tracing the system's recommendations many times over, they found, much as before, a vast, algorithmically generated cluster of far-right and conspiracy channels. Once again, the system used moderate voices as entry points to pull users toward the extremists, then kept them there, showing more and more video clips. If there had been any lingering doubt about whether Germany or America might somehow represent aberrations, Brazil settled it: YouTube's methods of right-wing radicalization at scale were too chillingly consistent to be anything but hard-coded in.

The real-world consequences of YouTube's rabbit-hole effect — the distortion imposed on millions of citizens, a substantial chunk of the electorate — were everywhere, starting with politics. Bolsonaro urged citizens to watch YouTube rather than reputable news. He replaced government technocrats with social media personalities, who used their power to act on the oddball conspiracies — about education, public health, minorities — that had appeased the Silicon Valley algorithm that got them there.

And the YouTubers who followed Bolsonaro into office continued posting feverishly on the platform, understanding that they relied on it to maintain the social media voters who were their base. That meant indulging, in everything they did in office, the needs and biases of the platform.

Ground zero for the new era of politics by YouTube was the São Paulo headquarters of Movimento Brasil Livre. Kim Kataguiri, the group's leader, had risen to YouTube fame as a teenager by posting videos refuting what he considered his teachers' leftist biases. (Maurício Martins, the official in Bolsonaro's party, had cited one of those videos, autoplayed for him by YouTube, as his introduction to politics.) In 2016, he and others had formed MBL to agitate for the impeachment of Brazil's then president. The group's members trended young, educated, right-wing, and extremely online — the YouTube demographic. That fall, at age twenty-two, he won a seat in the federal legislature.

Now a few months into his term, Kataguiri stopped by the group's offices, a concrete-floored hangout of hipsters slouching over laptops. A cameraman wearing a backward Make America Great Again hat directed him onto a leather sofa, where he recorded the day's video. After filming ended, Kataguiri told me that initially MBL had used Facebook but that after 2016, around the time that YouTube updated its algorithm, the video platform had proved more effective, and they switched. Plus, he added, Facebook had taken repeated action against his group for misinformation, whereas YouTube never did, though MBL posted the exact same content to both. This was something I heard repeatedly: YouTube was much more permissive, one reason that groups like his loved it.

Other YouTubers in MBL won office in 2018, too. Their channels all occupied the central node of Kaiser's map of Brazilian YouTube, heavily boosted by the site's recommendations. One of them, Arthur do Val, even after winning a seat in his state legislature, still went by the name of his YouTube channel, Mamãefalei, which means "Mommy said."

To underscore the platform's importance, do Val cited a super-viral video that another group had just posted. Titled "1964" for the year of Brazil's military coup, it claimed that the dictatorship's abuses — it had murdered hundreds of dissidents and tortured thousands more — had been fabricated by left-wing historians. It argued that the coup had been necessary to stamp out communism, implying that another such action might soon be required, too. "I was one of the biggest sharers of this video," do Val said.

The "1964" video was brought up everywhere I went in Brazil. Dominguez, the eighteen-year-old activist, called it "a milestone" that had persuaded him that the military regime had not been so bad. Valeria Borges, the history teacher, said it was "terrifying" to watch YouTube erase their country's history from young Brazilians' minds, even nudge them toward repeating it.

As we lingered at MBL headquarters, the activists let on that, for all their success, even they'd come to worry about the platforms' impact. "We have something here that we call the dictatorship of the like," said Pedro D'Eyrot, a man-bunned former rock guitarist who'd turned political and now made videos for MBL. They had watched, he said, as one YouTuber after another grew steadily more extreme, more untruthful, more reckless, "just because something is going to give you views, going to give engagement."

Everyone felt the pressure, he said. "Once you open that door there's no going back, because you always have to go further." He'd once believed in social media as a force for change, he said. Now it seemed to draw out tendencies that could only be harmful, too extreme even for a group of MAGA hat–wearing coup revisionists. "Flat Earthers, anti-vaxxers, conspiracy theorists in politics. It's the same phenomenon," he said. "You see it everywhere." If some of the greatest exploiters and beneficiaries of this system were suddenly speaking like Renée DiResta or Guillaume Chaslot, then the dangers, I realized, must have grown beyond even what I'd seen so far, here or in America. They had.

3. Dr. YouTube

IN MACEIÓ, ONE of Brazil's poorer cities, in a concrete courtyard on the outskirts of town, fifteen mothers huddled under a plastic canopy in the dripping rain, waiting for Mardjane Nunes. Since 2015, thousands of pregnant women in the Americas, infected by a new virus called Zika, have given birth to children with severe neurological impairment and misshapen skulls, a condition known as microcephaly. Brazil's northeast, where Maceió is, was hit hardest. Across neighborhoods like this one, mothers formed support groups to help one another navigate the poorly understood condition that had crippled their children.

Nunes, a leading expert on Zika, had come to answer questions. Within minutes, a mother stood, cradling her child, and said she'd heard on social media that Zika was caused not by a mosquito-borne virus, as doctors said, but by expired vaccines. Tormented by uncertainty, she was considering forgoing vaccinations. Heads nodded across the group. Nunes told her, gently but unambiguously, that the rumors were false. But, one after another, the mothers expressed doubt. They had all seen this, or something like it, online. Zika was a lie or a plot. Doctors couldn't be trusted. Vaccines were unsafe.

Nunes had previously heard from colleagues that the meetings often went like this, she said afterward. She had recently left a prestigious job at the health ministry to return to frontline work, fighting HIV and Zika at the local hospital and through community groups. Social media, she said, was becoming a subject of growing alarm in public-health circles. Field researchers came back with stories of whole towns refusing treatment, mothers terrified into denying their children lifesaving care. But she hadn't been prepared for the fear in the mothers' eyes, the totality of their community's break from reality. "If this group, who is already more engaged, already speaks with each other more, still has doubts," she said, "imagine what is in the minds of mothers who don't have a group like this."

It explained, she said, why her ministry had put more and more resources into educating young families like these, only to find itself outmatched by misinformation spreading even faster, via social media. Vaccine avoidance was rising in Brazil. So were reports of communities refusing to use mosquito larvicides, a preferred method for fighting Zika that is also often named in conspiracy videos. "Social media is winning," Nunes said.

It was not a new problem. DiResta had discovered Facebook systematically pushing Zika conspiracies as far back as 2015. The Brazilian Institute of Research and Data Analysis found that, in 2017, YouTube had been filled with conspiracies about the yellow fever vaccine. Cases of yellow fever surged around the same time, though it was unclear which had caused which. Either way, many of those conspiracies had been pushed by far-right politics channels. It was another piece of evidence for Kaiser's finding that YouTube's algorithm, by binding together once-distinct conspiracy and extremist channels, crossbred them into a new sort of threat.

"Everything you don't know, you can find on YouTube," Gisleangela Oliveira dos Santos, one of the mothers who had asked about vaccines, told my colleague Amanda in her home the next day. Though Oliveira dos Santos lived a day's journey away, Amanda, a young mother herself, urged that the film crew make the trip with her, recognizing that parents acting on these conspiracies, though easy to mistake as part of the problem, were victims of social media, too.

When Oliveira dos Santos's baby had been diagnosed with microcephaly three years earlier, information had been scarce. The virus, after all, was new. She'd sought out every scrap she could online, including YouTube.

Again and again, the platform served her videos blaming Zika on expired measles vaccines that the government had bought on the cheap. It was the fault of mercury in the needles. Of a cabal of shadowy foreigners who wanted to weaken Catholic families. Some videos had been staged to resemble news reports or public service announcements. Some showed a priest or other trusted figure imploring the good mothers of Brazil not to listen to the corrupt, foreigner-controlled doctors. The other mothers in her community had the same experience, sharing the clips on group WhatsApp threads, another web of peer-group confirmation.

Oliveira dos Santos had been pushed into the videos, she said, by

YouTube's recommendation system and its search engine. Even googling terms like "Zika" or "Zika vaccines" led her to the videos, which Google, again with its synergistic favoring of YouTube links that proved so lucrative, often put at the top of its search results. Oliveira dos Santos knew that the internet could be unreliable. But the videos paralyzed her with doubt. She had initially given her child standard childhood inoculations. But, she said, "I was scared to give any more vaccines to my daughter after that." She stopped accepting them herself.

Ever since, she has been wracked with doubts and, most of all, guilt. Had she, by accepting vaccines, caused her child's life-threatening illness? The doctors said she hadn't. But these American tech companies, deeply respected in Brazil, told her over and over that she had. They even showed her "proof," pushing it in front of her nearly every time she looked for information on caring for the child that YouTube and Google insisted she had crippled for life. "I feel powerless," she said. "I feel powerless and wounded." (Like countless other Brazilians, the more time she spent on YouTube, the more videos she saw in support of Bolsonaro. She found them persuasive, too, she said, and voted for him.)

Maceió's public hospital is not especially well funded. When I visited, many of the overhead lights were kept off to save electricity. But its place on the front line against Zika had attracted some of the country's top medical talent. When doctors there heard why I had come, they made time immediately, waving me into the mostly bare breakroom. "Fake news is a virtual war. We have it coming from every direction," said Flavio Santana, a pediatric neurologist. Discussions within the country's medical community, he said, focused more and more on frustration with social media platforms. "If you go to other places in Brazil, you're going to find the same issues."

Auriene Oliviera, an infectious-disease specialist, nodded. Patients increasingly defied her advice and contested her facts. "They say, 'No, I've researched it on Google, I've seen it on YouTube'," she said. She understood her patients' dilemma. Conspiracies offered a level of certainty that science could not. Homegrown remedies let mothers feel like they were retaking control of their children's health. And the platforms were ever-present in a way that Dr. Oliviera couldn't be, appearing day after day in the lives of mothers who, because they worked multiple jobs or lived far away, she might see once per month. They reached for smartphone apps not out of sloth or ignorance, but out of necessity.

Increasingly, however, the viral videos put children's lives at risk, by counseling mothers not only to refuse vaccines but also to treat certain conditions themselves, to refuse feeding tubes for children whose condition made them unable to swallow. A few times, the doctors said, they'd resorted to threatening to contact child services as a means of compelling mothers to listen. It was a power they felt terrible holding over mothers' heads, but sometimes it was the only option forceful enough to match the platforms' power.

How long had this been going on? I asked. If it had coincided with the arrival of Zika, in 2015, then it could arguably owe more to the confusion created by the virus than to any technological change. But the doctors gave the same answer as everyone else. It had started later, just after YouTube upgraded its algorithms. "More than once a week, this kind of thing comes up," Oliviera said. "It's more and more severe." Doctors and medical researchers often lamented, she said, that they were competing against "Dr. Google and Dr. YouTube." And they were losing.

I gathered the conspiracy videos that the mothers and health workers had cited, many of which had tens or hundreds of thousands of views, and sent them to Kaiser's team. Had these, and the channels that posted them, appeared at all in their network analysis? I asked. Not only did they appear, it turned out, but they were championed. The team identified an enormous network of algorithmically linked health and wellness channels, covering everything from medical reports to healing crystals. As with politics videos, the algorithm used more credible or familiar channels as gateways to direct users toward the worst conspiracies and misinformation. The very videos that distraught parents and doctors had shown to us sat near the center of the network, the algorithm's ultimate destination.

It was hard evidence that everyone we'd spoken to about medical misinformation in Brazil had been even more right about YouTube than they'd known. That the platform exploited normal user interest in medical matters, as it had with politics, to pull them down rabbit holes they would have otherwise never pursued. And that, much as YouTube had learned to sequence politics videos to turn casual viewers into digitally addicted radicals, it had come to array Zika and vaccine videos in precisely the right order to persuade loving mothers to deliberately endanger their children.

"There's always going to be borderline content on platforms. That's to be expected," Kaiser said, straining to sympathize with the tech companies. "The shocking thing," he added, "is that YouTube's algorithms basically are helping people to go in these directions."

4. The Pipeline

ON HEARING WHAT Amanda and I were investigating, Luciana Brito, a soft-spoken clinical psychologist we'd met at the mothers' center in Maceió, insisted that we talk. She was in town, visiting from her research center in Brazil's capital, for fieldwork with Zika families. Brito was busy all day — the parents were struggling — and it was after midnight by the time we sat down. Scrolling through her phone, she pulled up a WhatsApp message she had received from a father of a child with microcephaly. It was a video claiming that Zika had been spread by the Rockefeller Foundation as part of a plot to legalize abortion in Brazil. The father demanded to know if it was true.

This happened, Brito said, all the time now. In many parts of the world, people cannot afford full-sized computers or broadband, or even the data charges associated with streaming video. WhatsApp provided a workaround. With zero-rating deals often covering data charges incurred on the app, people who couldn't afford to stream YouTube could instead watch snippets that had been reuploaded on WhatsApp, and then forward them to friends and share them in supersized WhatsApp groups. In parts of Brazil where illiteracy is high, this is thought to be a primary means by which many families consume news. WhatsApp groups are their Google, their Facebook, and their CNN, all rolled into one.

Because it was everyday users copying over the clips, whatever trended on YouTube (or Facebook) became likelier to get reuploaded on Whats-App and go viral again there, like an infection jumping from one host to the next. Videos like the one that Brito's contact had sent her, she said, often spread in WhatsApp chat groups that had been set up to share information about coping with Zika, turning people's very efforts to manage their family's health against them. Brito and her colleagues joined the groups, where they tried to debunk the worst of it, but the questions kept coming. And content from YouTube and Facebook filtered in constantly, with no check against it.

Virgilio Almeida, the Federal University of Minas Gerais computer scientist, had been studying this exact phenomenon. He and his team tracked tens of thousands of messages in hundreds of Brazilian WhatsApp groups (all anonymized, of course), then looked for trends. WhatsApp users, they found, uploaded one video for every fourteen text messages, an astonishingly high rate. WhatsApp users also linked to YouTube more than any other site — ten times as frequently as they linked to Facebook — bolstering the theory of a YouTube-to-WhatsApp pipeline. They found similar trends in India and Indonesia, suggesting the effect might be universal.

That was something else, Brito said. As Zika conspiracies spread, far-right YouTubers had hijacked them, adding a twist. Women's rights groups, they claimed, had helped engineer the virus as an excuse to impose mandatory abortions. Often the videos named Brito's group. Viewers, already terrified of Zika, would take their cue. "Right after they launch a video, we start receiving threats," Brito said. The claims, she knew, offered psychic relief for families, letting them turn their guilt and fear outward. It was J. M. Berger's crisis-solution construct: much as American YouTubers had turned youth male dispossession into rage at feminists, now Brazil's were exploiting the terror of families faced with an implacable illness.

Threats against Brito and her colleagues had grown so frequent that the police set up a special channel for them to report any that seemed grave. They used it about once a week, she said. But she worried most about mothers who had internalized the conspiracies. More all the time were rejecting help from aid groups they now suspected of afflicting their children. And without medical and emotional support, they turned even deeper into YouTube. "These women are very vulnerable," she said. "It's very easy for them to fall into the trap of believing in these theories. So there is a lot of despair."

There was one name I heard over and over in Maceió, from doctors, health workers, the mothers pulled down YouTube rabbit holes. No one had seen Debora Diniz for months, but they all urged me to talk with her. Diniz, a slight woman with cropped gray hair who for years worked as a human rights lawyer, had, several years earlier, become a documentary filmmaker. Her film on the Zika outbreak had led her to Maceió. Moved by the mothers, doctors, and aid workers who'd pulled together, she stayed, advocating on the community's behalf.

One day, threats began overwhelming her phone and email. Diniz initially ignored them. As a veteran of Brazil's culture wars, especially around abortion, she was accustomed to it. But they became unusually numerous. And the accusations were outlandish: that she was working for George Soros, that she'd had a hand in the creation of Zika. Many cited the same source: Bernardo Küster.

He was, through and through, a creation of YouTube. The thirty-year-old ultraconservative had, from his home in the small city of Londrina, churned out years' worth of tirades against godless liberals, the Pope, journalists, "gender ideology" (code for LGBT rights), and especially feminists. Rewarded over and over by YouTube's systems, he had accrued 750,000 subscribers. Bolsonaro had once endorsed his channel. And since late 2017, Küster had named Diniz at the center of a plot to force abortions on unwilling mothers. As the videos did well, he made more and more of them, inventing new claims that sent his thousands of followers, enraged at this woman's sins, after her.

The threats filling Diniz's phone became more frequent and more graphic, long descriptions of the senders' plans to rape and torture her. Often they echoed whatever Küster had said in his last video. Some cited details of her daily routines. "They describe the way that they will kill me," Diniz told me when we met in New York, where she now lived, after having fled her native Brazil. As the film crew rolled, she picked up her phone to read to me: "It's God's will that I will kill you. I will commit suicide after that." Küster had winkingly mentioned the threats in his videos, though never explicitly endorsed them. YouTube refused to remove the videos, despite Diniz's pleas that they endangered her life.

After months of this, the university where Diniz taught received a warning. The sender said that he was coming to shoot Diniz, then her students, then himself. The police told Diniz they could no longer guarantee her safety. She worried, too, about her colleagues and elderly parents, who had begun receiving similar threats. She left Brazil, not knowing when or if she would return.

"I exposed her," Küster said in a much-watched video celebrating her exile. "You are not welcome here," he shouted, wagging a finger at the camera. But Küster was, Diniz believed, in many ways a product of forces larger than himself. Both he and the threats he inspired, she argued, came from an "ecosystem of hate" cultivated by YouTube. "The YouTube system of recommending the next video and the next video feeds the ecosystem," she said, speaking slowly as she picked each word in English, her third language. "'I heard here that she's an enemy of Brazil. I hear in the next one that feminists are changing family values. And the next one I hear that they receive money from abroad.' That loop is what leads someone to say, 'I will do what has to be done.'" The effect was so persuasive, she said, because "it feels like the connection is made by the viewer, but the connection is made by the system."

Exiles like Diniz's were growing common. After all, you cannot guard against a threat that comes from everywhere. A few months earlier, Marcia Tiburi, a left-wing activist who had run for the governorship of Rio de Janeiro state, fled Brazil to escape death threats fomented largely on social media. Jean Wyllys, the country's only openly gay lawmaker, had done the same.

The evening before our interview, Diniz said, she'd had dinner with Wyllys, who was in town. Someone must have recognized them, because a group of Brazilians gathered outside the restaurant, taking photos and pointing. The crowd menaced them as they left, following them down the street, shouting slurs and accusations echoing the conspiracies on You-Tube. It was why Diniz rarely went out, even here.

"We have a militia that is moved by algorithms," she said. "The algorithms are building the militia."

I asked if she still received threatening messages.

"It's every day," she said. "You never, ever feel comfortable with a situation like this."

We had been talking for an hour, the cameras and lights pressing in as I asked her to navigate, on film and in a foreign language, her own trauma. I told her that I couldn't imagine what it would take to continue speaking up, knowing the dangers had followed her even here.

She splayed her arms over the table that we sat across, and looked down. She was crying. "There are moments in your life that you face a dilemma," she said. "You have just two options. One is to let them win. And the other is to fight back. I don't want that language for my life. But I will dedicate my life to changing that situation. And they will not kill me. They will not kill me."

I offered to end the interview, but she shook her head. She said that she had followed the stories of doctors and activists targeted by YouTube videos, schoolteachers sent into hiding, lives ruined, and communities upended. "We need the companies to face their role," she said. She urged YouTube's executives to reflect on their own involvement. "My hope is that they understand that they are part of this community of hate," she said. "Ethically, they are responsible."

But YouTube continued to resist accountability. The company's corporate representatives repeated the familiar script. The company took safety and well-being seriously. But it rejected the Harvard and Federal University of Minas Gerais studies, saying that it did not consider their methodology sound. When it came to these questions, the company said it had conducted its own internal research, which had proved that the platform overwhelmingly promoted accurate and beneficial content. The representatives, who demanded to review hundreds of pages of evidence behind the studies Amanda and I cited, would not provide any data or methodology to support their own claim.

After conceding that some of the health misinformation videos that Kaiser had identified had broken the site's rules, the company removed them. The details of Kaiser's research, which I'd relayed to YouTube, implied that there were hundreds of videos, possibly thousands, urging mothers to withhold lifesaving care from their children. We'd sent only a few links as examples. YouTube never asked for the others. The company also did not ask for details on the videos that had inspired credible death threats against Diniz and others, many of which remain online.

Later that year, YouTube announced that it had made changes to its algorithm aimed at reducing "the spread of borderline content and harmful misinformation." But some of those changes had already been in effect when we'd done our reporting, raising questions about their effectiveness. The company touted a somewhat oblique metric for success: "A 70% drop in watch time of this content coming from non-subscribed recommendations in the U.S."

In May 2019, two months after returning from Brazil, I got a text message from Kaiser: he needed me to call him right away. He picked up on the first ring, his voice shaking. He and the others had been running more iterations of their platform-tracing program on Brazilian channels, he said. And they'd found something so disturbing they didn't know what to do with it. Kaiser wasn't calling about an article, I realized. He was calling for help.

5. *Training Grounds*

CHRISTIANE DIDN'T THINK anything of it when her ten-year-old daughter and a friend uploaded a video of themselves splashing in a backyard pool. "The video is innocent, it's not a big deal," said Christiane, who lives in a suburb of Rio de Janeiro. A few days later, her daughter shared exciting news: the video had thousands of views. Before long, it had 400,000. It was a staggering, inexplicable number for an unremarkable little clip uploaded to Christiane's channel, which normally got a few dozen clicks. "I saw the video again and I got scared by the number of views," Christiane said.

She had reason to be. YouTube's algorithm had quietly selected the video of her daughter for a vast and disturbing program. It was curating, from across its archives, dozens of videos of prepubescent, partially unclothed children. It plucked many of them from the home movies of unwitting families. It strung them all together, showing one clip after another of six- or seven-year-olds in bathing suits or underwear, doing splits or lying in bed, to draw in a very specific kind of viewer with content they would find irresistible. And then it built an audience for those videos the size of ten football stadiums. "I'm so shocked," Christiane said when she learned what had happened, terrified that her daughter's video had been presented alongside so many others, with the platform's intentions disturbingly clear.

Kaiser, along with Rauchfleisch and Córdova, had stumbled onto this while working on the Brazil study. As their test machine followed You-Tube's recommendation on sexually themed videos, the system pushed toward more bizarre or extreme sexual content. This in itself was not shocking; they had seen the rabbit-hole effect many times on other sorts of content. But some of the recommendation chains followed an unmistakable progression: each subsequent video led to another where the woman in its center put greater emphasis on youth and grew more erotic. Videos of women discussing sex, for example, led to videos of women in underwear or breastfeeding, sometimes mentioning their age: nineteen, eighteen, even sixteen. Some solicited "sugar daddies," a term for donations from lustful viewers. Others hinted at private videos where they posed nude for money. After a few clicks, the women in the videos played more and more overtly at prepubescence, speaking in baby talk or posing seductively in children's clothing.

From there, YouTube would suddenly shift to recommending clips of very young children caught in moments of unintended nudity. A girl perhaps as young as five or six changing her clothes, or contorting into a gymnastics pose. Then a near-endless stream of such videos, drawn from around the world. Not all appeared to be home movies; some had been uploaded by carefully anonymized accounts.

The ruthless specificity of YouTube's selections was almost as disturbing as the content itself, suggesting that its systems could correctly identify a video of a partially nude child and determine that this characteristic was the video's appeal. Showing a series of them immediately after sexually explicit material made clear that the algorithm treated the unwitting children as sexual content. The extraordinary view counts, sometimes in the millions, indicated that this was no quirk of personalization. The system had found, maybe constructed, an audience for the videos. And it was working to keep that audience engaged.

"It's YouTube's algorithm that connects these channels. That's the scary thing," Kaiser said, calling the recommendations "disturbingly on point." He'd known to proceed carefully with these videos. American laws against viewing child pornography offer few exceptions for researchers or journalists. Most of the clips fell, probably, just short of legally constituting child pornography. But some did not. And the context in which YouTube had placed them allowed no ambiguity as to their intent. Kaiser and I settled on procedures to track the videos responsibly and without exposing anyone to harm. But we also felt compelled to move quickly. View counts were ratcheting by thousands per day. Some, like that of Christiane's daughter, were posted under the parents' names, leaving the children in the videos easily trackable by the right kind of monster. Something had to be done.

Juliana Cunha, a psychologist with SaferNet, a Brazilian internet monitor, said her organization had seen this phenomenon before. But never involving girls so young. And never reaching such a large audience. Similar videos, traded on dark-web forums and file-sharing sites, might normally reach a few hundred people. This appeared to be the most widely viewed catalog of child-exploitation videos ever assembled, promoted to an audience of millions.

Most people who view sexualized imagery of children leave it at that, research suggests. But some viewers become likelier, on each viewing, to reach out to the children directly, a first step toward grooming victims for potential physical abuse. Child-safety groups worried that the videos could make that easier, even invite it, by pushing them to interested viewers over and over, wearing them down, and by identifying the names of family members or the kids' social media accounts.

There was, psychologists feared, another risk. YouTube had cultivated an enormous audience of viewers who had never sought the content out, but rather were pulled into it by the platform's recommendations. This was not just another rabbit hole. The pathway appeared to mimic, step by step, a process that psychologists had repeatedly observed in research on how people develop attractions to child pornography.

For some people, pedophilic impulses form early in life and remain more or less innate. But Kathryn Seigfried-Spellar and Marcus Rogers, Purdue University psychologists, have found that child-pornography consumers often developed that interest, rather than being born with it. People who undergo this process begin with adult pornography, then move to incrementally more extreme material, following an addiction-like compulsion to chase increasingly deviant sexual content, pornography a degree more taboo than what they'd seen before. "As they get desensitized to those pictures, if they're on that scale," Rogers said, "then they're going to seek out stuff that's even more thrilling, even more titillating, even more sexualized."

Their compulsions were shaped by whatever content they happened to encounter, akin to training. It was not at all inevitable that these people would follow their urge past any moral line. Nor that this compulsion, if they did follow it, would lead them toward children. But on YouTube, the second-most-popular website in the world, the system seemed to have identified people with this urge, walked them along a path that indulged it at just the right pace to keep them moving, and then pointed them in a very specific direction. "This is something that takes them on that journey," Rogers said of YouTube's sequencing. He called the recommendation engine a potential "gateway drug towards more hard-core child pornography."

Research into this subject is, he underscored, notoriously challenging. Few child-pornography consumers are willing to discuss their interest. Some will lie about their motives, to avoid the stigma of pedophilia. Controlled studies would be, for ethical reasons, impossible. As a result, studies like his tend to be relatively small and often focus on people who have been caught.

Still, every expert that Amanda and I consulted said there was evidence to suggest that Seigfried-Spellar and Rogers's conclusions, as well as their fears of its application to YouTube, had merit. Stephen Blumenthal, a clinical psychologist with Britain's National Health Service who treats people for deviant sexual interests and had published scholarly research on his work, said he had seen patients develop pedophilic desires by following a similar progression. "It's incredibly powerful, and people get drawn into that," he said. "They might never have gone down that route were it not for the possibilities that the internet opened up." While he was unaware of cases specifically involving YouTube, he said, the parallels concerned him. So did the unprecedented scale and efficiency of YouTube's methods.

YouTube responded with skepticism when presented with our findings. A spokesperson called the psychologists' concerns in particular "questionable." YouTube's position, she said, was that the science was not yet settled on whether pedophilic urges could be trained in or heightened by environmental factors, as Seigfried-Spellar, Rogers, and Blumenthal had found. The spokesperson cited an expert named Ethel Quayle, whose research, she said, challenged the existence of any "gateway" effect.

But, despite YouTube's responsibility-muddying claim of scientific uncertainty, when Amanda contacted Quayle, of the University of Edinburgh, Quayle said that in fact her research supported the theory of the gateway effect. Experts, she said, had long worried that machine-learning algorithms would create such pathways. "The algorithm doesn't have any kind of moral compass to it," she said. In a recent study of child-pornography offenders that she'd conducted, she said, "the majority talked about following links, originally from legitimate pornographic sites, and then chasing more and more deviant material."

For people with a predisposition to respond to such cues, Quayle said, algorithmic suggestions like YouTube's offer "almost a predetermined route for where they're going to go." That YouTube's handpicked expert believed the opposite of what YouTube had claimed she believed made me doubt how deeply the company had really researched the subject, for all its claims of taking child safety seriously. On top of this, Quayle and others warned, YouTube risked eroding viewers' internal taboo against pedophilia by showing videos of children alongside more mainstream sexual content, as well as displaying the videos' high view counts, demonstrating that they were widely viewed and thus presumably acceptable. As Rogers had said: "You normalize it."

Immediately after we notified YouTube of what we had found, a number of the videos we'd sent them as examples were removed. (Many we had not sent them, but which were part of the same network, remained online.) The platform's algorithm also immediately changed, no longer linking the dozens of videos together. When we asked YouTube about this, the company insisted that the timing was a coincidence. When I pushed, a spokesperson said it was hypothetically possible that the timing was related but that she could not say either way. It seemed as if YouTube was trying to tidy up without acknowledging there had been anything to tidy.

The company's spokespeople requested reams of information from us: studies, alternate studies, details on the researchers' methodology. They asked us to define terms like *network* and what we meant by users "finding" videos. They asked how many words the story would be. They asked us to clarify some detail, then a few days later asked the same question again. And they insisted on speaking to one of our editors at the paper before publication, whom they pressed for details on specific words the story would use to describe YouTube's role.

During my and Amanda's back-and-forth with YouTube, the analyses that Kaiser and his team were still running hit upon something. Soon after we contacted YouTube about the child-exploitation videos, notifying the company that Kaiser's team had found them in part by tracing the static "related channel" feature — just as he had done in every prior experiment, as a methodological check on his results — the company deleted the feature outright. Sitewide, after years in place, it was gone. When we asked the company whether the timing was related, the representatives claimed to be unaware that Kaiser had used the feature in his research at all. It was a strange claim, not only because we had told them he was doing so, but because YouTube had previously objected to Kaiser's research on exactly those grounds.

Before publication of my article with Amanda revealing what we'd found, the company linked me up with Jennifer O'Connor, YouTube's product director for trust and safety. She said that the company was committed to eradicating the exploitation of children on its platform outright. Still, she said, she did not accept the research suggesting that YouTube's algorithm pulled users toward more extreme content, in this case or others. Even on a subject this politically and legally sensitive — on which YouTube faced enormous incentive to reassure the world that it was taking every possible step in response — to publicly concede the system's role, and thereby acknowledge its radicalizing tendencies on this and so many other subjects, remained an impossibility.

I said that it was difficult to square this stance with the videos we had seen, the millions of views, the way the system routed users to them. She did not concede the point, but suggested that YouTube would hedge on the side of safety anyway. "When it comes to kids," she said, "we just want to take a much more conservative stance for what we recommend." O'Connor was vague on details, which she said were being worked out.

I thought back to something Kaiser had said. There was, he'd argued, only one sure way to stop this from happening again. On videos of children, turn off the algorithm. Just stop recommending videos of kids. This was easily within YouTube's technical capability. After an earlier controversy regarding comments beneath videos of kids, it had set up a system to automatically identify such videos and switch off their comments. Besides, for a $15-billion-per-year company, how much money could these videos really make? I asked O'Connor whether YouTube would consider something like this. To my surprise, she said that the company was "trending in that direction." She promised news soon.

I relayed the conversation to Kaiser's team, as well as to some monitoring groups, who were thrilled. They called it an enormously positive step, the internet made meaningfully safer for kids. But shortly before publication, YouTube "clarified" O'Connor's comment. YouTube video-makers rely on recommendations to drive traffic, they said, so the algorithm would stay switched on, even for videos of prepubescent children.

After our story published, Josh Hawley, a Republican senator who often criticized social media platforms, announced a bill in response to our findings. Just as Kaiser had urged, it would force YouTube and other platforms to shut down recommendations on videos of children. But the five-page bill, which never received a vote, seemed to have been mostly for show. Still, Senator Richard Blumenthal, a Democrat who'd advanced serious internet reforms, cosigned a letter with Senator Marsha Blackburn, a Republican, to YouTube's CEO regarding the story. It posed precise, on-target questions. One asked whether YouTube's policy managers for child safety would be "included in design decisions and the product lifecycle." This was a common issue in the Valley: people who study the platforms' impact, as non-engineers, have little say in their design. Blumenthal and Blackburn's letter also repeated Kaiser's primary question: why not simply turn off recommendations on videos of children?

That July, the Senate Judiciary Committee dedicated a full, though lightly attended, hearing to the subject. Its chair, Lindsey Graham, repeated Trump's long-standing threat to strip liability protections from the platforms. Blumenthal, the only Democrat to attend, said he was "frankly disappointed" in what he considered YouTube's nonresponse. "This report was sickening," Hawley said at the hearing, in reference to the story. "But I think what was more sickening was YouTube's refusal to do anything about it."

As Amanda and I were reporting the story, we'd checked the videos for any identifying information that might trace back to parents. When we could find it, we contacted local organizations that could alert the families to what was happening and provide help. After one such organization had contacted Christiane, the mother from Brazil, she offered to discuss her experience. Baffled and angry, she said she was struggling to absorb what had happened. She fretted over what to tell her husband. She expressed confusion at YouTube's practices, at one point asking whether it would be possible to sue the company. And she worried over what to do for her daughter, who had been displayed to a city-sized audience by a child-sexualizing algorithm. How could she keep her safe?

"The only thing I can do," she decided, "is forbid her to publish anything on YouTube."

Twelve

Infodemic

1. Don't Hug the Vaccinated

TWO YEARS BEFORE a strange new virus emerged in China, a World Health Organization official named Andy Pattison, who is Swiss, went to his boss with a plan for just such an event. Social media had become a vector for medical misinformation, Pattison told Tedros Adhanom Ghebreyesus, the WHO director-general. Frantic reports from health workers in Brazil and elsewhere had made clear that the platforms would be a major front line in any public-health emergency. They should begin preparing.

Tedros agreed, setting up an office at the agency's Geneva headquarters. Because the WHO, like other UN agencies, does much of its work by advising, and on good days persuading, governments, the office's half-dozen employees focused on cultivating ties with the major American tech companies that Pattison considered to be their own power centers. Progress was slow. They helped Pinterest improve its search results for vaccine-related queries. They advised Google on a fitness app. "The interest that I got was very minimal. I got very junior members of staff meeting me for a short amount of time," Pattison has said, adding that little action tended to follow.

Then, on January 21, 2020, Chinese scientists announced that the virus, which had killed four people, was spreading person to person. Within two days, the death toll jumped to seventeen. A week later, the WHO declared a global emergency. Pattison's office activated its contacts in Silicon Valley. "I made this pitch on a human level: 'Go back to your companies, get ready, start pulling together teams,'" he has recalled telling them. He set up calls between Tedros and the heads of Facebook,

Google, and other platforms. Mark Zuckerberg and Sheryl Sandberg suggested the WHO set up pages on WhatsApp and Facebook to post updates and answer user questions.

On February 13, two weeks after the spread of the virus now known as Covid-19 had been declared a global emergency, Pattison landed in California for a meeting, hosted at Facebook, with Silicon Valley's top firms. Life remained normal in the United States and Europe. But his sense of the crisis had already shifted. There was, he told CNBC on the day of the meeting, an "infodemic." The major social media platforms, including Twitter and YouTube, were "awash with misinformation," he said.

Facebook posts were already winning hundreds of thousands of interactions by insisting, a month and a half before Trump would project the same claim from the podium in the White House briefing room, that the virus could be cured by drinking diluted bleach. Instagram influencers explained that Bill Gates had invented the virus to justify forced vaccinations. A viral WhatsApp forward said the CIA was hoarding groceries. YouTube videos blaming the disease on 5G cell towers, implying there was no virus, suddenly won millions of views.

At Pattison's urging, the companies pledged to tighten some rules. YouTube would remove videos contravening WHO guidance. Facebook would send users notifications if they tried to share a Covid-related post that moderators had marked as false. The platforms promised Pattison, and the world, that they had learned from past mistakes. They would get this one right.

As the virus fanned across whole nations in those first weeks, fear and isolation spread with it. Shops and public spaces boarded up. An apocalyptic stillness hung over major thoroughfares and business districts, broken only by wailing sirens as hospital wards swelled — and, in some places, by the macabre idling of refrigerator trucks outside overfull morgues. Families braced at home as if preparing for an invasion, venturing out only for tense grocery runs during which, in our collective ignorance, many donned gloves or sprayed Windex on produce whose surfaces, for all we knew, might be fatally contaminated. Cities reanimated for a single minute each evening as cooped-up apartment dwellers threw open their windows to cheer in gratitude to frontline workers, though perhaps also as a way to grasp for some sense of community, for safety in numbers.

For the other 23 hours and 59 minutes of the day, the fearful or the lonely could turn to that other window to the outside world: their computer. Several years' worth of digital adoption happened overnight. Facebook reported a 70 percent increase in usage in some countries. Twitter's grew 23 percent. An internet services firm estimated that YouTube's share of worldwide internet traffic jumped from 9 to 16 percent. Overall internet usage rose 40 percent, the firm also said, suggesting that in actuality YouTube's traffic nearly tripled.

Despite Pattison's efforts to prepare the companies, a few fact-checking badges couldn't resolve the core problem. Social media was still a machine engineered to distort reality through the lens of tribal conflict and pull users toward extremes. And the pandemic — the specter of an invisible, omnipresent, uncontrollable threat — activated the very emotions that fed the machine, on a scale greater than any other event since the creation of the platforms themselves.

It was as if the entire world became a Zika-afflicted village whose mothers turned in desperation to online rumors, or a collective of lonely young men escalating one another's disillusionment and anomie into a shared struggle against some fabricated enemy. Coronavirus conspiracies, promising access to forbidden truths others did not hold, let believers feel certainty and autonomy amid a crisis that had taken away both. By pinning it all on some villain or plot, they gave a senseless tragedy some degree of meaning, however dark. And they offered users a way to take action, first by sharing their secret knowledge with others, then by telling one another that they would band together against whatever culprit the conspiracy blamed.

The overarching narrative — coronavirus is a plot by Them to control Us — was everywhere by April. Often, the conspiracies originated with everyday users with tiny followings. A small-town missionary's Facebook post accusing Bill Gates and China of spreading coronavirus to under-mine Trump. A Houston beautician's tweet listing past epidemics along-side corresponding election years (the dates were wrong) with the message "Coronavirus is a government made disease." A video, on YouTube, of two doctors presenting phony claims that Covid was mostly harmless and that masks could be forgone. Each reached audiences numbering in the mil-lions, all thanks to the platforms' promotional systems.

These were hardly outliers. Vaccine-misinformation videos mush-roomed across YouTube, instructing tens of millions of viewers not to believe the "medical mafia" seeking to embed microchips in their chil-dren. Facebook, too, experienced an "explosive growth in anti-vaccination views," according to a study in *Nature*, as the platform's recommendation system appeared to divert huge numbers of users from mainstream health pages to anti-vaccine groups.

Throughout 2020, three forces rose in parallel on social media plat-forms, of which coronavirus conspiracies were only the first. The other two would prove just as fateful: long-mounting strains of online extrem-ism, going by names that many Americans would have found ridiculous at the year's start and that were terrifying by its end; and, separately, among Americans more broadly, ultrapartisan outrage and misinformation exag-gerated to the point of rendering armed rebellion not only acceptable but, to many, necessary. All three forces drew on causes that existed apart from social media — the pandemic, white backlash to a wave of racial justice protests throughout the summer, and, especially, President Trump. But social media propelled and shaped those causes until, on January 6, 2021, they converged in an act of mass violence, organized online, that would change the trajectory of American democracy, perhaps for good.

All that spring, as the Covid lies and rumors spread, the social media giants insisted that they were taking every available measure. But internal documents suggest that Facebook executives, by April, realized that their algorithms were boosting dangerous misinformation, that they could have stemmed the problem dramatically with the flip of a switch, and that they refused to do so for fear of hurting traffic. Company researchers had found that "serial reshares" — posts shared repeatedly onward from user to user — were likelier to be misinformation. The algorithm, seeing these posts as good viral fodder, boosted their reach artificially. Simply turning off this boost, Facebook's researchers found, would curb Covid-related misinformation by up to 38 percent. But Zuckerberg nixed it. "Mark doesn't think we could go broad," an employee who'd briefed Zuckerberg wrote in a memo. "We wouldn't launch if there was a material trade-off with MSI," she added, using Facebook's engagement acronym, short for "meaningful social interactions."

That same month, Facebook researchers investigated "manufactured virality" pages, which repost already viral content to lure in followers, a favored tool of scammers, clickbaiters, and Russian influence peddlers. The viral hucksters, they found, drove 64 percent of misinformation and 19 percent of traffic across *all Facebook pages* — shocking figures, though a seemingly easy target for removal. But when they brought their findings to Zuckerberg, he "deprioritized" their work. Facebook kept both discoveries secret.

With the platforms spinning away as normal and 6,000 people dying every day from Covid, a third of them Americans, the world was, by May, primed for *Plandemic*. The video, a twenty-six-minute faux documentary, was uploaded, on May 4, to Facebook and YouTube. It presented a pioneering HIV scientist (in reality, a discredited former researcher) as revealing, according to the narrator, "the plague of corruption that places all human life in danger." The video asserted that the virus had been engineered to justify pushing dangerous vaccines for profit, masks cause illness, the antimalarial drug hydroxychloroquine could prevent Covid, and many other claims.

The video's route to virality revealed, and perhaps carved, the social media pathways through which much of 2020's chaos would flow. Starting on groups for anti-vaxxers, general conspiracists, and QAnon, its story affirmed each of their worldviews. It escalated their sense of fighting a great conflict. And it activated them around a cause: opposition to the shadowy forces behind Covid. Within a week, *Plandemic* spread to alternative medicine communities, then wellness influencers, then generic lifestyle and yoga pages. Separately, it circulated to pages and groups that opposed lockdowns, then to pro-Trump pages, then to pages for any cultural or social cause that was even vaguely conservative-aligned. Each took it on as a communal call to arms, weaving it into their collective identities. Many pushed the video to Twitter and Instagram, starting the process all over again. In a script that was by now becoming monotonous, the companies did not react until news agencies began calling them for comment. By then, it was too late. Though they removed the video itself, its claims and calls to action were well into the digital bloodstream, and have resurfaced in social media conspiracies ever since.

By August, Andy Pattison, the WHO official, concluded that he would have to change tacks entirely with Silicon Valley. "The challenge I've got with them is to put sustainability and maturity over absolute profit," he told a development publication, speaking more bluntly than he might have with news outlets. "And that's a tough conversation to have, because they've all got bottom lines."

He met regularly with corporate liaisons throughout the pandemic. But evidence of real-world harm only continued mounting. Americans who used Facebook, Twitter, or YouTube, one study found, became more likely to believe that vitamin C could successfully treat Covid or that the government had manufactured the virus. Millions were rejecting masks and social distancing and would later reject vaccines. Doctors reported more and more patients refusing lifesaving treatments based on something they'd seen online, much as Brazilian families tormented by Zika had done just one year earlier, and often citing the same conspiracies. Trump, both driving and driven by the online rage that suffused his base, encouraged every step, pushing phony Covid cures and pledging to "liberate" states with lockdown measures.

"More evidence of a Plandemic," a California man texted his cousin in October, linking to a TikTok video, in the sort of exchange that had become routine in American life. "Don't hug any of the vaccinated, symptoms are directly related to vaccine shedding," the cousin responded, referring to a Facebook-propagated conspiracy. Both men had Covid. For days, they texted back and forth, attributing their symptoms to scheming doctors or vaccines based on rumors they'd seen online, according to messages later recovered by the writer Rachel McKibbens, who was the sister of one of the men. "The Damned hospital made me way worse. My lungs were in no way in this bad of shape when I went in there," McKibbens's brother wrote. The hospital staff, he was convinced, was "in it for the money now."

As their health deteriorated, both men grasped for evidence that the social media rumors had been right, with one attributing his wife's heavy period to vaccines based on a falsehood promoted on Instagram. They recommended each other bogus treatments that had circulated on YouTube and Facebook. Most of all, they urged each other to resist advice from doctors, health authorities, even McKibbens. Her brother, his symptoms worsening, was hospitalized. But, certain the doctors were poisoning him as part of the plots he'd heard about over and over online, he refused treatment and left, bunkering up at home. A few days later, he died there, alone.

2. Looting and Shooting

AS WHOLE POPULATIONS tumbled into health misinformation that spring and summer, a second, parallel rabbit hole opened on social media, pulling in dejected young white men who were seeking community and purpose. It was a demographic that, though smaller than those succumbing to Covid conspiracies, would prove to be nearly as dangerous once the platforms had done their work. The online alt right, once focused on little more than Gamergate or Pepe the Frog memes, was recruited into a world of self-described militias prepping for the societal collapse they became sure was imminent.

For Steven Carrillo, a thirty-two-year-old Air Force staff sergeant, the slide from chest thumping on Facebook groups about violence to its actual execution began in March 2020, when a fellow user texted him, "Start drafting that op... I'ma green light some shit." He answered, "Sounds good, bro!"

Carrillo had come to the groups through a life of turmoil. He grew up poor, passed between parents in small-town California and grandparents in rural Mexico. In 2015, he suffered a head trauma in a car crash, which dulled his once-bright personality, and in 2018 lost his wife to suicide. After that, he surrendered their children to his in-laws and moved into a van.

"He was just in complete disconnect," his sister has said. But the Air Force deployed him to the Middle East for much of 2019. Friends on base introduced him to Facebook groups that called themselves militias. In reality, they were chat pages dedicated to fantasizing about insurrection or civil war. They offered members a way to make sense of the world by reframing it within the extremists' narrative of individual crisis answered by collective solution, much as Reddit incels had found community by imagining an uprising against feminists, or 8chan users by praising acts of genocide until Brenton Tarrant carried one out in New Zealand. Carrillo's group had named itself, in a similar ironic wink, Boogaloo. It had begun as a 4chan meme. Users there called for a nationwide insurrection, intended to topple the government and bring about a right-wing utopia, by invoking "Civil War 2: Electric Boogaloo," a play on the '80s dance movie *Breakin' 2: Electric Boogaloo.*

In spring 2020, as the platforms gave rise to communities that feared lockdowns as exactly the power grab foretold in viral conspiracies like those in *Plandemic* or QAnon, social media algorithms identified once-obscure militia pages like Boogaloo as just the sort of thing that would draw those users even deeper into online worlds. Boogaloo posts spread so rapidly across Facebook, Twitter, Instagram, and Reddit that an extremism-monitoring group warned that "viral insurgencies" were "developing in plain sight." Covid conspiracists, interlinked with militia causes by the platforms' algorithms, brought those militias recruits and a newly urgent cause, while militias gave the conspiracists a sense of purpose: a looming, final conflict with the government. Crisis and solution. As with similar 4chan-to-Facebook movements, Boogaloo and other militias whose adherents posted about triggering a civil war seemed mostly to be signaling in-group membership, not sincere intent. But some lost sight of the difference; instructions for homemade explosives and firearms proliferated. A "Boogaloo Tactics" file shared on Facebook and Instagram instructed that "assassinations" against "the pencil pushers" should wait until their "crimes" were "proven to the people," but nevertheless that, more immediately, "some people have to go." Boogaloo members began showing up at anti-lockdown protests, heavily armed, waiting for the shooting to start.

Throughout early 2020, Carrillo, now back in California, where he'd begun dating a local woman, spent more and more time on the group's pages, adopting Boogaloo as an identity. He adorned his Facebook profile with militia memes and, in March, purchased an AR-15 component through a website that advertised on Boogaloo Facebook groups and promised to donate some of its profits to the family of an alleged Boogaloo member who had been killed that month in a confrontation with police. A few weeks after his text exchange about planning an "op," Carrillo joined invitation-only Facebook and WhatsApp groups for local Boogaloo members, where they planned "firearm training" meetups and discussed vague plans to trigger their civil war by killing police officers. An "onboarding" file he filled out in April informed him, in the video game make-believe common to such groups, "Our Areas of Operations can take us from the dirt to downtown in a blink of an eye."

Boogaloo was just one group of many others like it. Also that month, far-right gun activists set up state-by-state Facebook pages calling on locals to protest stay-at-home orders. Though the activists had little preexisting reach, their groups attracted 900,000 users, a telltale sign of algorithmic promotion. Only a few dozen attended each rally, some carrying M15-style rifles. But thousands remained active on the pages, which, in time, merged with the larger communities of backlash and conspiracy that the platforms continued pulling together into a larger whole, encouraging those identities and causes to blur.

Facebook-organized violence grew more frequent and more extreme. In Arkansas that May, members of a Facebook militia stormed the grounds of the governor's mansion and burned him in effigy. In Washington, organizers hinted that a rally would culminate in attacks on local citizens who, the organizers learned from police records, had reported businesses that violated Covid closure orders. Though the attacks themselves never materialized, 1,500 ralliers attended, many of them armed.

The militias, Covid conspiracists, and sympathetic pro-Trump communities had also begun taking on the life-or-death urgency of another cause with which the platforms had repeatedly interlinked them: QAnon. With the algorithm's help, QAnon belief now infused all of these separate causes, much as Renée DiResta had discovered Facebook's groups feature blurring anti-vaxxers with Pizzagate (the QAnon predecessor conspiracy) as far back as 2016.

Nina Jankowicz, a disinformation researcher, stumbled into a typical pathway that summer. She would search Facebook for "alternative health," join one of the top-ranked groups, then follow Facebook's algorithmically generated "related groups" sidebar, which frequently led to Q pages. It was a brief and brutally efficient journey that threatened to pull in anyone searching for Covid remedies at a time when medical science as yet had none. The pattern was playing out across all the major platforms, converting Americans' fear and confusion first into softer conspiracy belief, then into full-blown QAnonism, a huge engagement booster on the platforms. Wellness channels on YouTube and fitness influencers on Instagram drifted from astrology to coronavirus conspiracies to QAnon. Facebook's largest anti-vaccine network filled with Q dog whistles. TikTok surged with Pizzagate conspiracies. One twenty-year-old TikToker, who'd helped spark the Pizzagate resurgence, said she'd learned about it from a viral YouTube video. When *Plandemic*'s producers released a sequel, the video was predominantly pushed via Q pages.

By the pandemic's outset, the QAnon cause, amid its now almost impenetrably dense lore and esoterica, had sharpened around a core belief: President Trump and loyal generals were on the verge of a glorious military coup that would overturn the cabal that had orchestrated Pizzagate and that secretly dominated American life. In the subsequent purge, the military would execute tens of thousands of traitorous Democrats, Jewish financiers, federal bureaucrats, and cultural liberals on the National Mall. Q adherents, most of whom gathered on Facebook or YouTube and never ventured to the hardcore forums where Q's "drops" initially appeared, were told they played a crucial role, if only by following along for clues and helping to spread the word.

That summer, ninety-seven professed QAnon believers would run in congressional primaries; twenty-seven of them would win. Two ran as independents. The other twenty-five were in-good-standing Republican nominees for the House of Representatives. QAnon memes and references especially dominated militia pages, escalating their sense that violence would be both righteous and inevitable.

In late May, Ivan Hunter, the Boogaloo member with whom Carrillo had texted about an "op," drove with several others to Minneapolis, where protests were raging over the police killing of George Floyd, an unarmed Black man. The men gathered outside a police precinct that had been taken over by a few hundred protesters. Hunter yelled, "Justice for Floyd," raised a Kalashnikov-style rifle, and fired thirteen times into the building. No one was injured. He had likely hoped, as Boogaloos often wrote online, to spark violence between protesters and police that would escalate into war.

A few days later, on May 28, Carrillo posted a video of Black Lives Matter protests to a Boogaloo Facebook group he frequented. "It's on our coast now, this needs to be nationwide...it's a great opportunity to target the specialty soup bois," he wrote, a reference to "alphabet-soup" agencies with acronym names, such as the FBI, whose agents Boogaloos talked of killing to trigger the all-out conflict they desired. He added, "We have mobs of angry people to use to our advantage." Another local user, Robert

Justus, responded, "lets boogie." That night, Carrillo proposed to his girl-friend with a twenty-five-dollar silicone ring, which he promised to replace with a diamond, and packed a bag to leave in the morning.

Boogaloo pages like his did not generate their sense of impending civil conflict on their own. They absorbed it from social media platforms, which were suffused in it. That same night, May 28, Trump, both driving and feeding off this sentiment, posted on Twitter and Facebook that, if authorities in Minneapolis did not suppress Black Lives Matter protests, he would "send in the National Guard & get the job done right." He added, "Any difficulty and we will assume control but, when the looting starts, the shooting starts." His last phrase, echoing a Miami police chief's infamous 1967 pledge to crack down on Black neighborhoods, seemed to encourage lethal violence at a moment when tensions were high, street clashes were rising, and both police and far-right militias were in a position to comply.

Twitter added a warning message to Trump's post, saying it violated rules against "glorifying violence," and limited the post's circulation. But Zuckerberg announced that, while he considered the post "divisive and inflammatory," Facebook would leave it up. "We think people need to know if the government is planning to deploy force," he explained. It was a strange justification — amplifying incitement for the sake of public awareness. Zuckerberg called Trump personally to reiterate Facebook's policies. He held a company-wide town hall to defend his decision, which employees internally denounced.

The platforms' tendencies were affecting everyone, not just those on the pro-Trump right. The same day as Trump's "looting and shooting" post, a Minneapolis reporter published photos of Black Lives Matter protests in the city. Left-wing Twitter users questioned whether the photos might put protesters at risk of arrest. Whatever the merits of the question, outrage one-upmanship overwhelmed it. Other users won more attention by saying the photos, more than just risking arrest, ensured the protesters' murders. They cited a long-debunked conspiracy claiming that demonstrators photographed at past BLM rallies tended to subsequently die under mysterious circumstances. Outrage snowballed, with tens of thousands of users accusing the photographer of deliberately endangering Black lives. Many expressed a wish to see him harmed or killed; others pledged to carry it out. Some circulated his phone number and home address. That night, a left-wing Twitter personality posted photos of the license plates of a CNN reporter's car, saying it belonged to "lying provocateurs" infiltrating BLM on behalf of police. The post won 62,000 interactions, likely reaching millions. That weekend, protesters attacked a Fox News cameraman in DC, while others stormed CNN's Atlanta headquarters. Incidents of protesters attacking reporters, though less frequent than attacks on reporters by police, continued all summer.

The next evening, May 29, Carrillo and Justus drove a van to the outskirts of a BLM protest in Oakland. After circling, Carrillo climbed in back, slid open the van door, and aimed a high-powered rifle at two Homeland Security guards outside a federal office building. He shot both, killing one of them. He and Justus abandoned the van, which was later found filled with guns and bomb-making equipment.

To the extent that Carrillo's motives were coherent, he had apparently hoped his attack would be mistaken as the work of Black Lives Matter and set off more violence. Thanks to social media's partisan-affirming tendencies, he got at least his first wish. Police had not even yet publicly identified Carrillo when pro-Trump Facebook pages won hundreds of thousands of interactions by blaming the Oakland officer's death on Black Lives Matter "riots," "left-wing domestic terrorists," and "another poorly managed Democrat city." They described it as the latest in a wave of violence stoked by "national Democrats, corporate media & Biden staffers," an extension of the tyranny of "Democrat lockdowns" and out-of-control minorities.

Over the next days, Carrillo messaged on WhatsApp with other group members, including Hunt, who was in hiding after firing into the Minneapolis precinct office, to plan more violence. But a week after his attack, police tracked Carrillo to his home in a rural town called Ben Lomond. By the time they arrived, he was on a nearby hillside, waiting in ambush.

He repeatedly fired a homemade AR-15 and flung homemade explosives, killing one officer and wounding several others. He had messaged his friends, asking for reinforcement, but after months of encouraging chatter, they ignored him. Carrillo, injured by return fire, fled in a stolen car, but was quickly caught. Police discovered he'd written "boog" in his own blood on the hood. The firefight had unfolded fewer than forty-five miles from Facebook's campus.

Carrillo, who remains unapologetic, later married, in a jailhouse ceremony, the girlfriend to whom he'd proposed on the eve of his killings. His friend Robert Justus, who was also arrested, has told prosecutors that Carrillo forced him to go along. In January 2022, the sister of one of the officers he'd murdered sued Facebook, alleging that the company knowingly allowed its algorithms to promote and facilitate the violent extremism that led to her brother's death. Though the suit's odds are poor, it represents a sense that Silicon Valley's seeming complicity in the nation's disintegration over 2020 could not be ignored — a sense that, within hours of Carrillo's crime, had already begun extending into the companies' own workforces.

3. Friction

ON MONDAY, JUNE 1, one week after George Floyd's murder and three days after Carrillo's attack, a few hundred Facebook employees set out-of-office messages announcing that, for one day, they were refusing to work. Some signed petitions demanding personnel and policy changes from their bosses. Many, in a first, publicly condemned their employer. "Facebook's inaction in taking down Trump's post inciting violence makes me ashamed to work here," Lauren Tan, an engineer, tweeted. "This isn't right. Silence is complicity."

The walkout was nominally to protest Facebook's refusal, a few days earlier, to remove Trump's post threatening to have the National Guard shoot racial justice protesters. But even this was, as many said, only the final affront. At a time of rising violence and deadly health misinformation,

Silicon Valley, after recruiting the world's top engineering talent on a promise that they would help save the world, seemed to instead be abetting, even driving, social ills that threatened to tear America apart, just as they had done in Myanmar and Sri Lanka. As if to underscore the employees' point, on the day of the walkout the dominant story on Facebook was the misinformation blaming Carrillo's double murder on Black Lives Matter.

The walkout marked the beginning of a public, high-stakes battle between the Valley's corporate heads and a mostly new alliance rising up against them: their own employees, their own advertisers, prominent civil rights activists, and, later, Democratic party leaders. This was categorically different from facing outside analysts or dissident programmers who had, up until then, led criticism of the Valley. It was a meaningful challenge to the Valley's core corporate interests, posed, according to its participants, on behalf of a world that increasingly saw those companies as a perilous threat.

Concerns about election misinformation had been mounting for months. In late May, the day after Floyd's murder, Trump had posted a stream of falsehoods opposing California's early-voting policies, writing, "This will be a Rigged Election." After years of enabling Trump, Twitter had finally acted, sort of. It appended a small box labeled "Get the facts," linking to a separate page that gently fact-checked Trump's claims. It was largely symbolic.

After the Facebook walkout, in a salve to employees, Zuckerberg announced that he supported BLM. Yet that same day, his platform's most popular post was a video by the right-wing personality Candace Owens claiming that "racially motivated police brutality is a myth" and that George Floyd was "a criminal" and "horrible human being." It was viewed 94 million times, about the same as the Super Bowl.

Throughout June, stories emerged of Joel Kaplan, the conservative lobbyist on Facebook's payroll, watering down the company's policies in ways that protected Trump from rules against misinformation, effectively abetting's the president's efforts to use the platform to pressure state officials to suppress voting and disrupt the election. For many, it was proof that, even with everything at stake, Silicon Valley could not be trusted to do the right thing. Civil rights groups led a campaign, Stop Hate for Profit, pressuring advertisers to boycott Facebook. A number of corporations and advertising agencies complied. Some pulled ad budgets worth $100,000 per day.

It's unlikely this dented Facebook's $80 billion per year in ad revenue. But the threat to its bottom line did inspire something like action, and not just at Facebook. In late June, Facebook and Instagram banned Boogaloo from their platforms. YouTube removed several prominent white extremists, including Unite the Right organizer Richard Spencer — almost three years after the events in Charlottesville. Perhaps most significant, Reddit closed two thousand communities it said had engaged in hate speech, including The_Donald, the unofficial meeting point of the online far right. The crackdowns were a turning point, implicit acknowledgment that hosting hate was effectively a policy in support of its spread. That good speech would not, on these platforms, naturally defeat bad. Still, the removals came, like so many before, too late. The insurrectionist, white-nationalist identity and way of thinking, along with the dozens of conspiracies and falsehoods justifying them, were already endemic, ingrained into the larger, real-world communities with which the platforms had so effectively inculcated them.

The Valley's critics kept pushing for deeper change. A Facebook programmer, whose last day at the company happened to fall on July 1, posted a twenty-four-minute goodbye message, warning, "Facebook is hurting people at scale." The company was "getting trapped by our ideology of free expression," said the programmer, flanked by plushy dolls and wearing a series of brightly colored Facebook T-shirts. "We are failing. And what's worse, we have enshrined that failure in our policies."

The mounting threat of tainting the company in advertisers' eyes was enough for Zuckerberg and Sandberg to meet, in early July, with the boycott groups. The civil rights leaders emerged enraged, telling reporters they felt patronized by empty promises and gaslit by claims of progress that seemed to deliberately misunderstand the company's own technology.

Their account rang familiar to any reporter who had interviewed Facebook policymakers.

Coincidentally, that week, an independent audit of Facebook's policies and practices, two years in the making, was published. Under public pressure over its role in the 2016 election and subsequent privacy scandals, Facebook had commissioned it in 2018 from a civil rights law firm, holding it out ever since as proof of its commitment to improving. But the auditors, granted access that Facebook had suggested would prove its critics wrong, instead concluded that its algorithms promoted polarization and extremism, its policies allowed election misinformation to run rampant, and its internal practices permitted little sensitivity to real-world harms. These were hardly new accusations. But, now levied by Facebook's own handpicked auditors, based partly on internal information, and made not on behalf of dissident techies or obscure academics but by a respected voice of civil rights law, they carried special weight with the public as authoritative confirmation beyond what had come before. The report put Valley leaders on the defensive: they might dismiss Guillaume Chaslot as aggrieved or Jonas Kaiser as misguided, but they could not slam the door on well-respected civil rights lawyers without risking further rebellion from employees or advertisers.

Finally, in August, Facebook and Twitter did the previously unthinkable: they deleted a Trump post. He had published a video calling children "almost immune" to Covid. Endangering kids' health was, finally, a bridge too far. YouTube followed suit. (The companies may have hoped this would serve as a warning shot, but it didn't alter his behavior. Two months and many lies later, they would pull another of his posts on much the same grounds.) All the while, Trump continued to benefit from algorithmic promotion whose value far exceeded the burden from any wrist slap: his engagement numbers on Facebook outpaced Joe Biden's by forty to one in that last month of the summer, even as Trump lagged in polls — further proof that the platforms did not reflect reality but create their own.

By September, America was careening toward an election in which democracy itself seemed at stake. Trump and some of his allies insinuated that they would intervene against mail-in voting, which was expected to favor Democrats. They also suggested that they expected the Supreme Court's conservative majority to overturn a loss. And that they might refuse to surrender power. Fears of voter suppression during the election, and of vigilante violence after it, were widespread. House Speaker Nancy Pelosi, lamenting the pervasiveness of QAnon misinformation on Facebook, said, "I don't know how the Facebook board of directors or their top employees can look themselves in the mirror. They have clearly chosen. Their business plan is to make money off of poison, and that's the path they have chosen to go."

Under pressure, Facebook announced that month that it would bar candidates from falsely declaring victory and would remove any posts that cited Covid to discourage in-person voting. It imposed a conspicuously lighter penalty for one of Trump's favored tactics: "Content that seeks to delegitimize the outcome of the election" or "the legitimacy of voting methods" would be merely appended with an "informational label." Facebook and Instagram would also accept no new political ads in the week before the election, preempting any attempt to slip voter-manipulating content onto the platforms last-minute. Instagram went further. Until the election was over, U.S.-based users who followed a hashtag, whatever the subject, would no longer be able to sort posts by most recent. "We're doing this to reduce the real-time spread of potentially harmful content that could pop up around the election," a press statement said. Both changes, though small, crossed an important threshold: curbing the products' basic features for the betterment of society.

A month out from the election, Twitter announced the most substantial changes of any platform. High-follower accounts, including politicians, would be put under tighter rules than others — the opposite of Facebook's special dispensations. Rule-breaking posts would be removed or hidden behind a warning label. Trump already had fourteen such labels, which functioned as both fact-checks and speed bumps, slowing the ease with which users could read or share them. Twitter later barred users from retweeting or liking the offending Trump posts at all. With those social elements gone, the impact of his tweets seemed to drop considerably.

Twitter also added an element long urged by outside experts: friction. Normally, users could share a post by hitting "retweet," instantly promoting it onto their own feeds. Now, pressing "retweet" would instead bring up a prompt urging the user to add some message of their own. It forced a pause, reducing the ease of sharing. The scale of the intervention was slight but its effect was significant: retweets declined 20 percent overall, the company said, and the spread of misinformation with it. Twitter had deliberately slowed engagement, violating its own financial self-interest along with decades of Silicon Valley dogma insisting that more activity online could only be beneficial. The result, seemingly, was to make the world less misinformed and therefore better off.

Most surprising, Twitter temporarily switched off the algorithm that pushed especially viral tweets into users' news feeds even if they did not follow the tweet's author. The company called the effort to "slow down" virality a "worthwhile sacrifice to encourage more thoughtful and explicit amplification." This was, as best I could tell, the first and only time that a major platform had voluntarily shut down its own algorithm. It was implicit admission of exactly the sort that the companies had avoided for so long: that their products could be dangerous, that societies would be safer with aspects of those products switched off, and that it was easily within their power to do so.

Then came the QAnon crackdowns. Partial bans earlier in the year, removing select accounts or groups, had proven ineffective. Finally, Facebook and Instagram imposed total bans on the movement in October, with Twitter gradually culling Q-linked accounts. YouTube's CEO, Susan Wojcicki, said only that YouTube would remove videos that accused people of involvement in Q-related conspiracies in order to harass or threaten them. The narrow rule tweak was YouTube's only significant policy change leading up to the election. But as with Boogaloo and so many other dark currents, it was too late. After years of these extremist communities having incubated on the platforms and cultivated themselves into mass movements, the levying of bans simply relocated them to more private platforms, where they were free to drift even further into extremism. Even on mainstream platforms, many continued lurking in some form. Also in October, FBI officers arrested several Boogaloo members who were stockpiling weapons and explosives for a plot to kidnap and potentially murder Michigan's governor. They had organized in part on a private Facebook group.

The platforms' broader natures remained unchanged. In the weeks before the election, Facebook filled with calls for violence targeting Trump's enemies. Digital researchers identified at least 60,000 posts invoking acts of political violence: "The Terrorist Democrats Are The Enemy And All Must Be Killed." "The next time we see SChiff, it should be him hanging from a noose #deathforschiff." (Adam Schiff is a Democratic Congressman who led the first impeachment effort against Trump.) Another 10,000 called for armed insurrection if Biden won. A staggering 2.7 million posts on political groups urged violence in more general terms such as "kill them" or "shoot them."

It was exactly what I'd seen in Sri Lanka and Myanmar — a rising chant for blood, explicit and in unison — just before those societies collapsed into the very acts of violence they'd threatened in huge numbers. I thought of Sudarshana Gunawardana, the Sri Lankan government minister who, watching Facebook-propagated incitement overrun his country, had helplessly pelted warnings at the company's unlistening representatives. After the riots finally receded, he'd lamented, "We're a society, we're not just a market." Now it was Americans' turn to beg Silicon Valley, with limited success, to remember before it was too late that we were not just a market for them to exploit.

On election day, two Q candidates won seats in Congress: Lauren Boebert of Colorado and Marjorie Taylor Greene of Georgia. Greene had also echoed Alex Jones's claims that school shootings were staged and, in a reminder that political violence was central to the cause, had once liked a Facebook post calling for Barack Obama to be hanged and another urging that House Speaker Nancy Pelosi should get "a bullet to the head."

QAnon's ascension, however, was overshadowed for Americans by another development: Trump had lost. Two days after the vote, with most news outlets yet to formally call the race, Facebook announced it had removed a group for election misinformation. Called "Stop the Steal," it claimed that Trump's supposed loss was in fact a coup by shadowy forces. The page gained 338,000 members in less than a day, making it one of the fastest-growing in Facebook's history. It filled with conspiracies, calls for violence, and especially invocations of QAnon.

Still, with Trump humbled and soon to leave office, maybe the online extremism that he'd long encouraged might dissipate as well. After all, Silicon Valley had always said its platforms merely reflected real-world sentiment and events. Perhaps the worst was over.

4. The Big Lie

ALL THAT FALL, Richard Barnett, a sixty-year-old construction contractor and gun enthusiast from small-town Arkansas, had been falling down the rabbit hole. A Facebook obsessive, he repeatedly reposted already-viral Covid, anti-vaccine, and pro-Trump conspiracies swirling across the platform — a typical Facebook superposter, not unlike Rolf Wassermann, the German artist who'd amplified whatever the platform pushed in front of him. But Barnett was absorbing a social media ecosystem now far more toxic than Germany's. He attended a Facebook-organized rally at his state capitol in September, carrying an AR-15, to protest Covid restrictions. He came to believe, a friend later said, that shadowy powers intended to exploit the pandemic to insert microchips in citizens' foreheads, a vague echo of *Plandemic* and QAnon beliefs. He organized a group in support of the charity Save Our Children, which had been co-opted by QAnon for its work opposing child trafficking. In a photo from an October meetup, he

and a dozen others held military-style rifles in front of a sign that read
DEAD PEDOPHILES DON'T REOFFEND, a coded reference to Democrats.

He was typical of the horde of social media users — some affiliated
with militia or QAnon groups, some, like Barnett, just riding the algorithm — that had been, throughout 2020, working themselves up for the
great battles that their conspiracies told them were gloriously nigh. When
viral Facebook posts claimed Biden's victory was fraudulent, they were
ready to believe, even to act.

"We need to put a stop to this corrupt government," a user posted,
three days after the election, in a Facebook militia group whose tens of
thousands of members were already calling themselves "ready and armed."
They moved to a private page, the better to plan. "If they are not elimi-
nated now they will eliminate us," one wrote. Another responded, "Time
to take them down."

The militia and Q groups, for all their influence across the platforms,
were just a small, hypercommitted faction of pro-Trump users. But the
platforms' systems began quickly pulling wider masses toward the extremists. And they did it by promoting content that pushed the same lie that
Trump was deploying to try to stay in office and that had animated the
quickly shuttered Stop the Steal group: Trump had won, Democrats had
instituted massive voter fraud, and patriots would have to overturn the
phony results. It became known as the Big Lie. It's impossible to know for
sure how far it would have gone without social media. But the platforms
promoted it on a scale that would have been otherwise impossible and,
perhaps most powerfully, trained users to repeat it back to one another as
urgent truth. In the week after the election, the twenty most-engaged
Facebook posts containing the word *election* were all written by Trump.
All twenty carried a label calling the post misleading, which had little
apparent effect. His posts accounted for twenty-two of the twenty-five
most-engaged Facebook posts in the United States.

Rumors validating the lie were sent viral over and over. Biden admitted that election fraud had been widespread, users were told. Democratic

ballots in Pennsylvania carried the names of dead people. A right-wing YouTube channel reported that Detroit poll workers had been caught wheeling in suitcases of fraudulent ballots. Another told its 1.8 million subscribers that pollsters had retracted their announcements that Biden had won. (When a reporter asked the channel's operator why YouTube hadn't enforced its own election-misinformation rules against him, he answered, "YouTube has been great.") A Twitter personality invented reports of Trump ballots being "dumped" in Michigan. A prominent mis-information account, @Breaking911, announced that a rogue postal worker had fled for Canada with stolen ballots.

By mid-November, Facebook researchers made a startling discovery: 10 percent of all U.S.-based views of political content, or 2 percent of over-all views, were of posts claiming the election had been stolen. On a plat-form this vast, consisting of billions of daily posts encompassing all news from every outlet in every city, billions of discussion groups on every con-ceivable topic, chitchat, family photos, business listings, the entirety of the human experience, for a single statement — especially a dangerously false statement — to overrun so much of the normal cacophony was shocking.

YouTube was no better. Newsmax TV, a channel heavily promoting conspiracies of Democratic voter fraud, saw its views skyrocket from 3 mil-lion in October to a staggering 133 million in November. Chaslot, once more tracking YouTube's recommendations, found the platform pushing Newsmax to people after they'd watched mainstream news outlets like the BBC, left-wing channels, even *The Ellen DeGeneres Show.* Newsmax was suddenly in the top 1 percent of YouTube's most-recommended channels. Chaslot found the same pattern with New Tang Dynasty TV, a cesspool of pro-Trump election misinformation run by the Falun Gong religious movement, whose audience exploded by a factor of ten. YouTube videos pushing the Big Lie were viewed 138 million times in the week following the election. By comparison, 7.5 million people had watched election-night coverage across all major TV networks. In early December, a few days after Chaslot released his findings, YouTube finally announced it would remove false claims of voter fraud — but, bizarrely, would not remove false videos already up, and would not punish rule-breaking until after January 20.

The platform remained saturated in election lies. Anyone who got news on social media had every reason to conclude, as Richard Barnett, the Arkansan superuser, did, that "mountains of evidence," as he wrote on his Facebook page, showed Trump had in fact won. Barnett amplified the conspiracy to his friends, engaging their outrage as the lie had engaged his, a dutiful cog in the social media machine.

On December 19, a month and a half after the election, Trump tweeted, "Big protest in D.C. on January 6th. Be there, will be wild!" Congress was to certify Biden's victory on that day. Trump was pressuring lawmakers to throw out Biden's electoral votes, overturning his victory in an effective coup d'état. Some Republican lawmakers had already signaled that they would agree to do so, and dozens ultimately did. Maybe a rally at the White House, Trump and his allies reasoned, could pressure the holdouts.

Online, many of Trump's supporters took his message as validation of everything they'd been telling one another for months. The child-abusing Democratic cabal was about to be exposed, probably executed. Trump would call in the military, and God-fearing militias had better be there to back him up. "#Patriots need to be as violent as BLM/Antifa! That's our go-ahead!!" a member of the Proud Boys, a white-nationalist group, wrote on Parler, a Twitter clone that had grown favored by the far right after bans by mainstream platforms. On TheDonald, a chat site modeled on the now-banned Reddit subsection, more than 80 percent of discussions referring to the January 6 event included overt calls for violence. Some posted maps of the Capitol building, marking out tunnels and entrances.

By December's end, many users were converging around a plan. Some would bring guns and explosives to Washington. Others would instigate a crowd large enough to overrun Capitol police. They would storm the building, stopping the vote certification by force. And then, as one Parler user wrote, "We're gonna kill Congress." An entire universe of Facebook groups, rising as one, promoted Trump's rally as the great battle they had been prepping for. Flyer-like memes, ubiquitous on the platform, urged attendance, often bearing militia slogans indicating the start of an armed revolt. Many included QAnon slogans calling it "the storm," the blood-soaked purge that Q had foretold. And they carried a hashtag that echoed the plans of far-right forums to which many of the groups linked back: #OccupyCongress.

"This is OUR COUNTRY!!!" Barnett wrote on his Facebook page a few days before Christmas, urging followers to join him at the rally. The same day, he posted a photo of himself bearing a rifle, along with a caption saying he had come into the world kicking and screaming, covered in blood, and was willing to leave it the same way. A few days later, on January 2, he carried a "Banana Republic USA" sign to a "Stop the Steal" rally in his small Arkansas hometown, where he told a reporter of his ambitions to reinstate Trump's supposed victory. "If you don't like it, send somebody after me, but I ain't going down easy."

As in so many cases before, whether with incels or Boogaloos, what had begun as online bluster for the sake of finding community amid disorientation became, on platforms that rewarded escalation and created a false sense of consensus around the most extreme views, a sincere will to action. "Today I had the very difficult conversation with my children, that daddy might not come home from D.C.," a user on TheDonald wrote the day before the rally. His message, upvoted by 3,800 users, said he intended to fulfill his military oath to "defend my country from all enemies, both Foreign & Domestic."

The forum filled with other stories like these. They were martyrdom messages, nearly word-for-word echoes of those made, in videotapes and social media posts, by jihadist suicide bombers the day before their deed. "I told my Mom goodbye today. I said I had a good life," another wrote. "If our 'leaders' do the wrong thing and we have to storm the Capitol, I am going to do it. See you there pedes," she wrote, signing off with a reference to the YouTube- and Reddit-inspired nickname that had bonded the community for years. "It will [be] the honor of my life to fight alongside you." Users posted dozens of supportive responses: *Those buildings belong to us … It's the House chambers that should be stormed if it comes to that, not the WH … Bring the wood, build the gallows outside congress, be mentally prepared to pull them out and string them up … I will be open carrying so will my friends. There is not enough cops in DC to stop what is coming.*

Barnett arrived early at the White House grounds on January 6. Waiting for Trump to appear, he took out his phone and posted a video to Facebook. "We're coming together," he said. "Get ready for the party." Around noon, south of the White House, Trump began speaking. As he wound down his speech, he told the crowd, "We're going to walk down to the Capitol," implying that it would be the next step in his effort, now weeks long, to halt Congress from certifying the electoral votes, as it was doing at that moment. "Because you'll never take back our country with weakness. You have to show strength, and you have to be strong," Trump said, to a roar of approval. Thousands crossed to the Capitol, though without Trump, who, despite assuring the crowd "I'll be there with you," had returned to the White House to watch on TV.

The insurrection's other leader, after all, maybe its real leader, was already on the ground, embedded in the pockets of every smartphone-carrying participant. January 6 was the culmination of Trumpism, yes, but also of a movement built on and by social media. It was an act that had been planned, days in advance, with no planners. Coordinated among thousands of people with no coordinators. And now it would be executed through digitally guided collective will. As people arrived at the Capitol, they found ralliers who had come earlier already haranguing the few police on guard. A wooden gallows, bearing an empty noose, had been erected on the grounds. Two blocks away, police discovered a pipe bomb at the Republican National Committee headquarters. Then another at the Democratic National Committee.

The police presence would remain sparse throughout much of the day. District and federal officials, despite being warned of the nature of online discussions, simply did not see the Trump rally for the threat that it was. Even once the violence began, their response was delayed by hours of bureaucratic dysfunction, an inspector general report found. Several top officials later resigned in disgrace.

As the ralliers joined crowds pressed against the fences, the simple math of their situation must have set in. They were thousands: angry, shouting, many in helmets and military-surplus gear. Their only hurdle, at some entrances, were twenty-pound metal barricades manned by three or four cops in baseball caps behind whom footpaths lay open all the way to the Capitol. Within an hour of Trump's exhortation, the crowd overpowered the outermost perimeter. In another hour, they breached the building itself. Lawmakers inside, going about the business of certifying the vote, had little idea anything was wrong until police rushed in and barricaded the doors behind them.

"We're in, we're in! Derrick Evans is in the Capitol!" Evans, a West Virginia state lawmaker, shouted into his smartphone, streaming live on Facebook, where he had been posting about the rally for days. In virtually every photo of the Capitol siege, you will see rioters holding up smartphones. They are tweeting, Instagramming, livestreaming to Facebook and YouTube. This was, like the Christchurch shooting a year before or incel murders a year before that, a performance, all conducted for and on social media. It was such a product of the social web that many of its participants saw no distinction between the lives they lived online and the real-world insurrection they were committing as an extension of the identities shaped by those platforms.

Many of those who forced their way inside wore QAnon-branded shirts and hats. Jake Angeli, a thirty-two-year-old social media obsessive, had dressed in American-flag face paint, animal horns, and a fur headdress, calling himself "Q shaman." Others wore military-style camo bearing patches with the names of Facebook militias. One hid behind a giant Pepe the Frog mask. "We just pushed, pushed, and pushed, and yelled 'go' and yelled 'charge,'" a thirty-six-year-old florist from West Texas, Jenny

Cudd, narrated on Facebook live as she entered the halls. "We got up to the top of the Capitol and there was a door open and we went inside," she went on. "We did break down Nancy Pelosi's office door and somebody stole her gavel and took a picture in the chair flipping off the camera."

The man she had seen was Richard Barnett, the Arkansas Facebook conspiracist. And the photo he took — his feet on Pelosi's desk, in flannel and jeans, arms outstretched in apparent glee, a lit-up smartphone in his hand — became, before the siege had even ended, a symbol of the unreality and humiliation of the day. Barnett, smiling at us all, became the face of something grotesque in American life, something whose strength many of us had not understood until that moment, when it marched into the halls of power and put its feet up.

Some had come for more than livestreaming. A group of eight men and one woman, wearing military-style gear over Oath Keepers T-shirts, pushed past the crowd into the Capitol. They stayed in contact on Zello, a push-to-talk app, and on Facebook, the platform on which their militia had risen and recruited. "You are executing citizen's arrest. Arrest this assembly, we have probable cause for acts of treason, election fraud," one of them said. "Inside," one wrote on Facebook. "All legislators are down in the Tunnels 3floors down," another responded. A third issued an order: "All members are in the tunnels under capital seal them in. Turn on gas."

Others shared the Oath Keepers' intent. Peter Stager, a forty-one-year-old Arkansan, said in a Twitter video, "Everybody in there is a treasonous traitor," and "Death is the only remedy for what's in that building." He carried an American flag up the Capitol steps, found a policeman who'd been knocked off his feet by the crowd, and beat the officer with the flagpole. Angeli, the "Q shaman," left a note for Pence at his desk in the Senate chamber: "It's only a matter of time, justice is coming." Pence had escaped the invaders by mere yards. Lawmakers later emerged saying they had huddled in back offices or behind locked doors, fearing for their lives as angry crowds roamed the hallways. Dominic Pezzola, a Proud Boys member later charged with breaking through a Capitol window with a police shield, "said that anyone they got their hands on they would have killed, including Nancy Pelosi," an FBI informant reported. The informant said Pezzola and his friends planned to come to Washington for the inauguration and "kill every single 'm-fer' they can." Former friends told *Vice News* that Pezzola had grown hyperactive on Facebook; one described him as having fallen down a social media "rabbit hole."

Five people died during the insurrection. None had been targeted specifically; the animal violence of the uncontrolled mob killed them. Brian Sicknick, a forty-two-year-old policeman overrun by the crowd and pepper-sprayed twice, returned to headquarters, collapsed, and succumbed the next day. A medical examiner attributed the stroke that killed him to natural causes exacerbated by the violence.

Most of the rest were themselves members of the mob — like so many others pulled into extremist causes, simultaneously participants and victims. Kevin Greeson, a fifty-five-year-old Parler user and Proud Boys supporter from Alabama — who'd posted, "Load your guns and take to the streets!" — died of a heart attack in the crowd. Benjamin Philips, a fifty-year-old from Pennsylvania who'd started an alternative social network called Trumparoo, died of a stroke. Roseanne Boyland, a thirty-four-year-old Facebook obsessive from Georgia, collapsed in a crush at a Capitol tunnel and died. Boyland's family said she had found the online far right, and then QAnon, while searching for meaning in the aftermath of long struggles with addiction.

Then there was Ashli Babbitt, a thirty-five-year-old Californian, Air Force veteran, and owner of a pool-supply company who'd reoriented her life around QAnon and tweeted fifty-plus times per day. Babbitt, wearing a Trump flag as a cape, forced herself through a broken glass window in a barricaded doorway and, within feet of the lawmakers her community had insisted must be killed, was shot by a Capitol police officer. She died immediately. Like many others in the crowd, John Sullivan, a heavy social media user, filmed Babbitt's death. "That got me moved, that got me heated!" Sullivan said on the recording. As Babbitt slumped back into the crowd, blood pouring from her mouth, he awed, "Dude, this shit's gonna go viral."

On the Capitol lawn, Matthew Rosenberg, a *New York Times* reporter who had rushed over to cover the mayhem, bumped into Barnett, who was already recognizable from the photo taken in Pelosi's office just minutes earlier. Barnett had wandered onto the lawn, his shirt now ripped open from some melee in the Capitol, clutching a letter from Pelosi's desk. Chatting freely with Rosenberg, Barnett waved Pelosi's letter proudly, telling him, "I wrote her a nasty note, put my feet up on her desk, and scratched my balls." He strolled back into the crowd that was now milling casually in front of the sacked Capitol building, drinking beers and waving flags, projecting an air of victory.

Afterward, with hundreds arrested (including Barnett) and with Trump impeached for a second time, shock waves would echo for months. But before the siege had even ended, they had already rippled all the way to Silicon Valley. "Can we get some courage and actual action from leadership in response to this behavior?" a Facebook employee wrote on the company's internal message board as the riot unfolded. "Your silence is disappointing at the least and criminal at worst."

In a stream of internal posts, employees fumed at Facebook's decision to leave up a Trump post, written amid the siege, that winkingly encouraged it to press on: "These are the things and events that happen," he wrote, when a "sacred landslide" victory is "stripped away from great patriots." The company's relationship with its 50,000-some workers was already at a nadir from the previous year's conflicts. Now, as Facebook allowed Trump to use the platform to urge an ongoing insurrection, frustration boiled over. "We need to take down his account right now. This is not a moment for half measures," another employee wrote. But rather than acting against Trump, the company froze comments on the internal discussion.

The next day, the workers' union at Alphabet, which had formed only that week, put out a statement condemning their employers' inaction. (Alphabet is the parent company to Google and YouTube.) "Social media has emboldened the fascist movement growing in the United States and we are particularly cognizant that YouTube, an Alphabet product, has played a key role in this growing threat," they wrote. Alphabet workers, they continued, had repeatedly warned executives of YouTube's role in "hate, harassment, discrimination, and radicalization" but had been "ignored or given token concessions." It urged the company, at the least, to "hold Donald Trump accountable to the platform's own rules."

There was, if not a sea change in the Valley, then at least a flash of reckoning. Chris Sacca, one of Twitter's earliest investors, tweeted, "You've got blood on your hands, Jack and Zuck. For four years you've rationalized this terror. Inciting violent treason is not a free speech exercise. If you work at those companies, it's on you too. Shut it down." Asked why he'd called out the employees as well, Sacca responded, "Frankly, the only people they listen to are the employees that surround them. In tech, if you lose talent, you lose power."

The day after the riot, Facebook announced it would block Trump from using its services at least until the inauguration two weeks later. The next day, as Trump continued tweeting in support of the insurrectionists, Twitter pulled the plug, too. YouTube, the last major holdout, followed four days later. Most experts and much of the public agreed that banning Trump was both necessary and overdue. Still, there was undeniable discomfort with that decision falling in the hands of a few Silicon Valley executives. And not just because they were unelected corporate actors. Those same executives' decisions had helped bring the social media crisis to this point in the first place. After years of the industry appeasing Trump and Republicans, the ban was widely seen as self-interested. It had been implemented, after all, three days after Democrats won control of the Senate, in addition to the House and White House.

Democrats, whose anger only rose, viewed the ban as a superficial measure undertaken only when Trump's exit from power was foregone. The Biden campaign had written privately to Facebook, throughout the election, expressing first concern, then outrage, over what it considered the company's failures to act. "I've never been a fan of Facebook, as you probably know," Biden had earlier told the *New York Times* editorial board, suggesting his administration might revoke certain legal protections for social media platforms. "I've never been a big Zuckerberg fan. I think he's a real problem."

The day after Biden's inauguration, two Democratic members of Congress sent letters to the CEOs of Facebook, Google, YouTube, and Twitter. They were written by Tom Malinowski, once a hard-charging human rights official at the State Department, and Anna Eshoo, who had represented the California district including Silicon Valley since 1993. Democratic leaders had championed the Valley for decades. Now the companies' own congresswoman had coauthored a letter telling them, "Perhaps no single entity is more responsible for the spread of dangerous conspiracy theories at scale or for inflaming anti-government grievance than the one you started and that you oversee today."

The letters placed much of the responsibility for the insurrection on the companies. "The fundamental problem," they wrote to the CEOs of Google and YouTube, "is that YouTube, like other social media platforms, sorts, presents, and recommends information to users by feeding them content most likely to reinforce their existing political biases, especially those rooted in anger, anxiety, and fear." The letters to Facebook and Twitter were similar. All demanded sweeping policy changes, ending with the same admonition: that the companies "begin a fundamental reexamination of maximizing user engagement as the basis for algorithmic sorting and recommendation." The language pointedly signaled that Democrats had embraced the view long advanced by researchers, social scientists, and dissident Valleyites: that the dangers from social media are not a matter of simply moderating better or tweaking policies. They are rooted in the fundamental nature of the platforms. And they are severe enough to threaten American democracy itself.

There was another change that January: QAnon all but collapsed. "We gave it our all. Now we need to keep our chins up and go back to our lives as best we are able," Ron Watkins, the administrator of 8chan (now rebranded as "8kun") widely suspected to have written Q's material, posted the morning of Biden's inauguration. On Telegram — a social app that had grown popular with QAnon as Twitter had applied greater friction — he urged followers to respect Biden's legitimacy. He added, "As we enter into the next administration please remember all the friends and happy memories we made together over the past few years." Watkins was effectively telling the movement, suspected to number in the millions, all bracing for a final battle against the evils responsible for every ill in their lives, to stand down. After that, posts from Q, who had already gone mysteriously silent since December 8, ceased.

The sense of an ending pervaded. An 8kun moderator purged the site's "QResearch" archives, writing, "I am just performing euthanasia to something I once loved very much." Some began posting their goodbyes. Others tried to come to grips: "Mods please explain why Biden isn't arrested yet." One compared watching Biden's inauguration to "being a kid and seeing the big gift under the tree…only to open it and realize it was a lump of coal the whole time." Without mainstream platforms to accelerate their cause or interlink it with the wider social web, the remaining believers had few places to apply their once-mighty energies. They spun and spun, looking for validation they never got, pining for resolution to the psychological crisis that years of radicalization had opened in them.

"EVERYTHING will be happening in the next 45 minutes," one user wrote in a Q forum during Biden's swearing in. The Democrats onstage, he promised, "will be arrested live on television with tens of millions watching in amazement!" It would be "the greatest day since D-Day" and "America will be united in celebration!" When the swearing in proceeded normally, another user asked if he was okay. He insisted that victory was still coming and, with it, a return to the life that had been taken from him. "I have lost friends and a girlfriend over the last year because they refused to see the truth, now at last I am being redeemed," he wrote. "Soon they will all come back and apologize, this is the happiest day of my life."

epilogue

whistleblowing

A WINDOW OPENED in the weeks after the Capitol siege. Unlike in the faltered reckonings of 2016 and 2018, there was, finally, broad understanding of social media's consequences. Reimagining the platforms, down to their cores, felt necessary in a way that it had not before and, with much of Silicon Valley itself aghast, maybe even possible. Tech experts and writers buzzed over new possibilities. Maybe subscription-based services, with users paying monthly fees to log on, could break the industry's addiction to ad revenue and therefore to engagement. Maybe tightened liability laws could realign their incentives.

But the window quickly closed. The social media giants were invested too deeply in status quo financial and ideological models for such radical change. Mostly, they built on the methods they knew best: automated technology and at-scale content moderation. Twitter, for instance, dialed up its "friction," adding prompts and interstitials ("Want to read the article first?") to slow users from compulsively sharing posts. It was a meaningful change, but far short of Jack Dorsey's suggestions of rethinking the platform's underlying mechanics, which remained in place. Dorsey later stepped down as CEO, in November 2021, his bold promises unfulfilled.

A few weeks after the insurrection, Zuckerberg announced that Facebook's recommendation system would no longer promote political groups — a potentially landmark step toward blunting one of the platform's most dangerous elements. But in an indication that the company's reforms reflected grudging sops to external pressure rather than a sincere change in thinking, it was the third time Facebook had announced this change. Earlier pledges, in October 2020 and on January 6, had been mostly

329

empty, independent researchers found. Only under pressure from Democratic lawmakers did this latest promise actually bear out.

Facebook's reversals had begun even before the insurrection. During the election, Facebook had tweaked its algorithm to promote "authoritative" news outlets over hyperpartisan links. In December, it rolled back the change, reinstating the algorithms' original preferences. That month, Facebook had also announced that it would lift its recently imposed ban on political ads, but only in Georgia, where two looming Senate elections would determine control of the chamber. The company claimed that it was deferring to unnamed "experts" who had supposedly called political ads crucial to "the importance of expressing voice." In reality, democracy groups widely opposed the change. The effect was immediate. Before Facebook had lifted its political ad ban in Georgia, user feeds had largely shown *Wall Street Journal* and *Atlanta Journal-Constitution* articles. The day after Facebook flipped the switch, *Breitbart* articles, partisan content, and political ads replaced them. After January 6, critics pressed Facebook to reinstate the algorithm tweak and the ban on political ads. The company, after all, had initially presented both policies as essential for protecting democracy. How could it possibly go back? But the algorithm stayed in its more dangerous form and, that March, Facebook lifted its ban on political ads nationwide.

Just as quickly as they rolled back reforms, Silicon Valley leaders also began questioning how much responsibility they really had to change anything at all. "I think these events were largely organized on platforms that don't have our abilities to stop hate, don't have our standards, and don't have our transparency," Sheryl Sandberg, Facebook's second in command, said of the January 6 insurrection. Her comments, though widely derided outside the Valley, sent a clear signal within it: we're digging in.

A few days later, Adam Mosseri, the former news-feed chief who now ran Instagram, said that while January 6 would "mark a big shift" in society's relationship to technology, it was important not to overcorrect. "Every new technology has gone through these waves," he said, drawing a set of comparisons I'd heard before in the Valley: "That happened with VHS. That happened with writing. That happened with bicycles." But no one was ever able to pinpoint for me which genocides had been attributed to VHS.

Facebook and others shifted from promising that they had learned their lesson and would finally change to insisting, even more stridently than they had before January 6, that all the evidence pointing to their responsibility was simply wrong. "Facebook's systems are not designed to reward provocative content," Facebook's PR chief, the former British Deputy Prime Minister Nick Clegg, wrote in a 5,000-word blog post titled "You and the Algorithm: It Takes Two to Tango." It was really users who pushed "sensational content," Clegg wrote.

The companies largely reverted to their old ways. Enforcement against election disinformation dropped precipitously over the course of 2021, the watchdog group Common Cause found, as lies that undermined democracy were "left to metastasize on Facebook and Twitter." Movements born on social media continued to rise, seeping into the fabric of American governance.

By early 2022, one study found, more than one in nine state lawmakers nationwide belonged to at least one far-right Facebook group. Many promoted the conspiracies and ideologies that had first grown online into law, passing waves of legislation that curbed voting rights, Covid policies, and LGBT protections. Amid an internet-fueled panic over teachers supposedly "grooming" schoolchildren into homosexuality, some pushed legislation encouraging kids to record their teachers for proof—a disturbingly crisp echo of the "gay kit" YouTube conspiracy that had caused such chaos in Brazil. The Texas GOP, which controlled the state senate, state house, and the governor's mansion, changed its official slogan to "We are the storm," the QAnon rallying cry. In two separate instances, in Colorado and Michigan, election officials loyal to QAnon were caught tampering with voting systems. By the next election, in 2022, QAnon-aligned candidates were on the ballot in 26 states.

The social media giants continued surfacing so many Covid-related lies and conspiracies that Vivek Murthy, the surgeon general, issued a formal advisory in July that the platforms "enabled misinformation to poison our information environment, with little accountability to their users," which he called an "urgent crisis." A day later, Biden said that Facebook was "killing people."

Democrats, along with many others, put much of their hope in federal regulatory investigations into the companies. The effort had begun, in late 2020, with the Democrat-controlled House antitrust subcommittee, which had released a 449-page report that October recommending sweeping regulations against Facebook, Google, Amazon, and Apple that would, in some cases, break them up. Though the report focused on monopolistic behaviors, the lawmakers did not hide that they worried about the companies' control over matters beyond the marketplace, warning, "Our economy and democracy are at stake."

The Justice Department had filed suit against Google that October, implicating it and YouTube in abuses in line with those in the House report. The Federal Trade Commission had filed a similar suit against Facebook in December, suggesting it might seek to break the company up. Both cases, joined in parallel suits by several state attorneys general, proceeded throughout 2021 and 2022. But while antitrust enforcement can be a powerful tool, it is a blunt one. Splintering Facebook from Instagram, or Google from YouTube, would weaken the companies, maybe even drastically. But it would not change the underlying nature of their products. Neither would it remove the economic or ideological forces that had produced those products in the first place.

For all its talk of rebuilding trust, Silicon Valley showed, in an episode only a month after Biden's inauguration, that it would wield the full weight of its power against whole societies to deter them from acting. Australian regulators had moved to target the Valley's greatest vulnerability: revenue. As of February 2021, Facebook and Google would be required to pay Australian news outlets for the right to feature links to their work. The platforms, after all, were siphoning the news industry's ad revenue by trading on their journalism. The new rule included a powerful provision. If the tech firms and news agencies couldn't agree on a price by the imposed deadline, government arbiters would set it for them. In truth, the rules favored News Corp, the mega-conglomerate run by Australian-born Rupert Murdoch, who in 2016 had threatened Zuckerberg with just this sort of action.

But whatever the merits, as a test case of governments' power over social media platforms, the results were telling. Google, just short of the deadline, struck a deal with News Corp and others, bringing it into compliance. Facebook refused. Instead, one morning, Australians woke to find Facebook had blocked all news content. An entire nation's preeminent information source — 39 percent of Australians said they got their news there — suddenly included no news. Much more had gone dark, too: politicians running for re-election, groups that worked with victims of domestic violence, the state weather service. Even, in the middle of a pandemic, government health offices. The company had finally done what it wouldn't in Myanmar, over a months-long genocide it had been credibly accused of abetting. Or in Sri Lanka or India. In no case had spiraling violence, however deadly, led the company to flip the "off" switch, even on just one component of the platform. But the week that Australia threatened its revenue, it was lights out.

Australians could, of course, access news or government websites directly. Still, Facebook had, by deliberate design, made itself essential, training users to rely on its platform as the end-all for news and information. With news content gone, rumor and misinformation filled the vacuum. Evelyn Douek, an Australian scholar studying the governance of social media platforms at Harvard Law School, called the blackout "calculated for impact and unconscionable." Human Rights Watch described the intervention as "alarming and dangerous." An Australian lawmaker warned that blocking the state weather service might disrupt citizens' access to updates that, on a week when floods and wildfires both raged, could mean life or death. A few days later, Australia's government capitulated, allowing Facebook sweeping exceptions from the regulations.

European governments continued to impose fines and regulations. Officials implicitly acknowledged that they had little more capability to force structural change on Silicon Valley than had their counterparts in Australia or, for that matter, the hapless officials I'd met in Sri Lanka — many of whom were, by 2021, out of office anyway, having been replaced by an ultranationalist strongman who'd risen, in part, by stirring up hate and rumors online. But the Europeans hoped to pilot policies that might become models for others. The French government opened a center on digital regulation, for which it hired, among others, Guillaume Chaslot, the former YouTube engineer. He has been especially preoccupied with finding ways to show web users how algorithms guide their experiences as they navigate the platforms, even reveal to them the system's choices and habits in real time. He compared it to the labels on cigarettes warning consumers that smoking causes lung cancer. In early 2022, the European Union began developing new regulations that would restrict how American tech companies could use European consumers' personal data. Facebook, in an annual report issued that February, threatened an even harsher version of its Australia strategy, warning that, if the E.U. went ahead, it would "likely be unable to offer a number of our most significant products and services, including Facebook and Instagram, in Europe." Germany's finance minister shrugged off the coercion, telling reporters that, ever since he had given up social media four years earlier, "life has been fantastic." France's finance minister, almost daring the company to follow through, announced, "we would live very well without Facebook."

Public pressure in the United States was more uneven. Former president Obama, in a 2022 speech in the heart of Silicon Valley, warned that social media was "turbocharging some of humanity's worst impulses." He called "the profound change...in how we communicate and consume information" a major driver of democracy's worsening travails, urging citizens and governments to rein in the companies. Still, the Biden administration was consumed with stabilizing the public health and economic emergencies wrought by the pandemic, then with Russia's invasion of

Ukraine. Meanwhile, the companies hired up many of the outside analysts and academics who'd embarrassed them with investigations of their products. Typically, they were recruited by would-be reformers within middle management, who probably meant it when they said that pressuring the companies from within was likelier to bring change. And many were driven into Silicon Valley's arms by the collapsing academic job market, where opportunities for PhD holders laden with student debt disintegrated just as Americans saw their healthcare and childcare costs spike from the pandemic. Whatever their motivations for joining the Valley, their public-facing work ceased as a result.

But a few, thanks perhaps in part to their notoriety for the shocking discoveries they'd already made about social media, secured stable enough perches in academia to continue. Jonas Kaiser, the YouTube-mapping German media scholar, was one of them, joining the faculty at Boston's Suffolk University in late 2020. Another was William Brady, who became an assistant professor at Northwestern in 2022. Both continue the work of understanding social media's consequences, as do dozens like them, with untold findings still to come.

Some did find ways to pressure the industry from within. Among them is Renée DiResta, who tracks online causes and bad actors, like the anti-vaxxers that first prompted her journey, at a Stanford University research center in the heart of the Valley. Much as she was careful, in her 2018 testimony before the Senate, to engage the Democrats likeliest to take action while still finding common ground with Republicans, DiResta has leveraged her and Stanford's links to the social media companies, contributing to successful campaigns to remove government-aligned influence campaigns from the platforms, all without ever, as best I can tell, pulling a single punch on her public criticisms of those same corporations.

There is one group with the leverage, access, and technical know-how to effectively pressure Silicon Valley: its own workforce. After January 6, workers' anger only grew, with 40 percent of the big-tech workforce saying in March of 2021 that giants like Google or Facebook should be broken up. But for all the muscle that workers had flexed in 2020, their activism largely ceased. Unionization — the five fingers that become a fist — remains anathema among Valley workers, making organizing across 50,000-worker companies almost impossible. And with pay, perks, and job security virtually unmatched in the modern era, why not clock in and out for a few years, make your fortune, and retire in peace?

But not everyone chose to look the other way. By May 2021, a Facebook employee named Frances Haugen, who worked on a team combating election-related misinformation overseas, had had enough. Her corporate overlords, she came to believe, were willfully sacrificing the safety of users, whole societies, even democracy itself for the sake of maximizing profit.

Haugen copied thousands of internal research reports, meeting memos, and corporate directives, photographing her screen rather than downloading the files directly to avoid triggering security measures. For months, she had been in touch with Jeff Horwitz, a *Wall Street Journal* reporter whom she had first contacted in December 2020, impressed with his reporting on social media's damaging influence in India, where she had spent time. But it would be some months before she formulated her plan for the files.

"I just don't want to agonize over what I didn't do for the rest of my life," Haugen texted a friend, in September 2021, as she considered whether to go public. Soon afterward, she sent the files to the Securities and Exchange Commission, a federal regulator that oversees market practices, as part of eight whistleblower complaints alleging corporate malfeasance at Facebook. She also sent them to Congress and to Horwitz, who began revealing the secrets they contained.

Collectively, the documents told the story of a company fully aware that its harms sometimes exceeded even critics' worst assessments. At times, the reports warned explicitly of dangers that later became deadly, like a spike in hate speech or in vaccine misinformation, with plenty of notice for the company to have acted and, had it not refused to do so, possibly saved lives. In undeniable reports and unvarnished language, they showed Facebook's own data and experts confirming the allegations that the company had so blithely dismissed in public. Facebook's executives, including Zuckerberg, had been plainly told that their company posed tremendous dangers, and those executives had intervened over and over to keep their platforms spinning at full speed anyway. The files, which Facebook downplayed as unrepresentative, largely confirmed long-held suspicions. But some went even further. An internal presentation on hooking more children on Facebook's products included the line "Is there a way to leverage playdates to drive word of hand/growth among kids?"

As public outrage grew, *60 Minutes* announced that it would air an interview with the leaker of the documents. Until that point, Haugen's identity had still been secret. Her interview cut through a by-then years-old debate over this technology for the clarity with which she made her charges: the platforms amplified harm; Facebook knew it; the company had the power to stop it but chose not to; and the company continually lied to regulators and to the public. "Facebook has realized that if they change the algorithm to be safer," Haugen said, "people will spend less time on the site, they'll click on less ads, they'll make less money."

Two days later, she testified to a Senate subcommittee. She presented herself as striving to reform the industry to salvage its potential. "We can have social media we enjoy, that connects us, without tearing apart our democracy, putting our children in danger, and sowing ethnic violence around the world," she told the senators. Working with Lawrence Lessig, a Harvard legal scholar who had volunteered as her lawyer, along with a communications firm that Lessig hired, Haugen also sent the documents to eighteen American and European news agencies. She briefed members of Congress whose committee seats gave them the power to shape new regulations. She circulated European capitals, meeting with high-level officials whose governments had led the way on regulating social media.

Throughout, Haugen consistently called back to Facebook's failures in poorer countries. That record, she argued, highlighted the company's callousness toward its customers' well-being, as well as the destabilizing power of platform dynamics that, after all, played out everywhere. "What we see in Myanmar, what we see in Ethiopia," she said at a panel, "are only the opening chapters of a novel that has an ending that is far scarier than anything we want to read."

Democrats and rights groups, leveraging the outrage Haugen generated and the threat of ongoing antitrust suits, have focused on pushing for forceful regulation of social media companies. The American government, after all, may be the one remaining entity in the world with the power to force the companies to change. Still, it is difficult to imagine a few dozen lawmakers, operating one of the most dysfunctional legislatures in the Western world, able to perpetually keep pace with thousands of engineers whose every incentive would be to replace whatever feature or policy had been regulated into submission with something else that could achieve the same result.

Coercing the companies into regulating themselves is also an uncertain path. The social media giants, as currently constituted, may be simply unable to roll back their systems' worst tendencies. Technically, it would be easy. But the cultural, ideological, and economic forces that led executives to create and supercharge those systems in the first place still apply. Lawmakers and activists can yell at Zuckerberg, Wojcicki, and others all they want. The founders and CEOs of these companies, for all their fabulous wealth, have been, whether they realized it or not, prisoners of their creations from the day that a venture capitalist first cut them a check in return for the promise of permanent, exponential growth.

When asked what would most effectively reform both the platforms and the companies overseeing them, Haugen had a simple answer: turn off the algorithm. "I think we don't want computers deciding what we focus on," she said. She also suggested that if Congress curtailed liability protections, making the companies legally responsible for the consequences of anything their systems promoted, "they would get rid of engagement-based ranking." Platforms would roll back to the 2000s, when they simply displayed your friends' posts by newest to oldest. No A.I. to swarm you with attention-maximizing content or route you down rabbit holes.

Her response followed a reliable pattern that has emerged in the years I've spent covering social media. The longer that someone spends studying the platforms, whatever their discipline, the likelier they are to converge on Haugen's answer: turn it off. Sometimes the recommendation is narrower. Jonas Kaiser urged YouTube to turn off its algorithms on sensitive topics like health or things related to children. Sometimes it is wider. Benedict Evans, a former Andreessen Horowitz venture capitalist, proposed "to remove whole layers of mechanics that enable abuse." After all, algorithms are hardly the only feature behind social media's chaos. Casino-style interfaces, share buttons, publicly displayed "like" counters, groups recommendations — all are intrinsic to the platforms and their harms.

There are, as in any matter this contentious, a handful of dissenting experts, who argue that social media's impact is overblown. They do not dispute the evidence for the technology's role in harms like radicalization, but rather use different methods that produce milder results. Still, their view remains a minority, and one of relative emphasis, akin to arguing that car exhaust's role in climate change is less than that of coal plants.

Virtually none of these experts or dissidents argue that the world would benefit from shuttering social media altogether. All had come to their work in the first place, after all, on a belief that social media brought undeniable good and, freed from its revenue-boosting mechanics, might still prove revolutionary. But whatever the counsel, for a great many serious researchers, analysts, or human rights advocates, it comes down to some version of turning it off. It would mean a less enticing, less engaging internet, one where surprising YouTube videos or emotion-grabbing Facebook groups were rarer and less readily at hand. But all available evidence also suggested that it would be a world with fewer schoolteachers chased into hiding, fewer families burned alive in their homes by rumor-fueled riots, fewer lives ruined by undeserved infamy or by the false promise of extremism. Fewer children deprived of lifesaving vaccines or exposed to unwitting sexualization. Maybe even fewer democracies torn asunder by polarization, lies, and violence.

One reason that many experts converge on this answer, I think, is that many of them, by their fourth or fifth major study, have been to Silicon Valley to meet its engineer-overlords. And they have come to understand that one aspect of their public defense is true: they believe they are not deliberately promoting misinformation, hate, or tribalism. To the extent that they think about these effects, it is to curb them. But that is what makes visiting the Valley so disturbing. Some combination of ideology, greed, and the technological opacity of complex machine-learning blinds executives from seeing their creations in their entirety. The machines are, in the ways that matter, essentially ungoverned.

The more I spoke with psychologists and network analysts, regulators and reformed engineers, the more that the terms they used to describe this technology kept reminding me of HAL 9000, the artificial intelligence from *2001: A Space Odyssey*, the Kubrick film whose salience had imposed itself over and over in my investigation of social media. In the film, HAL, though responsible for the crew's safety, overinterprets programming instructing it to ensure arrival at their preplanned destination no matter what, and attempts to kill everyone aboard the ship. HAL is not meant to be a villain. If there was one, it was the engineers who, in their hubris, assumed their creation's actions would be as benevolent as their intentions, or per-haps the astronauts who entrusted themselves to a machine possessing the power of life and death, with incentives that might diverge from their own.

The lesson of *2001* was hardly to upgrade HAL with further algorith-mic tweaks, in the hopes that, next time, it might behave a little more responsibly. Nor was it that HAL's engineers should say they were sorry and promise to do better. And it certainly wasn't that HAL's corporate maker should take on greater and greater control of their customers' lives while lawmakers and journalists mused on the robot's nature. The lesson was unambiguous: shut HAL off. Even if it meant losing whatever benefits HAL brought. Even if it was difficult, in the film's final scenes, to rip HAL's tentacles from the systems governing every facet of the astronauts' lives. Even if the machine fought back with all its power.

Acknowledgments

Any value to this book is due in large part to its editor, Ben George, whose passion, care, and infectious spirit never once flagged, even during marathon sixteen-hour editing sessions with an infant on his knee. Thank you as well to Bruce Nichols, Katharine Myers, and everyone at Little, Brown for your enthusiasm and your faith.

The book would not have been possible without Jennifer Joel of ICM Partners, who shepherded it through opportunity and obstacle alike with steadfastness and wisdom.

I am indebted to many of my colleagues at the *New York Times*. Michael Slackman, the assistant managing editor for International, first suggested the idea that became this project, as well as oversaw and supported reporting that grew into or inspired sections of this book. Eric Nagourney, Juliana Barbassa, and Doug Schorzman edited that reporting, putting blood and sweat into stories that should really bear their names. Amanda Taub, with whom I started the Interpreter column in 2016, co-authored stories from Sri Lanka, Germany, and Brazil. I was also fortunate to report alongside or co-author with Wai Moe in Myanmar; Katrin Bennhold and Shane Thomas McMillan in Germany; Dharisha Bastians in Sri Lanka; and, in Brazil, Mariana Simões and Kate Steiker-Ginzberg; along with Alyse Shorland and Singeli Agnew as producers for *The Weekly*. Pui-Wing Tam, Kevin Roose, Paul Mozur, and others offered support and solidarity in covering social media. Thank you to the leadership at the *Times* for supporting that reporting and granting me the space for this book.

A great many academics, researchers, and others freely gave their energy, ideas, and sometimes original work in support of this project. So did doctors, engineers, human rights workers, and others on the front lines of these issues, not to mention the people we euphemistically call "sources": survivors, insiders, witnesses. They are too many to name here but are referenced throughout the text. This is, in many ways, their book.

Thank you, especially, to Mom, Dad, and Joanna for believing in me and making me who I am. And to Jordan for keeping me going, in body and spirit, and making it all feel worthwhile.

Notes

prologue: consequences

3   spent $300 million: "Facebook Just Opened an Epic $300 Million Gehry-Designed Campus with a Redwood Forest and Rooftop Garden," Andrew Evers, CNBC, September 4, 2018.

3   by priceless murals: "Tina Vaz on Facebook's Artist in Residence Program," Whitewall.art, January 15, 2020.

7   "There's nothing new": Interview with Monika Bickert, Facebook's head of global policy management, in October 2018.

7   "As a society": Interview with Nathaniel Gleicher, Facebook's head of security policy, in October 2018.

9   "As we have greater": Interview with Sara Su, then director for product management on Facebook's news feed integrity team, in October 2018.

9   "Our algorithms exploit": From "Facebook Executives Shut Down Efforts to Make the Site Less Divisive," Jeff Horwitz and Deepa Seetharaman, *Wall Street Journal*, May 2020.

10   "driving people toward": "Facebook's Civil Rights Audit — Final Report," Laura W. Murphy and the law firm Relman Colfax, About.fb.com, July 8, 2020.

Chapter One: Trapped in the Casino

15   returned a stream: "How Facebook and YouTube Help Spread Anti-Vaxxer Propaganda," Julia Carrie Wong, *The Guardian*, February 1, 2019.

18   a silicon Galápagos: *The Code: Silicon Valley and the Remaking of America*, Margaret O'Mara, 2019, establishes, in great detail, how the Valley's founding traits and personalities produced the modern social networks and made them as they are.

19   "fondness for humiliating": From *The Man Behind the Microchip: Robert Noyce and the Invention of Silicon Valley*, Leslie Berlin, 2005, one of many biographies of Shockley contemporaries, detailing his abuses. For greater detail, particularly on his turn toward eugenics and racism, see *Broken Genius: The Rise and Fall of William Shockley, Creator of the Electronic Age*, Joel N. Shurkin, 2006.

19   kept in the Valley: O'Mara, 2019: 7–9.

20   tended to fund: Interview with Leslie Berlin, a Stanford University historian, in May 2020.

21   Facebook had 8 million users: Userbase source for Facebook: "Inside Mark Zuckerberg's Controversial Decision to Turn Down Yahoo's $1 Billion Early Offer to Buy Facebook," Mike Hoefflinger, *Business Insider*, April 16, 2017. For Friendster: "The Friendster Autopsy: How a Social Network Dies," Robert McMillan, *Wired*, February 27, 2013, and "Friendster Patents Social Networking," Pete Cashmore, *Mashable*, July 7, 2006. For Orkut: "Google's Orkut Captivates Brazilians," by Seth Kugel, *New York Times*, April 9, 2006. For Myspace: "The Decline of Myspace: Future of Social Media," Karl Kangur, *DreamGrow*, August 13, 2012.

21 get off the startup roller coaster: *Facebook: The Inside Story*, Steven Levy, 2020, relays detailed, firsthand accounts from Zuckerberg and other high-ranking employees of the decision to turn down the Yahoo offer, as well as the subsequent news feed episode.

22 a matter of consensus: This phenomenon, known to social scientists as common knowledge, is perhaps best captured in "How Does Media Influence Social Norms? Experimental Evidence on the Role of Common Knowledge," Eric Arias, *Political Science Research and Methods*, July 2019. See also *Rational Ritual: Culture, Coordination, and Common Knowledge*, Michael Suk-Young Chwe, 2013 reissue, or the work of Princeton University's Betsy Levy Paluck, explored later in this book.

22 testy public apology: "Calm down. Breathe. We hear you," Mark Zuckerberg on now-defunct Facebook Notes, September 2006.

23 valued at $15 billion: "Microsoft Buys Stake in Facebook," Brad Stone, *New York Times*, October 25, 2007.

23 When the news feed launched: All statistics in this paragraph from *Social Media Fact Sheet*, Pew Research Center, April 7, 2021.

23 by the summer of 2016: Facebook usage statistics are from "10 Facts About Americans and Facebook," John Gramlich, Pew Research Center, June 1, 2021. In-person socializing statistics are from the Bureau of Labor Statistics and "Facebook Has 50 Minutes of Your Time Each Day. It Wants More," James B. Stewart, *New York Times*, May 5, 2016.

24 "I'm not on social media": Parker's comments are from a business conference hosted by the news site Axios in November 2017, where he was interviewed by reporter Mike Allen.

25 generated $1 million: "The Formula for Phone Addiction Might Double as a Cure," Simone Stolzoff, *Wired*, February 1, 2018.

26 social media's accomplice: The textbook overview of dopamine and its uses and abuses, including by Pavlov, is the academic article "A Selective Role for Dopamine in Stimulus–Reward Learning," Shelly B. Flagel et al., *Nature*, 2011.

26 The psychologist B. F. Skinner: For an approachable overview of Skinner's findings, as well as elaboration on dual amplifiers of variable and intermittent rewards (social media provides both), try "Schedules of Reinforcement," Annabelle G.Y. Lim, *Simply Psychology*, July 2, 2020. Greater detail, along with citations to supporting neurological research, can be found in chapter 2 of *Behave: The Biology of Humans at Our Best and Worst*, Robert M. Sapolsky, 2017.

27 checks their smartphone: "The Top 10 Valuable Facebook Statistics," Zephoria Research, 2021.

27 to open social media: "47 Facebook Stats That Matter to Marketers in 2021," Christina Newberry, *Hootsuite*, January 11, 2021.

27 In 2018, a team of economists: "The Welfare Effects of Social Media," Hunt Allcott, Luca Braghieri, Sarah Eichmeyer, and Matthew Gentzkow, *American Economic Review*, March 2020.

28 "considered a cursed project": "What's the History of the 'Awesome Button' (That Eventually Became the Like Button) on Facebook?," Andrew Bosworth, *Quora*, October 16, 2014.

29 "a psychological gauge": "Sociometer Theory," by Mark R. Leary, is chapter 33 in *Handbook of Theories of Social Psychology*, vol. 2, 2011.

29 up to about 150 members: A fuller discussion of this number, its origins, and implications takes place later in this book. Its progenitor, Robin Dunbar, provides a useful overview in "Dunbar's Number: Why My Theory That Humans Can Only Maintain 150 Friendships Has Withstood 30 Years of Scrutiny," *The Conversation*, May 12, 2021.

Notes

29 "survival of the friendliest": *Survival of the Friendliest*, Brian Hare and Vanessa Woods, 2021.

29 We process that information: Further discussion of these emotions' uniquely human origins and function in *Humankind: A Hopeful History*, Rutger Bregman, 2019.

30 "Even though at the time": "The Binge Breaker," Bianca Bosker, *The Atlantic*, November 2016.

30 "that button having a number": "Jack Dorsey on Twitter's Mistakes," *The Daily*, a *New York Times* podcast, August 7, 2020.

30 neural activity flares: Unless noted otherwise, all references to the neurological effects of social media use in this section draw from the research of Dar Meshi, a Michigan State University neuroscientist. See, in particular, "The Emerging Neuroscience of Social Media," Meshi et al., in *Trends in Cognitive Sciences*, December 2015.

30 smaller nucleus accumbens: "Facebook Usage on Smartphones and Gray Matter Volume of the Nucleus Accumbens," Christian Montag et al., *Behavioural Brain Research*, June 2017.

31 "When Facebook changed their algorithm": "The Inventor of the 'Like' Button Wants You to Stop Worrying About Likes," Julian Morgans, *Vice News*, July 5, 2017.

31 "It is very common": "'Our Minds Can Be Hijacked': The Tech Insiders Who Fear a Smartphone Dystopia," Paul Lewis, *The Guardian*, October 6, 2017.

32 "remains a deep mystery": "Individuals and Groups in Social Psychology," Henri Tajfel, *British Journal of Social & Clinical Psychology* 18, no. 2, 1979.

32 He and several peers launched: For an effective overview, see "The Social Identity Theory of Intergroup Behavior," Henri Tajfel and John C. Turner, *Psychology of Intergroup Relations*, 1986.

32 Social identity, Tajfel demonstrated, is how we bond: "Social Psychology of Intergroup Relations," Henri Tajfel, *Annual Review of Psychology* 33, 1982.

33 In one experiment: "Social Categorization and Discriminatory Behavior: Extinguishing the Minimal Intergroup Discrimination Effect," Anne Locksley, Vilma Ortiz, and Christine Hepburn, *Journal of Personality and Social Psychology* 39, no. 5, 1980.

33 The same behavior: An overview of many such studies can be found in "Ingroup Favoritism and Prejudice," in *Principles of Social Psychology, First International Edition*, Charles Stangor, Hammond Tarry, and Rajiv Jhangiani, 2014.

33 During lunch breaks: Heston has recounted this in several interviews, with the first appearing in "The Arts," Jeff Rovin, *Omni Magazine*, November 1980: 140. His co-star, Natalie Trundy, independently described the incident at least once: "The Day of the Apes," Tom Weaver, *Starlog* magazine, September 2001: 20.

33 social-identity instincts drive us: Tafjel, "Social Psychology of Intergroup Relations."

33 It also makes us more distrustful: This effect has been repeatedly demonstrated, perhaps best in "A New Stress-Based Model of Political Extremism," Daphna Canetti-Nisim, Eran Halperin, Keren Sharvit, and Stevan E. Hobfoll, *Journal of Conflict Resolution* 53, no. 2, June 2009.

34 "Identity was the slingshot": *Why We're Polarized*, Ezra Klein, 2020: 143.

35 "I'm convinced that you all": "Google Chief Says Internet Freedom Key for Myanmar," Agence France-Presse video, March 22, 2013.

36 "a person without a Facebook": reported in "Fears over Facebook Regulation Proposal," Tim McLaughlin, *Myanmar Times*, July 15–21, 2013.

36 From 2012 to 2015: *Sticks and Stones: Hate Speech Narratives and Facilitators in Myanmar*, by the nonprofit research group C4ADS, February 2016.

36 many there remain unaware: *Internet Health Report: 2019*, published by the Mozilla Foundation, provides survey data showing that majorities of users in several zero-rated countries "have no idea there is an internet beyond Facebook."

37 his posts circulated: See the C4ADS *Sticks and Stones* report for deep and often disturbing detail on Facebook hate speech in Myanmar at this time.

37 The managers told Callan: "How Facebook's Rise Fueled Chaos and Confusion in Myanmar," Timothy McLaughlin, *Wired*, July 2018, captures this episode in detail. See also "Why Facebook Is Losing the War on Hate Speech in Myanmar," Steve Stecklow, Reuters, August 15, 2018.

Chapter 2: Everything Is Gamergate

39 *You just got helldumped: Crash Override: How Gamergate (Nearly) Destroyed My Life, and How We Can Win the Fight Against Online Hate*, Zoë Quinn, 2017: 2.

40 "i just want to see": Logs of these discussions are accessible at "GamerGate — #GameOverGate IRC Logs Explanation," Knowyourmeme.com, undated. See also "Zoe Quinn's Screenshots of 4chan's Dirty Tricks Were Just the Appetizer. Here's the First Course of the Dinner, Directly from the IRC log," David Futrelle, Wehuntedthemammoth.com, September 8, 2014.

40 "I tried to focus": Quinn: 4.

40 "If I ever see": "Game of Fear," Zachary Jason, *Boston Magazine*, April 28, 2015.

41 "If you think": "Zoë and the Trolls," Noreen Malone, *New York Magazine*, July 2017.

42 One favored method: "That Time the Internet Sent a SWAT Team to My Mom's House," Caroline Sinders, Narratively.com, July 17, 2015.

42 In 2017, police arrested: "His 'Swatting' Call Led to the Death of a Man. Now He is Going to Prison for 20 Years," Steve Almasy and Melissa Alonso, CNN, March 30, 2019.

42 Two other serial: "FBI Arrests Man Suspected of Orchestrating Dozens of 'Swatting' Calls," Timothy B. Lee, Arstechnica.com, January 14, 2020.

42 When an industry-news: "Intel Pulls Ads from Gamasutra, and Then Apologizes for It," Dean Takahashi, Venturebeat.com, October 3, 2014.

44 "Software increasingly defines": "I'm Brianna Wu, and I'm Risking My Life Standing Up to Gamergate," Brianna Wu, *Daily Dot*, February 12, 2015.

45 Through the 1960s: O'Mara: 90–92.

46 "We are really the revolutionaries": Berlin: 194.

46 PCC's newsletter: O'Mara: 136–39.

46 It had grown out: *From Counterculture to Cyberculture: Stewart Brand, the Whole Earth Network, and the Rise of Digital Utopianism*, Fred Turner, 2010: 71–72.

47 The site's founders: Cliff Figallo, one of the platform's architects, has said, for example, "Principles of tolerance and inclusion, fair resource allocation, distributed responsibility, management by example and influence, a flat organizational hierarchy, cooperative policy formulation, and acceptance of a libertarian-bordering-on-anarchic ethos were all carryovers from our communal living experience." Source: Turner: 148.

47 A near-absence of rules: Ibid.

48 "We reject: kings": "A Cloudy Crystal Ball / Apocalypse Now," presentation by David Clark, July 1992, to the 24th annual Internet Engineering Task Force conference.

48 A former WELL board member: "A Declaration of the Independence of Cyberspace," John Perry Barlow, February 8, 1996. Initially circulated to dozens of websites simultaneously, now available at Eff.org/cyberspace-independence.

48 "Our general counsel and CEO": "Twitter's Tony Wang: 'We Are the Free Speech Wing of the Free Speech Party,'" Josh Halliday, *The Guardian*, March 22, 2012.

48 "the founding ideal": Levy, *Facebook: The Inside Story*: 458.

48 While Apple was: This is according to Dave Morin, a former senior engineer at Facebook, as paraphrased in Levy: 149.

48 "We're kind of fundamentally": "The Facebook Dilemma," *PBS Frontline*, October 29, 2018.

48 a letter to shareholders: "Zuckerberg's Letter to Investors," Reuters, February 1, 2012.

48 "There's this fundamental": Levy, 7.

49 "The reason we nerds": *Hackers and Painters*, Paul Graham, 2004: 9.

49 has said he looks for: "What We Look for in Founders," Paul Graham, Paulgraham.com, October 2010.

49 "These guys want to": "What I Did This Summer," Paul Graham, Paulgraham.com, October 2005.

49 "If you're less sensitive": *Zero to One: Notes on Startups, or How to Build the Future*, Peter Thiel and Blake Masters, 2014: 40.

51 "Max Levchin, my co-founder": Ibid: 122.

52 A pair of videos: Screenshots documenting the incident can be found at "Kenny Glenn Case / Dusty the Cat," Knowyourmeme.com, September 10, 2011.

52 made it wildly popular: "Media Manipulation and Disinformation Online," Alice Marwick and Rebecca Lewis, *Data & Society*, May 2017.

54 "Ultimately," Christopher Poole: "The Trolls Among Us," Mattathias Schwartz, *New York Times Magazine*, August 3, 2008.

54 Adolescents also have: *Behave: The Biology of Humans at Our Best and Worst*, Robert M. Sapolsky, 2017: 163–164.

54 heavier use of social networks: *Teens, Social Media, and Privacy*, Mary Madden et al., Pew Research Center, May 21, 2013.

55 A '90s message board had defined: "From LOL to LULZ, the Evolution of the Internet Troll over 24 Years," Kristen V. Brown, Splinternews.com, March 18, 2016.

56 In 2010, one of the community's: "How the Internet Beat Up an 11-Year-Old Girl," Adrian Chen, *Gawker*, July 16, 2010.

57 The local band she'd named in her initial posts recorded: "Myspace-Famous Musician Dahvie Vanity Was Accused of Child Sex Abuse for Years. Now the FBI is Involved," Kat Tenbarge, Insider.com, July 2, 2020.

57 Amid an FBI: Ibid.

57 "regularly framed their activity": *You Are Here: A Field Guide for Navigating Polarized Speech, Conspiracy Theories, and Our Polluted Media Landscape*, Whitney Phillips and Ryan M. Milner, 2021: 58.

57 "an outcome they prodded": Ibid.

57 "Trolling is basically": Schwartz.

57 "the perfect conditions": Phillips and Milner: 78.

58 Auernheimer bragged of his role: "The End of Kindness: Weev and the Cult of the Angry Young Man," Greg Sandoval, *The Verge*, September 12, 2013.

58 In 2010, *TechCrunch*: "We're Awarding Goatse Security a Crunchie Award for Public Service," Michael Arrington, *TechCrunch*, June 14, 2010.

58 "journalists drank alongside hackers": "Lulz and Leg Irons: In the Courtroom with Weev," Molly Crabapple, *Vice News*, March 19, 2013.

59 "We're making a blue-ocean bet": "The Kleiner Perkins sFund: A $250 Million Bet That Social Is Just Getting Started," Michael Arrington, *TechCrunch*, October 21, 2010.

59 "three themes that you CEOs": "CEO 2.0," address by Bing Gordon to Endeavor Entrepreneur Summit in San Francisco, California, June 28, 2011.

60 the North American video game crash: A comprehensive account of this history can be found in "No Girls Allowed," Tracey Lien, Polygon.com, December 2, 2013.

62 "They weren't fighting for the right": "How the Alt-Right's Sexism Lures Men into White Supremacy," Aja Romano, *Vox*, April 26, 2018.

63 "I remember people saying": *Facebook: The Inside Story*, Steven Levy, 2020: 213.

63 Robin Dunbar had proposed: "Coevolution of Neocortical Size, Group Size, and Language in Humans," Robin Dunbar, *Behavioral and Brain Sciences* 16, 1993.

63 the average Facebook user had about 130 friends: This was reported by Facebook's now-defunct statistics page as of 2010. See, for example, "10 Fascinating Facebook Facts," *Mashable*, July 22, 2010.

63 Friendster even capped: "Friends, Friendsters, and Top 8: Writing Community into Being on Social Network Sites," Danah Boyd, *First Monday* 11, no. 12, December 2006.

63 "escaping the Dunbar curse": "Like, How Many Friends Does Facebook Need?" Edo Elan, *The Product Guy*, May 10, 2010.

63 Zuckerberg spoke publicly: Zuckerberg had said, "There's this famous Dunbar's number — humans have the capacity to maintain empathetic relationships with about 150 people. I think Facebook extends that." From Levy, *Facebook: The Inside Story*: 226.

64 studies of rhesus monkeys and macaques: Sapolsky: 428-436.

Chapter 3: Opening the Portal

68 11 percent of technology venture-capital: "New Survey Reflects Lack of Women and Minorities in Senior Investment Roles at Venture Capital Firms," National Venture Capital Association press release, December 14, 2016.

68 98 percent of their investment dollars: "Funding for Female Founders Stalled at 2.2% of VC Dollars in 2018," Emma Hinchliffe, *Fortune*, January 28, 2019.

69 "We will not ban legal": "Reddit CEO Addresses Violentacrez Controversy," Sean Hollister, *The Verge*, October 18, 2012.

70 "understand the harm that misusing": Sections of the post, which Reddit has since removed, can be found at: "Reddit's Confusing Response to the Distribution of Nudes," Alex Goldman, NPR, September 8, 2014.

72 she announced the policy: "From 1 to 9,000 Communities, Now Taking Steps to Grow Reddit to 90,000 Communities (and Beyond!)," Ellen Pao et al., Reddit, February 24, 2015.

73 Keegan Hankes, a researcher for: "How Reddit Became a Worse Black Hole of Violent Racism than Stormfront," Keegan Hankes, *Gawker*, March 10, 2015.

73 warning that even the worst: "Reddit's Racists 'Celebrate' Charleston Terror — and Worry About the Blowback," Jacob Siegel, *The Daily Beast*, July 12, 2017.

74 "Gamergate seems to have alerted": "Weev and the Rise of the Nazi Troll Army," Andrew Anglin, *Daily Stormer*, October 4, 2014.

74 "too extreme" even for: This is according to Brad Griffin, a far-right activist. "Dylann Roof, 4chan, and the New Online Racism," Jacob Siegel, *Daily Beast*, April 14, 2017.

74 One study later estimated: *A Comparative Study of White Nationalist and ISIS Online Social Media Networks*, J. M. Berger, George Washington University Program on Extremism, September 2016.

74 "The trolls are winning": "The Trolls Are Winning the Battle for the Internet," Ellen Pao, *Washington Post*, July 16, 2015.

76 "Every time you write one of your": "How Stephen Bannon Made Milo Dangerous," Keegan Hankes, Southern Poverty Law Center, February 23, 2017.

76 "If rape culture was real": Ibid.

76 "I realized Milo could connect": *Devil's Bargain: Steve Bannon, Donald Trump, and the Nationalist Uprising*, Joshua Green, 2017: 147.

76 "Finally doing my big feature": "Here's How Breitbart and Milo Smuggled White Nationalism into the Mainstream," Joseph Bernstein, *BuzzFeed News*, October 5, 2017.

77 "The alt-right is a movement": "An Establishment Conservative's Guide to the Alt-Right," Allum Bokhari and Milo Yiannopoulos, *Breitbart*, March 29, 2016.

77 The portmanteau is thought to have originated: "Behind the Racist Hashtag That Is Blowing Up Twitter," Joseph Bernstein, *BuzzFeed News*, July 27, 2015.

77 "They call it 'meme magic'": "Meme Magic: Donald Trump Is the Internet's Revenge on Lazy Elites," Milo Yiannopoulos, *Breitbart*, May 4, 2016.

77 "The unindoctrinated should not": "This Is *The Daily Stormer*'s Playbook," Ashley Feinberg, *HuffPost*, December 13, 2017.

78 "He has a character and a style": Bokhari and Yiannopoulos.

78 a Harvard study later found: *Partisanship, Propaganda, and Disinformation: Online Media and the 2016 U.S. Presidential Election*, Robert M. Faris et al., Berkman Klein Center for Internet & Society research paper, 2017.

78 which 43 percent of Americans did: "Key Findings About the Online News Landscape in America," A. W. Geiger, Pew Research Center, September 11, 2019.

78 Facebook appointed *Breitbart*: "Mark Zuckerberg Is Struggling to Explain Why *Breitbart* Belongs on Facebook News," Adi Robertson, *The Verge*, October 25, 2019.

79 the Harvard study concluded: All findings in this paragraph and the next are from Faris et al.

Chapter 4: Tyranny of Cousins

81 "I've been among people": "Full transcript: Walter Palmer Speaks About Cecil the Lion Controversy," Paul Walsh, *Minneapolis Star Tribune*, September 7, 2015.

81 "I don't understand that level": Ibid.

81 the BBC had run: "Zimbabwe's 'Iconic' Lion Cecil Killed by Hunter," BBC News, July 27, 2015.

82 text a toll-free number: "Odeo Releases Twttr," Michael Arrington, *TechCrunch*, July 15, 2006.

83 in an early sketch: "twttr sketch," Jack Dorsey, Flickr, March 24, 2006.

83 "Twitter revolution": In a representative reaction, Mark Pfeifle, a deputy national security adviser in the George W. Bush White House, urged a Nobel Peace Prize for Twitter, without which, he wrote, "the people of Iran would not have felt empowered and confident to stand up for freedom and democracy." "A Nobel Peace Prize for Twitter?" Mark Pfeifle, *Christian Science Monitor*, July 6, 2009.

83 In a single day: "Outrage and Backlash: #CecilTheLion Racks Up 670K Tweets in 24 Hours," Jordan Valinsky, Digiday.com, July 29, 2015.

83 "I'll pay £35k+": "The Entire World Is Enraged with Walter Palmer, the American Dentist Who Killed Cecil the Lion," Hanna Kozlowska, QZ.com, July 28, 2015.

84 "I hope that #WalterPalmer": "Stars Blast Minnesota Dentist over Killing of Cecil the Lion," Justin Ray, NBC News, July 31, 2015.

84 Hundreds posted negative reviews: "Killer of Cecil the Lion Finds Out That He Is a Target Now, of Internet Vigilantism," Christina Capecchi and Katie Rogers, *New York Times*, July 29, 2015.

84 "His employees are better off": Comment on "Meanwhile, Outside Walter Palmer's Dentistry Office" by user CinnamonDolceLatte, Reddit, July 29, 2015.

84 shared 3.6 million times: "Where Clicks Reign, Audience Is King," Ravi Somaiya, *New York Times*, August 16, 2015.

84 augured a seismic change: "The Clickbait Candidate," James Williams, *Quillette*, October 3, 2016.

85 "The truth is": Ibid.

86 you feel compelled to broadcast: "The New Synthesis in Moral Psychology," Jonathan Haidt, *Science*, May 18, 2007.

86 In a set of experiments, children: "How Infants and Toddlers React to Antisocial Others," Kiley Hamlin et al., *Proceedings of the National Academy of Sciences*, December 13, 2011. See also *Just Babies: The Origins of Good and Evil* (2013), by Paul Bloom, a co-author on the Hamlin studies.

87 Sentimentalism says it is actually motivated: Haidt, 2007.

87 Neurological research supports this: "The Emotional Dog and Its Rational Tail: A Social Intuitionist Approach to Moral Judgment," Jonathan Haidt, *Psychological Review*, October 2001.

89 A software developer named Adria Richards: "A Dongle Joke That Spiraled Way Out of Control," Kim Mai-Cutler, *TechCrunch*, March 21, 2013.

89 "Low cost, anonymous, instant": "Re-Shaming the Debate: Social Norms, Shame, and Regulation in an Internet Age," Kate Klonick, *Maryland Law Review* 76, no. 4, 2016.

90 tended to be "over-determined": Ibid.

90 "as if shamings were now happening": "How One Stupid Tweet Blew Up Justine Sacco's Life," Jon Ronson, *New York Times Magazine*, February 12, 2015.

90 A small-town Wisconsin class photo: "The Nazi Salute Picture That Divided an American Town," Chris McGreal, *The Guardian*, January 10, 2019.

90 A rookie reporter from Des Moines: "Twitter Hates Me. The *Des Moines Register* Fired Me. Here's What Really Happened," Aaron Calvin, *Columbia Journalism Review*, November 4, 2019.

91 "You think it's easy for me": "The CEO of Holy Land Hummus I Know Doesn't Match the Social Media Monster," Rob Eshman, *The Forward*, June 8, 2020.

91 "It's perplexing that people who": "Bogus Social Media Outrage Is Making Authors Change Lines in Their Books Now," Laura Miller, *Slate*, June 8, 2021.

91 A Black student at Smith College: "Inside a Battle Over Race, Class, and Power at Smith College," Michael Powell, *New York Times*, February 24, 2021.

92 A 2013 study of the Chinese platform Weibo: "Anger Is More Influential than Joy: Sentiment Correlation in Weibo," Rui Fan et al., *PLOS One* 9, no. 10, October 2014.

92 Studies of Twitter and Facebook: "Experimental Evidence of Massive-Scale Emotional Contagion Through Social Networks," Adam D.I. Kramer et al., *Proceedings of the National Academy of Sciences* 111, no. 24, June 2014. "Hostile Emotions in News Comments: A Cross-National Analysis of Facebook Discussions," Edda Humprecht et al., *Social Media + Society* 6, no. 1, March 2020. "Behavioral Effects of Framing on Social Media Users: How Conflict, Economic, Human Interest, and Morality Frames Drive News Sharing," Sebastián Valenzuela et al., *Journal of Communication* 67, no. 5, October 2017. "Emotion Shapes the Diffu-

sion of Moralized Content in Social Networks," William J. Brady et al., *Proceedings of the National Academy of Sciences* 114, no. 28, July 2017. "Critical Posts Get More Likes, Comments, and Shares than Other Posts," Pew Research Center, February 21, 2017.

93   unraveled by a seventy-year-old Russian geneticist: For an overview of the experiment and its findings: "How to Tame a Fox and Build a Dog," Lee Alan Dugatkin and Lyudmila Trut, *American Scientist*, July–August 2017. "The Silver Fox Domestication Experiment," Lee Alan Dugatkin, *Evolution: Education and Outreach* 11, 2018.

94   "eager to establish human: "Early Canid Domestication: The Farm-Fox Experiment," Lyudmila Trut, *American Scientist* 87, no. 2, March–April 1999.

95   resolving a longstanding mystery about humans: The extrapolation of Trut's research into this and the immediately subsequent lessons for human anthropology and behavior are the basis of Richard Wrangham's *The Goodness Paradox: The Strange Relationship Between Virtue and Violence in Human Evolution*, 2019. Though these connections and conclusions are far from Wrangham's alone, he is most associated with the overarching theory.

95   "Language-based conspiracy was the key": Wrangham: 274.

96   "tyranny of the cousins": *Conditions of Liberty: Civil Society and Its Rivals*, Ernest Gellner, 1994.

96   "To be a noncomformist": Wrangham: 275.

96   "proactive" and "coalitional": "Evolution of Coalitionary Killing," Richard Wrangham, *Yearbook of Physical Anthropology* 42, no. 1, 1999. Also see Wrangham, *Goodness Paradox*: 244.

97   Brain scans find that: "Perceptual Dehumanization of Faces Is Activated by Norm Violations and Facilitates Norm Enforcement," Katrina M. Fincher and Philip E. Tetlock, *Journal of Experimental Psychology* 145, no. 2, 2016.

97   "In a quest to impress peers": "Moral Grandstanding: There's a Lot of It About, All of It Bad," Justin Tosi and Brandon Warmke, *Aeon*, May 10, 2017.

97   "a moral arms race": Ibid.

98   "homogeneity, ingroup/outgroup biases": "Moral Grandstanding in Public Discourse: Status-Seeking Motives as a Potential Explanatory Mechanism in Predicting Conflict," Joshua B. Grubbs et al., *PLOS One* 14, no. 10, 2019.

98   In a disturbing experiment: "Reputation Fuels Moralistic Punishment That People Judge To Be Questionably Merited," Jillian J. Jordan and Nour S. Kteily, working paper, 2020. See also "Signaling When No One Is Watching: A Reputation Heuristics Account of Outrage and Punishment in One-Shot Anonymous Interactions," Jillian J. Jordan and D. G. Rand, *Journal of Personality and Social Psychology* 118, no. 1, 2020.

99   it ended Memorial Day 2020: For a comprehensive account of the incident, see "How Two Lives Collided in Central Park, Rattling the Nation," Sarah Maslin Nir, *New York Times*, June 14, 2020.

101   "certain dark societal impulses": "The Bird Watcher, That Incident and His Feelings on the Woman's Fate," Sarah Maslin Nir, *New York Times*, May 27, 2020.

101   The Coopers demonstrated: Of the many reflections on the shift in social mores animated by social media, one that perhaps best captures the ambivalence of that moment: "Karens All the Way Down," Kat Rosenfield, *Arc Digital*, May 26, 2020.

104   When two scholars analyzed 300: "Political Rumoring on Twitter During the 2012 US Presidential Election: Rumor Diffusion and Correction," Jieun Shin et al., *New Media & Society* 19, no. 8, 2017.

Chapter 5: Awakening the Machine

106 "In September 2011, I sent a provocative email": *Measure What Matters: How Google, Bono, and the Gates Foundation Rock the World with OKRS*, John Doerr, 2017: 161.

106 "is ten minutes long": Ibid: 162

106 "begets more advertising": Ibid.

107 By 2002, spam accounted for 40 percent: "Spam Wars," Evan I. Schwartz, *MIT Technology Review*, July 1, 2003.

108 the company credits its algorithm: "The Netflix Recommender System: Algorithms, Business Value, and Innovation," Carlos A. Gomez-Uribe and Neil Hunt, *ACM Transactions on Management Information Systems* 6, no. 4, January 2016.

108 Spotify acquired: "The Amazing Ways Spotify Uses Big Data, AI and Machine Learning to Drive Business Success," Benard Marr, *Forbes*, October 30, 2017.

109 Men were spending 40 percent more: This figure has been independently corroborated by, e.g., "The Demographics of YouTube, in 5 Charts," Eric Blattberg, Digiday.com, April 24, 2015.

110 an executive pulled aside Goodrow: The executive was Shishir Mehrota. All quotes and paraphrases in this and the next paragraph are from Doerr: 163.

111 "There's this kind of shift": "Beware Online 'Filter Bubbles,'" Eli Pariser, speech at TED2011, Long Beach, California, May 2, 2011.

111 In one 2015 experiment: "The Search Engine Manipulation Effect (SEME) and Its Possible Impact on the Outcomes of Elections," Robert Epstein and Ronald E. Robertson, *Proceedings of the National Academy of Sciences* 112, no. 33, August 18, 2015.

112 "America's next president could be eased": "How Google Could Rig the 2016 Election," Robert Epstein, *Politico*, August 19, 2015.

112 "There's this epic struggle": Pariser.

112 Facebook tweaked its algorithm: "How Facebook Shapes Your Feed," Will Oremus, Chris Alcantara, Jeremy B. Merrill, and Artur Galocha, *Washington Post*, October 26, 2021.

113 lecturing women on their duty: "Teen Vine Stars Enrage Followers by Telling Girls How to Be More Attractive," Aja Romano, *Daily Dot*, December 29, 2013.

115 "There is a right answer": "Letter to Shareholders," Jeff Bezos, Security and Exchange Commission filings, 1997.

115 "The billion daily hours": Doerr: 166–167.

117 "Forget strategy": *Zucked: Waking Up to the Facebook Catastrophe*, Roger McNamee, 2019: 41.

119 "the true scarce commodity": The original memo, a fascinating snapshot of the industry's shift to an attention economy, can be found in full at "Microsoft's CEO Sent a 3,187-Word Memo and We Read It So You Don't Have To," Polly Mosendz, *The Atlantic Wire*, July 10, 2014.

120 "We are not going to meet": Doerr.

120 "fundamental paradigm shift": "Deep Neural Networks for YouTube Recommendations," Paul Covington, Jay Adams, and Emre Sargin, *Proceedings of the 10th ACM Conference on Recommender Systems*, September 2016.

120 "So, when YouTube claims": "Reverse Engineering the YouTube Algorithm (Part 2)," Matt Gielen, Tubfilter.com, February 2017.

120 "Product tells us": "YouTube Executives Ignored Warnings, Letting Toxic Videos Run Rampant," Mark Bergen, Bloomberg, April 2, 2019.

120–121 The company estimated that 70 percent: This is according to comments by Neel Mohan, YouTube's chief product officer, at the industry Consumer Electronics Show in January 2018. See, for example, "YouTube's AI Is the Puppet Master over Most of What You Watch," Joan E. Solsman, *CNet*, January 10, 2018.

121 "We design a lot of algorithms": "The Facebook Dilemma," *PBS Frontline*, October 29, 2018.

121 "It is designed to make": Ibid. Speaker is Sandy Parakilas, Facebook's former platform operations manager.

121 "That's the key": Ibid. Speaker is Antonio García Martínez, a former product manager.

121 in-house researchers tracked 10 million users: "Exposure to Ideologically Diverse News and Opinion on Facebook," Eytan Bakshy, Solomon Messing, and Lada A. Adamic, *Science* 348, no. 6239, May 7, 2015.

121 "associated with adopting more extreme": Ibid.

122 "Which of the big questions": Exchange is from the comments field in "For the Next Hour I'll Be Here Answering Your Questions on Facebook," Mark Zuckerberg, Facebook.com, June 30, 2015.

122 "Every time you use Facebook": "Inside Facebook's AI Machine," Steven Levy, *Wired*, February 2017.

122 "If they do these": "News Feed: Getting Your Content to the Right People," Adam Mosseri, presentation to Facebook F8 conference in San Francisco, April 21, 2016.

122 "When users spend more": Doerr: 161.

123 Facebook engineers were automatically: "I was an eng leader on Facebook's NewsFeed," Krishna Gade, Twitter, February 11, 2021. Twitter.com/krishnagade/status/135990889 7998315521

123 "You start thinking about": "Can Mark Zuckerberg Fix Facebook Before It Breaks Democracy?" Evan Osnos, *The New Yorker*, September 17, 2018.

123 "A machine-learning algorithm significantly": "TikTok and the Sorting Hat," Eugene Wei, Eugenewei.com, August 4, 2020.

123 "We'll just give it": Speaker is Jim McFadden. "How YouTube Drives People to the Internet's Darkest Corners," Jack Nicas, *Wall Street Journal*, February 7, 2018.

125 bombarded with the phrase: "On Believing What We Remember," Ian Begg, Victoria Armour, and Thérèse Kerr, *Canadian Journal of Behavioral Science* 17, 1985.

125 When he searched YouTube for *Pope Francis*: All findings from Chaslot's 2016 election research project were later published at "How YouTube's A.I. Boosts Alternative Facts," Guillaume Chaslot, Medium.com, March 31, 2017.

126 circulated a memo: "The Binge Breaker," Bianca Bosker, *The Atlantic*, November 2016.

126 "They didn't do anything": Osnos.

126–127 "I realized: this is": "'Our Minds Can Be Hijacked': The Tech Insiders Who Fear a Smartphone Dystopia," Paul Lewis, *The Guardian*, October 6, 2017.

127 "There's no good analogue": *Stand Out of Our Light: Freedom and Resistance in the Attention Economy*, James Williams, 2017: 29.

127 Pacing the stage with a wireless: "The Lunatics Are Running the Asylum," Renee DiResta, speech to GoogleIO conference, Mountain View, California, June 8, 2016.

128 "Algorithms are influencing policy": Ibid.

128 "The average curated tweet": "Twitter's Algorithm Does Not Seem to Silence Conservatives," *The Economist*, August 1, 2020.

128 "some of the most salacious": "Jack Dorsey on Twitter's Mistakes," Lauren Jackson, *New York Times*, August 7, 2020.

129 "can i just say": "Microsoft's Chat Bot Was Fun for Awhile, Until It Turned into a Racist," Mathew Ingram, *Fortune*, March 24, 2016.

129 "You absolutely do NOT": "How to Make a Bot That Isn't Racist," Sarah Jeong, *Motherboard*, March 25, 2016.

130 "Our engineers were hunting": Doerr: 169.

130 "We'd achieved": Ibid.

130 "Stretch OKRs tend": Ibid.

Chapter 6: The Fun House Mirror

132 highly associated with "anomie": "The Psychology of Conspiracy Theories," Karen M. Douglas, Robbie M. Sutton, and Aleksandra Cichocka, *Current Directions in Psychological Science* 26, no. 6, December 2017.

132 "Cheese pizza," one suggested: A beat-by-beat chronology of Pizzagate's rise, including references to individual posts, can be found at "Anatomy of a Fake News Scandal," Amanda Robb, *Rolling Stone*, November 16, 2017; and "How the Bizarre Conspiracy Theory Behind 'Pizzagate' Was Spread," Craig Silverman, *BuzzFeed News*, December 5, 2016.

133 14 percent of Trump supporters: "Trump Remains Unpopular; Voters Prefer Obama on SCOTUS Pick," Tom Jenson, Public Policy Polling, December 9, 2016.

133 another poll tested: *The Economist*/YouGov Poll, December 20, 2016.

134 Wojcicki convened her shell-shocked: "YouTube Executives Ignored Warnings, Letting Toxic Videos Run Rampant," Mark Bergen, Bloomberg, April 2, 2019.

134 "The results of the 2016 Election show": All quotes in this paragraph from *Facebook: The Inside Story*, Steven Levy, 2020: 360–361.

134 Company executives went so far: "Facebook, in Cross Hairs After Election, Is Said to Question Its Influence," Mike Isaac, *New York Times*, November 12, 2016.

134 a Facebook researcher had presented: "Facebook Executives Shut Down Efforts to Make the Site Less Divisive," Jeff Horwitz and Deepa Seetharaman, *Wall Street Journal*, May 26, 2020.

134 Zuckerberg overruled his own: "Zuckerberg Once Wanted to Sanction Trump. Then Face-Book Wrote Rules That Accommodated Him," Elizabeth Dwoskin, Craig Timberg, and Tony Romm, *Washington Post*, June 28, 2020.

135 "Personally I think": "Zuckerberg: The Idea That Fake News on Facebook Influenced the Election Is 'Crazy,' " Casey Newton, *The Verge*, November 10, 2016.

135 had in its own 2010 experiment empirically demonstrated: "Facebook Experiment Boosts US Voter Turnout," Zoe Corbyn, *Nature*, 2012.

135 Only 1 percent of user: "I want to share some thoughts on Facebook and the election," Mark Zuckerberg, Facebook.com, November 12, 2016.

135 "It really did seem to have helped": "Twitter Board Member: Twitter Helped Trump Win The Election," Charlie Warzel, *BuzzFeed News*, November 30, 2016.

136 "Facebook's prioritization": "Media in the Age of Algorithms," Tim O'Reilly, Oreilly.com, November 16, 2016.

136 "More than 80 percent": "YouTube's A.I. Was Divisive in the US Presidential Election," Guillaume Chaslot, Medium.com, November 27, 2016.

137 *Raiding a pedo ring*: Welch's attack and YouTube's response are detailed in "John Podesta Is Ready to Talk About Pizzagate," Andy Kroll, *Rolling Stone*, December 9, 2018.

138 His team scraped half a million: The methodology and results detailed in these pages were first published as "Emotion Shapes the Diffusion of Moralized Content in Social Net-

works," William J. Brady, Julian A. Wills, John T. Jost, Joshua A. Tucker, and Jay J. Van Bavel, *Proceedings of the National Academy of Sciences* 114, no. 28, July 11, 2017.

139 "Negative posts about political out-groups": "Twitter's Research Shows That Its Algorithm Favors Conservative Views," Emma Roth, *The Verge*, October 22, 2021.

139 a later study that drew on Brady's: "Out-Group Animosity Drives Engagement on Social Media," Steve Rathje, Jay J. Van Bavel, and Sander van der Linden, *Proceedings of the National Academy of Sciences* 118, no. 26, June 29, 2021.

139 systematically boosted conservative politics: "Examining Algorithmic Amplification of Political Content on Twitter," Rumman Chowdhury and Luca Belli, Twitter corporate blog, October 21, 2021.

139–140 one sixth the userbase of Facebook or YouTube: Twitter reported 328 million monthly active users in the first quarter of 2017. Facebook reported 1.94 billion. YouTube does not consistently release comparable data, but has at times claimed to have over 2 billion monthly active users. Sources: "Twitter's Surprising User Growth Bodes Well For 2017," Trefis Team, *Forbes*, April 27, 2017. "Facebook Beats in Q1 with $8.03B Revenue, Faster Growth to 1.94B Users," Josh Constine, *TechCrunch*, May 3, 2017.

140 market capitalization worth only 2.5 percent: Twitter's market capitalization as of April 2017 was $10.68 billion and Facebook's was $417 billion. By comparison, Google's was $594 billion. All figures from Macrotrends.net.

140 "You're hanging out with people": "Why I'm Breaking Up with Twitter," Alisyn Camerota, CNN, July 12, 2017.

140 pressured Dorsey to change course: "Elliott Management's Paul Singer Seeks to Replace Twitter CEO Jack Dorsey, Source Says," Alex Sherman, CNBC, February 28, 2020.

141 Other executives described him as indecisive: "'Did We Create This Monster?' How Twitter Turned Toxic," Austin Carr and Harry McCracken, *Fast Company*, April 4, 2018.

141 silent-meditation retreats, including to Myanmar: Tweet by Jack Dorsey (@jack), December 8, 2018. Twitter.com/jack/status/1071575088695140353

141 move part-time to Africa: "Jack Dorsey's Planned Move to Africa Divides Square and Twitter Investors," Kate Rooney, CNBC, December 2, 2019.

142 He opposed or diluted post-election changes: Kaplan's role has been exhaustively and independently reported, for example in Dwoskin et al.; Horwitz and Seetharaman; "15 Months of Fresh Hell Inside Facebook," Nicholas Thompson and Fred Vogelstein, *Wired*, April 16, 2018; and "Delay, Deny, and Deflect: How Facebook's Leaders Fought Through Crisis," Sheera Frenkel, Nicholas Confessore, Cecilia Kang, Matthew Rosenberg, and Jack Nicas, *New York Times*, November 14, 2018.

142 "bring humanity together": "Read Mark Zuckerberg's Full 6,000-Word Letter on Facebook's Global Ambitions," Kurt Wagner and Kara Swisher, *ReCode*, February 16, 2017.

142 entertained pushing different-minded users: Jackson.

142 described its actual aim: "The Making of a YouTube Radical," Kevin Roose, *New York Times*, June 8, 2019.

142–143 "how opinions are formed": "Inside Facebook's A.I. Machine," Steven Levy, *Wired*, February 23, 2017.

143 guide users toward differing: Ibid.

143 this process works only under: "A Meta-Analytic Test of Intergroup Contact Theory," Thomas F. Pettigrew and Linda R. Tropp, *Journal of Personality and Social Psychology* 90, no. 5, June 2006.

143   follow a bot that retweeted voices: "Exposure to Opposing Views on Social Media Can Increase Political Polarization," Christopher A. Bail et al., *Proceedings of the National Academy of Sciences* 115, no. 37, September 11, 2018.

143   perceive out-groups as monoliths: Social scientists call this the "outgroup homogeneity effect." See, for example: "Out-Group Homogeneity Effects in Natural and Minimal Groups," Thomas M. Ostrom and Constantine Sedikides, *Psychological Bulletin* 112, no. 3, 1992.

144   "false polarization": For a comprehensive account of false polarization, see "The Great and Widening Divide: Political False Polarization and Its Consequences," Victoria Parker, master's thesis, Wilfrid Laurier University, 2018.

144   false polarization is worsening: "On Trolls and Polls: How Social Media Extremists and Dissenters Exacerbate and Mitigate Political False Polarization," presentation by Victoria Parker, Wilfrid Laurier University, 2019.

144   leads people to develop more extreme views: "Thinking Fast and Furious: Emotional Intensity and Opinion Polarization in Online Media," David Asker and Elias Dinas, *Public Opinion Quarterly* 83, no. 3, fall 2019.

144   groups heighten their sensitivity: "The Spreading of Misinformation Online," Michela Del Vicario et al., *Proceedings of the National Academy of Sciences* 113, no. 3, January 19, 2016.

144   "When we encounter opposing views": "How Social Media Took Us from Tahrir Square to Donald Trump," Zeynep Tufekci, *MIT Technology Review,* August 14, 2018.

145   "the problem with Facebook": "Interview with Siva Vaidhyanathan," David Greene, National Public Radio, *Morning Edition,* December 26, 2017.

145   "I would read something": "Screaming into the Void: How Outrage Is Hijacking Our Culture, and Our Minds," National Public Radio, *Hidden Brain,* October 7, 2019.

145   "It was like coming out of a trance": Ibid.

145   a short but influential paper: "Moral Outrage in the Digital Age," Molly J. Crockett, *Nature Human Behaviour* 1, 2017.

147   "I think they need to be extremely": "Mark Warner to Facebook: Tell Me What You Know," Elaine Godfrey, *The Atlantic,* September 28, 2017.

147–148   "how you would try to wrangle": "The Facebook Dilemma," PBS *Frontline,* October 29, 2018.

148   They couldn't help wondering: Ibid.

148   later termed this "ampliganda": "It's Not Misinformation. It's Amplified Propaganda," Renee DiResta, *The Atlantic,* October 2021.

150   according to an MIT Media Lab analysis: "Who's Influencing Election 2016?," William Powers, Medium.com, February 23, 2016.

150   begun posting 200-plus times per day: For an account of Mackey's story, including details from the federal indictment issued against him, see "Trump's Most Influential White Nationalist Troll Is a Middlebury Grad Who Lives in Manhattan," Luke O'Brien, *HuffPost,* April 5, 2018; and "FBI Arrests Prolific Racist Twitter Troll 'Ricky Vaughn' For 2016 Election Interference," Luke O'Brien, *HuffPost,* January 27, 2021.

151   shared 36,000 times: "Debunking 5 Viral Images of the Migrant Caravan," Kevin Roose, *New York Times,* October 24, 2018.

151   Republicans were shown a false headline: "Shifting Attention to Accuracy Can Reduce Misinformation Online," Gordon Pennycook et al., *Nature* 592, 2021.

151   "Most people do not want to spread": Ibid.

152 heavily favored the candidates: "Does YouTube's Algorithm Promote Populist Candidates in the French Presidential Elections?," Guillaume Chaslot et al., Mediashift.org, April 21, 2017.

153 "the methodology, data and, most importantly": "How an Ex-YouTube Insider Investigated Its Secret Algorithm," Paul Lewis and Erin McCormick, *The Guardian*, February 2, 2018.

153 "Our only conclusion is that": Ibid.

154 reshaping not just online behavior: Except where otherwise noted, all subsequent references to Brady and Crockett's study in this chapter draw from "The MAD Model of Moral Contagion: The Role of Motivation, Attention, and Design in the Spread of Moralized Content Online," William J. Brady, Molly J. Crockett, and Jay J. Van Bavel, *Perspectives on Psychological Science* 15, no. 4, June 2020.

155 showed participants a fake social media stream: "Attentional Capture Helps Explain Why Moral and Emotional Content Go Viral," William J. Brady, Ana P. Gantman, and Jay J. Van Bavel, *Journal of Experimental Psychology* 149, no. 4, 2020.

156 leads users to express more calls: "Moral-Emotional Content and Patterns of Violent Expression and Hate Speech in Online User Comment," Jeffrey Javed and Blake Miller, working paper, April 2019. (Javed subsequently took a job at Facebook, on a team that optimizes ad placement.)

Chapter 7: The Germs and the Wind

158 would arrive at a village: See, for example: *Massacre by the River: Burmese Army Crimes Against Humanity in Tula Toli*, Human Rights Watch report, December 19, 2017.

158 "People were holding the soldiers' feet": "Rohingya Recount Atrocities: 'They Threw My Baby into a Fire,'" Jeffrey Gettleman, *New York Times*, October 11, 2017.

159 A twenty-year-old woman told a Human Rights Watch: *Sexual Violence Against Rohingya Women and Girls in Burma*, Human Rights Watch report, November 16, 2017.

161 had flown to Facebook's headquarters: "How Facebook's Rise Fueled Chaos and Confusion in Myanmar," Timothy McLaughlin, *Wired*, July 2018.

162 with hate speech only growing more common: All examples in this and the next paragraph from: *Hate Speech Narratives and Facilitators in Myanmar*, Center for Advanced Defense Studies (C4ADS) report, February 2016.

162 analyzed a sample of 32,000: Ibid.

163 38 percent of people in the country: *Survey of Burma/Myanmar Public Opinion*, Center for Insights in Survey Research, April 1, 2017.

163 Madden flew to Facebook's headquarters: McLaughlin, 2018.

163 "I have to thank Facebook": "Across Myanmar, Denial of Ethnic Cleansing and Loathing of Rohingya," Hanna Beech, *New York Times*, October 24, 2017.

163 "There has never been a more": "Genocide in the Modern Era: Social Media and the Proliferation of Hate Speech in Myanmar," Ashley Kinseth, *Tea Circle Oxford*, May 2018.

164 "honest question — what's": Tweet by Max Read (@max_read), March 15, 2018 (since deleted).

164 "There are real issues": Tweet by Adam Mosseri (@mosseri), March 15, 2018 (since deleted).

165 in a bizarre episode in India: "When Is Government Web Censorship Justified? An Indian Horror Story," Max Fisher, *The Atlantic*, August 22, 2012.

165 pushing 300,000 people: "Panic Seizes India as a Region's Strife Radiates," Jim Yardley, *New York Times*, August 17, 2012.

165 rose in Indonesia: See, for example: "Beredar Hoax Penculikan Anak, Gelandangan Disiksa Nyaris Tewas," Fajar Eko Nugroho, *Liputan6*, March 7, 2017. "Justice by Numbers," Sana

Jaffrey, *New Mandala*, January 12, 2017. "The Muslim Cyber Army: What Is It and What Does It Want?" Damar Juniarto, Indonesiaatmelbourne.unimelb.edu.au, 2017.

165 "This revolution started": "Social Media Sparked, Accelerated Egypt's Revolutionary Fire," Sam Gustin, *Wired*, February 11, 2011.

165 "The same tool": "Let's Design Social Media That Drives Real Change," Wael Ghonim, TED Talk, January 14, 2016.

165 "I feel tremendous guilt": "Former Facebook Exec Says Social Media Is Ripping Apart Society," James Vincent, *The Verge*, December 11, 2017.

170 launched zero-rated services: *Free Internet and the Costs to Media Pluralism: The Hazards of Zero-Rating the News*, Daniel O'Maley and Amba Kak, CIMA digital report, November 8, 2018.

170 "As the usage expands": *Facebook: The Inside Story*, Steven Levy, 2020: 435.

170 "The history of progress": *Zero to One*, Thiel and Masters, 2014: 32.

171 a 6,000-word essay: "Building Global Community," Mark Zuckerberg, Facebook.com, February 16, 2017.

Chapter 8: Church Bells

180 She was finding in Mexico: "La Otra Violencia: El Linchamiento de José Abraham y Rey David," Gema Santamaría, *Nexos*, October 22, 2015.

180 Cancun suburb: "Un Ruso sobrevive a un intento de linchamiento en Cancún por insultar a los mexicanos," L.P.B., *El País*, May 20, 2017.

180 village of quiet families: "In Frightened Mexico Town, a Mob Kills 2 Young Pollsters," Alberto Arce, Associated Press, October 22, 2015.

180 in another village, the same pattern: "When Fake News Kills: Lynchings in Mexico Are Linked to Viral Child-Kidnap Rumors," Patrick J. McDonnel and Cecilia Sanchez, *Los Angeles Times*, September 21, 2018.

180 is a communal impulse: For more, see *In the Vortex of Violence: Lynching, Extralegal Justice, and the State in Post-Revolutionary Mexico*, Gema Kloppe-Santamaría, 2020.

181 BBC reporters in northern Nigeria: "Like. Share. Kill," Yemisi Adegoke, *BBC Africa Eye*, November 12, 2018.

181 feel at risk of losing their position: For an explication of the research status threat and its relevance to the Trump coalition, see, for example: "Trump-ing Foreign Affairs: Status Threat and Foreign Policy Preferences on the Right," Rachel Marie Blum and Cristopher Sebastian Parker, *Perspectives on Politics* 17, no. 3, August 2019.

182 "our group identities are more salient": "The MAD Model of Moral Contagion: The Role of Motivation, Attention, and Design in the Spread of Moralized Content Online," William J. Brady, Molly J. Crockett, and Jay J. Van Bavel, *Perspectives on Psychological Science* 15, no. 4, June 2020.

183 tried to burn down a refugee group house: "Eine rechtsradikale Einstellung besteht aus mehr als Fremdenhass," *Der Spiegel*, October 12, 2015.

184 gathered data on every anti-refugee attack: "Fanning the Flames of Hate: Social Media and Hate Crime," Karsten Müller and Carlo Schwarz, *Journal of the European Economic Association* 19, no. 4, August 2021.

186 "irony poisoned": See, for example: "How the Parkland Teens Give Us a Glimpse of a Post-Irony Internet," Miles Klee, *Mel Magazine*, February 28, 2018.

186 Denkhaus's lawyer emphasized: "Brandstifterprozess Altena," Akantifahagen.blogsport.eu, May 31, 2016.

189 "relatively unchangeable, unjustified certainty": "Political Tolerance, Dogmatism, and Social Media Uses and Gratifications," Chamil Rathnayake and Jenifer Sunrise Winter, *Policy & Internet* 9, no. 4, 2017.

189 Another: grandiose narcissism: "Why Narcissists Are at Risk for Developing Facebook Addiction: The Need to Be Admired and the Need to Belong," Silvia Casale and Giulia Fioravanti, *Addictive Behaviors* 76, January 2018.

189 Unusually low self-esteem: "The Relationship Between Addictive Use of Social Media, Narcissism, and Self-Esteem: Findings from a Large National Survey," Cecilie Schou Andreassen, Ståle Pallesen, and Mark D. Griffiths, *Addictive Behaviors* 64, January 2017.

189 "Online political hostility is committed": "The Psychology of Online Political Hostility: A Comprehensive, Cross-National Test of the Mismatch Hypothesis," Alexander Bor and Michael Bang Peterson, *American Political Science Review*, 2021.

189 Neurological experiments confirmed: "Snapchat vs. Facebook: Differences in Problematic Use, Behavior Change Attempts, and Trait Social Reward Preferences," Dar Meshi, Ofir Turel, and Dan Henley, *Addictive Behaviors* Report 12, December 2020.

189 She was right, an outside: "The Efficacy of Reddit's 2015 Ban Examined Through Hate Speech," Eshwar Chandrasekharan et al., *Proceedings of the ACM on Human-Computer Interaction* 1, November 2017.

189 exploring how social norms influence: For an accessible overview of Paluck's work, see "Romeo & Juliet in Rwanda: How a Soap Opera Sought to Change a Nation," NPR, *Hidden Brain*, July 13, 2020.

190 Schoolkids bully or don't: "Changing Climates of Conflict: A Social Network Experiment in 56 Schools," Elizabeth Levy Paluck, Hana Shepher, and Peter M. Aronow, *Proceedings of the National Academy of Sciences* 113, no. 3, January 19, 2016.

190 experiment in rural Mexico: "How Does Media Influence Social Norms? Experimental Evidence on the Role of Common Knowledge," Eric Arias, *Political Science Research and Methods* 7, no. 3, July 2019.

191 identifying which students were influential: Paluck et al., 2016.

196 "Now, in that case": "Mark Zuckerberg on Facebook's Hardest Year, and What Comes Next," Ezra Klein, *Vox*, April 2, 2018.

196 "overreliance on third parties": "Open Letter to Mark Zuckerberg," Phandeeyar et al., April 5, 2018.

196 sent the groups an email apologizing: "Zuckerberg Was Called Out Over Myanmar Violence. Here's His Apology," Kevin Roose and Paul Mozur, *New York Times*, April 9, 2018.

196–197 formal report on the genocide: *Report of Independent International Fact-Finding Mission on Myanmar*, United Nations Human Rights Council, August 27, 2018.

197 "You can't just snap": "Can Mark Zuckerberg Fix Facebook Before It Breaks Democracy?" Evan Osnos, *The New Yorker*, September 17, 2018.

197 $55 billion: "Facebook Reports Fourth Quarter and Full Year 2018 Results," press release, Facebook Investor Relations, January 30, 2019.

Chapter 9: The Rabbit Hole

199 "This was new": "As Germans Seek News, YouTube Delivers Far-Right Tirades," Max Fisher and Katrin Bennhold, *New York Times*, September 7, 2018.

200 Serrato applied a set: "Revealed: Facebook hate speech exploded in Myanmar during Rohingya crisis," Libby Hogan and Michael Safi, *The Guardian*, April 2, 2018.

Notes

201 Google often promotes YouTube: "Searching for Video? Google Pushes YouTube Over Rivals," Sam Schechner, Kirsten Grind, and John West, *Wall Street Journal*, July 14, 2020.

203 didn't reflect real-world communities: Kaiser later published his findings in "Public Spheres of Skepticism: Climate Skeptics' Online Comments in the German Networked Public Sphere," Jonas Kaiser, *International Journal of Communication* 11, 2017.

204 had gotten their start: See, for example, "Feeding Hate with Video: A Former Alt-Right YouTuber Explains His Methods," Cade Metz, *New York Times*, April 15, 2021.

204 trained a computer to track YouTube: The researchers later published their results in "The German Far-right on YouTube: An Analysis of User Overlap and User Comments," Adrian Rauchfleisch and Jonas Kaiser, *Journal of Broadcasting and Electronic Media* 64, no. 3, 2020. The research first appeared in "YouTubes Algorithmen sorgen dafür, dass AfD-Fans unter sich bleiben," Adrian Rauchfleisch and Jonas Kaiser, *Vice Germany*, September 22, 2017.

205 scraped every comment: Ibid.

206 centered on a teeming: "The Alt-Right Can't Disown Charlottesville," Ashley Feinberg, *Wired*, August 13, 2017.

206 declared a "summer of hate": "Summer of Hate Challenged in Companion Civil Lawsuits," Bill Morlin, Southern Poverty Law Center, October 19, 2017.

206–207 "We memed alt right": "Our Extended Interview with Richard Spencer on White Nationalism," *Vice News*, December 10, 2016.

207 endorsed the event: Feinberg, 2017.

207 1,870 far-right Facebook groups: "Analysis of 2017 Unite the Right Event, One Year Later," Megan Squire, Megansquire.com, August 2018.

208 told a Harvard seminar: "The Dark Side of the Networked Public Sphere," lecture by Jonas Kaiser to Berkman Klein Luncheon Series at Harvard University, Cambridge, Massachusetts, January 23, 2018.

208 opened a discussion thread: "McInnes, Molyneux, and 4chan: Investigating Pathways to the Alt-Right," Cassie Miller, Southern Poverty Law Center, April 19, 2018.

208 credited with the ((((echo)))): Ibid.

208 On flyers advertising: "Birth of a White Supremacist," Andrew Marantz, *The New Yorker*, October 9, 2017.

208 "I used to be a part": All the Right Stuff quotes from Miller, 2018.

209 "hours in political-debate": Marantz, 2018.

209 most important gateways: See, for example, "Alternative Influence: Broadcasting the Reactionary Right on YouTube," Rebecca Lewis, *Data & Society*, September 2018.

209 "the masculine spirit": "Jordan Peterson, Custodian of the Patriarchy," Nellie Bowles, *New York Times*, May 18, 2018.

209 searches for "depression": "The Alt-Right Is Recruiting Depressed People," Paris Martineau, *The Outline*, February 26, 2018.

209 "aggrieved entitlement": *Angry White Men: Masculinity at the End of an Era*, Michael Kimmel, 2017: 31–68.

210 "People in these communities": Tweet by @SadMarshGhost, February 23, 2018. twitter.com/SadMarshGhost/status/967029954016874497

210 subsequently become twice: "On Jordan Peterson, the Alt Right and Engagement across Difference," Joel Finkelstein, *Heterodox Academy*, November 18, 2019.

211 "crisis-solution construct": *Extremism*, J. M. Berger, 2018: 62–89.

211 "The scale of the crisis": Ibid: 96.

211 "revenge against humanity": "Elliot Rodger, Isla Vista Shooting Suspect, Posted Misogynistic Video before Attack," Josh Glasstetter, Southern Poverty Law Center, May 24, 2014.

211 call themselves "incels": "The Alt-Right Is Killing People," Keegan Hankes and Alex Amend, Southern Poverty Law Center, February 5, 2018. See also "Understanding the Incel Community on YouTube," Kostantinos Papadamou et al., *Proceedings of the ACM on Human-Computer Interaction*, October 2021.

212 Views became more extreme: "The Evolution of the Manosphere across the Web," Manoel Horta Ribeiro et al., *Proceedings of the Fifteenth International AAAI Conference on Web and Social Media*, 2021.

212 fifty killings had been claimed: "The Misogynist Incel Movement Is Spreading," Lois Beckett, *The Guardian*, March 3, 2021.

212 lionized as a hero: "In the Years Since the Isla Vista Shooting, the Incel Subculture Continues to Inspire Gunmen," Jennifer Mascia, *The Trace*, May 23, 2019.

212 surveyed its 25,000 members: "How Do People Join Militias? A Leaked Oath Keepers Roster Has Answers," Ali Breland, *Mother Jones*, October 27, 2021.

213 a system it called Reinforce: "The Making of a YouTube Radical," Kevin Roose, *New York Times*, June 9, 2019.

213 "One of my closest friends": Tweet by Chris Sacca (@sacca), January 12, 2021. twitter.com /sacca/status/1349055880348663808

213 his descent had started: "How YouTube Built a Radicalization Machine for the Far-Right," Kelly Weill, *Daily Beast*, December 19, 2018.

213 Bellingcat scoured an archive: "From Memes to Infowars: How 75 Fascist Activists Were 'Red-Pilled,'" Robert Evans, Bellingcat.com, October 11, 2018.

213 "YouTube's algorithms bounced": "My Affair with the Intellectual Dark Web," Meghan Daum, Medium.com, August 24, 2018.

214 Kaiser and Rauchfleisch ran automated: Kaiser and Rauchfleisch provided me, in interviews over 2019 and 2020, with several working papers that detail their methods and findings, as well as much of the underlying data. These later became the basis for multiple peer-reviewed articles and book chapters, some still forthcoming. See, for example: "Birds of a Feather Get Recommended Together: Algorithmic Homophily in YouTube's Channel Recommendations in the United States and Germany," Jonas Kaiser and Adrian Rauchfleisch, *Social Media + Society* 6, no. 4, October 2020.

216 published his findings: "How YouTube's Channel Recommendations Push Users to the Fringe," Craig Silverman, *BuzzFeed News*, April 12, 2018.

216 "pushes many channels towards": "Unite the Right? How YouTube's Recommendation Algorithm Connects the U.S. Far-Right," Jonas Kaiser and Adrian Rauchfleisch, *Data & Society*, April 11, 2018.

217 confirmed the "radicalization pipeline": "Auditing radicalization pathways on YouTube," Manoel Horta Ribeiro et al., *Proceedings of the 2020 Conference on Fairness, Accountability, and Transparency*, January 2020.

217 combined 50 million views: "Untrue-Tube: Monetizing Misery and Disinformation," Jonathan Albright, Medium.com, February 25, 2018.

217 policy team recommended: "YouTube Executives Ignored Warnings, Letting Toxic Videos Run Rampant," Mark Bergen, Bloomberg, April 2, 2019.

218 "an almost inconceivable battle": "An open letter to Mark Zuckerberg," Leonard Pozner and Veronique De La Rosa, *The Guardian*, July 25, 2018.

218 "We created Facebook": "Facebook Touts Fight on Fake News, but Struggles to Explain Why InfoWars Isn't Banned," Oliver Darcy, CNN, July 11, 2018.

218 "I'm Jewish, and": "Zuckerberg: The Recode Interview," Kara Swisher, *Recode*, October 8, 2018.

219 "We're going to hold Jones": Tweet by Jack Dorsey (@jack), August 7, 2018. twitter.com/jack /status/1026984245925793792

219 "I don't believe that it is the right": "Can Mark Zuckerberg Fix Facebook before It Breaks Democracy?" Evan Osnos, *The New Yorker*, September 17, 2018.

219 "We didn't fully predict": Tweet by Jack Dorsey (@jack), March 1, 2018. twitter.com/jack /status/969234275420655616

219 largely quit in frustration: "Jack Dorsey's Push to Clean Up Twitter Stalls, Researchers Say," Deepa Seetharaman, *Wall Street Journal*, March 15, 2020.

220 discovered one in Denver: Landrum published her findings in "Differential Susceptibility to Misleading Flat Earth Arguments on YouTube," Asheley Landrum, Alex Olshansky, Othello Richards, *Media Psychology* 24, no. 1, 2021.

221 repeated exposure to a claim: Social scientists call this the "illusory truth effect." See, for example: "Knowledge Does Not Protect against Illusory Truth Effect," Lisa K. Fazio et al., *Journal of Experimental Psychology* 144, no. 5, October 2015.

221 impression that the claim is widely accepted: This is the "common knowledge" effect referenced in Chapter 1. See Arias 2019 and Chwe 2013.

222 "Social camaraderie": *Understanding Racist Activism: Theory, Methods, and Research*, Kathleen M. Blee, 2017: 70.

222 promise resolution for feelings: Among the studies to establish a link between feelings of powerlessness and conspiracy belief: "Beliefs in conspiracies," Marina Abalakina-Paap, *Political Psychology* 20, no. 3, 1999.

222 sent into disorienting: "QAnon High Priest Was Just Trolling Away as Citigroup Tech Executive," William Turton and Josh Brustein, Bloomberg, October 7, 2020.

222 Reframing chaos as order: Among the studies to find that conspiracy belief often serves a way to reassert lost feelings of autonomy and control: "Measuring Individual Differences in Generic Beliefs in Conspiracy Theories across Cultures: Conspiracy Mentality Questionnaire," Martin Bruder et al., *Frontiers in Psychology* 4, 2013.

223 slid QAnon into the slipstream: This process will be discussed further in a later chapter. See, among many others: "The Prophecies of Q," Adrienne LaFrance, *The Atlantic*, June 2020. "QAnon Booms on Facebook as Conspiracy Group Gains Mainstream Traction," Deepa Seetharaman, *Wall Street Journal*, August 13, 2020. "Seven: 'Where We Go One,'" Kevin Roose et al., *New York Times*, May 28, 2020.

223 most popular downloads: "Apple, Google Cashed in on Pizzagate-Offshoot Conspiracy App," Ben Collins and Brandy Zadrozny, NBC News, July 16, 2018.

223 reached #2 on Amazon's: "How a Conspiracy Theory about Democrats Drinking Children's Blood Topped Amazon's Best-Sellers List," Kaitlyn Tiffany, *Vox*, March 6, 2019.

224 many law-enforcement officers: "QAnon Is Attracting Cops," Ali Breland, *Mother Jones*, September 28, 2020.

224 yoga moms and lifestyle influencers: "The Yoga World Is Riddled with Anti-Vaxxers and QAnon Believers," Cecile Guerin, *Wired UK*, January 28, 2021.

224 "Gonna be honest patriots": Tweet by @_qpatriot1776_, June 28, 2020, now removed by Twitter. Copy available at tweet by Travis View (@travis_view), June 29, 2020, twitter.com /travis_view/status/1277634756927033345

224 "I'm in the Same Boat": Ibid.

225 set up a series of test accounts: " 'Carol's Journey': What Facebook Knew about How It Radicalized Users," Brandy Zadrozny, NBC News, October 22, 2021.

225 through "gateway groups": Ibid.

225 "I can't emphasize enough": Tweet by Renee DiResta (@noUpside), February 18, 2018. twitter.com/noupside/status/965340235251920896

225 "Seventy percent of the top 100": "Facebook Knew Calls for Violence Plagued 'Groups,' Now Plans Overhaul," Jeff Horwitz, *Wall Street Journal*, January 31, 3031.

226 "where the bubble generation begins": "Mark in the Middle," Casey Newton, *The Verge*, September 23, 2020.

226 "Their theory about what": Facebook post by Dominic Fox, August 8, 2019. www.facebook .com/reynardine/posts/10156003037586991

229 4,000 who watched: "Facebook: New Zealand Attack Video Viewed 4,000 Times," BBC News, March 19, 2019.

229 jammed up office fax: "Twitter User Hacks 50,000 Printers to Tell People to Subscribe to PewDiePie," Catalin Cimpanu, ZD Net, November 30, 2018.

230 On 8chan, users, watching live, were rapturous: All user posts from thread titled "*ahem*" by Anonymous, 8chan, March 15, 2019. Formerly at 8ch.net/pol/res/12916717.html.

230 site should be shut down: " 'Shut the Site Down,' Says the Creator of 8chan, a Megaphone for Gunmen," Kevin Roose, *New York Times*, August 4, 2019.

231 the greater culpability lay: Royal Commission of Inquiry into the Terrorist Attack on Christchurch Mosque on March 15, 2019, Royal Commission of New Zealand, December 2020.

231 "YouTube was, for him": Ibid.

231 "This is a point": "Christchurch Inquiry Report Released," Helen Sullivan, *The Guardian*, December 7, 2020.

Chapter 10: The New Overlords

234 Those guidelines had once been: "Post No Evil," WNYC, *Radiolab*, August 17, 2018.

234 A vast archipelago of thousands: Key aspects of Jacob's account of Facebook moderation's inner workings, as well as the experiences of its moderators, have been independently established. See "Behind the Walls of Silence," Till Krause and Hannes Grassegger, *Süddeutsche Zeitung Magazine*, December 15, 2016. "The Low-Paid Workers Cleaning Up the Worst Horrors of the Internet," Gillian Tett, *Financial Times*, March 16, 2018. "The Secret Lives of Facebook Moderators in America," Casey Newton, *The Verge*, February 25, 2019.

240 The Facebook executive who oversaw: Interview with Justin Osofsky, then Facebook's vice president for global operations, October 2, 2018. "We, Obviously, Are Always Working to Make Sure that We Have the Right Controls and Relationships in Place. My Instinct in What You're Uncovering Here Is Probably Less an Issue at a Partner Level, at a Company to Company Level, and More of What You're Saying. Which Is Like, You Have Someone on the Front Lines That's Just Saying Something That's Inappropriate."

241 "Why are most chess masters": "Startup Advice for Entrepreneurs from Y Combinator," Mark Coker, *VentureBeat*, March 26, 2007.

241 "in software, you want to invest": "The Hardest Lessons for Startups to Learn," talk by Paul Graham to Y Combinator Startup School, April 2006.

242 The perks were intended: *The Code: Silicon Valley and the Remaking of America*, Margaret O'Mara, 2019: 201, 271–272.

243 "spent a few years": *Zucked: Waking Up to the Facebook Catastrophe*, Roger McNamee: 2019: 48.

243 "Their impact transformed": Ibid.

243 "I no longer believe": "The Education of a Libertarian," Peter Thiel, CatoUnbound.com, April 13, 2009.

243 corporation-run floating cities: "Mouthbreathing Machiavellis Dream of a Silicon Reich," Corey Pein, *The Baffler*, May 19, 2014.

243 incumbents: A widely used term of art, it is referenced, for example, in "The History of Progress Is a History of Better Monopoly Businesses Replacing Incumbents," *Zero to One*, Thiel and Masters, 2014: 33.

244 "This problem is one": Open Hearing on Foreign Influence Operations' Use of Social Media Platforms, Select Committee on Intelligence of the United States Senate, August 1, 2018.

244 "Responsibility for the": Ibid.

245 "One of the biggest issues social": "A Blueprint for Content Governance and Enforcement," Mark Zuckerberg, Facebook, November 15, 2018. www.facebook.com/notes/7514490020 72082

246 "even when they tell us": Ibid.

246 overhauled its algorithm: "Facebook Overhauls News Feed in Favor of 'Meaningful Social Interactions,'" Julia Carrie Wong, *The Guardian*, January 11, 2018.

246 Likes were worth one point: "Five Points for Anger, One for a 'Like': How Facebook's Formula Fostered Rage and Misinformation," Jeremy B. Merrill and Will Oremus, *Washington Post*, October 26, 2021.

247 "Misinformation, toxicity": "Facebook Tried to Make Its Platform a Healthier Place. It Got Angrier Instead," Keach Hagey and Jeff Horwitz, *Wall Street Journal*, September 15, 2021.

247 "unhealthy side effects": Ibid.

247 "forced them to skew": "Whistleblower: Facebook Is Misleading the Public on Progress against Hate Speech, Violence, Misinformation," Scott Pelley, *60 Minutes*, October 4, 2021.

247 Stanford and New York University economists: "The Welfare Effects of Social Media," Hunt Allcott et al., *American Economic Review* 110, no. 3, March 2020.

247 calling it a "turning point": "'Turning point': Mitch Fifield Flags Further Government Regulation of the Internet," Michael Koziol, *Sydney Morning Herald*, October 8, 2018.

248 "If we do not see": "European Union Says Facebook Must Change Rules by End of 2018," Alexander Smith and Jason Abbruzzese, NBC News, September 19, 2018.

248 "Facebook Morale Takes a Tumble Along with Stock Price," Deepa Seetharaman, *Wall Street Journal*, November 14, 2018.

248 internal poll of 29,000: "15 Months of Fresh Hell Inside Facebook," Nicholas Thompson and Fred Vogelstein, *Wired*, April 16, 2019.

249 their lock on democracy is over: Political scientists refer to democracy mediated by institutional gatekeepers as "Schumpeterian democracy," after the theorist Joseph Schumpeter. For more on the causes and consequences of this system's decline, see *How Democracies Die*, Steven Levitsky and Daniel Ziblatt, 2018: 97–117.

249 "rather than through": "Mark Zuckerberg's Letter to Investors: The Hacker Way," CNN Money, February 1, 2012.

249 called this new era: "What Happened to the Public Sphere? The Networked Public Sphere and Public Opinion Formation," Jonas Kaiser et al., *Handbook of Cyber-Development, Cyber-Democracy, and Cyber-Defense,* 2016: 433–459.

249 most charged posts rose: "The Yellow Vest Riots In France Are What Happens When Facebook Gets Involved with Local News," Ryan Broderick and Jules Darmanin, *BuzzFeed News,* December 5, 2018.

250 issued a cacophony: "Demands of France's Yellow Vests," France Bleu, Opendemocracy .net, November 29, 2018.

250 frequency of mass-protest: "Trends in Nonviolent Resistance and State Response: Is Violence towards Civilian-Based Movements on the Rise?" Erica Chenoweth, *Global Responsibility to Protect* 9, no. 1, January 2017.

251 easier for activists to organize: *Twitter and Tear Gas: The Power and Fragility of Networked Protest,* Zeynep Tufekci, 2017.

252 under the headline: "Former Facebook Workers: We Routinely Suppressed Conservative News," Michael Nunez, *Gizmodo,* May 9, 2016.

253 "Facebook has the power": "Republicans Press Facebook over Allegations of Bias against Conservative News," Andrea Peterson, *Washington Post,* May 11, 2016.

253 directed more acrimony: Levy, 2020: 343.

253 By Monday, its top story: "Three Days after Removing Human Editors, Facebook Is Already Trending Fake News," Abby Ohlheiser, *Washington Post,* August 29, 2016.

253 identified as one of the top: The blog in question is called *Ending the Fed.* Source on its role in the 2016 election: "Partisanship, Propaganda, and Disinformation: Online Media and the 2016 U.S. Presidential Election," Robert M. Faris et al., Berkman Klein Center for Internet & Society Research Paper, 2017.

253 confronted at a financial: "Inside the Two Years that Shook Facebook — and the World," Nicholas Thompson and Fred Vogelstein, *Wired,* February 2, 2018.

254 Fox News grew outspoken: See, for example: "Is Facebook as Left-Leaning as Everyone Suspects?" John Brandon, Fox News, September 26, 2016.

254 "It's not even close": "Facebook's Mark Zuckerberg Met with Conservatives over the 'Trending' Bias Spat," Arjun Kharpal, CNBC, May 19, 2016.

254 *Vice News* story headlined: "Twitter Is 'Shadow Banning' Prominent Republicans," Alex Thompson, *Vice News,* July 25, 2018.

255 based on a technical: "Twitter's Not 'Shadow Banning' Republicans, but Get Ready to Hear that It Is," Laura Hazard Owen, NiemanLab.com, July 27, 2018.

255 punishing him for questioning: Tweet by Matt Gaetz (@RepMattGaetz), July 25, 2018. twitter.com/RepMattGaetz/status/1022224027673219072

255 "suppresses conservative voices": Tweet by Ronna McDaniel (@GOPChairwoman) July 25, 2018. twitter.com/gopchairwoman/status/1022289868620267522

255 "Enough is enough": Tweet by Donald Trump, Jr. (@donaldtrumpjr), July 25, 2018. twitter .com/donaldjtrumpjr/status/1022198354468593665

255 break up IBM: Overviews of the IBM and Microsoft episodes are recounted in, for example, "IBM and Microsoft: Antitrust Then and Now," CNet, January 2, 2002. For greater detail and discussion of the cases legacy, see O'Mara, 2017: 341–346.

255 slid so dramatically: "Dominance Ended, I.B.M. Fights Back," Sandra Salmans, *New York Times,* January 9, 1982.

256 "I said, 'Get an office'": Osnos, 2018.

256　argued a 2018 op-ed: "What the Microsoft Antitrust Case Taught Us," Richard Blumenthal and Tim Wu, *New York Times*, May 18, 2018.

256　a leader who "violates protocol": "Peacetime CEO/Wartime CEO," Ben Horowitz, A16z .com, April 15, 2011.

257　drew an extended parallel: "To Create Culture, Start a Revolution," talk by Ben Horowitz to Startup Grind Global Conference, February 2017.

257　read a Horowitz-authored book: "How Mark Zuckerberg Became a Wartime CEO," Casey Newton, *The Verge*, November 20, 2018. The book: *The Hard Thing about Hard Things*, Ben Horowitz, 2014.

257　gathered the company's: "With Facebook at 'War,' Zuckerberg Adopts More Aggressive Style," Deepa Seetharaman, *Wall Street Journal*, November 19, 2018.

258　hired a dark-arts PR: "Delay, Deny and Deflect: How Facebook's Leaders Fought through Crisis," Sheera Frenkel, Nicholas Confessore, Cecilia Kang, Matthew Rosenberg, and Jack Nicas, *New York Times*, November 14, 2018.

258　Prominent investors in the venture-capitalist: "Safe Space: Silicon Valley, Clubhouse, and the Cult of VC Victimhood," Zoe Schiffer and Megan Farokhmanesh, *The Verge*, July 16, 2020.

258　"We get it": Tweet by Balaji Srinivasan (@balajis), July 1, 2020. twitter.com/balajis/status /1278198087404515328

258　urging Valley-wide bans: Schiffer and Farokhmanesh.

258　meeting to consider retooling: Thompson and Vogelstein, 2019.

258　Kaplan successfully pushed: "Facebook Executives Shut Down Efforts to Make the Site Less Divisive," Jeff Horwitz and Deepa Seetharaman, *Wall Street Journal*, May 26, 2020.

259　off-the-record dinners: "Inside Mark Zuckerberg's Private Meetings with Conservative Pundits," Natasha Bertran and Daniel Lippman, *Politico*, October 14, 2019.

259　"the death of free speech": "Tucker Carlson: Facebook's Zuckerberg Dictating Which Political Opinions You're 'Allowed to Have,'" Ian Schwartz, Realclearpolitics.com, May 2, 2019.

259　allow politicians to lie: "Facebook, Elections and Political Speech," Nick Clegg, About .fb.com, September 24, 2019. See also "Facebook Says It Won't Remove Politicians' Posts for Breaking Its Rules," Adi Robertson, *The Verge*, September 24, 2019.

259　"I'd been at FB for less": Tweet by Sophie Zhang (@szhang_ds), June 6, 2021. twitter.com /szhang_ds/status/1401392039414046720

259　Zhang flagged dozens: Zhang has told her story several times, most comprehensively in "She Risked Everything to Expose Facebook. Now She's Telling Her Story," Karen Hao, *MIT Technology Review*, July 29, 2021.

259　"I know that I have": Ibid.

259　Vietnam's communist dictatorship: "The Case against Mark Zuckerberg: Insiders Say Facebook's CEO Chose Growth Over Safety," Elizabeth Dwoskin, Tory Newmyer, Shibani Mahtani, *Washington Post*, October 25, 2021.

259　estimated that Facebook's Vietnam presence brings in $1 billion: Let us breathe! Censorship and criminalization of online expression in Viet Nam, Amnesty International Report, November 30, 2020.

259–260　no longer screen political advertisements: "Dissent Erupts at Facebook over Hands-Off Stance on Political Ads," Mike Isaac, *New York Times*, October 28, 2019.

260　About 250 employees signed: "Read the Letter Facebook Employees Sent to Mark Zuckerberg about Political Ads," compiled by *New York Times*, October 28, 2019.

260　published a column on: "I Worked on Political Ads at Facebook. They Profit by Manipulating Us.," Yaël Eisenstat, *Washington Post*, November 4, 2019.

262 issue explicitly in August 2019: "Facebook Wrestles with the Features It Used to Define Social Networking," Mike Isaac, *New York Times*, October 25, 2021.

262 "promoting these types of activities": Ibid.

263 breezy 32-slide PowerPoint: The file, and others, can be seen at "Inside Facebook's Secret Rulebook for Global Political Speech," Max Fisher, *New York Times*, December 27, 2018.

264 "time well spent": "Quality Time, Brought to You by Big Tech," Arielle Pardes, *Wired*, December 31, 2018.

264 "We will start to realize": Tweet by B.J. Fogg (@bjfogg), September 11, 2019. twitter.com /bjfogg/status/1171883692488183809

264 publishing a book with the title: "Addicted to Screens? That's Really a You Problem," Nellie Bowles, *New York Times*, October 6, 2019.

264 Harris called the campaign: Pardes, 2018.

265 "The CEOs, inside": "Where Silicon Valley Is Going to Get in Touch with Its Soul," Nellie Bowles, *New York Times*, December 4, 2017.

265 an American moderator filed a lawsuit: "Ex-Content Moderator Sues Facebook, Saying Violent Images Caused Her PTSD," Sandra E. Garcia, *New York Times*, September 25, 2018.

265 In 2020, Facebook settled: "Facebook Will Pay $52 Million in Settlement with Moderators Who Developed PTSD on the Job," Casey Newton, *The Verge*, May 12, 2020.

Chapter 11: Dictatorship of the Like

266 a far-right lawmaker edited footage: "É horrível ser difamado pelo Bolsonaro," Débora Lopes, *Vice Portuguese*, May 11, 2013.

267 millions of acres: "With Amazon on Fire, Environmental Officials in Open Revolt against Bolsonaro," Ernesto Londoño and Letícia Casado, *New York Times*, August 28, 2019.

267 "I wouldn't rape you": "A Look at Offensive Comments by Brazil Candidate Bolsonaro," Stan Lehman, Associated Press, September 29, 2018.

267 festered on the fringes of Brazil's: "URSAL, Illuminati, and Brazil's YouTube Subculture," Luiza Bandeira, Digital Forensic Research Lab, August 30, 2018.

267 Dozens more conspiracies: "Fast and False in Brazil," Luiza Bandeira, Digital Forensic Research Lab, September 19, 2018.

267 second-largest market; "Pesquisa Video Viewers: como os brasileiros estão consumindo vídeos em 2018," Maria Helena Marinho, Google Marketing Materials, September 2018.

271 Almeida had some ideas: Almeida and his team provided us with several separate reports documenting their methodology and findings, along with the underlying raw data, in a series of interviews conducted throughout early 2019. I shared much of this material with YouTube prior to publication of our *New York Times* story. Almeida et al. have not yet published this research in full and in a formal journal article, though they have used similar methodology (and produced similar findings) in subsequent peer-reviewed studies. See "Auditing Radicalization Pathways on YouTube," Manoel Horta Ribeiro et al., *Proceedings of the 2020 Conference on Fairness, Accountability, and Transparency*, January 2020. "Misinformation, Radicalization and Hate through the Lens of Users," Manoel Horta Ribeiro, Virgilio Almeida, and Wagner Meira Jr., dissertation, June 30, 2020.

272 encouraging schoolchildren to clandestinely: See, for example: "Snitch on a Teacher: Bolsonaro Win Sparks Push against 'Indoctrination,'" Dom Phillips, *The Guardian*, October 30, 2018.

Notes

273 A wave of such incidents: "Education Is in the Crosshairs in Bolsonaro's Brazil," Michael Fox, *The Nation*, November 12, 2018. See also "Brazil's Classrooms Become a Battleground in a Culture War," *The Economist*, December 1, 2018.

275 Bolsonaro urged citizens: Tweet by Jair Bolsonaro (@jairbolsonaro), November 11, 2018. twitter.com/jairbolsonaro/status/1061809199196368896

275 He replaced government technocrats: For example: "Brazil Replaces Far-Right Education Minister with Conspiracy Theorist," Dom Phillips, *The Guardian*, April 9, 2019.

276 taken repeated action against: "Facebook Removes Pages of Brazil Activist Network before Elections," Brad Haynes, Reuters, July 25, 2018.

278 Vaccine avoidance was rising: "Vaccine Confidence and Hesitancy in Brazil," Amy Louise Brown et al., *Cadernos de Saúde Pública* 21, September 2018.

278 refusing to use mosquito larvicides: "The Effects of Corrective Information About Disease Epidemics and Outbreaks: Evidence from Zika and Yellow Fever in Brazil," John M. Carey et al., *Science Advances* 6, no. 5, January 2020.

279 Brazilian Institute of Research and Data Analysis: "Mapeando propagação de boatos no YouTube — Febre Amarela," Isabela Pimentel, Instituto Brasileiro de Pesquisa e Análise de Dados, February 8, 2018.

281 The team identified: Kaiser et al. shared their findings and methodology with me as it proceeded, along with supporting documentation and underlying data. I shared relevant selections of this with YouTube prior to publication. Much on this research later appeared in: "Fighting Zika with Honey: An Analysis of YouTube's Video Recommendations on Brazilian YouTube," Kaiser, Rauchfleisch, and Yasodara Cordova, *International Journal of Communication*, February 2021.

283 studying this exact phenomenon: Much of the methodology, data, and findings referenced in this research can be found in these two published studies: "Analyzing and Characterizing Political Discussions in WhatsApp Public Groups," Josemar Alves Caetano et al., working paper, 2018. "Characterizing Attention Cascades in WhatsApp Groups," Caetano et al., *Proceedings of the 10th ACM Conference on Web Science*, June 2019.

287 "YouTube announced that it had made": "The Four Rs of Responsibility, Part 2: Raising authoritative content and reducing borderline content and harmful misinformation," YouTube Official Blog, December 3, 2019.

288 Kaiser, along with Rauchfleisch and Córdova: The researchers later published some of their findings and methods in "The Implications of Venturing Down the Rabbit Hole," Jonas Kaiser and Adrian Rauchfleisch, *Internet Policy Review*, June 27, 2019.

290 Most people who view sexualized: For an overview of the research: "The Science of Sex Abuse," Rachel Aviv, *The New Yorker*, January 6, 2013.

290 consumers often developed that interest: "Does Deviant Pornography Use Follow a Guttman-Like Progression?" Kathryn Seigfried-Spellar and Marcus Rogers, Computers in *Human Behavior* 29, no. 5, September 2013.

292 study of child-pornography offenders: See, among others: "An Integrative Review of Historical Technology and Countermeasure Usage Trends in Online Child Sexual Exploitation Material Offenders," Chad M. S. Steel et al., *Forensic Science International* 33, June 2020. "Online Sexual Deviance, Pornography and Child Sexual Exploitation Material," Ethel Quayle, *Forensische Psychiatrie, Psychologie, Kriminologie* 14, 2020. "Prevention, Disruption and Deterrence of Online Child Sexual Exploitation and Abuse," Ethel Quayle, *ERA Forum* 21, 2020.

294 an earlier controversy regarding: "YouTube Bans Comments on Videos of Young Children in Bid to Block Predators," Daisuke Wakabayashi, *New York Times*, February 28, 2019.

294 Josh Hawley, a Republican Senator: "Senate Bill Targets YouTube's Kids Content amid Probe Report," Rebecca Kern, Bloomberg, June 20, 2019.

294 cosigned a letter with Senator Marsha Blackburn: Richard Blumenthal and Marsha Blackburn to Susan Wojcicki, June 6, 2019. www.blumenthal.senate.gov/imo/media/doc/2019 .06.03%20-%20YouTube%20-%20Child%20Abuse.pdf

295 said he was "frankly disappointed": "Protecting Innocence in a Digital World," Senate Judiciary Committee Hearing, July 9, 2019.

Chapter 12: Infodemic

296 went to his boss with a plan: "W.H.O. Fights a Pandemic Besides Coronavirus: An 'Infodemic,'" Matt Richtel, *New York Times*, February 6, 2020.

296 "The interest that I got:" "Q&A: Solidifying Social Media Platforms' Role in Global Health," Devex Partnerships, Devex.com, November 29, 2021.

296 "I made this pitch on a human": "How WHO Is Engaging Big Tech to Fight Covid-19," Catherine Cheney, Devex.com, August 14, 2020.

297 an "infodemic": "Facebook, Amazon, Google and More Met with WHO to Figure Out How to Stop Coronavirus Misinformation," Christina Farr and Salvador Rodriguez, CNBC, February 14, 2020.

297 Facebook posts were already winning: "Coronavirus Cannot be Cured by Drinking Bleach or Snorting Cocaine, despite Social Media Rumors," Christina Capatides, CBS News, March 9, 2020.

297 Instagram influencers explained: "Coronavirus Conspiracy Video Spreads on Instagram among Black Celebrities," Brandy Zadrozny, NBC News, March 13, 2020.

297 the CIA was hoarding: Tweet by Brody Logan (@BrodyLogan), March 16, 2020. twitter .com/BrodyLogan/status/1239406460188020736

297 blaming the disease on 5G cell towers: "Why Coronavirus Conspiracy Theories Flourish. And Why It Matters," Max Fisher, *New York Times*, April 8, 2020.

298 Facebook reported a 70 percent: "Eight: 'We Go All,'" Kevin Roose, *New York Times*, June 4, 2020.

298 jumped from 9 to 16 percent: "YouTube Controls 16% of Pandemic Traffic Globally: Sandvine," Daniel Frankel, Next TV, May 7, 2020.

298 was everywhere by April: In April 2020, the advocacy group Avaaz identified 100 Covid-conspiracy posts on Facebook with 1.7 million combined shares. "How Facebook Can Flatten the Curve of the Coronavirus Infodemic," Avaaz, April 15, 2020.

298–299 small-town missionary's Facebook: His post received 18,000 shares. "Fact-Checking a Facebook Conspiracy about Bill Gates, Dr. Fauci and Covid-19," Daniel Funke, Politifact, April 14, 2020.

299 "Coronavirus is a government made": Her post received 90,000 shares and 350,000 likes. Tweet by @krisssnicolee, March 7, 2020. twitter.com/krisssnicolee/status/123630959554 4584192

299 two doctors presenting phony: Their video received 4.3 million views. "Cue the debunking: Two Bakersfield Doctors Go Viral with Dubious COVID Test Conclusions," Barbara Feder Ostrov, *Cal Matters*, April 27, 2020.

299 mushroomed across YouTube: "How Has Covid-19 Affected the Anti-Vaccination Movement? A Social Media Analysis," Commetric, June 2, 2020.

299 "explosive growth in anti-vaccination": "The Online Competition between Pro- and Anti-Vaccination Views," Neil F. Johnson et al., *Nature* 582, May 2020.

299 internal documents suggest that Facebook: "The Case against Mark Zuckerberg: Insiders Say Facebook's CEO Chose Growth over Safety," Elizabeth Dwoskin, Tory Newmyer, Shibani Mahtani, *Washington Post*, October 25, 2021.

300 Zuckerberg nixed it: Ibid.

300 researchers investigated "manufactured virality": "Facebook Employees Found a Simple Way to Tackle Misinformation. They 'Deprioritized' It after Meeting with Mark Zuckerberg, Documents Show," Billy Perrigo and Vera Bergengruen, *Time*, November 10, 2021.

300 The video's route to virality: "Virality Project (US): Marketing Meets Misinformation," Renée DiResta and Isabella Garcia-Camargo, Stanford Internet Observatory, May 26, 2020.

301 spread to alternative medicine communities: Ibid.

301 did not react until news agencies: "How the 'Plandemic' Movie and Its Falsehoods Spread Widely Online," Sheera Frenkel, Ben Decker, Davey Alba, *New York Times*, May 20, 2020.

301 "The challenge I've got with them": Cheney, August 2020.

301 more likely to believe that vitamin C: "The Relation between Media Consumption and Misinformation at the Outset of the SARS-CoV-2 Pandemic in the US," Kathleen Hall Jamieson and Dolores Albarracin, *Harvard Kennedy School Misinformation Review* 1, no. 2, 2020.

301 Doctors reported more and more patients: "Coronavirus Doctors Battle Another Scourge: Misinformation," Adam Satariano, *New York Times*, August 17, 2020.

301 "More evidence of a Plandemic": Tweet by Rachel McKibbens (@rachelmckibbens), November 15, 2021. twitter.com/RachelMcKibbens/status/1460268133302738947

302 a Facebook-propagated conspiracy: "No, Covid-19 Vaccines Do Not 'Shed,'" Arijeta Lajka, Associated Press, April 29, 2021.

302 they texted back and forth: Tweet by Rachel McKibbens (@rachelmckibbens), November 11, 2021. twitter.com/RachelMcKibbens/status/1458881015917678594

303 "Start drafting that op": Criminal complaint, *United States of America v. Ivan Harrison Hunter*, Case 20-mj-758-hb, May 27, 2020.

303 "He was just in complete disconnect": "I Felt Hate More than Anything: How an Active Duty Airman Tried to Start a Civil War," Gisela Pérez de Acha, Kathryn Hurd, and Ellie Lightfoot, *Frontline* and ProPublica, April 13, 2021.

303 warned that "viral insurgencies": "Cyber Swarming, Memetic Warfare and Viral Insurgency," Alex Goldenberg and Joel Finkelstein, Network Contagion Research Institute, February 2020.

304 A "Boogaloo Tactics" file: Tech Transparency Project, April 22, 2020.

304 purchased an AR-15 component: Criminal complaint, *United States of America v. Timothy John Watson*, Case 3:20-mj-000127-RWT, October 30, 2020.

304 they planned "firearm training": Criminal complaint, *United States of America v. Jessie Alexander Rush, Robert Jesus Blancas, Simon Sage Ybarra, and Kenny Matthew Miksch*, Case CR-21-0121-JD, March 23, 2021.

304 their groups attracted 900,000 users: "Facebook Removes Some Events Calling for Protests of Stay-at-Home Orders," Brandy Zadrozny, NBC News, April 20, 2020.

304 But thousands remained active on the pages: See, for example: "Extremists Are Using Facebook to Organize for Civil War amid Coronavirus," Tech Transparency Project Report, April 22, 2020.

305 QAnon belief now infused: "QAnon Booms on Facebook as Conspiracy Group Gains Mainstream Traction," Deepa Seetharaman, *Wall Street Journal*, August 13, 2020.

305 Nina Jankowicz, a disinformation: Tweet by Nina Jankowicz (@wiczipedia), May 27, 2020. twitter.com/wiczipedia/status/1265629272988954625

305 filled with Q dog whistles: "Facebook Bans One of the Anti-Vaccine Movement's Biggest Groups for Violating QAnon Rules," Aatif Sulleyman, *Newsweek*, November 18, 2020.

305 TikTok surged with Pizzagate: "'PizzaGate' Conspiracy Theory Thrives Anew in the Tik-Tok Era," Cecilia Kang and Sheera Frenkel, *New York Times*, June 27, 2020.

306 That summer, ninety-seven: "Here are the QAnon Supporters Running for Congress in 2020," Alex Kaplan, Media Matters, January 7, 2020 (updated through July 27, 2021).

306 Hunter yelled, "Justice for Floyd": *USA v. Hunter*, 2020.

306 "It's on our coast now": The details of Carrillo and Justus's actions are according to federal criminal complaints. See, for example: "Alleged 'Boogaloo' Extremist Charged in Killing of Federal Officer during George Floyd Protest," Andrew Blankstein and Ben Collins, NBC News, June 16, 2020.

307 Carrillo proposed to his: De Acha, Hurd, and Lightfoot, April 2021.

307 he would "send in the National Guard": Tweet by Donald J. Trump (@realDonaldTrump), May 29, 2020. Since deleted.

307 "divisive and inflammatory": "Zuckerberg Says He's 'Struggling' with Trump's Latest Posts but Leaving Them Up," David Ingram, NBC News, May 29, 2020.

307 a long-debunked conspiracy: "Show Me State of Mind," Jelani Cobb, *This American Life* 671, March 29, 2019.

308 Some circulated his phone number: Tweet by Andy Mannix (@andrewmannix), May 29, 2020. twitter.com/AndrewMannix/status/1266253783408930816. As if to underscore that his antagonists perhaps had the wrong man, Mannix later shared a Pulitzer Prize for the *Minneapolis Star Tribune*'s reporting on the police abuses that had inspired the protests.

308 posted photos of the license plates: Tweet by Max Blumenthal (@MaxBlumenthal), May 30, 2020. Since deleted.

309 sued Facebook, alleging that: "Facebook Promoted Extremism Leading to Federal Officer Dave Patrick Underwood's Murder: Lawsuit," Aaron Katersky, ABC News, January 6, 2020.

309 "Facebook's inaction in taking down": Tweet by Lauren Tan (@sugarpirate_), June 1, 2020. twitter.com/sugarpirate_/status/1266470996162146304

310 Yet that same day, his platform's most popular: "How Facebook Is Undermining 'Black Lives Matters,'" *The Daily*, a *New York Times* podcast, June 22, 2020.

310 Throughout June, stories emerged: See, for example: "Zuckerberg Once Wanted to Sanction Trump. Then Facebook Wrote Rules that Accommodated Him," Elizabeth Dwoskin, Craig Timberg, Tony Romm, *Washington Post*, June 28, 2020.

311 Civil rights groups led a campaign: "Facebook's Tipping Point," Judd Legum, Popular Information, June 27, 2020.

311 banned Boogaloo from their: "Banning a Violent Network in the US," Facebook Newsroom, About.fb.com, June 30, 2020.

311 YouTube removed several prominent: "YouTube Bans Stefan Molyneux, David Duke, Richard Spencer, and More for Hate Speech," Julia Alexander, *The Verge*, June 29, 2020.

311 Reddit closed two thousand: "Reddit Bans The_Donald, Forum of Nearly 800,000 Trump Fans, over Abusive Posts," Bobby Allyn, NPR, June 29, 2020.

311 posted a twenty-four-minute goodbye message: "'Facebook Is Hurting People at Scale,'" Ryan Mac and Craig Silverman, *BuzzFeed News*, July 23, 2020.

311 telling reporters they felt: "Facebook Fails to Appease Organizers of Ad Boycott," Mike Isaac and Tiffany Hsu, *New York Times*, July 7, 2018. "When a Critic Met Facebook: 'What They're Doing Is Gaslighting,'" Charlie Warzel, *New York Times*, July 9, 2020.

312 an independent audit of Facebook's policies: "Facebook's Civil Rights Audit — Final Report," Laura W. Murphy and the law firm Relman Colfax, About.fb.com, July 8, 2020.

312 But the auditors, granted access: Ibid.

312 outpaced Joe Biden's by forty: Data from Crowdtangle.com.

313 "I don't know how the Facebook board": "Nancy Pelosi Wonders How Top Facebook Employees Can 'Look Themselves in the Mirror' because They 'Make Money Off Poison,'" Avery Hartmans, *Business Insider*, September 21, 2020.

313 It imposed a conspicuously lighter penalty: "New Steps to Protect the US Elections," Facebook Newsroom, About.fb.com, September 3, 2020.

313 "We're doing this to reduce": Tweet by @instagramcommes, October 29, 2020. mobile .twitter.com/InstagramComms/status/1321957713476280320

313 A month out from the election: "With Election Day Looming, Twitter Imposes New Limits on U.S. Politicians — and Ordinary Users, Too," Elizabeth Dwoskin and Craig Timberg, *Washington Post*, October 9, 2020.

314 the effort to "slow down" virality: "Additional Steps We're Taking Ahead of the 2020 US Election," Vijaya Gadde and Kayvon Beykpour, Twitter corporate blog, October 9, 2020.

314 imposed total bans on the movement in October: "Facebook Amps Up Its Crackdown on QAnon," Sheera Frenkel, *New York Times*, October 6, 2020. "Twitter, in Widening Crackdown, Removes over 70,000 QAnon Accounts," Kate Conger, *New York Times*, January 11, 2021.

314 YouTube's CEO, Susan Wojcicki, said only: "YouTube Tightens Rules on Conspiracy Videos, but Stops Short of Banning QAnon," Jennifer Elias, CNBC, October 15, 2020.

315 at least 60,000 posts: Social Media in 2020: Incitement, Counteraction report, November 25, 2020.

316 "a bullet to the head": "Marjorie Taylor Greene Indicated Support for Executing Prominent Democrats in 2018 and 2019 before Running for Congress," Em Steck and Andrew Kaczynski, CNN, January 26, 2021.

316 gained 338,000 members: "The Rise and Fall of the 'Stop the Steal' Facebook Group," Sheera Frenkel, *New York Times*, November 5, 2020.

316 shadowy powers intended to exploit: "Richard Barnett, Arkansas Man Pictured Sitting at Nancy Pelosi's Desk, Arrested," The Associated Press, January 8, 2021.

316 He organized a group in support of the charity: "Save Our Children Raises over $1,000 for Nonprofit," *Westside Eagle Observer*, October 28, 2020.

317 "We need to put a stop to this": "Capitol Attack Was Months in the Making on Facebook," *Tech Transparency Project Report*, January 19, 2021.

317 the twenty most-engaged Facebook posts: Data from Crowdtangle.com.

318 Detroit poll workers: "No Evidence Ballots Were Smuggled into Detroit Counting hub," Clara Hendrickson, *Detroit Free Press*, November 5, 2020.

318 "YouTube has been great": "Critics Call Gary Franchi's YouTube Channel, the Next News Network, a Hive of Conspiracy Theories. So How Has It Survived the Platform's Conspiracy Crackdown?" John Keilman, *Chicago Tribune*, October 31, 2020.

318 ballots being "dumped": Tweet by @j_epp_, November 4, 2020. Since deleted.

318 rogue postal worker had fled: Tweet by @breaking911, November 5, 2020. Since deleted.

318 10 percent of all U.S.-based views: "Internal Alarm, Public Shrugs: Facebook's Employees Dissect Its Election Role," Ryan Mac and Sheera Frenkel, *New York Times*, October 22, 2021.

318 top 1 percent of YouTube's: Tweet by Guillaume Chaslot (@gchaslot), December 3, 2020. twitter.com/gchaslot/status/1334615047197380610

318 viewed 138 million times: "Election Fraud Narrative," *Transparency.tube Report*, November 17, 2020.

319 The platform remained saturated: "YouTube Still Awash in False Voter Fraud Claims," *Tech Transparency Report*, December 22, 2020.

319 "mountains of evidence": "Trump's Far-Right Supporters Promise Violence at Today's DC Protests," Jordan Green, *Raw Story*, January 6, 2021.

319 more than 80 percent of discussions: "On Far-Right Websites, Plans to Storm Capitol Were Made in Plain Sight," Laurel Wamsley, NPR, January 7, 2021.

319 "We're gonna kill Congress": Green, January 6, 2021.

320 "This is OUR COUNTRY!!!": Swaine, April 2021.

320 "If you don't like it": "Richard Barnett Benton County Republican Rally," KNWA Fox 24, January 6, 2021.

320 "Today I had the very difficult": "How the Insurgent and MAGA Right Are Being Welded Together on the Streets of Washington D.C.," Robert Evans, Bellingcat.com, January 5, 2021.

320 "I told my Mom goodbye": Ibid.

320 YouTube- and Reddit-inspired nickname: "What Does 'Pedes' Mean?" naterich_stl, Reddit, March 16, 2019.

321 "honor of my life": Evans.

322 an inspector general report found: "Capitol Police Told to Hold Back on Riot Response on Jan. 6, Report Finds," Luke Broadwater, *New York Times*, April 13, 2021.

322 "We're in, we're in!": "West Virginia Lawmaker Records Himself Storming the U.S. Capitol: 'We're in!'" The Associated Press, January 7, 2021.

322 posting about the rally for days: Criminal complaint, *United States of America v. Derrick Evans*, Case 1:21-CR-337, January 8, 2021.

322 "We just pushed, pushed": Criminal complaint, *United States of America v. Jenny Cudd*, Case 1:21-cr-00068-TNM, October 13, 2021.

323 "You are executing citizen's": Criminal complaint, *United States of America v. Thomas Edward Caldwell, Donovan Ray Crowl, and Jessica Marie Watkins*, Case 1:21-mj-00119, January 19, 2021.

323 "Everybody in there is a treasonous": Criminal complaint, United States of America v. Peter Francis Stager, Case 1:21-mj-00057, January 14, 2021.

324 "said that anyone they got their hands": Criminal complaint, United States of America v. Dominic Pezzola, Case 1:21-mj-00047, January 13, 2021.

324 Former friends told Vice News: "The Proud Boy Who Smashed a US Capitol Window Is a Former Marine," Tess Owen and Mack Lamoureux, Vice News, January 15, 2021.

324 "Load your guns and take": "The Radicalization of Kevin Greeson," Connor Sheets, ProPublica and *Birmingham News*, January 15, 2021.

324 Boyland's family said: "Death of QAnon Follower at Capitol Leaves a Wake of Pain," Nicholas Bogel-Burroughs and Evan Hill, *New York Times*, May 30, 2021.

324 filmed Babbitt's death: "The Story of the Man Who Filmed Ashli Babbitt's Death," Samuel Benson, *Deseret News*, August 11, 2021.

324 "That got me moved": "John Sullivan, Who Filmed Shooting of Ashli Babbitt in Capitol, Detained on Federal Charges," Robert Mackey, *The Intercept*, January 14, 2021.

325 "Can we get some courage": "Twitter, Facebook Freeze Trump Accounts as Tech Giants Respond to Storming of U.S. Capitol," Elizabeth Culliford, Katie Paul, and Joseph Menn, Reuters, January 6, 2021.

325   "We need to take down": "Facebook Forced Its Employees to Stop Discussing Trump's Coup Attempt," Ryan Mac, *BuzzFeed News*, January 6, 2021.

325–326   "Social media has emboldened": "Alphabet Workers Union Statement on Yesterday's Insurrection," Alphabet Workers Union, January 7, 2021.

326   "You've got blood": Tweet by Chris Sacca (@sacca), January 6, 2021. twitter.com/sacca/status/1346921144859783169

327   "I've never been a fan": "Joe Biden," The Editorial Board, *New York Times*, January 17, 2020.

327   "Perhaps no single entity": Tom Malinowski and Anna G. Eshoo to Mark Zuckerberg, January 21, 2021. malinowski.house.gov/sites/malinowski.house.gov/files/Letter%20to%20Facebook%20 — %20Malinowski_Eshoo_final_0.pdf

327   "The fundamental problem": Tom Malinowski and Anna G. Eshoo to Sundar Pichai and Susan Wojcicki, January 21, 2021. malinowski.house.gov/sites/malinowski.house.gov/files/Letter%20to%20YouTube%20 — %20Malinowski_Eshoo_final_0.pdf

327   "We gave it our all": Post by Ron Watkins (@codemonkeyz), Telegram, January 20, 2021.

328   "As we enter into the": Ibid.

328   An 8kun moderator purged: Post by Pillow, 8kun, January 20, 2021. archive.is/lG6er

328   "Mods please explain": Post by StartAgain, Greatawakening.win, January 20, 2021.

328   "being a kid and seeing": Post by FL350, Greatawakening.win, January 20, 2021.

328   "EVERYTHING will be happening": Post by Bubba1776, Greatawakening.win, January 20, 2021.

328   "I have lost friends": Ibid.

epilogue: whistleblowing

329   no longer promote political: "Facebook to Stop Recommending Civic and Political Groups," BBC News, January 28, 2021.

329–330   had been mostly empty: "Facebook Said It Would Stop Pushing Users to Join Partisan Political Groups. It Didn't," Leon Yin and Alfred Ng, *The Markup*, January 19, 2021.

330   under pressure from Democratic: "Facebook Says 'Technical Issues' Were the Cause of Broken Promise to Congress," Alfred Ng and Leon Yin, *The Markup*, February 12, 2021.

330   rolled back the change: "Facebook Reverses Postelection Algorithm Changes that Boosted News from Authoritative Sources," Kevin Roose, *The New York Times*, December 16, 2020.

330   The company claimed: "An Update on the Georgia Runoff Elections," Sarah Schiff, About.fb.com, December 15, 2020.

330   The day after Facebook: "In Georgia, Facebook's Changes Brought Back a Partisan News Feed," Corin Faife, *The Markup*, January 5, 2021.

330   that March, Facebook lifted: "Facebook Ends Ban on Political Advertising," Mike Isaac, *The New York Times*, March 3, 2021.

330   "I think these events": "Facebook's Sandberg Deflected Blame for Capitol Riot, but New Evidence Shows How Platform Played Role," Elizabeth Dwoskin, *Washington Post*, January 13, 2021.

330   "mark a big shift": "Banning President Trump Was the Right Decision, Says Instagram's Adam Mosseri," Nilay Patel, *The Verge*, January 19, 2021.

331   "Facebook's systems are not designed": "You and the Algorithm: It Takes Two to Tango," Nick Clegg, Medium.com, March 31, 2021.

331   "left to metastasize": Trending in the Wrong Direction: Social Media Platforms' Declining Enforcement of Voting Disinformation, Common Cause Report, September 2, 2021.

331 "at least one far-right Facebook group": *Breaching the Mainstream: A National Survey of Far-Right Membership in State Legislatures*, Institute for Research and Education on Human Rights, May 2022.

331 "encouraging kids to record their teachers": "Florida GOP pushes 'intellectual diversity' survey for colleges," Ana Ceballos, *The Tampa Bay Times*, April 6, 2021.

331 tampering with voting systems: "Voting Machine Missing after Michigan Clerk Stripped of Election Power," Jonathan Oosting, *Bridge Michigan*, October 28, 2021. "Several Interruptions from Tina Peters Caused Commissioners to Almost Throw Peters Out of Public Hearing," *Western Slope Now*, October 25, 2021.

331 "on the ballot in 26 states:" "QAnon candidates are on the ballot in 26 states," Steve Reilly, et al., *Grid*, April 12, 2022.

331–332 issued a formal advisory: "Surgeon General Assails Tech Companies over Misinformation on Covid-19," Sheryl Gay Stolberg and Davey Alba, *New York Times*, July 15, 2021.

332 Biden said that Facebook: "'They're Killing People': Biden Denounces Social Media for Virus Disinformation," Zolan Kanno-Youngs and Cecilia Kang, *New York Times*, July 16, 2021.

332 released a 449-page report: *Investigation of Competition in Digital Markets*, House Subcommittee on Antitrust, Commercial and Administrative Law, October 6, 2020.

332 pay Australian news outlets: "Can Australia Force Google and Facebook to Pay for News?" Celina Ribeiro, *Wired*, August 30, 2020.

333 39 percent of Australians: Digital News Report: Australia 2020, University of Canberra News & Media Research Centre, 2020.

333 Much more had gone dark: "Facebook's New Look in Australia: News and Hospitals Out, Aliens Still In," Damien Cave, *New York Times*, February 18, 2021.

333 "calculated for impact": Tweet by Evelyn Douek (@evelyndouek), February 17, 2021. twitter.com/evelyndouek/status/1362171044136710144

333 Human Rights Watch described: Tweet by Sophie McNeill (@sophiemcneill), February 17, 2021. twitter.com/Sophiemcneill/status/1362187114431975426

333 Australian lawmaker warned: Tweet by Anthony Albanese (@albomp), February 17, 2021. twitter.com/AlboMP/status/1362177819304812544

334 "likely be unable to offer": "Meta Says It May Shut Down Facebook and Instagram in Europe over Data-Sharing Dispute," Sam Shead, *CNBC*, February 7, 2022.

334 "life has been fantastic": "We're Fine without Facebook, German and French Ministers Say," William Horobin and Zoe Schneeweiss, *Bloomberg News*, February 7, 2022.

335 40 percent of the big-tech workforce: "How Tech Workers Feel about China, AI and Big Tech's Tremendous Power," Emily Birnbaum and Issie Lapowsky, *Protocol*, March 15, 2021.

336 For months, she had been in touch: "Inside the Big Facebook Leak," Ben Smith, *New York Times*, October 24, 2021.

336 "I just don't want to agonize": "The education of Frances Haugen: How the Facebook Whistleblower Learned to Use Data as a Weapon from Years in Tech", Cat Zakrzewski and Reed Albergotti, *Washington Post*, October 11, 2021.

337 "Facebook has realized": "Whistleblower: Facebook Is Misleading the Public on Progress against Hate Speech, Violence, Misinformation," Scott Pelley, *60 Minutes*, October 4, 2021.

337 "We can have social media we enjoy": Frances Haugen Opening Statement, Senate Hearing on Children and Social Media, October 5, 2021.

337 "What we see in Myanmar": Zakrzewski and Albergotti, October 2021.

Index

Index

Index

Index

Index

social media companies' crackdownon, 312–316
  and viral outrage, 85
Trumparoo, 324
Trut, Lyudmila, 94
Tufekci, Zeynep, 144, 198, 251
Twitter
  affect of algorithms on, 128–129
  and Black Lives Matter, 307–308
  Cecil the lion on, 82–84
  Jack Dorsey as CEO at, 140–141
  and election of 2016, 135
  and election of 2020, 254–255
  following Capitol siege, 329
  founding of, 50
  intermittent variable reinforcement by, 27
  and January 6th Capitol attack, 326–328
  Alex Jones on, 219
  and Like button, 30
  and moral-emotional words, 138–139
  and political polarization, 138–143, 150
  and Donald Trump, 310, 312–314, 318
  value of attention on, 56
2001: A Space Odyssey (film), 23, 263, 340
"tyranny of the cousins," 96

Uber, 115, 244
Uhle, Sören, 199, 201
Unite the Right Rally (Charlottesville), 183, 205–208, 311
United Nations, 196–197
University of California, Berkeley, 197
University of North Carolina, 198, 251
University of Warwick, 184, 194
upvotes, on Reddit, 67–68
Upworthy, 34, 112
URSAL, 268

Vaidhyanathan, Siva, 145
venture capitalists, 19–20, 50–51, 68, 71, 117, 241–243, 258, 338, 339
The Verge, 226
Vice News, 6, 31, 58, 254–255, 324
video game culture, 59–62
Vietnam, 259
virality, headlines constructed for, 34
Vox, 34, 166, 196

Wahabzada, Abdul Aziz, 228
Wall Street Journal, 9, 134, 330, 336
Warmke, Justin, 97, 98
Warner, Mark, 147, 148
Washington Post, 34, 74
Wassermann, Rolf, 187–188, 194, 316
Watkins, Ron, 223, 327–328
Weedon, Jen, 172, 197
Weerasinghe, Amith, 173–176
Wei, Eugene, 123
Weibo, 92
Weiner, Anthony, 131
Weinstein, Harvey, 101–102
Welch, Edgar Maddison, 137
WELL (Whole Earth 'Letrconic Link), 46–47
Wells Fargo, 23
Wesemann, Anette, 185
WhatsApp, 8, 174, 186, 234, 282–283, 297, 304, 308
whistleblowing, 329–340
white nationalism, 74, 133, 206, 207, 216, 311
Whole Earth Catalog, 47
Whole Earth Truck Store, 47
Wickrematunge, Raisa, 172
WikiLeaks, 132
Williams, James, 84, 102, 126–127
Winfrey, Oprah, 54
Winter, Brian, 267–268
Wirathu, 37–38, 162, 263
Wired magazine, 248
Wojcicki, Susan, 105–106, 115, 119–121, 134, 314
Wolff, Natascha, 192, 193
Wong, Yishan, 50, 67, 69–71
World Health Organization (WHO), 296–297
Wozniak, Steve, 17
Wrangham, Richard, 95–96
Wu, Brianna, 43–44, 61, 62, 79, 80, 88, 93, 140, 232–233
Wyllys, Jean, 286

Y Combinator, 116
Yahoo, 21
Yale University, 145
yellow fever, 279

Index

About the Author

Max Fisher is a reporter and columnist for the international desk of the *New York Times*, where he authors a column called "The Interpreter," which explains global trends and major world events, and where he was part of a team reporting on social media that was a finalist for the Pulitzer Prize in 2019. Fisher previously covered international affairs at *The Atlantic* and the *Washington Post*. He lives in Washington, DC.